DIETRICH BONHOEFFER WORKS, VOLUME 4

Discipleship

This series is a translation of
DIETRICH BONHOEFFER WERKE
Edited by
Eberhard Bethge†, Ernst Feil,
Christian Gremmels, Wolfgang Huber,
Hans Pfeifer, Albrecht Schönherr,
Heinz Eduard Tödt†, Ilse Tödt

In memoriam Eberhard Bethge
1909–2000

This volume has been made possible through
the generous support of the Aid Association for
Lutherans, the Lilly Endowment, Inc., the Stif-
tung Bonhoeffer Lehrstuhl, the Bowen H. and
Janice Arthur McCoy Charitable Foundation,
St. Matthew Lutheran Church, Avon, Conn.; the
New England Synod of the Evangelical Lutheran
Church in America, the Lusk-Damen Charitable
Gift Fund, and numerous members and friends
of the International Bonhoeffer Society.

DIETRICH BONHOEFFER WORKS

General Editor
Wayne Whitson Floyd, Jr.

DIETRICH BONHOEFFER

Discipleship

Translated from the German Edition
Edited by
MARTIN KUSKE† AND ILSE TÖDT

English Edition
Edited by
GEFFREY B. KELLY AND JOHN D. GODSEY

Translated by
BARBARA GREEN AND REINHARD KRAUSS

FORTRESS PRESS   MINNEAPOLIS

DIETRICH BONHOEFFER WORKS, Volume 4

First Fortress Press paperback edition 2003

Originally published in German as *Dietrich Bonhoeffer Werke,* edited by Eberhard Bethge et al., by Chr. Kaiser Verlag in 1989; Band 4 edited by Martin Kuske and Ilse Tödt. First English-language edition of *Dietrich Bonhoeffer Works,* Volume 4, published by Fortress Press in 2001.

Nachfolge first published in German by Christian Kaiser Verlag in 1937. Original, abridged English-language edition of *Nachfolge* published in 1949 as *The Cost of Discipleship* by SCM Press Ltd., London, and the Macmillan Company, New York. Revised, unabridged edition of *The Cost of Discipleship* published in 1959 by SCM Press Ltd., London, and the Macmillan Company, New York. New English-language translation of *Nachfolge* with new supplementary material first published in 2001 by Fortress Press as part of *Dietrich Bonhoeffer Works.*

Cover photo: Dietrich Bonhoeffer, August 1935. © Chr. Kaiser/Gütersloher Verlagshaus, Gütersloh, Germany. Used by permission.
Jacket design: Cheryl Watson
Internal design: The HK Scriptorium, Inc.

ISBN 0-8006-8324-2

Library of Congress has cataloged the hardcover edition as follows:

Bonhoeffer, Dietrich, 1906–1945.
    [Nachfolge. English]
    Discipleship / Dietrich Bonhoeffer ; translated from the German edition edited by Martin Kuske and Ilse Tödt ; English edition edited by Geffrey B. Kelly and John D. Godsey ; translated by Barbara Green and Reinhard Krauss.
        p. cm. — (Dietrich Bonhoeffer works ; v. 4)
    Includes bibliographical references and index.
    ISBN 0-8006-8304-8 (alk. paper)
        1. Sermon on the mount. I. Kelly, Geffrey B. II. Godsey, John D. III. Title.

BR45 .B6513 1996 vol. 4
[BT380]
230'.044 s—dc21
[241.5'3]   00-037627

The paper used in this publication meets the minimum requirements of American National Standard for Information Sciences—Permanence of Paper for Printed Library Materials, ANSI Z329.48-1984.

Manufactured in the U.S.A.

CONTENTS

General Editor's Foreword to Dietrich Bonhoeffer Works

Since the time that the writings of Dietrich Bonhoeffer (1906–45) first began to be available in English after World War II, they have been eagerly read both by scholars and by a wide general audience. The story of his life is compelling, set in the midst of historic events that shaped a century.

Bonhoeffer's leadership in the anti-Nazi Confessing Church and his participation in the *Abwehr* resistance circle make his works a unique source for understanding the interaction of religion, politics, and culture among those few Christians who actively opposed National Socialism. His writings provide not only an example of intellectual preparation for the reconstruction of German culture after the war but also a rare insight into the vanishing world of the old social and academic elites. Because of his participation in the resistance against the Nazi regime, Dietrich Bonhoeffer was hanged in the concentration camp at Flossenbürg on April 9, 1945.

Yet Bonhoeffer's enduring contribution is not just his moral example but his theology as well. As a student in Tübingen, Berlin, and at Union Theological Seminary in New York—where he also was associated for a time with the Abyssinian Baptist Church in Harlem—and as a participant in the European ecumenical movement, Bonhoeffer became known as one of the few figures of the 1930s with a comprehensive and nuanced grasp of both German- and English-language theology. His thought resonates with a prescience, subtlety, and maturity that continually belies the youth of the thinker.

In 1986 the Chr. Kaiser Verlag, now part of Gütersloher Verlagshaus, marked the eightieth anniversary of Bonhoeffer's birth by issuing the first of the sixteen volumes of the definitive German edition of his writings, the *Dietrich Bonhoeffer Werke* (*DBW*). The final volume of this monumental critical edition appeared in Berlin in the spring of 1998.

Preliminary discussions about an English-language edition began even as the German series was beginning to emerge. As a consequence, the International Bonhoeffer Society, English Language Section, formed an editorial board, initially chaired by Robin Lovin, assisted by Mark Brocker, to undertake this project. Since 1993 the *Dietrich Bonhoeffer Works* (*DBWE*) translation project has been located in the Krauth Memorial Library of the Lutheran Theological Seminary at Philadelphia, under the leadership of its general editor and project director—Wayne Whitson Floyd, Jr., who directs the seminary's Dietrich Bonhoeffer Center—and its executive director—Clifford J. Green of Hartford Seminary.

The *Dietrich Bonhoeffer Works* provides the English-speaking world with an entirely new, complete, and unabridged translation of the written legacy of one of the twentieth century's most notable theologians. The success of this edition is based foremost upon the gifts and dedication of the translators producing these new volumes, upon which all the other contributions of this series depend.

The *DBWE* includes a large amount of material appearing in English for the first time. Key terms are now translated consistently throughout the corpus, with special attention being paid to accepted English equivalents of technical theological and philosophical concepts.

This authoritative English edition strives, above all, to be true to the language, the style, and—most importantly—the theology of Bonhoeffer's writings. Translators have sought, nonetheless, to present Bonhoeffer's words in a manner that is sensitive to issues of gender in the language it employs. Consequently, accurate translation has removed sexist formulations that had been introduced inadvertently or unnecessarily into earlier English versions of his works. In addition, translators and editors generally have employed gender-inclusive language, insofar as this was possible without distorting Bonhoeffer's meaning or dissociating him from his own time.

At times Bonhoeffer's theology sounds fresh and modern, not because the translators have made it so, but because his language still speaks with a hardy contemporaneity even after more than half a century. In other instances, Bonhoeffer sounds more remote, a product of another era, not due to any lack of facility by the translators and editors, but because his concerns and rhetoric are in certain ways bound inextricably to a time that is past.

Volumes include introductions written by the editor(s) of each volume of the English edition, footnotes provided by Bonhoeffer, editorial notes added by the German and English editors, and afterwords composed by the editor(s) of the German edition. In addition, volumes provide tables of abbreviations used in the editorial apparatus, as well as bibliographies which list sources used by Bonhoeffer, literature consulted by the editors, and other works related to each particular volume. Finally, volumes contain pertinent chronologies, charts, and indexes of scriptural references, names, and subjects.

The layout of the English edition has retained Bonhoeffer's manner of dividing works into chapters and sections, as well as his original paragraphing (exceptions are noted by a ¶-symbol to indicate any paragraph break added by the editors of the English edition or by conventions explained in the introductions written by the editor[s] of specific volumes). The pagination of the *DBW* German critical edition is indicated in the outer margins of the pages of the translated text. At times, for the sake of precision and clarity of translation, a word or phrase that has been translated is provided in its original language, set within square brackets at the appropriate point in the text. Biblical citations come from the New Revised Standard Version (NRSV), unless otherwise noted. Where versification of the Bible used by Bonhoeffer differs from the NRSV, the verse number in the latter is noted in the text in square brackets.

Bonhoeffer's own footnotes—which are indicated in the body of the text by plain, superscripted numbers—are reproduced in precisely the same numerical sequence as they appear in the German critical edition, complete with his idiosyncrasies of documentation. In these, as in the accompanying editorial notes, existing English translations of books and articles have been substituted for their counterparts in other languages whenever available. The edition of a work that was consulted by Bonhoeffer himself can be ascertained by consulting the bibliography at the end of each volume. When a non-English title is not listed individually in the bibliography (along with an English translation of the title), a translation of each title has been provided for the English reader within the footnote or editorial note in which it is cited.

The editorial notes, which are indicated in the body of the text by superscripted numbers in square brackets—except *DBWE* volume five where they are indicated by plain, superscripted numbers—provide information on the intellectual, ecclesiastical, social, and political context of Bonhoeffer's pursuits during the first half of the twentieth century. These are based on the scholarship of the German critical edition; they have been supplemented by the contributions of the editors and translators of the English edition. Where the editors or translators of the English edition have substantially augmented or revised a German editor's note, the initials of the person making the change(s) appear at the note's conclusion, and editorial material that has been added in the English edition is surrounded by square brackets. When any previously translated material is quoted within an editorial note in altered form— indicated by the notation [trans. altered]—such changes should be assumed to be the responsibility of the translator(s).

Bibliographies at the end of each volume provide the complete information for each written source that Bonhoeffer or the various editors have mentioned in the current volume. References to the archives, collections, and personal library of materials that had belonged to Bonhoeffer and that survived the war—as cataloged in the *Nachlaß Dietrich Bonhoeffer* and collected in the Staatsbibliothek in Berlin—are indicated within the *Dietrich Bonhoeffer Works* by the abbreviation *NL* followed by the corresponding reference code within that published index.

The production of any individual volume of the *Dietrich Bonhoeffer Works* requires the financial assistance of numerous individuals and organizations, whose support is duly noted on the verso of the half-title page. In addition, the editor's introduction of each volume acknowledges those persons who have assisted in a particular way with the production of the English edition of that text. A special note of gratitude, however, is owed to all those prior translators, editors, and publishers of various portions of Bonhoeffer's literary legacy who heretofore have made available to the English-speaking world the writings of this remarkable theologian.

This English edition depends especially upon the careful scholarship of all those who labored to produce the critical German edition, completed in April 1998, from which these translations have been made. Their work has been overseen by a board of general editors—responsible for both the concept and the content of the German edition—composed of Eberhard Bethge†, Ernst Feil, Christian Gremmels, Wolfgang Huber (spokesperson for the German editorial board), Hans Pfeifer (ongoing liaison between the German and English editorial boards), Albrecht Schönherr, Heinz Eduard Tödt†, and Ilse Tödt.

The present English edition would be impossible without the creativity and unflagging dedication of the members of the editorial board of the *Dietrich Bonhoeffer Works:* Victoria Barnett, Mark Brocker, James H. Burtness, Keith W. Clements, Wayne Whitson Floyd, Jr., Barbara Green, Clifford J. Green, John W. de Gruchy, Barry A. Harvey, James Patrick Kelley, Geffrey B. Kelly, Reinhard Krauss, Robin W. Lovin, Michael Lukens, Nancy Lukens, Paul Matheny, Mary Nebelsick, and H. Martin Rumscheidt.

The deepest thanks for their support of this undertaking is owed, as well, to all the various members, friends, and benefactors of the International Bonhoeffer Society; to the National Endowment for the Humanities, which supported this project during its inception; to the Lutheran Theological Seminary at Philadelphia and its former Auxiliary who established and still help to support the Dietrich Bonhoeffer Center on its campus, specifically for the purpose of facilitating these publications; and to our publisher, Fortress Press, as represented with uncommon patience and *Gemütlichkeit* by Michael West, Ann Delgehausen, Joe Bonyata, Rachel Riensche, and Henry French. The privilege of collaboration with professionals such as these is fitting testimony to the spirit of Dietrich Bonhoeffer, who was himself always so attentive to the creative mystery of community—and that ever-deepening collegiality that is engendered by our social nature as human beings.

Special mention must be made of the priceless contribution made to all Bonhoeffer scholarship, especially the *Dietrich Bonhoeffer Werke,* by Eberhard Bethge, who died on March 18, 2000, while the manuscript of *DBWE* 4, *Discipleship,* was being copyedited. Eberhard was Dietrich's student, then friend and collaborator, and later his editor and biographer. His impact on this English Edition of the *Dietrich Bonhoeffer Works*—and all those persons whose labor has brought it about—is immeasurable. All who meet Dietrich Bonhoeffer in the form of his printed words owe a never-ending debt of gratitude to this remarkable human being, Eberhard Bethge, who almost single-handedly was responsible for assuring that Bonhoeffer's legacy would endure for us and generations to come.

Wayne Whitson Floyd, Jr., General Editor and Project Director
January 27, 1995
The Fiftieth Anniversary of the Liberation of Auschwitz
Fourth revision on March 18, 2000

ABBREVIATIONS

AB (*DBW* 2)	*Act and Being* (*DBW*, German edition)
AB (*DBWE* 2)	*Act and Being* (*DBWE*, English edition)
CC	*Christ the Center* (U.K. title *Christology*)
CD	*The Cost of Discipleship* (*Discipleship* [*DBWE* 4] previously was published in English as *The Cost of Discipleship*.)
CF (*DBWE* 3)	*Creation and Fall* (*DBWE*, English edition)
CS	*The Communion of Saints* (U.K. title *Sanctorum Communio*)
DB-ER	*Dietrich Bonhoeffer: A Biography* (Fortress Press, 2000 revised edition)
DBW	*Dietrich Bonhoeffer Werke*, German edition
DBWE	*Dietrich Bonhoeffer Works*, English edition
E	*Ethics*
FP (*DBWE* 7)	*Fiction from Tegel Prison* (*DBWE*, English edition)
GS	*Gesammelte Schriften* (Collected works)
LPP	*Letters and Papers from Prison*, 4th edition
LT (*DBWE* 5)	*Life Together* (*DBWE*, English edition)
LW	[Martin] *Luther's Works*, American edition
NL	*Nachlaß Dietrich Bonhoeffer*
NRS	*No Rusty Swords*
NRSV	New Revised Standard Version
SC (*DBW* 1)	*Sanctorum Communio* (*DBW*, German edition)
SC (*DBWE* 1)	*Sanctorum Communio* (*DBWE*, English edition)
TF	*A Testament to Freedom*
TP	*True Patriotism*
WA	*Weimar Ausgabe* (Weimar edition), Martin Luther
WF	*The Way to Freedom*

GEFFREY B. KELLY AND JOHN D. GODSEY

EDITORS' INTRODUCTION
TO THE ENGLISH EDITION

DISCIPLESHIP, previously published in a popular edition as *The Cost of Discipleship*, has been acclaimed in both Protestant and Catholic circles as a classic in Christian spirituality. *Discipleship* was the largest and most influential book published by Dietrich Bonhoeffer during his lifetime. Within its pages he confronts his readers time and again with his own stark challenges to their facile, less than Christlike ways of being Christian. What did it mean to declare oneself a follower of Jesus Christ? What were Christians to do about the seemingly "impossible demands" of Jesus' Sermon on the Mount? How effective and relevant were the Matthean Beatitudes against the materialism, militarism, and ruthless dictatorship that had come to dominate Germany in Bonhoeffer's own time? How were Christians to act responsibly in the Church Struggle created by Hitler and Nazism?

These were the issues that had disturbed Bonhoeffer during the gestation period of this book. He declares at the outset that his sole concern is to search not for new battle cries and catchwords but "for Jesus himself." Bonhoeffer's questions are shocking in their directness: "What did Jesus want to say to us? What does he want from us today? How does he help us to be faithful Christians today?" He goes on in the opening paragraph of *Discipleship* to say that he does not want to know what some church leader desires of Christians; instead, he wants "to know what Jesus wants."[1] Indeed, Bonhoeffer's attempts to ascertain "what Jesus wants" become the main guideline of every chapter that follows, not in the sense that Jesus assumes total control over the disciples, who then would be excused from personal responsibility. Rather, Bonhoeffer insists that

---

[1.] See below, page 37.

Jesus' word can liberate the followers of Christ to brave the responsible deeds demanded by their calling.

The Challenge of Discipleship

Though this book was put in its final form in 1935 and 1936, prior to its publication in 1937, most of the formulations that still excite readers' imaginations were first spoken much earlier in Bonhoeffer's seminars, sermons, and study groups. The conceptual underpinnings that form the inspirational core of *Discipleship* stand in the lineage of his earliest experiences as a budding theologian and young pastor. When the time came for him to compose this book for eventual publication, Bonhoeffer already was immersed in the unruly and risky task of serving an opposition church against a popular political movement and against churches that supported it.

Discipleship soon became a pivotal book in Bonhoeffer's collected writings. In it he crafted a Christ-centered spirituality that took the insights developed in his doctoral dissertation, *Sanctorum Communio,* and his *Habilitationsschrift, Act and Being,* into the practical level of church life in the midst of inimical, heathen forces, which in his opinion were corrupting an entire nation. He was convinced that a new way of being church had to come about to counteract the corroding attraction of a popular ideology that appealed to the baser elements in the human psyche by which people can be manipulated to evil ends.

Bonhoeffer was a leading figure in the Confessing Church, which stood in open conflict with the German Reich Church. The leaders of this Reich Church supported the Nazi government and accused the opposition churches of being disloyal citizens. The Barmen and Dahlem Synods of the Confessing Church had already issued declarations of faith and church policy that set Bonhoeffer's Confessing Church in open hostility to the regnant Nazi ideology. Subsequent state regulations had squeezed this opposition church into narrow enclaves tarred with ecclesiastical illegality. Acts of brutality and psychological coercion followed, as well as imprisonment of dissident pastors, as the Nazi government tightened its control over the ecclesiastical sphere and thus impeded any putative church opposition.[2] Beatings, arrests, police terror, and

---

[2.] See below, "Editors' Afterword to the German Edition," pages 294–99.

rampant injustice were commonplace in the years in which the Nazi government reinforced its grip on every aspect of life in Germany. It was not lost on Bonhoeffer that these developments and the sluggish reaction of many church leaders were in sharp contrast to those daring, even shocking, sayings of Jesus, the Beatitudes. For Bonhoeffer, Jesus' words seemed to be addressed as much to persecuted Jews and Christians in Germany as to Jesus' closest followers during his public life.

In the midst of the turmoil of those years, Bonhoeffer delivered his lectures on the Sermon on the Mount that later became a principal theme of *Discipleship.* He was determined to break the church out of its standard mode of compromise with, and accommodation to, political powers for the sake of its own survival as church. That self-serving, ecclesiastical tactic—while eminently practical if the church's sole purpose was to be a sacramental system and an easygoing provider of grace—had convinced Bonhoeffer that the churches of Germany had, in effect, cheapened themselves. He believed that, by not resisting an evil government's temptations, they had misled the ordinary citizens in their understanding of salvation. The Protestant principle of "faith alone" appeared to be retooled to justify inaction and indifference. The church seemed awash in pietistic evasions that softened the force of the Reformation's insistence on "God's word alone." Patriotic Germans gave glory to Adolf Hitler and thus unwittingly denied the glory due to God alone.

Bonhoeffer recognized this central Reformation issue—namely, the church's cheapening of grace through the enfeebling vacuity of its interpretations of Jesus' challenges to his followers—as a priority to be dealt with at the outset of his book. Christians seemed primed to dismiss the Beatitudes as impossible ideals. Everywhere he turned, Bonhoeffer seemed to encounter in the churches an ill-defined refusal to bear Christ's cross. These were all crucial aspects in Bonhoeffer's assessment of the crises of faith that Christians and their churches were now being asked to confront. These issues, unpacked so dramatically in the opening pages of *Discipleship,* set an exciting tempo for the reader. The catchphrases "cheap grace" and "costly grace" seemed to sum up so well the problems posed by the bondage of the churches to secular powers and the reductionist faith of traditional churchgoers which proved so fatal under the Nazi regime.[3]

[3.] See below, pages 43–47.

Future generations of readers would summarize the book through these phrases. The initial English translation of the title would even speak directly of "the cost of discipleship." Yet Bonhoeffer gave the original book a simpler title, *Nachfolge* or *Discipleship*—literally, "following after." This following of the call of Jesus Christ, or Christian discipleship, is the theme of the entire book, and not the concept of grace, at least as "grace" was understood by many at that time and even now. The chief questions with which he was wrestling, as he explained in a letter to Karl Barth, were "those of the exposition of the Sermon on the Mount and the Pauline doctrine of justification and sanctification."[4] This new English edition, therefore, has restored Bonhoeffer's original title, translated as *Discipleship*.

The opening chapter moves at a breathtaking pace straight to the problem of following Christ at a time when so many were in thrall to a seductive earthly lord. Bonhoeffer puts the reader on notice that Christian discipleship must be lived with utmost seriousness. Faith in Christ and membership in the church were, in fact, at a crossroads. The direction Christians and their churches were to take would determine whether or not they were the true followers of Jesus—that is, whether or not the churches honestly represented Jesus Christ. In the typical church life around him, however, Bonhoeffer detected only "cheap grace," a "bargain-basement" Christianity, creeds without costs, and a denial of God's living word.[5] "Cheap grace," as Jonathan Sorum has pointed out, "is *not* grace" at all. Costly grace, on the other hand, "is *simply* grace."[6] The cheapening of grace is contrasted by Bonhoeffer with Jesus' call to the "costly grace" of discipleship, demanding a response of immediate obedience. Costly grace demands not a new confession of faith, not a religious decision to be more regular in church attendance, but obedience to the call of Jesus Christ! Christian discipleship offers no program, no set of principles, no elitist ideal, no new set of laws. Discipleship means, quite simply, Jesus Christ and Jesus Christ alone; the sole content of discipleship is to "follow Christ."

Bonhoeffer's first recorded use of the phrase "cheap grace" came in an address titled "Christ and Peace," to members of the German Student Christian Movement in Berlin in 1932. He insisted that Jesus' commands be taken just as seriously when they "affect civil life and, indeed, the

---

[4.] *TF* 430 (*DBW* 14:235f.).
[5.] See below, page 43.
[6.] Sorum, "Cheap Grace, Costly Grace, and Just Plain Grace," 20.

entire earthly existence of people." For Bonhoeffer, it was an unwarrant-
ed presumption to claim purity in one's faith "if we refuse to follow the
path of obedience by sinning in expectation of the easy grace of forgiveness." In so doing, "We thus make grace cheap," he argued, "and with
the justification of the sinner through the cross of Christ, we thereby
forget the cry of the Lord who never justifies sin."[7] It is intriguing that
Bonhoeffer's uncompromising arguments in 1932 were relevant to the
peace issues he would raise in 1934 and 1936 and continue to be the core
issues of pacifism today, even after the completion of a century unparal-
leled for the wars waged by so-called Christian politicians.

Bonhoeffer's logic is disarming in its simplicity: "The command, 'you
shall not kill,' and the word, 'love your enemy,' are given to us simply to
obey."[8] The implication of these remarks is clear. One does not separate Jesus' commands from one's secular life—an insistence that will be
made even more forcefully in his later writings.

The connection made between obedience and faith in the first part of
Discipleship was not, as some critics contended, a dangerous swing away
from the Pauline/Protestant doctrine of justification by faith alone toward
a more Catholic emphasis on good works. On the contrary, Bonhoeffer
saw himself engaged in a struggle for the very soul of the Reformation,
namely, personal faith lived in obedience to the call of Jesus Christ in correlation and simultaneity with the commands of Christ inspirited by the
gift of faith. Such discipleship does not derive from abstract theologies
or neatly packaged doctrinal systems. Nor is it expressed in punctilious
obedience to approved laws or ritual correctness. The idea of Christ is
not the force behind the call to discipleship, but the very living Christ, to
whom the Christian must be exclusively attached.

Although in the doctrine of justification the coupling of faith in
Christ with obedience to Christ suggests a theological sequence from
faith to obedience, the two can never be separated chronologically. Obedience to Christ, inextricably bonded to the gift of faith, is Bonhoeffer's
recurring theme in *Discipleship*. Bonhoeffer is not offering a book-length
inventory of the personal, financial, and emotional costs of following
Jesus. Neither is he writing an exposé of the manner in which churches
pandered to their congregants, angling for easier ways of being Christian, content with the mediocrity of mere Sunday observance.

[7.] "Christ and Peace," *TF* 94–95 (*DBW* 17: 117–18).
[8.] Ibid., 95 (*DBW* 17: 118).

Bonhoeffer's emphasis on the obedient deeds of discipleship in response to God's word in Jesus Christ is in his view a restoration of the meaning of faith in a world that had become increasingly bereft of compassion, peace, forgiveness of enemies, purity of heart, and meekness, yet increasingly willing to exploit the poor and oppress those who struggle for justice. In short, the perspective of the Beatitudes of Jesus' Sermon on the Mount quickly became Bonhoeffer's way of elucidating the meaning of discipleship for Christians and their churches. If, in a nation that has turned away from Christianity, faith is ever to be restored, the church must preach once again what is central in the Christian faith, the call of Jesus Christ to follow him.

The emphasis on concrete obedience in one's faith did not begin, however, with Bonhoeffer taking stock of the Church Struggle and of the political malevolence to which many churches had succumbed. References abound throughout the collected writings of Bonhoeffer concerning the necessity of being obedient, doing concrete deeds that emanate from faith, and living theology in a practical fashion by applying it to real people who suffer.

As early as a student sermon from 1926, for example, we find the young Bonhoeffer blending the themes of faith and obedience in words that find their echo in *Discipleship:* "Either we say yes or we say no; I believe or I do not believe. Here we gently embrace in trust the word and the way of God or we arrogantly refuse, trusting in our own ways. Simply saying yes, listening to the word in obedience, that is faith. . . ."[9]

This dialectical pairing of faith with obedience did not change throughout his career as a theologian and pastor. We see it incorporated into his Berlin dissertations in relationship to the necessity of Christian love at the core of genuine community in Jesus Christ and in his recurring emphasis on obedience to God's word. Speaking of authority and freedom in the empirical church, Bonhoeffer makes the daring claim that "the absolute authority of the word demands absolute obedience, that is, absolute freedom. . . ."[10] And in one of his most self-revealing sentences from *Act and Being,* he states matter-of-factly that "only a way of thinking that, bound in obedience to Christ, 'is' from the truth can place into the truth."[11] The same dialectical simultaneity of faith and

---

[9.] *DBW* 9:541.
[10.] *SC* (*DBWE* 1):250.
[11.] *AB* (*DBWE* 2):80.

obedience defined the young pastors' life together at the Finkenwalde
Seminary that Bonhoeffer directed and that constituted the immediate
context for his observations in *Discipleship*.

If there is a logical progression to Bonhoeffer's analysis of the call
to follow Jesus and his challenges to Christians and their churches, it
begins with the call of Jesus in the matrices of the Sermon on the Mount,
the cross, and the commissioning of his twelve disciples. This core, as
attested in the Synoptic Gospels, is correlated in a shorter second part of
Discipleship with the demands of following the risen Christ who is present
in the church-community. Here the call to discipleship during Jesus' lifetime is conjoined with the baptismal call of every Christian to enter into
new life in Christ, to share in the cross of discipleship, and thereby to
be transformed into Christ's very image. The shift is not an entirely new
direction. Bonhoeffer uses Pauline imagery to show the unity of the biblical witness to the lived, risky reality of discipleship, for following Jesus
Christ to the cross outside Jerusalem is not unlike the path to present-day
Golgothas, where Christ suffers anew in the community of saints, at the
hands of a godless world.

Luther, Kierkegaard, Pacifism, and the Sermon on the Mount

Not untypical of his theological and, at times, unabashed eclecticism,
Bonhoeffer engaged theologians like Karl Barth, Emil Brunner, Paul
Althaus, Karl Holl, and others in vigorous dialogue as his text unfolded.
Bonhoeffer was unique in his ability to balance the liberal views of his
teachers at Berlin University with the Barthian rebellion against what
he sensed were the false values of Protestant liberalism. Bonhoeffer's
philosophical-theological joustings with these influential thinkers sharpened his critical reflections on the conceptual dimensions of Christian
discipleship, thereby helping him to refine his text in view of its eventual
publication. The editors of the German text have meticulously traced
these sources through extensive textual annotations as well as in their
afterword. Their observations will not be repeated here. Nonetheless,
some remarks about the significant influences on Bonhoeffer's assessment of Christian discipleship are in order.

It is clear that here, as throughout his theology, Bonhoeffer's framework is Luther's doctrine of justification by faith alone. Second, for a
person so insistent on community, Bonhoeffer borrows extensively from

the great existentialist and individualist Søren Kierkegaard and from Karl Barth, who also was influenced at that time by Kierkegaard. Finally, Bonhoeffer was himself confronted by the gospel of peace and, indeed, by the full force of the Sermon on the Mount as his outlook on the issues of compassion, peace, and justice, which were apparently addressed by Jesus' Sermon, was transformed. His subsequent comments become central to the themes of *Discipleship*.

Bonhoeffer's text can be understood from one important perspective as a daring attempt to retrieve Luther from the shambles of his irrelevance in the Hitler era. For Bonhoeffer, Luther seemed to have been eclipsed by the reductionism of Protestant liberalism in which Jesus became a mere teacher of moral truths and the Protestant doctrine of faith alone was tamed by humanistic acculturation.[12] For Luther, though, faith and ethical convictions were one reality; the world of Jesus Christ and the world of human struggles were a single world.

Bonhoeffer's Luther saw the need for the comfort of the gospel, which the Scriptures alone could give to human beings in their agonizing separation from God and their overpowering despair over futile efforts to control their own destiny. In Luther's view, believers clinging to Christ in faith could, paradoxically, become Christ. In faith, God's word in Christ and the catalytic power of the Holy Spirit converge on the sinner, prompting the free deeds of the Christian, a point that Bonhoeffer had incorporated into a lifelong insistence, highlighted in *Discipleship*, that theology, church, and discipleship itself were the work of the Lord. If that work came under the control of the human self, it would run into the dead end of sinful distortion. Bonhoeffer agreed with Luther's interpretation of Jesus' word as leading to the recognition of Christ in one another, the sense of 'otherness' that one needed to break out of the sinful patterns of human existence that yielded only what Luther called a "heart turned in on itself."

Here two issues in Luther's theology emerged that Bonhoeffer, if his retrieval of Luther was to be successful, had to make the focus of his work. First was the doctrine of the two kingdoms and, second, the obedience shown in the free deeds of following Christ. What Bonhoeffer would describe in his *Ethics* as "thinking in two spheres" had its roots

---

[12.] This section draws heavily from Sorum's analysis of Bonhoeffer's interpretation of Luther in "The Eschatological Boundary in Dietrich Bonhoeffer's *Nachfolge*," 1–70 *et passim*.

in his refusal in *Discipleship* to see in the Lutheran doctrine of the two kingdoms any approval for an opening in which those who professed to be Christians could transfer their lives' allegiance from Jesus Christ to an earthly lord. But the danger of this attitude, depicted with uncommon pungency in Bonhoeffer's *Discipleship*, was that such compartmentalization went together with turning the everyday demands of Jesus' Sermon on the Mount into cheap platitudes. Bonhoeffer's interpretation of the Lutheran doctrine of the two kingdoms understood it to affirm only one reality, not two distinct realities in which Jesus is exiled from the political, militaristic, and moneymaking realms of secular life. In Luther's teaching on the subject, church and state can limit each other, to be sure, but they are not to be confused with each other—a Nazified church allied with the Nazi government would, for Luther, hardly constitute two distinct realms. The boundary is always Jesus Christ and his cross. No state can claim ultimacy for itself against the demands of Jesus Christ. No church can ignore its duty to call the state to account for its actions.

Throughout Bonhoeffer's theology the church's critical relationship to the state is always profoundly this-worldly. The Christian life that emerges from the empowering presence of Jesus Christ in people's lives is the life of Christ himself, always directed to being for others, being for God's world. In Christ one embraces both God and the world, never God or the world. As Bonhoeffer had written earlier, also in reflection on one's Christian life in the world, "God wants us to honor God on earth; God wants us to honor God in our fellow man and woman—and nowhere else."[13] Throughout *Discipleship*, Bonhoeffer picks up on this Christ-centered, other-centered mode of following Jesus.

Yet he was equally aware that the church he knew and loved had itself turned from the light of Jesus Christ toward a new, glowing light of the nation. The church had come perilously close to transforming itself into a national church that honored the Teutonic gods of blood, soil, and conquest, all under the banner of Martin Luther in the "mighty fortress" of Nazi Germany. This prompted Bonhoeffer in a sermon during the Reformation Festival, November 6, 1932, to decry Germany's revival of triumphalist nationalism, which he viewed as part of a lethal illness and as evidence of the church's slow death as an effective voice in German society. That sermon expresses clearly Bonhoeffer's way of setting straight the theological record on what Luther really

---

[13.] "Thy Kingdom Come," *TF* 92 (*DBW* 12:276).

thought about Christian 'works' and the present, attractive 'work' of building a new earthly kingdom in tandem with the growing glorification of the Nazi nation. In words that would resound even more clearly in *Discipleship*, Bonhoeffer calls for true Christian deeds in obedience to Jesus Christ.

> It may sound highly inappropriate to speak of works on Reformation Day. But it would be a terrible misunderstanding of the gospel were we to intend faith, confession, to be a thing only for pious evening and morning prayers. Faith, our confession, means letting God be God—even in our deeds—and especially being obedient to God in those deeds. Do the first work—since it is highly important to say this today. No one who knows the church can complain that the church does nothing. No, the church never stops doing many things . . . but we all do so many works that belong in second, third, or fourth place, yet we do not do the first work. Not even the church does that . . . to love God and one's brothers and sisters. . . .[14]

Here we see as early as 1932 the emergence of Bonhoeffer's emphasis on obedience to the divine command to love as the first work inspirited by faith. We see, too, his growing hesitance and distrust regarding the church's willingness to hail the new nationalism—in the guise of honoring one of Luther's two kingdoms, apart from the other.

In his retrieval of Luther, Bonhoeffer found an unexpected ally in the Danish philosopher Søren Kierkegaard. Despite their differences, principally over what Bonhoeffer believed to be an exaggerated individualism in Kierkegaard, he believed that Kierkegaard alone of nineteenth-century thinkers had correctly perceived the true dialectic of faith and obedience in Luther's interpretation of the gospel. Bonhoeffer's complaint that Luther's doctrine of faith alone had been vitiated by a neglect of active obedience echoed Kierkegaard's own passionate appeal in several of his polemical writings against the bourgeois complacency of Danish Lutheranism for a return to the authentic principles of the Reformation. Bonhoeffer had even listed Kierkegaard in the line of "genuine Christian thinking" that went from Paul, Augustine, and Luther to Kierkegaard and Barth. Wondering whether Luther himself would be able to recognize contemporary Christendom, Kierkegaard had written: "The misfortune of Christianity is clearly that the dialectical factor has been taken from Luther's doctrine of faith so that it has become a hiding

---

[14.] *DBW* 12:429–30 [*GS* 4:99–100].

place for sheer paganism and epicureanism. People forget that Luther was urging the claims of faith against a fantastically exaggerated asceticism."[15]

In writing *Discipleship* Bonhoeffer had been greatly influenced by Kierkegaard's study of Luther, *Der Einzelne und die Kirche: Über Luther und den Protestantismus*, which served as a direct source for several sections of Bonhoeffer's text.[16] In the book, Kierkegaard mentions the cheapness and costliness of faith in Luther's historical context and writings. Among the issues raised by Kierkegaard's analysis of Luther are the reduction of faith to a doctrine, the directness of the gift of faith as opposed to theological reflection on faith, and grace as the outcome of justification, not as its principle.[17]

This latter point in Kierkegaard's text seems to have struck Bonhoeffer as extremely significant, as evidenced by his heavy underlining in his copy of it. For Kierkegaard, as for Bonhoeffer, Luther's followers fell into the trap of inverting Luther's own erroneous tactics with God in his monastic life. Luther knew he possessed within himself the principle of his good works. He believed he could clutch at this principle by strenuous acts of obedience and thus attain righteousness sufficient to make him acceptable before his God. Then, in his tower experience, Luther discovered that the only true righteousness came from outside and beyond himself, bestowed by God. And that righteousness or justice was Jesus Christ, whose death on the cross and resurrected presence was pure grace for the sinner. But Luther's followers turned Luther's insight into an abstract principle. This could be called the 'principle of grace'. In effect, one has God's righteousness by merely possessing the principle. But one does not have to actualize this principle. Simply holding it and defending it against the counterprinciple of good works was sufficient. The theological flaw in that argument, however, was that Luther understood grace as outcome, not as presupposition. The word of God in Christ can only be heard and believed by living the life of simple obedience. And so in nineteenth-century Danish Lutheranism, understood by

---

[15.] *The Journals of Søren Kierkegaard*, 300.

[16.] Throughout the present translation of *Discipleship*, Bonhoeffer's quotations from *Der Einzelne und die Kirche* have been rendered in the English version of *The Journals of Søren Kierkegaard* and/or *Søren Kierkegaard's Journals and Papers*.

[17.] See Kelly, "The Influence of Kierkegaard on Bonhoeffer's Concept of Discipleship," 148–51.

Bonhoeffer to be paralleled by German Lutheranism in the 1930s, Luther's doctrine became a mere presupposition demanding that good Christians refrain from simple obedience, lest they expose themselves to the ironic accusation that they were denying the all-sufficiency of grace. And so, as the twisted logic went, the Christian simply had to conform to the world.[18]

This is a crucial issue for Bonhoeffer. Klerkegaard's analysis of the misguided strategies of latter-day Lutherans enlightened Bonhoeffer to the depth of the distortion against which he was struggling. When grace becomes a principle of righteousness, rather than the outcome of God's gift of righteousness, there is no new existence in Jesus Christ, no boundary between the life of sin and the new life of holiness, no need to embrace the cross. Such Christians have merely to let grace do it all and to accommodate themselves to the orders of creation as the only true way to obey God. This was the cheap grace against which Bonhoeffer inveighed. His sarcasm in rejecting such thinking is directed as much against the distortion of Luther as against the easy way in which so-called Christians could twist Luther's teachings to justify their noninvolvement in the urgent, courageous deeds that were needed for that time, such as rejecting the evil core of Nazism and speaking up for the Jews.

The best illustration of what Luther actually meant—and adjunct to Bonhoeffer's efforts to restore the Protestant principle in a nation whose leaders were increasingly without ethical principles—came through Bonhoeffer's attachment to the Sermon on the Mount. If Luther is the perennial mentor of Bonhoeffer's theology, the Sermon on the Mount appears to be the special word of God that transformed Bonhoeffer from a self-serving theologian, turning "the doctrine of Jesus Christ into something of personal advantage for myself," into a Christian. "It was," he wrote, "a great liberation. It became clear to me that the life of a servant of Jesus Christ must belong to the church, and step by step it became plainer to me how far that must go."[19] How that encounter with the Sermon on the Mount came about is a question still shrouded in conjecture. Some suppose the encounter may have begun at Union Theological Seminary in his weekend mission to the young blacks of Harlem. Perhaps it was his long discussions with the French pacifist Jean Lasserre, who helped open his eyes to the real meaning of "Blessed are

---

[18.] See Sorum, "The Eschatological Boundary," 147–50.
[19.] *TF* 424–25 (*DBW* 14:113).

the peacemakers!" Or did the harsh treatment of the Jews of Germany and the growing militarism of world governments as seen in the light of God's word—on which he reflected and prayerfully meditated daily—help him become a Christian in faith and deed? Or was it a bolt of lightning, as happened to Luther?

Whatever the nature of the transformation to which Bonhoeffer alludes, he was convinced that only the pure teaching of Christ's Sermon on the Mount, not the self-serving ways in which university professors pursued truth in the abstract, offered hope for a nation that was enshrining a secular leader where only God belonged.[20] The seminary of Finkenwalde became the setting for Bonhoeffer's lectures on the Sermon on the Mount, which are at the center of *Discipleship*.

Bonhoeffer's manner of integrating Jesus' declarations of who was blessed, in all the Beatitudes' irony and paradox, spelled out the risky tasks of those who answered the call of Jesus Christ. The challenges are neither softened nor minimized. The poor in spirit are those who accept privations for the sake of Jesus Christ. Those who mourn are those who refuse to be in tune with the world, who mourn on account of its guilt, its fate, its fortune, and who bear the sorrow and suffering that come their way as they follow Christ. The meek are those who renounce every right of their own and live solely for the sake of Jesus Christ. Those who hunger and thirst for righteousness are those who renounce their own righteousness, who look for no praise for their achievements or sacrifices, and who must always look forward to the renewal of the earth and the hoped-for advent of God's righteousness. The merciful are those who can renounce their own honor and dignity for the sake of Jesus Christ and who show their compassion by seeking out those enmeshed in sin or subject to oppression, distress, and humiliation. The pure in heart are those who have surrendered their hearts completely to Jesus so that Jesus alone may reign in their hearts. The peacemakers are those who have found their peace in Jesus Christ and who now renounce all violence and endure suffering for the sake of peace and justice. Those who are persecuted for the sake of righteousness are those, including the imprisoned pastors, who suffer for any just cause. Does such a beatitudinal community exist on this earth? Bonhoeffer answers that it exists only

---

[20.] Bonhoeffer shared his conviction about the Sermon on the Mount with Erwin Sutz as he was deciding to return to Germany to take over the training of seminarians in the Confessing Church, in opposition to the Reich Church. See below, page 24.

where the poorest, the meekest, the most viciously afflicted of all people are to be found: at the cross of Jesus Christ at Golgotha! The church-community of the Beatitudes is the community of the crucified Jesus Christ. It is the cross that makes living the Beatitudes possible and that makes the contemporary crucifixion of Jesus' followers the exemplar of Christian discipleship.[21]

The sections on not resisting evil, forgiveness and love of enemies, and the way of the pacifist have been among the most problematic elements in *Discipleship*. The editors of the German critical edition have shown conclusively that Bonhoeffer's views on peace and nonviolence underwent a major change after his time as an assistant pastor in Barcelona, during which he dismissed the pacifist refusal to serve in war as a violation of the orders of creation. All that would change by the time he returned to Berlin and began his career as a theologian and lecturer in theology. The German editors mention Bonhoeffer's encounters with the French pacifist Jean Lasserre as one of the sources of his growing pacifist convictions. This view is supported by interviews with Lasserre himself, who was able to speak of the change he had noted in his friend Dietrich, who had come to accept the way of peace as the only course for Christians who recognize the presence of Jesus Christ in one another.[22]

So pronounced was the change from "realist" to pacifist that few statements in support of the peace movement, even today, can match the fire and passion of Bonhoeffer's Berlin lecture "Christ and Peace";[23] his denunciation of the idolatry of national security at the ecumenical conference in Gland, Switzerland, in August 1932;[24] his disturbing challenge to the churches to be advocates for peace in a sermon, "The Church and the People of the World," at the ecumenical gathering in Fanø, Denmark, in September 1934.[25] In *Discipleship* the issues of peace, nonresistance to evil, and forgiveness of enemies coalesced to such an extent that some critics saw the book as too otherworldly and impractical in how Christians had to deal with an enemy such as Nazism—so dangerous to Christian civilization and so entrenched in power militarily.

[21.] Godsey, *The Theology of Dietrich Bonhoeffer*, 156–57.

[22.] See Kelly, "An Interview with Jean Lasserre," and Nelson, "The Relationship of Jean Lasserre to Dietrich Bonhoeffer's Peace Concerns in the Struggle of Church and Culture."

[23.] "Christ and Peace," *TF* 93–95 (*DBW* 17:116–20).

[24.] "The Church Is Dead," *TF* 103–4 (*DBW* 11:350–57).

[25.] "The Church and the People of the World," *TF* 227–29 (*DBW* 13:302–5).

Some critics see *Discipleship* as more of a detour along the way to the more realistic actions of Bonhoeffer the conspirator, the affirmer of a world come of age in the prison letters.

In his strongest condemnations of war and violence Bonhoeffer relies on the commands of Jesus Christ, which in their starkness and counter-culturalism are given to us not to dissect in endless casuistry, but only to obey. Christ is the prime reality; hence, attacks on people are, for Bonhoeffer, attacks on none other than Jesus Christ. In the sermon at Fanø, mentioned above, Bonhoeffer proclaims again the simple logic of obeying the peace commands of Jesus Christ: "The brothers and sisters in Christ obey his word; they do not doubt or question, but keep his commandment of peace. They are not ashamed, in defiance of the world, even to speak of eternal peace. They cannot take up arms against Christ himself—yet this is what they do if they take up arms against one another!"[26] Bonhoeffer's struggles against violence and war may have begun in New York under the influence of the pacifist Lasserre, but they took on additional urgency when, back in Germany, he realized more fully that his own people appeared to have created a mystique about war and the manly glory that could be attained only on the battlefield.

Bonhoeffer's advocacy for the restoration of peace, forbearance, and Christian community in Nazi Germany that he weaves into the text of *Discipleship* was both daunting and unpopular. Yet he was not, as history and statements from his *Ethics* have shown, uncompromising about using violence to prevent the greater evil of war and genocide. But even in the matter of the political conspiracy, he associated the well-intentioned acts of violence against the evil government of Adolf Hitler with sin, guilt, and the need for repentance. Christians were still challenged to hold fast to the command of Jesus Christ and to repent of deviation from it, even if acting to restore the order of Christ in the world. Knowing well the risks he was taking in agitating for the restoration of Christ's teachings on peace, forgiveness, and nonviolence in Nazi Germany, Bonhoeffer wrote to his agnostic brother, Karl Friedrich, that there were realities for which one had to take an uncompromising stand. "And it appears to me that peace and social justice, really Christ himself, are these."[27] Here Bonhoeffer identifies the cause of peace with that of social justice and Jesus Christ.

[26.] Ibid., 228 (*DBW* 13:303).

[27.] *DBW* 13:273 (*GS* 3:25).

These are the realities that must be restored if Christians and their churches can again live by the pure demands of Christ's Sermon on the Mount, or by Paul's teachings on the need for Christians to live and die in Christ through their baptism and the freedom granted by grace to be Christians in the world. Bonhoeffer was writing for a church under attack by an ideologically bent state. He was also writing in the ambience of a powerful government that had abrogated all criticism and that had taken control over the conduct of church affairs, forcing acceptance of racist, bellicose, and nationalistic policies as the price for survival. It is not surprising that in many of Bonhoeffer's assessments of the world, anything that could encourage church leaders in their facile incensing of the Nazi altar was avoided in favor of a more countercultural perspective. This countercultural perspective was not a flight *from* the world, but a struggle to establish a critical church presence *in* the world. Hence *Discipleship* contains ample exhortations for Christians to engage positively with the world.

The world of Bonhoeffer's original readers, however, was in open rebellion against the limits that constituted Christian values in a civil society. In *Discipleship,* Bonhoeffer attempts to confront the seductive lure held out to Germany's citizens, asking them to divorce themselves from what Nazi ideology portrayed as the less than fully Germanic world redeemed by Jesus Christ—a world portrayed as 'polluted' by subhumans like Jews and gypsies, in addition to those out of favor with the government through their dissenting ways. This to Bonhoeffer was a demonic attack on the real world, on real persons created in God's image, on the Christ.

Here as elsewhere, Bonhoeffer's writings are infused with a theology of the cross. The cross of Christ gives the lie to human claims that the world of cravings for domination is the world of Christ. Bonhoeffer makes it clear that followers of Jesus Christ live immersed in the world, only to be called forth by their Lord to live in genuine worldliness. The Sermon on the Mount for Bonhoeffer is, after all, a worldly document. Paul's understanding of baptism and his directives for practical living in community entail dying to a world that, without Christ, is itself dying and in decay. Bonhoeffer is on solid theological ground when he delivers Christ's mandate for his followers to break with any world and culture that, in denying the dignity of people whom Christians are to affirm in faith as their brothers and sisters, denies Jesus Christ himself.

The Vicarious Representative Action
of Jesus Christ and the Freedom to Be Christian

It would not be an exaggeration to claim that within *Discipleship* one can discover a reiteration, in some form, of almost everything Bonhoeffer had previously written. Nor was it an overstatement on Bonhoeffer's part when, in his prison letters, he could say that, despite all later misgivings, he still stood by what he had written on discipleship in Christ.[28] From his earliest writings, to his sermons, courses, and conferences of the 1930s, to the final letters from prison, one can see the thoughts of a person of very deep faith who has, throughout his life, attempted to come to terms with the call of Jesus Christ to follow along the path of Christian discipleship. Bonhoeffer's convictions on how to follow Jesus in one's faith were well set by the time he was developing the philosophical-theological insights needed to express what he felt in his heart.

No fully accurate reading of *Discipleship* is possible, therefore, without an appreciation of the foundational concepts of Christian community and the impact of God's revelation on Christian freedom and faith contained in the Berlin dissertations. Coursing through *Sanctorum Communio*, his doctoral dissertation, are references to the dynamic reality of Jesus Christ, whose vicarious representative action in the Christian church is affirmed as the life-giving spirit of the visible community of Christians.[29] Readers would miss the point Bonhoeffer wishes to make in *Discipleship* were they unable to appreciate Bonhoeffer's depiction of Jesus as the enfleshment both of God and of humanity so that Christians are moved to what, without the presence and grace of Jesus Christ, they would be unable to do: to live together in faith and self-giving love, to follow Jesus even to the cross, to take the risks necessary to deliver their society from evil, and to trust in the divine promise to provide sustenance in a hostile world. The Jesus of *Discipleship* is the binding force of the Christian community. Bonhoeffer urges this community to forgo the cheap grace of an easy Christianity and to accept the cross in loving others, even enemies, as Christ has loved them.

Jesus' vicarious representative action on behalf of his brothers and sisters, depicted carefully by Bonhoeffer in his doctoral dissertation,

---

[28.] *LPP* 269 (*DBW* 8:542).
[29.] See Clifford J. Green, "Editor's Introduction to the English Edition," *SC* (*DBWE* 1):1–17.

likewise provides the Christocentric foundation for all the associations
Bonhoeffer makes between the gospel presentation of the call of Christ
to discipleship and the Pauline emphasis on how the resurrected Christ
becomes vicariously present in every community gathered in his name
and faithful to his teachings. Bonhoeffer's approach to the demands
of discipleship depends on the strong conviction, reinforced in his student days, that Jesus is speaking vicariously in present-day words that call
Christians to action on his behalf. The themes of *Discipleship* thus center on Jesus Christ, who has never left his community, who is the costly
grace of Christians, and whose presence is in danger of being denied in
churches and by Christians who twist the idea of discipleship into following an anti-Christian idol. They substitute faith in Christ, who is present
vicariously in the actions of his present-day followers, with platitudes,
theological distortions, and criminal violence against innocent people.
In many ways *Discipleship* can be viewed as a concrete description of the
practical life to which Christ calls all Christians who would be "Christ
existing as church-community."

One can only wonder how incisive Bonhoeffer's powerful denunciation of misleading theologies, questionable church attitudes, and vapid
but attractive political slogans would be without the rigorous foundation
he acquired in investigating the dynamics of faith and revelation, as well
as belief systems, philosophical presuppositions, intellectual arrogance,
distortions of the nature of freedom, and appealing but superficial solu-
tions to the problems and crises in human history. *Act and Being*, Bonhoeffer's second dissertation, has been described as a tour de force in
helping Bonhoeffer secure an academic appointment. It is much more.

The effort at understanding the human search for truth and meaning
that Bonhoeffer invested in *Act and Being* provided a unique ability to
detect distortions of the truth, to identify flaws in manipulative systems
of domination, and to expose fraudulent attempts to control God and
domesticate Jesus Christ.[30] Throughout *Act and Being*, Bonhoeffer criticizes efforts to place human autonomy, rather than God, at the center
of Christian maturity. He saw God being yoked to human consciousness
and to intellectual systems that masked egocentric pretentiousness while
denigrating human freedom. Bonhoeffer cautions against sliding into
thought that would equate theological or philosophical reflection with

---

[30.] See Wayne Whitson Floyd, Jr., "Editor's Introduction to the English Edition," *AB*
(*DBWE* 2):1–20.

the direct act of God on the human being in faith. Gifting a human being with faith, Bonhoeffer tells us, is an act of direct relationship with God in Christ. As such it necessarily evades control by human reflection and human categorizations. God is free in the manner in which God has created human freedom—namely, not to be free *from* but to be free *for* others.

God is depicted in *Act and Being* as free from all human efforts to manipulate God's words and to domesticate God's dynamic presence within the books, academic podiums, and pulpits of a church system that can become easy prey to forceful political ideology. In short, Bonhoeffer in this foundational book develops the conceptual strengths for his perennial refusal to hand over faith's creative energies either to the domination of the thinking, reflecting 'I', or to manipulation by ecclesiastical establishments turned in upon themselves or by political systems that demand absolute allegiance. The connections to the principal arguments that Bonhoeffer uses in *Discipleship*—offsetting distortions of the gospel's portrait of Christ's faithful followers—are unmistakable. Both of his doctoral dissertations provided Bonhoeffer with many of the conceptual keys he needed to expose the dangers that the denial of Jesus Christ and the intellectual dishonesty of the churches and the criminality of the Nazi government posed to Christian faith and to civil life in Germany.

Faith, Freedom in Following Christ, and Subthemes of Discipleship

Although *Discipleship* bonded closely with the conceptual foundations set in *Sanctorum Communio* and *Act and Being,* the insights and inspiration of this book go far beyond the philosophical-theological convictions he had worked out in those earlier writings. *Discipleship* is set, not in comfortable academe, but in the steamier cauldron of political conflict and ecclesiastical fecklessness. The troubled times called for more than faith seeking to understand church dogma, to purify ritual, or to gauge attendance at worship. Bonhoeffer was demanding no less than following Jesus Christ through acts of self-sacrificing valor against the idolatries and apostasies that were eroding church integrity and destroying civility within Germany.

Discipleship, more so than any of his other writings, reveals a Bonhoeffer who, with uncommonly vehement language, gave vent to his anger and frustrations at the failure of Christians and their churches to react with prophetic force against the entrenched injustices of the Nazi government. Bonhoeffer's ire shaped the harsh rhetoric with which he described what he sensed was a lethal combat between the forces of Christ and those of Satan, between the kingdom of God and the world now become Satan's realm, between the Spirit who frees the human will for faith and the bondage of one's flesh to the appeal of a malevolent dictator. In all the conflicts that Bonhoeffer confronts in this book, his weapons are the word of God, the unyielding commands of Jesus Christ in the Sermon on the Mount, the Pauline exhortations to imitate the exemplary deeds of Jesus, and, in the face of inevitable suffering, acceptance of the paradoxical power of Jesus in the "weakness" of his cross.

All these subthemes are held together by Bonhoeffer's personal conviction that the freedom of a Christian is rooted in the Reformation principle of faith, lived in complete reliance on God's word in the Bible for direction and support. The Christocentrism of this book is unmistakable. The Christ encountered in *Discipleship* does not avoid the dangers of Jerusalem and the pain of confronting corruption within the temple; he sets out on his relentless journey to the cross. Indeed, the Christ and the Christians of *Discipleship* stand firm despite the crucifixions to which empires like Rome and Nazi Germany subjected their enemies. This is a Christ who frees the disciple to be a genuine person of faith, liberated from the bondage of self-will and its consequent infidelity to the word of God now collapsed into the words of a hypnotic earthly leader.

As we have seen, some critics have disdained this book as an interruption in the straight line from Bonhoeffer's early activism against the Hitler regime and from the affirmations of secularity and pragmatic action in *Ethics* and the prison letters. These critics fail to appreciate Bonhoeffer's ever-shifting dialectic in pitting the Christian disciple against the wiles and twisted values of what he depicts as a world plunged into widespread iniquity. When he wrote *Discipleship*, that world was centered in the totalitarian, anti-God, but wildly popular regime of Adolf Hitler. While many expected Lutheran Bonhoeffer to bring Luther's insistence on faith alone to bear on the Church Struggle with this latter-day Teutonic paganism, he offered instead the revolutionary values of Christ's Sermon on the Mount and his prophetic teachings against calamitous political systems and reductionist religious practices that masqueraded as the easily measured, tension-free path to salvation. Moreover, the final section of *Discipleship*, in which Bonhoeffer speaks of the image of Jesus

Christ, connects readily with that section of *Ethics* in which Bonhoeffer analyzes "Ethics as Formation" and declares that becoming like Jesus "is achieved only when the form of Jesus Christ itself works upon us in such a manner that it molds our form in its own likeness."[31] He goes on to speak of being conformed with the incarnate, crucified, and glorified Jesus. Concluding his thoughts on following Jesus in *Discipleship*, Bonhoeffer writes similarly that "we must be assimilated to the form of Christ in its entirety, the form of Christ incarnate, crucified, and glorified." Because the wording of the two texts is so very close, we can surmise that Bonhoeffer took elements from the last chapter of *Discipleship* in order to incorporate "Ethics as Formation" into the first part of his *Ethics*. Neither text suffers from pious spiritualizing. For Bonhoeffer, the primary challenge of ethical thinking is how to conform one's life to the teachings of Jesus and the patterns of his life lived in obedience to his Father's will. None of the practical sections that follow, such as the paradoxical telling of lies to restore truth in a country dominated by mendacity, fails to take faith in Jesus Christ into account.

There are connections to the prison letters as well. One can hardly miss the close relationship between the theology of the cross throughout the pages of *Discipleship* and Bonhoeffer's theology of a suffering God whose power lies in God's paradoxical weakness that animated several sections of the prison letters. Far from being a detour along the path to the worldliness of the prison letters, *Discipleship* stands, instead, as a pivotal text that explains the steps that led Bonhoeffer from the academic podium to his imprisonment and, despite the "dangers" he conceded,[32] serves to illuminate some of the more moving passages of the prison letters that address the problem of human suffering.

[31.] *E* 80; compare this section of *Ethics*, 80–88, with pages 284–88 below.

[32.] In his prison letters Bonhoeffer admitted that he could "see the dangers of that book, though I still stand by what I wrote" (*LPP* 369). Among those dangers, one can infer that he was alluding to the possibility of a Christian life that could easily be turned in on itself. By the time of his arrest, Bonhoeffer had seen the counteraction to the evil of Nazism emanate as much from nonreligious, nonbelieving good people as from himself and others who were motivated by their concerns of faith and human dignity to deliver their nation and the world from the evil of Nazism. *Discipleship* is very much a book written for Christians, exhorting them to take their Christian faith seriously. In addition to Christianly motivated people like Bonhoeffer, the resistance was equally animated by generous, self-sacrificing people whose motivation was in their humanistic values and innate sense of compassion for the suffering, vulnerable victims of Nazi tyranny.

Nor is it accurate to use Bonhoeffer's continual concern with the problem of affirming personal autonomy over against submission to the commanding authority of Jesus to argue that, in *Discipleship,* he is preoccupied with an internal conflict. Such a view asserts that in *Discipleship* Bonhoeffer vacillates between acting with personal determination, confident in the power of Jesus Christ to convey ultimate victory, and a theology of the cross that accepts suffering, even death—that accepts becoming "weak" in the manner of Jesus, who accepted his own crucifixion at the hands of his enemies. It is more evident that the *power* that Christ's commands engender in active resistance to the evil ideology then rampaging in every corner of civic life in Germany, and the *weakness* of being rendered defenseless in Nazi prisons or at the hands of criminal executioners, are a constant dialectic in Bonhoeffer's *Discipleship.* Bonhoeffer is relentless in urging the Christians of Germany to "confess" their faith and to resist.

Bonhoeffer's insistence on faith and active resistance to societal evil makes it a stretch to claim that Bonhoeffer's invocation of and submission to the absolute authority of Christ's teachings and moral commands represent "a power struggle within himself."[33] On the contrary, the themes of obedience to Christ, submission to Christ's commands,[34] and acceptance of suffering, even death, in following Jesus "all the way" to the cross are not necessarily arenas of Bonhoeffer's inner conflicts as he submitted his enormous self-will to the will of Jesus Christ. Submission to the teachings of Jesus became, instead, an intense experience of the freedom for which he had longed in the disparate paths of his lifelong search for meaning and fulfillment. As he would acknowledge in a letter contemporary to the phases in which *Discipleship* was composed, "[T]he Bible, and in particular the Sermon on the Mount, freed me from that [turning Jesus' teachings "into something of personal advantage" and being "quite

---

[33.] Green, *Bonhoeffer: A Theology of Sociality,* 175. The overall value of this book for understanding Bonhoeffer's early theology and its foundational impact on all of his later writings is well established. Green's exploration of the autobiographical elements in the earlier texts is particularly illuminating in showing how Bonhoeffer's struggle to integrate his ardor for personal autonomy into a wholehearted submission to Jesus Christ would become a driving force in his personal life and influence his Christology. Green, however, may be overstating his case in depicting *Discipleship* as evidence of the continuing personal conflict engendered by Bonhoeffer's personal ego strengths and his willful need for personal autonomy, over against the authority and power of the Christ who commands absolute obedience.

[34.] Ibid., 174–77.

pleased" with himself]. Since then everything has changed. . . . It was a great liberation."[35] The stages of discipleship that lead to the cross are, for Bonhoeffer, liberating moments that he acknowledges as crucial to the truth of the Christian life's journey, in which persons of faith must remain true to what they had accepted in their baptismal consecration as God's way for them. As he wrote in *Life Together*, which elucidates the immediate context of *Discipleship*, namely, his lectures to the seminarians of Finkenwalde on the call to follow Jesus in their common life and in their ministry, Christians had to "be ready to allow [themselves] to be interrupted by God" and not "pass by the visible sign of the cross raised in our lives to show us that God's way, and not our own, is what counts."[36] Passages abound, particularly in the second part of *Discipleship*, in which Bonhoeffer's words represent not a struggle against the negativity of a self-willed person but the positive confidence of becoming renewed in the community of Christ through accepting and living according to Jesus' words. Christians, he believed, were thus empowered to face any danger, even the loss of physical freedom and life itself, for the sake of Jesus Christ.

Discipleship is from beginning to end a call to follow Jesus along the paths already illuminated by God's word and the cross of Christ. The book is as much about what being a Christian demands of those who claim to follow Jesus as it is an exhortation to live and enjoy the only true freedom of a Christian. In the introductory description of his intentions, therefore, Bonhoeffer states clearly his convictions on how following the paths set by Christ's commands is at the center of that free, fulfilling life to which every Christian aspires.

> When holy scripture speaks of following Jesus, it proclaims that people are free from all human rules, from everything which pressures, burdens, or causes worry and torment of conscience. In following Jesus, people are released from the hard yoke of their own laws to be under the gentle yoke of Jesus Christ. . . . In the gentle pressure of this yoke they will receive the strength to walk the right path without becoming weary. . . . Jesus demands nothing from us without giving us the strength to comply. Jesus' commandment never wishes to destroy life, but rather to preserve, strengthen, and heal life.

A little later he adds: "Discipleship is joy."[37]

[35.] *TF* 424–25 (*DBW* 14:113).
[36.] *LT* (*DBWE* 5):99–100.
[37.] See below, page 40.

The Writing of *Discipleship*

To trace the stages during which Bonhoeffer's book was shaped into final form is to study manuscripts, notes, and biographical commentary pertaining to his lectures on Christian discipleship that spanned several years.[38] Bonhoeffer's insights on following Jesus Christ in a world in which Jesus appeared to have less and less relevance were first explored at length in scriptural context, then prayerfully pondered before being spoken to diverse audiences of students and seminarians. His ideas were likewise floated among friends and discussed at length during the 1930s before being put into final form for publication in 1937. The events of the Church Struggle with which he was involved in that troubled decade confirmed Bonhoeffer's convictions about the challenge of Jesus to his disciples to follow him by taking up their cross daily.

That Bonhoeffer desired to preach and teach on Christian discipleship is attested by letters he wrote in 1934 to his Swiss friend and fellow pastor, Erwin Sutz, whom he had come to know at Union Theological Seminary in New York, and to Reinhold Niebuhr, his former teacher at Union. Writing from his pastorate in London on September 11, 1934, Bonhoeffer confided to Sutz that he was struggling over whether to return to Germany to become director of one of the new Preachers' Seminaries or to remain in London, from whence he could go to India to study under Gandhi. He stated that he did not believe that pastors could be trained in the universities any longer, adding:

> The entire training of young seminarians belongs today in church-monastic schools in which the pure doctrine, the Sermon on the Mount, and worship can be taken seriously—which is really not the case with all three things at the university and, in present-day circumstances, is impossible.[39]

Once he had accepted the invitation to direct one of the five Confessing Church seminaries, Bonhoeffer would have the opportunity to put his convictions into practice and into written form.

The letter of July 13, 1934, to Niebuhr, which antedates his letter to Sutz, mentions that he was already writing a text "dealing with the question of the Sermon on the Mount."[40] During his London ministry, too,

---

[38.] This section draws heavily from the meticulous analysis of the stages of composition leading to the final published text of *Discipleship* as recounted in the foreword or *Vorwort* to the German edition (*DBW* 4:8–13).

[39.] *TF* 412 (*DBW* 13:204).

[40.] *DBW* 13:171 (*GS* 6:297).

Bonhoeffer took time to deepen his understanding of the Matthean portrayal of the call of Jesus and to discuss its implications for his own ministry as a member of an opposition church. Evidence of this interest comes from Bonhoeffer's close friend and fellow pastor of Jewish ancestry, Franz Hildebrandt, who had lived with him in London and who recalled Bonhoeffer's several conversations on the Sermon on the Mount during that same period.[41]

The progression from an avid reading of the biblical proclamation of Christ's call to follow him, to writing down insights from prayerful meditations on the Sermon on the Mount, to his formal lectures on Christian discipleship can best be seen, however, in connection with Bonhoeffer's role as director of the Confessing Church seminary in Finkenwalde. Preachers' Seminaries of the Confessing Church, such as the one at Finkenwalde, held courses for groups of young theologians which lasted about half a year. The first course that Bonhoeffer conducted ended in October 1935. The second course began in November 1935 and ended in March 1936. During each of the five courses up to September 1937, Bonhoeffer gave New Testament lectures twice or three times a week. By the opening of the seminary's first location in Zingst on the Baltic coast of Pomerania on April 29, 1935, Bonhoeffer was already prepared to present his first lecture on the New Testament. He was to teach five full-length courses on Christian discipleship when the seminary moved to its second location, a rambling, abandoned schoolhouse at Finkenwalde. During the winter semester of 1935–36 he also traveled each week from the seminary to Berlin University to teach an hour-long class on discipleship in Christ. This continued until the Reich Ministry of Education permanently revoked his teaching permit on August 5, 1936.

The disparate original segments of what later became *Discipleship* exist in the extant fragments of Bonhoeffer's lectures, related conferences, and seminarians' notes.[42] Bonhoeffer's biographer, Eberhard Bethge, recalls that his first lectures to the new seminarians, pastors in training, on discipleship were a "breath-taking surprise."[43] For students, these lectures became an initiation into revolutionary new approaches to the Gospels' description of Jesus' call to ministry. Unfortunately, there

---

[41.] Foreword to the German edition (*DBW* 4:8).

[42.] For references to these student notes, see editorial annotations with the abbreviation *NL*.

[43.] *DB-ER* 450.

are only remnants of Bonhoeffer's original manuscripts, but the seminarians' notes reveal clearly the preliminary stages of the final text. There one reads how Bonhoeffer interpreted the Sermon on the Mount in the context of the call to follow Jesus even to the cross. Each Beatitude was depicted as Jesus' demand to renounce a pseudovalue prized by society in order to be blessed with the freedom bestowed through such renunciation.

This first course ended in October 1935, when Bonhoeffer withdrew to a house owned by his family in Friedrichsbrunn in the Harz Mountains to prepare the next set of lectures. There he advanced his conviction that the entirety of scripture proclaims the one Lord Jesus, calling us to discipleship. This approach became, in essence, the published structure of *Discipleship,* namely, the correlation of the Pauline texts in the second part with the Synoptic Gospels' integration of the Sermon on the Mount and the call of Jesus—the theme of the first part.

Bonhoeffer's annual report of December 21, 1936,[44] notes that, after the initial lectures on discipleship in Christ, he addressed the related themes of "The Visible Church" in the second course and "New Life in Paul" in the third course. He mentioned, too, that in the semester of 1936–37 he was presenting lectures on "Concrete Ethics in Paul." In the final course at the seminary, the theme became "Community Building and Discipline in the New Testament."

Discipleship was to be crafted from these New Testament lectures.[45] For example, Part One of *Discipleship* developed out of his lectures on the call to follow Jesus in the summer courses of 1935 and 1936. Bonhoeffer's presentations on the Sermon on the Mount were delivered in segments of the first, second, and third courses, during 1935–36. Part Two of the book was shaped in a preliminary way through lectures based on Bonhoeffer's reading of the Pauline texts. He incorporated his thoughts on the church as 'new humanity' in courses that spanned the 1935–36, 1936–37, and 1937 terms at Finkenwalde. He covered the topic the sphere of the church in 1935–36 and 1937. His thoughts on living in this sphere were incorporated into courses in the 1936, 1936–37, and 1937 terms.

A careful comparison of these early forms reveals that the chapters dealing with "The Call to Discipleship," "Discipleship and the Cross,"

[44.] *DBW* 14:258–64 (*GS* 2:506–12).
[45.] See *DB-ER* 450–51, and the foreword to the German edition (*DBW* 4:9–12).

"Discipleship and the Individual," and those on the Sermon on the Mount derived from his lectures to the seminarians. Further, Bonhoeffer used in Part Two the Pauline-based lectures on the church as 'new humanity' to produce the chapter "The Body of Christ." His explication of the sphere of the church was used for the chapter on the visible church-community. His comments on living in the sphere of the church, which form a parallel to his exegesis of the Sermon on the Mount, were used for his chapter "The Saints."

It was only after the summer course of 1936 that Bonhoeffer began to revise his New Testament lectures for eventual publication. At that point he composed the chapter "Simple Obedience." Using his Greek-German New Testament he interpreted Matthew 10 for his chapter "The Messengers." After this, he added passages to his original manuscript on the Sermon on the Mount, especially to his commentary on Matthew 5 and 6.

In an introductory chapter to Part Two, Bonhoeffer underscored his conviction that the Pauline emphasis on baptism corresponds to the Synoptics' call to discipleship. He added his commentary on Philemon and Romans 13 to the chapter "The Visible Church-Community" and offered this portion of the manuscript to his seminarians in the summer course of 1937. Next he expanded his chapter "The Saints" with portions of "Statements on the Authority of the Keys and Communal Discipline in the New Testament," which had been copied and distributed for pastors of the Confessing Church in May 1937.[46] The concluding chapter, "The Image of Christ," deals with God's incarnate presence in the church and in all ethical decisions. It reminds one of the concluding part of Bonhoeffer's Christology lectures in the summer of 1933. At the last stages of preparing the book Bonhoeffer composed the "Preliminary Questions" to Part Two and his "Preface" to the book. He reworked the beginnings of his 1935 lectures on following Jesus into the now famous chapter "Cheap Grace."

Comparison of the published text with Bonhoeffer's earlier manuscripts has been doubly complicated by the fact that most of his manuscripts and part of the books of that period did not survive. They had been stored in the attic of a house in Stettin-Altdamm, placed at his disposal by two members of the Finkenwalde Confessing congregation. Although he did send crates of the books to Berlin, the manuscripts

---

[46.] *DBW* 14:836–43 (*GS* 3:374–81); *DBW* 12:340–48 (*GS* 3:231–42).

themselves remained in that house and have disappeared, including the material he used for his New Testament lectures and the original manuscript of the book version of *Discipleship* in 1937. Only one page of the book manuscript has been preserved, the Vilmar excerpt on love of the enemy, found in Bethge's own copy of 1937.

His special group of young pastors, whom Bonhoeffer had formed into a tight-knit community or "Brothers' House" within the seminary,[47] used typed circular letters to keep the former candidates abreast of the book's progress. Their interest in seeing the published version of the lectures, which earlier had so captivated them as listeners, attests to the lasting impression made on his students when Bonhoeffer shared his convictions on Christian discipleship. Some of the remarks in those informative circular letters are replete with humorous allusions to the plodding pace toward eventual publication. We thus read in Eberhard Bethge's report in the twelfth circular letter from Finkenwalde on September 28, 1936, that "our dear director has been trying ever anew to get to his book—to that end he is allegedly living incognito among us." Informing these pastors about the details of Bonhoeffer's birthday celebration of February 4, the seventeenth circular letter of March 3, 1937, relates that "this time the wishes have been reversed and the fourth course made up its own wish list asking that *Discipleship* might please be finished before we ourselves retire. . . ." The letter, however, goes on to reassure the readers that "the section on the 'Sermon on the Mount' is finished, so that not much is lacking for the book's completion." In the eighteenth circular letter of April 17, 1937, Bethge informed the pastors that "I can now report that Brother Bonhoeffer during the holiday has finished a considerable portion of his work, thus prompting great hopes that it will soon be completed." Finally, in the circular letter of August 26, 1937, Horst Lekszas revealed that the book was ready to be handed over to the publisher's typesetter. Lekszas noted that "despite the various delays plaguing any work, the anticipated book is now completed and in the hands of the typist and now awaiting only additional tender loving care."[48]

[47.] See Geffrey B. Kelly, "Editor's Introduction to the English Edition," *LT* (*DBWE* 5):17–20.

[48.] See *NL* A 48 and the foreword to the German edition (*DBW* 4:12).

Publication History in German and English

By the time the Gestapo had closed down the Finkenwalde seminary, the manuscript was on the desk of Otto Solomon, director of the Chr. Kaiser Publishing House in Munich. Solomon, who had published Barth's books and Bonhoeffer's 1933 commentary on Genesis 1–3, *Creation and Fall*,[49] was deeply moved by *Discipleship*. No other book had so stirred him since Barth's *The Epistle to the Romans*.[50] Over the objections of his theological advisors he immediately published the book. Bonhoeffer received his complimentary copies during Advent 1937.

According to the initial publication agreement there would be a run of one thousand copies. A second edition of *Nachfolge* appeared in 1940. The book was reprinted in 1950, a year after the publication of Bethge's posthumous edition of the fragmented manuscripts for Bonhoeffer's *Ethics*. The publishers changed the print from Gothic to Latin script for the seventh edition of *Nachfolge* in 1961. This seventh edition corrected printing and indexing mistakes that had been noted in handwriting by an unknown editor on a printed copy of the sixth edition of 1958. An afterword by Eberhard Bethge was added beginning with the twelfth edition of 1981. By 1987 there had been sixteen editions of *Nachfolge*. In the meantime over 80,000 copies of the German-language editions of the book had been sold.

This new English edition of *Discipleship* is based on the German text published as *DBW* 4 in 1989 and revised in 1994. This German critical edition in turn was based on the first edition of 1937, but with printing errors and other obvious mistakes corrected. *Discipleship* and *Life Together*, despite their mistranslations and glaring omissions, have been Bonhoeffer's most popular books among the English-language readership.

The previous English translation of *Discipleship* by Reginald Fuller was initiated by Bonhoeffer's brother-in-law, Gerhard Leibholz, husband of Bonhoeffer's twin sister, Sabine. It appeared in an abbreviated version in 1948 under the electrifying title *The Cost of Discipleship*. It was the first of Bonhoeffer's books to be published in English. For that first English edition Bonhoeffer's closest British friend, Bishop George Bell of Chichester, wrote the foreword. Gerhard Leibholz also contributed a memoir that supplied a biographical and historical context and served as an introduction for the book.

[49.] *CF* (*DBWE* 3).
[50.] Zimmermann, *I Knew Dietrich Bonhoeffer*, 170.

The first U.S. edition, also abridged, was published by Macmillan in 1949. This book included a preface by Reinhold Niebuhr, Bonhoeffer's former professor and friend at Union Theological Seminary. Omitted from this abridged edition were ten sections of Bonhoeffer's book: "Single-Minded Obedience" from Part One; the whole of "The Messengers," with its sections "The Harvest," "The Apostles," "The Work," "The Suffering of the Messengers," "The Decision," and "The Fruit"; and three sections from Part Two: "Preliminary Questions," "The Visible Community," and "The Saints."

The second edition, published in London by SCM in 1959 and in New York by Macmillan in 1960, restored these missing sections. This edition also contained translation revisions by Irmgard Booth. A paperback edition of this version was issued by Macmillan in 1963 and by SCM in 1964. Unfortunately, considering future citations of *The Cost of Discipleship,* the pagination of this paperback edition differed from the hardcover edition. A hardcover reissue of the 1963 Macmillan edition was marketed by Peter Smith of Gloucester Press in 1983. In 1995, Simon and Schuster issued the first Touchstone edition in paperback.

Matters of Translation

Besides the confusion of differing editions and paginations, English-speaking readers face two problems in understanding Bonhoeffer's original text. The first has to do with the division of the book into four chapters rather than the two parts intended by the author. The table of contents of the German edition makes Bonhoeffer's strategy clear. The first part, which encompasses the first three chapters in the previous, popular English edition, sets forth the meaning of discipleship as disclosed in the Synoptic Gospels—that is, during Jesus' life and ministry with his disciples in Israel. The second part, which is chapter 4 in the previous edition, contains Bonhoeffer's attempt to show that, according to the witness of Paul and other apostles in the New Testament, the resurrected Jesus Christ continued the same call to discipleship, now through baptism, and the same life with his followers, now in the church-community. According to Bonhoeffer, the terminology regarding discipleship changed after the death and resurrection of Jesus, but the reality of discipleship remained the same. If anything, he argues, the call to discipleship is thereafter even more powerful, because it now comes from the risen and glorified Jesus

Christ, who is present in the church that issues the call through word and sacrament. Bonhoeffer's book, then, intended to confirm that the call by the earthly Jesus to follow him continues unbroken in and through the church-community, from the days of Paul and the apostles to the present. The table of contents of the new *DBW* edition makes this clear by using Bonhoeffer's own two-part division for the book and not the arbitrary, artificial division of the popular English-language versions.

The second problem concerns the translation itself. Being an art more than a science, translation is never perfect. Nevertheless, the translators of this new edition not only have corrected mistranslations in the former editions and completed translations of hitherto omitted words, phrases, or sentences. They also have attempted to bring the whole into conformity with Bonhoeffer's usage in the Germany of his day and into consistency with translations in the other volumes of the new English edition of the Dietrich Bonhoeffer Works. Moreover, the translators have kept the language as gender-inclusive as possible when Bonhoeffer's reference is to human beings in general and as gender-free as possible when the reference is to God.

A few examples of specific words that heretofore have received widely differing translations and which have received consistent treatment in *Discipleship* are *Stellvertretung*, rendered as "vicarious representative action"; *Gemeinde*, which can mean "congregation" but is commonly translated here as "church-community" and, at times, "faith-community"; and *Gemeinschaft*, which ordinarily is translated as "community," although at times "communion" is used when it refers to an intimate relation between persons. The variations from the more customary translations are indicated by putting the German word in brackets after the English word or phrase. *Volkskirche* was a particularly difficult German word to translate. We might simply have left the word untranslated, convinced that phrases such as "church of the people" or "people as church" or "national church" or even "state church" were not adequate to describe the Protestant church in Germany in Bonhoeffer's time, a church to which membership seemed to have been bestowed by birth. For the so-called German Christians who had assimilated the Nazi political ideology into their church policies, a *Volkskirche* was a nationalist, *völkisch* (consisting of a certain kind of people), and, therefore, culturally and racially determined social body with a common religion, which in this case was a Teutonic transformation of Christianity. Bonhoeffer categorically criticizes and rejects any such ecclesiology.

As a result of the new title of *Discipleship,* the structuring of the book into two parts—not four—and the fresh, more accurate translation, those accustomed to the earlier English text because of the popularity of the paperback edition may think they are reading a completely new book. However, they will soon discover that, at bottom, the message is exactly the same: the challenging call to the costly but joyful following of Jesus Christ in the modern world. The principal difference is that, in reading this new edition, Christians and their churches will now be challenged by Bonhoeffer's convictions on Christian discipleship in a manner as faithful as possible to Bonhoeffer's original thought.

Acknowledgments

The editors of this volume are profoundly grateful to the two gifted translators who have so artfully used their expert knowledge of the German language to render Bonhoeffer's writing into English that is both accurate and readable. Barbara Green, who translated the first part, is an American who has spent many years in Germany, first as a student and then as the liaison officer of the National Council of Churches in the United States to the Federation of Protestant Churches in the German Democratic Republic (East Germany). Reinhard Krauss, who translated the second part and the German editors' afterword, grew up in postwar Germany but has lived since 1986 in the United States and now pastors a church in California. Both are Presbyterian ministers, and both are veteran translators. We acknowledge, too, the assistance of Albrecht Schönherr, a former seminarian and colleague of Bonhoeffer whom Barbara Green was able to consult. Translations of certain phrases benefited from the insights of someone who was at the seminary at which Bonhoeffer delivered his exciting lectures on Christian discipleship. Likewise, we are grateful for the meticulous reading of the entire translation by Ilse Tödt, one of the editors of *DBW* 4, *Nachfolge,* on which our work is based.

We are also most grateful to Wayne Whitson Floyd, Jr., who, as general editor of the Dietrich Bonhoeffer Works English Edition, provided general oversight to the project from beginning to end, offering invaluable advice on writing style, refereeing debates between the editors and translators, helping with the notes and bibliography, coaxing fidelity to deadlines out of us, and, in the book's last stages before publication, reading and editing the entire text with a critical eye toward consistency and accuracy. In addition, we extend a hearty thanks to the librarians and staff members of the libraries of the Lutheran Theological Seminary in Philadelphia and Wesley Theological Seminary in Washington, D.C., for their gracious assistance in bibliographical research.

Finally, we pay tribute to our wives, Cozette Godsey and Joan Kelly, and to the families of the translators, who have shown admirable patience and support during what seemed more like epochs than years of translating and editing this book, a process that took much longer than any of us ever imagined.

DISCIPLESHIP

PREFACE

IN TIMES OF CHURCH renewal holy scripture naturally becomes richer in content for us. Behind the daily catchwords and battle cries needed in the Church Struggle, a more intense, questioning search arises for the one who is our sole concern, for Jesus himself. What did Jesus want to say to us? What does he want from us today? How does he help us to be faithful Christians today? It is not ultimately important to us what this or that church leader wants. Rather, we want to know what Jesus wants. When we go to hear a sermon, his own word is what we want to hear. This matters to us not only for our own sakes, but also for all those who have become estranged from the church and its message. It is also our opinion that if Jesus himself and Jesus alone with his word were among us in our preaching, then quite a different set of people would hear the word and quite a different set of people would again turn away from it. It is not as if our church's preaching were no longer God's word, but there are so many dissonant sounds, so many human, harsh laws, and so many false hopes and consolations, which still obscure the pure word of Jesus and make a genuine decision more difficult. We surely intend our preaching to be preaching Christ alone. But it is not solely the fault of others if they find our preaching harsh and difficult because it is burdened with formulations and concepts foreign to them. It is simply not true that every word critical of our preaching today can be taken as a rejection of Christ or as anti-Christianity. Today there are a great number of people who come to our preaching, want to hear it, and then repeatedly have to admit sadly that we have made it too difficult for them to get to know Jesus. Do we really want to deny being in community with these people? They believe that it is not the word of Jesus itself that they wish to evade, but that too much of what comes between them and Jesus is merely human, institutional, or doctrinaire. Who among us would not instantly know all the answers which could be given to these people and with which we could easily evade responsibility for them? But would an answer not also demand that we ask whether we ourselves get in the way of Jesus' word by depending perhaps too much on certain formulations, or on a type of sermon intended for its own time, place, and social structure? Or by preaching too "dogmatically" and not enough "for use in life"?[1] Or by preferring to repeat certain ideas from scripture over and over and thus too heedlessly passing over other important passages? Or by preaching our own opinions and convictions too much and Jesus Christ himself too little? Nothing would contradict our own intention more deeply and would be more ruinous for our proclamation than if we burdened with difficult human rules those who are weary and heavy laden, whom Jesus calls unto himself. [2] That would drive them away from him again. How that would mock the love of Jesus Christ in front of Christians and heathen! But since general questions and self-accusations do not help here, let us be led back to scripture, to the word and call of Jesus Christ himself. Away from the poverty and narrowness of our own convictions and questions, here is where we seek the breadth and riches which are bestowed on us in Jesus.

We desire to speak of the call to follow Jesus. In doing so, are we burdening people with a new, heavier yoke? Should even harder, more inexorable rules be added to all the human rules under which their souls and bodies groan? Should our admonition to follow Jesus only prick their uneasy and wounded consciences with an even sharper sting? For this latest of innumerable times in church history, should we make impossible, tormenting, eccentric demands, obedience to which would be the pious luxury of the few? Would such demands have to be rejected by people who work and worry about their daily bread, their jobs, and their families, as the most godless tempting of God? Should the church be trying to erect a spiritual reign of terror over people by threatening earthly and eternal punishment on its own authority and commanding everything a person must believe and do to be saved? Should the church's word bring new tyr-

---

[1.] See letter to Rüdiger Schleicher, April 8, 1936 (*DBW* 14:144–48 [*GS* 3:26]).

[2.] "Those who are weary and heavy laden"; cf. Matt. 11:28. "Human rules rejected" is the caption in the Luther Bible over Matt. 15:1-20. [Bonhoeffer is aware here that Jesus associated the prohibition of human rules with the burdens ordinary people had to bear.] [JG/GK] In the latter passage Luther translated παράδοσις (handing down, as of teachings or commandments, *Menschensatzungen*) with "rules," whereas the NRSV uses "tradition" to express this Greek word.

anny and violent abuse to human souls? It may be that some people yearn for such servitude. But could the church ever serve such a longing?

When holy scripture speaks of following Jesus, it proclaims that people are free from all human rules, from everything which pressures, burdens, or causes worry and torment of conscience. In following Jesus, people are released from the hard yoke of their own laws to be under the gentle yoke of Jesus Christ. Does this disparage the seriousness of Jesus' commandments? No. Instead, only where Jesus' entire commandment and the call to unlimited discipleship remain intact are persons fully free to enter into Jesus' community. Those who follow Jesus' commandment entirely, who let Jesus' yoke rest on them without resistance, will find the burdens they must bear to be light. In the gentle pressure of this yoke they will receive the strength to walk the right path without becoming weary.[3] Jesus' commandment is harsh, inhumanly harsh for someone who resists it. Jesus' commandment is gentle and not difficult for someone who willingly accepts it. "His commandments are not burdensome" (1 John 5:3). Jesus' commandment has nothing to do with forced spiritual cures. Jesus demands nothing from us without giving us the strength to comply. Jesus' commandment never wishes to destroy life, but rather to preserve, strengthen, and heal life.

But the question still troubles us: What could the call to follow Jesus mean today for the worker, the businessman, the farmer, or the soldier? Could it bring an intolerable dilemma into the existence of persons working in the world who are Christian? Is Christianity, defined as following Jesus, a possibility for too small a number of people? Does it imply a rejection of the great masses of people and contempt for the weak and poor? Does it thereby deny the great mercy of Jesus Christ, who came to the

24

[3.] On the image of *yoke*, see Bonhoeffer's sermon on Matt. 11:28-30, London, September 1934 (*DBW* 13:372–78 [*GS* 5:531–32]): "A burden which would simply press a person to the ground becomes bearable through a yoke"; a person can bear it "under the yoke of Jesus, hitched together with him." See Søren Kierkegaard's *Der Einzelne und die Kirche*, 166, where he writes of both discipleship and Christ's yoke. "And just why must 'imitation' be emphasized? Could it be in order to lay a yoke upon men's consciences, or could it mean ascetic self-torturing and that we have learned nothing from the past? . . . No. Discipleship should be emphasized in order to maintain a little justice in Christianity and where possible to bring back a little meaning into Christendom, in order to humiliate with the help of the ideal and to learn how to take refuge in grace" (*Journals and Papers*, 2:346 [trans. altered] [JG/GK]). Bonhoeffer's use of "discipleship," "following Christ" (*Nachfolge*), was heavily influenced by Kierkegaard's extensive use of *Efterfølgelsen* (following-after). English translators of Kierkegaard's original Danish translate *Efterfølgelsen* as "imitation."

sinners and tax collectors,[4] the poor and weak, the misguided and despairing? What should we say to that? Is it a few, or many, who belong with Jesus? Jesus died on the cross alone, abandoned by his disciples. It was not two of his faithful followers who hung beside him, but two murderers. But they all stood beneath the cross: enemies and the faithful, doubters and the fearful, the scornful and the converted, and all of them and their sin were included in this hour in Jesus' prayer for forgiveness God's merciful love lives in the midst of its foes.[5] It is the same Jesus Christ who by grace calls us to follow him and whose grace saves the thief on the cross in his last hour.[6]

Where will the call to discipleship lead those who follow it? What decisions and painful separations will it entail? We must take this question to him who alone knows the answer. Only Jesus Christ, who bids us follow him, knows where the path will lead. But we know that it will be a path full of mercy beyond measure. Discipleship is joy.

Today it seems so difficult to walk with certainty the narrow path of the church's decision[7] and yet to remain wide open to Christ's love for all people, and in God's patience, mercy, and loving-kindness[8] (Titus 3:4) for the weak and godless. Still, both must remain together, or else we will follow merely human paths. May God grant us joy in all seriousness of discipleship, affirmation of the sinners in all rejection of sin, and the overpowering and winning word of the gospel in all defense against our enemies. "Come to me, all who are weary and heavy laden, and I will give you rest. Take my yoke upon you, and learn from me; for I am gentle and humble in heart, and you will find rest for your souls. For my yoke is easy, and my burden is light" (Matt. 11:28-30).

25

[4.] Matt. 9:10f.

[5.] Similar to Ps. 110:2b. Cf. Luther's 1518 interpretation of Psalm 110 (*WA* 1:696–97), as quoted by Karl Witte (*Nun freut euch lieben Christen gemein*, 226). In his 1938 book, *Life Together*, Bonhoeffer took the quote directly from Witte's condensation of it (*LT* [*DBWE* 5]:28).

[6.] See Luke 23:32ff.

[7.] The "church's decision" refers specifically to the Confessing Church and its decision to resist incorporation into the Reich Church. The direction the Confessing Church took was decided in May 1934 at the Barmen Synod and October 1934 at the Second Confessional Synod in Dahlem. Those supporting the Dahlem decisions, known as "Dahlemites," rejected any intervention of the state (i.e., the Nazi regime) into the order of the church. Bonhoeffer belonged to that minority. They were viewed in other church circles in 1937 as unnecessarily stubborn. On Bonhoeffer's evaluation of the "church's decision," see his April 1933 lecture "The Church on the Jewish Question" (*DBW* 12:354 [*GS* 2:49]); and his April 22, 1936, lecture on church union (*DBW* 14:655–80 [*GS* 2:225]). His reference to the "narrow path" derives from Matt. 7:14.

[8.] Bonhoeffer uses "philanthropy" (φιλανθρωπία, loving-kindness, in Titus 3:4) in the literal sense, meaning "love for human persons."

PART ONE

CHAPTER ONE

COSTLY GRACE

CHEAP GRACE IS THE mortal enemy of our church.[1] Our struggle today is for costly grace.

Cheap grace means grace as bargain-basement goods, cut-rate forgiveness, cut-rate comfort, cut-rate sacrament; grace as the church's inexhaustible pantry, from which it is doled out by careless hands without hesitation or limit. It is grace without a price, without costs. It is said that the essence of grace is that the bill for it is paid in advance for all time. Everything can be had for free, courtesy of that paid bill. The price paid is infinitely great and, therefore, the possibilities of taking advantage of and wasting grace are also infinitely great. What would grace be, if it were not cheap grace?

Cheap grace means grace as doctrine, as principle, as system. It means forgiveness of sins as a general truth; it means God's love as merely a Christian idea of God. Those who affirm it have already had their sins forgiven. The church that teaches this doctrine of grace thereby confers such grace upon itself. The world finds in this church a cheap cover-up for its sins, for which it shows no remorse and from which it has even less desire to be set free. Cheap grace is, thus, denial of God's living word, denial of the incarnation[2] of the word of God.

Cheap grace means justification of sin but not of the sinner. Because grace alone does everything, everything can stay in its old ways. "Our action is in vain." The world remains world and we remain sinners "even

---

[1.] Part One of the book, which begins with this introduction, is not titled in the printed edition. In 1936 Bonhoeffer called it "Discipleship in the Synoptics," that is, in the first three Gospels (*DBW* 14:618 [*NL* B9, 5 (41)]).

[2.] The word "incarnation" appears in seminarians' notes from Finkenwalde only on February 3, 1936—especially in what would become the final chapter, "The Image of Christ" (see *DBW* 14:461).

30 in the best of lives."[3] Thus, the Christian should live the same way the world does. In all things the Christian should go along with the world and not venture (like sixteenth-century enthusiasts) to live a different life under grace from that under sin! The Christian better not rage against grace or defile that glorious cheap grace by proclaiming anew a servitude to the letter of the Bible in an attempt to live an obedient life under the commandments of Jesus Christ! The world is justified by grace, therefore—because this grace is so serious! because this irreplaceable grace should not be opposed—the Christian should live just like the rest of the world! Of course, a Christian would like to do something exceptional! Undoubtedly, it must be the most difficult renunciation not to do so and to live like the world. But the Christian has to do it, has to practice such self-denial so that there is no difference between Christian life and worldly life. The Christian has to let grace truly be grace enough so that the world does not lose faith in this cheap grace. In being worldly, however, in this necessary renunciation required for the sake of the world—no, for the sake of grace!—the Christian can be comforted and secure (*securus*)[4] in possession of that grace which takes care of everything by itself. So the Christian need not follow Christ, since the Christian is comforted by grace! That is cheap grace as justification of sin, but not justification of the contrite sinner who turns away from sin and repents. It is not forgiveness of sin which separates those who sinned from sin. Cheap grace is that grace which we bestow on ourselves.

Cheap grace is preaching forgiveness without repentance; it is baptism without the discipline of community; it is the Lord's Supper without confession of sin; it is absolution without personal confession. Cheap grace is grace without discipleship, grace without the cross, grace without the living, incarnate Jesus Christ.

Costly grace is the hidden treasure in the field, for the sake of which

---

[3.] This is a citation from the second verse of Martin Luther's hymn based on Psalm 130, "Out of the Depths I Have Cried to You" (*The Lutheran Hymnary*, no. 273, and *Lutheran Book of Worship*, no. 295 ["Aus tiefer Not schrei ich zu dir" (*Evangelisches Gesangbuch für Brandenburg und Pommern*, 140, 2; *Evangelisches Gesangbuch*, 299, 2)]). In his book *The Divine Imperative*, Emil Brunner referred to this line in connection with *iustitia civilis* (civil justice), which Bonhoeffer underlined in his copy. This accords with Eberhard Bethge's student notes of the first lectures on "Discipleship" during the summer term of 1935. *NL* B 8 (1).

[4.] See Luther, *Lectures on Romans*, *LW* 25:20 [*WA* 56]. In 1935 Bonhoeffer illustrated 'false security' (*securitas* in contrast to *certitudo* or certainty) using King David: he "sinned against the promise; he sinned against grace" (*DBW* 14:895–96 [*GS* 4:311–12]).

[5.] Matt. 13:44.

people go and sell with joy everything they have.[5] It is the costly pearl, for whose price the merchant sells all that he has;[6] it is Christ's sovereignty, for the sake of which you tear out an eye if it causes you to stumble.[7] It is the call of Jesus Christ which causes a disciple to leave his nets and follow him.[8]

31

Costly grace is the gospel which must be sought again and again, the gift which has to be asked for, the door at which one has to knock.[9]

It is costly, because it calls to discipleship; it is grace, because it calls us to follow *Jesus Christ*. It is costly, because it costs people their lives; it is grace, because it thereby makes them live. It is costly, because it condemns sin; it is grace, because it justifies the sinner. Above all, grace is costly, because it was costly to God, because it costs God the life of God's Son—"you were bought with a price"[10]—and because nothing can be cheap to us which is costly to God. Above all, it is grace because the life of God's Son was not too costly for God to give in order to make us live. God did, indeed, give him up for us. Costly grace is the incarnation of God.

Costly grace is grace as God's holy treasure which must be protected from the world and which must not be thrown to the dogs.[11] Thus, it is grace as living word, word of God, which God speaks as God pleases. It comes to us as a gracious call to follow Jesus; it comes as a forgiving word to the fearful spirit and the broken heart.[12] Grace is costly, because it forces people under the yoke of following Jesus Christ; it is grace when Jesus says, "My yoke is easy, and my burden is light."[13]

[6.] Matt. 13:45f.

[7.] Mark 9:47 (parallel in Matt. 5:29). The word βασιλεία, which Luther translated *Reich*, suggests the word "king." The expression "sovereignty of Christ," *Königsherrschaft Christi*, was used mainly by Reformed theologians, but less so by Lutherans.

[8.] Mark 1:16–20.

[9.] Matt. 7:7

[10.] 1 Cor. 6:20.

[11.] Matt. 7:6. As early as Finkenwalde, Bonhoeffer called this way of protecting the faith an "arcane discipline," or "discipline of the secret." This term derives from the practice in the early church called "arcani disciplina." See *NL* B 12, 2 (2), which comes from 1936–37 (*DBW* 14:549–50), and *LPP* (286) from 1944. On the "discipline of the secret," see Godsey, *The Theology of Dietrich Bonhoeffer*, 254, and Kelly, *Liberating Faith*, 133–38. See also John W. Matthews, "Responsible Sharing of the Mystery of Christian Faith: *Disciplina Arcani* in the Life and Theology of Dietrich Bonhoeffer." [JG/GK]

[12.] Ps. 51:17.

[13.] Matt. 11:30.

Twice the call went out to Peter: Follow me! It was Jesus' first and last word to his disciple (Mark 1:17; John 21:22). His whole life lies between

32 these two calls. The first time, in response to Jesus' call, Peter left his nets, his vocation, at the Sea of Galilee and followed him on his word. The last time, the Resurrected One finds him at his old vocation, again at the Sea of Galilee, and again he calls: Follow me! Between the two lies a whole life of discipleship following Christ. At its center stands Peter's confession of Jesus as the Christ of God. The same message is proclaimed to Peter three times: at the beginning, at the end, and in Caesarea Philippi,[14] namely, that Christ is his Lord and God. It is the same grace of Christ which summons him—Follow me! This same grace also reveals itself to him in his confessing the Son of God.

Grace visited Peter three times along his life's path. It was the one grace, but proclaimed differently three times. Thus, it was Christ's own grace, and surely not grace which the disciple conferred on himself. It was the same grace of Christ which won Peter over to leave everything[15] to follow him, which brought about Peter's confession which had to seem like blasphemy to all the world, and which called the unfaithful Peter into the ultimate community of martyrdom and, in doing so, forgave him all his sins. In Peter's life, grace and discipleship belong inseparably together. He received costly grace.

The expansion of Christianity and the increasing secularization of the church caused the awareness of costly grace to be gradually lost. The world was Christianized; grace became common property of a Christian world. It could be had cheaply. But the Roman church did keep a remnant of that original awareness. It was decisive that monasticism did not separate from the church and that the church had the good sense to tolerate monasticism. Here, on the boundary of the church, was the place where the awareness that grace is costly and that grace includes discipleship was preserved.[16] People left everything they had for the sake of

33 Christ and tried to follow Jesus' strict commandments through daily exer-

---

[14.] The place where Peter confessed; see Matt. 16:13ff. Matthew 16:24 recounts Jesus' call to follow him.

[15.] Mark 10:28. Bonhoeffer had worked with the article by Gerhard Kittel on ἀκολυθεῖν ("following") in Kittel, *Theological Dictionary of the New Testament*, 1:213–14.

[16.] See Bonhoeffer's letter to his brother Karl-Friedrich, January 14, 1935, in which he writes: "The restoration of the church will surely come from a sort of new monasticism which has in common with the old only the uncompromising attitude of a life lived according to the Sermon on the Mount in the following of Christ" (*TF* 424 [*DBW* 13:273; *GS* 3:25]). [JG/GK]

cise.[17] Monastic life thus became a living protest against the secularization of Christianity, against the cheapening of grace. But because the church tolerated this protest and did not permit it to build up to a final explosion, the church relativized it. It even gained from the protest a justification for its own secular life. For now monastic life became the extraordinary achievement of individuals, to which the majority of church members need not be obligated. The fateful limiting of the validity of Jesus' commandments to a certain group of especially qualified people led to differentiating between highest achievement and lowest performance in Christian obedience. This made it possible, when the secularization of the church was attacked any further, to point to the possibility of the monastic way within the church, alongside which another possibility, that of an easier way, was also justified. Thus, calling attention to the original Christian understanding of costly grace as it was retained in the Roman church through monasticism enabled the church paradoxically to give final legitimacy to its own secularization. But the decisive mistake of monasticism was not that it followed the grace-laden path of strict discipleship, even with all of monasticism's misunderstandings of the contents of the will of Jesus. Rather, the mistake was that monasticism essentially distanced itself from what is Christian by permitting its way to become the extraordinary achievement of a few, thereby claiming a special meritoriousness for itself.

During the Reformation, God reawakened the gospel of pure, costly grace through God's servant Martin Luther by leading him through the monastery. Luther was a monk. He had left everything and wanted to follow Christ in complete obedience. He renounced the world and turned to Christian works. He learned obedience to Christ and his church, because he knew that only those who are obedient can believe. Luther invested his whole life in his call to the monastery. It was God who caused Luther to fail on that path. God showed him through scripture that discipleship is not the meritorious achievement of individuals, but a divine commandment to all Christians. The humble work of discipleship had become in monasticism the meritorious work of the holy ones.[18] The

34

[17.] Bonhoeffer used the Latin word for "exercise," *exercitium,* in his lectures of 1932 (*DBWE* 3:23, note 11) and 1933 (*DBW* 12:199). *NL* B 5, 2 (1) and *NL* B 2, 3 (49).

[18.] See Bethge's 1935 notes, *NL* B 8 (1): "In *Catholicism* discipleship was corrupted, not because some entered the monastery, but because that was portrayed as meritorious, extraordinary." See Kierkegaard, *Søren Kierkegaard's Journals and Papers:* "Then came meritoriousness, but how in the world could meritoriousness otherwise have arisen if discipleship [*Efterfølgelsen*] had been clearly maintained simply as the requirement" (2:356 [trans. altered]).

self-denial of the disciple[19] is revealed here as the final spiritual self-affirmation of the especially pious. This meant that the world had broken into the middle of monastic life and was at work again in a most dangerous way. Luther saw the monk's escape from the world as really a subtle love for the world.[20] In this shattering of his last possibility to achieve a pious life, grace seized Luther. In the collapse of the monastic world, he saw God's saving hand reaching out in Christ. He seized it in the faith that "our deeds are in vain, even in the best life."[21] It was a costly grace, which gave itself to him. It shattered his whole existence. Once again, he had to leave his nets and follow.[22] The first time, when he entered the monastery, he left everything behind except himself, his pious self. This time even that was taken from him. He followed, not by his own merit, but by God's grace. He was not told, yes, you have sinned, but now all that is forgiven. Continue on where you were and comfort yourself with forgiveness! Luther had to leave the monastery and reenter the world, not because the world itself was good and holy, but because even the monastery was nothing else but world.[23]

Luther's path out of the monastery back to the world meant the sharpest attack that had been launched on the world since early Christianity. The rejection which the monk had given the world was child's play compared to the rejection that the world endured through his returning to it. This time the attack was a frontal assault.[24] Following Jesus now had to be lived out in the midst of the world. What had been practiced in the special, easier circumstances of monastic life as a special accomplishment now had become what was necessary and commanded for every Christian in the world. Complete obedience to Jesus' commandments had to be carried out in the daily world of work. This deepened the conflict between the life of Christians and the life of the world

35

[19.] Mark 8:34.

[20.] See Kierkegaard, *Søren Kierkegaard's Journals and Papers:* "And 'the extraordinary' found pleasure in this recognition—again the secular mentality" (2:357).

[21.] Line from the hymn "Out of the Depths I Have Cried to You." See above, page 44, editorial note 3.

[22.] See Mark 1:18.

[23.] In his 1936 draft of a catechism for a confirmation lesson plan, Bonhoeffer wrote: "'[W]orld' [in scripture] is everything which wants to pull my heart away from God" (*DBW* 14:798 [*GS* 3:346]).

[24.] See Kierkegaard, *Søren Kierkegaard's Journals and Papers:* "If the established order wants to have a direct attack, well, here it is— . . . Luther rescued 'discipleship, the imitation of Christ' from a fantastic misunderstanding . . ." (3:87 [trans. altered]).

in an unforeseeable way. The Christian had closed in on the world. It was hand-to-hand combat.

Luther's deed cannot be misunderstood more grievously than by thinking that through discovering the gospel of pure grace, Luther proclaimed a dispensation from obeying Jesus' commandments in the world. The Reformation's main discovery would then be the sanctification and justification of the world by grace's forgiving power. For Luther, on the contrary, a Christian's secular vocation is justified only in that one's protest against the world is thereby most sharply expressed. A Christian's secular vocation receives new recognition from the gospel only to the extent that it is carried on while following Jesus. Luther's reason for leaving the monastery was not justification of the sin, but justification of the sinner. Costly grace was given as a gift to Luther. It was grace, because it was water onto thirsty land, comfort for anxiety, liberation from the servitude of a self-chosen path, forgiveness of all sins. The grace was costly, because it did not excuse one from works. Instead, it endlessly sharpened the call to discipleship. But just wherein it was costly, that was wherein it was grace. And where it was grace, that was where it was costly. That was the secret of the Reformation gospel, the secret of the justification of the sinner.

Nonetheless, what emerged victorious from Reformation history was not Luther's recognition of pure, costly grace, but the alert religious instinct of human beings for the place where grace could be had the cheapest.[25] Only a small, hardly noticeable distortion of the emphasis was needed, and that most dangerous and ruinous deed was done. Luther had taught that, even in their most pious ways and deeds, persons cannot stand before God, because they are basically always seeking themselves. Faced with this predicament, he seized the grace of free and unconditional forgiveness of all sins in faith. Luther knew that this grace had cost him one life and daily continued to cost him, for he was not excused by grace from discipleship, but instead was all the more thrust into it. Whenever Luther spoke of grace, he always meant to include his own life, which was only really placed into full obedience to Christ through grace. He could not speak of grace any other way than this.

36

[25.] Ibid.: "It was found that the Pope had become too expensive—and then . . . through the turn which [Luther] gave to the matter men thought to get salvation a little cheaper, absolutely free" (3:91); also see Kierkegaard's comment that ". . . as soon as 'imitation' is taken away 'grace' is essentially [the sale of] indulgences" (2:174). And see *DBW* 14:751: "Gospel = cheap indulgence."

Luther said that grace alone did it,[26] and his followers repeat it literally, with the one difference that very soon they left out and did not
consider and did not mention what Luther always included as a matter of
course: discipleship. Yes, he no longer even needed to say it, because he
always spoke as one whom grace had led into a most difficult following
of Jesus. The followers' own teaching ["by grace alone"] was, therefore,
unassailable, judged by Luther's teaching, but their teaching meant the
end and the destruction of the Reformation as the revelation of God's
costly grace on earth. The justification of the sinner in the world became
the justification of sin and the world. Without discipleship, costly grace
would become cheap grace.

When Luther said that our deeds are in vain, even in the best of lives,
and that, therefore, nothing is valid before God "except grace and favor to
forgive sins,"[27] he said it as someone who knew himself called to follow Jesus, called to leave everything he had up until this moment, and
in the same moment called anew to do it again. His acknowledgment of
grace was for him the final radical break with the sin of his life but never its
justification. Grasping at forgiveness was the final radical rejection of self-
willed life; the acknowledgment of grace itself his first really serious call to
discipleship. It was a "conclusion" for him,[28] although a divine conclusion,
not a human one. His descendants made this conclusion into a principled
presupposition on which to base their calculations. That was the whole
trouble. If grace is the "result" given by Christ himself to Christian life, then
this life is not for one moment excused from discipleship. But if grace is a
principled presupposition of my Christian life, then in advance I have justification of whatever sins I commit in my life in the world. I can now sin on
the basis of this grace; the world is in principle justified by grace. I can thus
remain as before in my bourgeois-secular existence. Everything remains
as before, and I can be sure that God's grace takes care of me. The whole
world has become "Christian" under this grace, but Christianity has become
the world under this grace as never before. The conflict between a Christian and a bourgeois-secular vocation is resolved. Christian life consists of
my living in the world and like the world, my not being any different from

37

[26.] In Luther's translation of Rom. 3:28, this is emphasized by the interpretive addition of "alone": "so now we believe that the human person is justified without works of the
law, by faith alone"—justified by "grace" (cf. Rom. 3:24 and 4:4).

[27.] Line from the hymn "Out of the Depths I Have Cried to You."

[28.] Bonhoeffer avails himself here of Kierkegaard's use of the word; see the following
paragraph.

it, my not being permitted to be different from it—for the sake of grace!—
but my going occasionally from the sphere of the world to the sphere of the
church, in order to be reassured there of the forgiveness of my sins. I am
liberated from following Jesus—by cheap grace, which has to be the bitter-
est enemy of discipleship, which has to hate and despise true discipleship.
Grace as presupposition is grace at its cheapest; grace as a conclusion is
costly grace. It is appalling to see what is at stake in the way in which a gospel
truth is expressed and used. It is the same word of the justification by grace
alone, and yet false use of the same statement can lead to the complete　　38
destruction of its essence.

　　When Faust says at the end of his life of seeking knowledge, "I see
that we can know nothing,"[29] then that is a conclusion, a result. It is
something entirely different than when a student repeats this statement
in the first semester to justify his laziness (Kierkegaard).[30] Used as a
conclusion, the sentence is true; as a presupposition, it is self-deception.
That means that knowledge cannot be separated from the existence in
which it was acquired. Only those who in following Christ leave everything they have can stand and say that they are justified solely by grace.
They recognize the call to discipleship itself as grace and grace as that
call. But those who want to use this grace to excuse themselves from
discipleship are deceiving themselves.

　　But doesn't Luther himself come dangerously close to this complete
distortion in understanding grace? What does it mean for Luther to say:
"Pecca fortiter, sed fortius fide et gaude in Christo"—"Sin boldly, but
believe and rejoice in Christ even more boldly!"*[31] So you are only a
sinner and can never get out of sin; whether you are a monk or a secu-

---

*Enders III, 208, 118ff.[31]

[29.] See Goethe, *Faust*, pt. 1, v. 364.

[30.] See Kierkegaard, *Søren Kierkegaard's Journals and Papers*: "And just as I, if I were
an innkeeper, . . . because I would be aware of not having the presuppositions which that
scholar had, presuppositions which gave him the right to say 'It is not scholarship that matters'—would not dare to take it as a conclusion and repeat it, just so would I far less (for
the matter is far more important) take the Lutheran principle as a result . . ." (3:94 [trans.
altered]. Bonhoeffer marked "as a conclusion" strongly.

[31.] This is a reference to the edition of Luther's letters entitled *Dr. Martin Luthers Briefwechsel*. The same source (Luther's letter to Melanchthon, August 1, 1521) is cited in Holl,
Luther, 235, note 3. Bonhoeffer used this quotation in *Act and Being* (*DBWE* 2):123. See *Briefwechsel* 2:372, 84f. The complete citation is found in *Briefwechsel* (ed. Enders), 3:208, lines
121ff.: "Esto peccator et pecca fortiter, sed fortius fide et gaude in Christo, qui victor est

lar person, whether you want to be pious or evil, you will not flee the bonds of the world, you will sin. So, then, sin boldly, and on the basis of grace already given! Is this blatant proclamation of cheap grace carte blanche for sin, and rejection of discipleship? Is it a blasphemous invitation to sin deliberately while relying on grace? Is there a more diabolical abuse of grace than sinning while relying on the gift of God's grace? Isn't the Catholic catechism right in recognizing this as sin against the Holy Spirit?[32]

To understand this, everything depends on how the difference between result and presupposition is applied. If Luther's statement is used as a presupposition for a theology of grace, then it proclaims cheap grace. But Luther's statement is to be understood correctly not as a beginning, but exclusively as an end, a conclusion, a last stone, as the very last word. Understood as a presupposition, pecca fortiter becomes an ethical principle. If grace is a principle, then pecca fortiter as a principle would correspond to it. That is justification of sin. It turns Luther's statement into its opposite. "Sin boldly"—that could be for Luther only the very last bit of pastoral advice, of consolation for those who along the path of discipleship have come to know that they cannot become sin-free, who out of fear of sin despair of God's grace. For them, "sin boldly" is not something like a fundamental affirmation of their disobedient lives. Rather, it is the gospel of God's grace, in the presence of which we are sinners always and at every place. This gospel seeks us and justifies us exactly as sinners. Admit your sin boldly; do not try to flee from it, but "believe much more boldly." You are a sinner, so just be a sinner. Do not want to be anything else than what you are. Become a sinner again every day and be bold in doing so. But to whom could such a thing be said except to those who from their hearts daily reject sin, who every day reject everything that hinders them from following Jesus and who are still unconsoled about their daily unfaithfulness and sin? Who else could hear it without danger for their faith than those who are called anew by such consolation to follow Christ? In this way, Luther's

---

peccati, mortis et mundi" (Be then a sinner and sin boldly, but believe and rejoice still more boldly in Christ, who is victor over sin, death, and the world [*LW* 48:282, trans. altered]).

[32.] Matt. 12:31f. Bonhoeffer bases his observation on the Roman Catechism of 1566, a copy of which is in the surviving remnant of Bonhoeffer's library. The text refers to this in the fifth chapter of the second part: "19. In what sense it is meant that some sins cannot be forgiven." See the catechism of Deharbe, as found in Schmitt, *Von den Geboten*, 554.

statement, understood as a conclusion, becomes that costly grace which alone is grace.

Grace as a principle, pecca fortiter as a principle, cheap grace—all these are finally only a new law, which neither helps nor liberates. Grace   40 as a living word, pecca fortiter as comfort in a time of despair and a call to discipleship, costly grace alone is pure grace, which really forgives sins and liberates the sinner.

Like ravens we have gathered around the carcass of cheap grace. From it we have imbibed the poison which has killed the following of Jesus among us. The doctrine of pure grace experienced an unprecedented deification. The pure doctrine of grace became its own God, grace itself.[33] Luther's teachings are quoted everywhere, but twisted from their truth into self-delusion. They say if only our church is in possession of a doctrine of justification, then it is surely a justified church! They say Luther's true legacy should be recognizable in making grace as cheap as possible. Being Lutheran should mean that discipleship is left to the legalists, the Reformed, or the enthusiasts, all for the sake of grace. They say that the world is justified and Christians in discipleship are made out to be heretics. A people became Christian, became Lutheran, but at the cost of discipleship, at an all-too-cheap price. Cheap grace had won.

But do we also know that this cheap grace has been utterly unmerciful against us?[34] Is the price that we are paying today with the collapse of the organized churches anything else but an inevitable consequence of grace acquired too cheaply?[35] We gave away preaching and sacraments cheaply; we performed baptisms and confirmations; we absolved an entire people, unquestioned and unconditionally; out of human love we handed over what was holy to the scornful and unbelievers. We poured out rivers of grace without end, but the call to rigorously follow Christ was seldom

---

[33.] See Kierkegaard, *Søren Kierkegaard's Journals and Papers:* "The definition of 'Church' found in the Augsburg Confession" overlooked "the communion of saints (in which there is the qualification in the direction of the existential [Existentielle]) . . .—but the "doctrine" is correct. . . . This is really paganism" (1:244). Here Bonhoeffer used the word "apotheosis," meaning "deification."

[34.] See Bethge's 1935 notes, *NL* B 8: "'Principle of grace'—no way!! Otherwise merciful grace becomes unmerciful grace."

[35.] On the situation of the Protestant church, see Bonhoeffer's 1936 essay on church union. There he states categorically that "The nature of the church is not determined by those who belong to it but by the word and sacrament of Jesus Christ which, where they are effective, gather for themselves a community in accordance with the promise" (*TF* 164–65 [*DBW* 14:673–76 (*GS* 2:236–38)]).

heard. What happened to the insights of the ancient church, which in the baptismal teaching watched so carefully over the boundary between the church and the world, over costly grace?[36] What happened to Luther's warnings against a proclamation of the gospel which made people secure in their godless lives? When was the world ever Christianized more dreadfully and wickedly than here? What do the three thousand Saxons whose bodies Charlemagne killed compare with the millions of souls being killed today?[37] The biblical wisdom that the sins of the fathers are visited on the children unto the third and fourth generation has become true in us.[38] Cheap grace was very unmerciful to our Protestant church.

Cheap grace surely has also been unmerciful with most of us personally. It did not open the way to Christ for us, but rather closed it. It did not call us into discipleship, but hardened us in disobedience. Moreover, was it not unmerciful and cruel when we were accosted by the message of cheap grace just where we had once heard the call to follow Jesus as Christ's call of grace, where we perhaps had once dared to take the first steps of discipleship in the discipline of obedience to the commandments? Could we hear this message in any other way than that it tried to block our way with the call to a highly worldly sobriety which suffocated our joy in discipleship by pointing out that it was all merely the path we chose ourselves, that it was an exertion of strength, effort, and discipline which was unnecessary, even very dangerous? For, after all, everything was already prepared and fulfilled by grace! The glowing wick was mercilessly extinguished.[39] It was unmerciful to speak to such people since

---

[36.] In Finkenwalde, Bonhoeffer discussed at length the catechization of the early church (including "the discipline of the secret") in light of the church's behavior in his time. See Joachim Kanitz's 1935 notes from Finkenwalde, and Erich Klapproth's notes from the winter semester 1936–37 (*DBW* 14:546–51).

[37.] In 782 c.e., Charlemagne had thousands of people from the Saxon tribe executed. The National Socialist propaganda machine used this historical fact against the church. Bonhoeffer always mentioned Charlemagne's name in the context of the *filioque* formula in the Nicene Creed: ". . . the Spirit proceeds from the Father *and the Son*." Charlemagne imposed this christological formula on the territory he ruled. See the student notes of Eberhard Bethge from 1935, Wolf-Dieter Zimmermann from 1936, and Erich Klapproth from 1936–37 (*DBW* 14:467, 472, 774). In 1933 the German Christians, equating a people with a church, proclaimed a national spirit that was not judged by Christ, but built on their *völkisch* traditions. During Bonhoeffer's work on the Bethel Confession in 1933, which contained a passage on the renewal of the *filioque* teaching, he wrote to his grandmother on August 20, 1933: "The issue really is: Germanism or Christianity" (*DB-ER* 302 [*DBW* 12:118 (*GS* 2:79)]). Cf *DBW* 14:369–70.

[38.] Exodus 20:5 and Deut. 5:9.

[39.] See Isa. 42:3 (Matt. 12:20).

they, confused by such a cheap offer, were forced to leave the path to which Christ called them clutching instead at cheap grace. Cheap grace would permanently prevent them, from recognizing costly grace. It could not happen any other way but that possessing cheap grace would mislead weaklings to suddenly feel strong,[40] yet in reality, they had lost their power for obedience and discipleship. The word of cheap grace has ruined more Christians than any commandment about works.

In everything that follows, we want to speak up on behalf of those who are tempted to despair, for whom the word of grace has become frightfully empty. For integrity's sake someone has to speak up for those among us who confess that cheap grace has made them give up following Christ, and that ceasing to follow Christ has made them lose the knowledge of costly grace. Because we cannot deny that we no longer stand in true discipleship to Christ, while being members of a true-believing church with a pure doctrine of grace, but no longer members of a church which follows Christ, we therefore simply have to try to understand grace and discipleship again in correct relationship to each other. We can no longer avoid this. Our church's predicament is proving more and more clearly to be a question of how we are to live as Christians today.

Blessed are they who already stand at the end of the path on which we wish to embark and perceive with amazement what really seems inconceivable: that grace is costly, precisely because it is pure grace, because it is God's grace in Jesus Christ.[41] Blessed are they who by simply following Jesus Christ are overcome by this grace, so that with humble spirit they may praise the grace of Christ which alone is effective. Blessed are they who, in the knowledge of such grace, can live in the world without losing themselves in it. In following Christ their heavenly home has

43

[40.] On Bonhoeffer's reference to "weak" and "strong" people, see Romans 14. In the confrontation with German Christians in the new auditorium of Berlin University on June 22, 1933, Bonhoeffer described the "weak" as those aggressive ones who wanted to prohibit all that was Jewish from the German church (*DB-ER* 287; cf. *DBW* 12:85).

[41.] In the year 1937 alone, twenty-seven former Finkenwalde seminarians were imprisoned for shorter or longer periods for disobeying wanton government prohibitions, according to Bonhoeffer's annual report on 1937 (*DBW* 15:14–15 [*GS* 2:524]). A letter from Willi Brandenburg from the police prison in Frankfurt/Oder was enclosed with the tenth newsletter from Finkenwalde, July 22, 1936: ". . . the Lord Christ! This is life, this is blessedness, for this is forgiveness of sins. As a good theologian, one knows this, but in such a situation one really experiences it" (*DBW* 14:202 [*GS* 2:497]). Bonhoeffer comments on this letter: "It is strange how every word counts which comes from such a situation" (*DBW* 14:199–200 [*GS* 2:494]).

become so certain that they are truly free for life in this world. Blessed are they for whom following Jesus Christ means nothing other than living from grace and for whom grace means following Christ. Blessed are they who in this sense have become Christians, for whom the word of grace has been merciful.

CHAPTER TWO

THE CALL TO DISCIPLESHIP

"As Jesus was walking along, he saw Levi son of Alphaeus sitting   45
at the tax booth, and he said to him, 'Follow me.' And he got up and followed him" (Mark 2:14).

The call goes out, and without any further ado the obedient deed of
the one called follows. The disciple's answer is not a spoken confession of
faith in Jesus. Instead, it is the obedient deed. How is this direct relation
between call and obedience possible? It is quite offensive to natural reason. Reason is impelled to reject the abruptness of the response. It seeks
something to mediate it; it seeks an explanation. No matter what, some
sort of mediation has to be found, psychological or historical. Some have
asked the foolish question whether the tax collector had known Jesus
previously and therefore was prepared to follow his call.[1] But the text
is stubbornly silent on this point; in it, everything depends on call and
deed directly facing each other. The text is not interested in psychological explanations for the faithful decisions of a person. Why not? Because
there is only one good reason for the proximity of call and deed: *Jesus
Christ himself.* It is he who calls. That is why the tax collector follows. This
encounter gives witness to Jesus' unconditional, immediate, and inex-
plicable authority. Nothing precedes it, and nothing follows except the
obedience of the called. Because Jesus is the Christ, he has authority to
call and to demand obedience to his word. Jesus calls to discipleship, not
as a teacher and a role model, but as the Christ, the Son of God. Thus, in
this short text Jesus Christ and his claim on people are proclaimed, and

---

[1.] This solution, which Bonhoeffer thought was to an artificial problem, was offered
by Weiss, *The Life of Christ,* 2:124, and before him by Neander, *The Life of Jesus Christ,* 213.

nothing else. No praise falls on the disciple or on his espoused Christianity.[2] Attention should not fall to him, but only to the one who calls,
46   to his authority. Not even a path to faith, to discipleship, is aimed at;
there is no other path to faith than obedience to Jesus' call.

What is said about the content of discipleship? Follow me, walk
behind me! That is all. Going after him is something without specific
content. It is truly not a program for one's life which would be sensible
to implement. It is neither a goal nor an ideal to be sought. It is not even
a matter for which, according to human inclination, it would be worth
investing anything at all, much less oneself. And what happens? Those
called leave everything they have, not in order to do something valuable.
Instead, they do it simply for the sake of the call itself, because otherwise
they could not walk behind Jesus. Nothing of importance is attached
to this action in itself. It remains something completely insignificant,
unworthy of notice. The bridges are torn down, and the followers simply
move ahead. They are called away and are supposed to "step out" of their
previous existence, they are supposed to "exist" in the strict sense of the
word.[3] Former things are left behind; they are completely given up.
The disciple is thrown out of the relative security of life into complete
insecurity (which in truth is absolute security and protection in community with Jesus); out of the foreseeable and calculable realm (which
in truth is unreliable) into the completely unforeseeable, coincidental
realm (which in truth is the only necessary and reliable one); out of the
realm of limited possibilities (which in truth is that of unlimited possibilities) into the realm of unlimited possibilities (which in truth is the
only liberating reality).[4] Yet that is not a general law; it is, rather, the
47   exact opposite of all legalism. Again, it is nothing other than being

---

[2.] Bonhoeffer refers here to youth associations for "Espoused Christianity" ("EC"),
which were founded in 1881 and existed in Germany from 1894 onward.

[3.] The concept of 'existence', coming from Heidegger's philosophy, had become
important in theology of the period in which Bonhoeffer worked. See *AB* (*DBWE* 2):27.
We read in Bethge's notes of 1935: "Question of the existence of persons in discipleship.
Encounter not above real human existence, not within it, not beneath it, but when Christ
steps up to Levi, his entire real existence is affected" (*NL* B 8 [3]).

[4.] Bonhoeffer is using the pair of philosophical concepts, 'possibility/reality' or
'potentiality/actuality'. Aristotle uses δύναμις/ἐνέργεια. For Bonhoeffer the concept of
reality takes precedence over that of possibility in theological statements. As early as 1927,
for example, his fourth proposition in defense of his doctoral dissertation states: "Introduc-
ing the concept of potentiality into *Christian* thought means a limitation of divine omnipo-
tence" (*DBW* 9:477). See also *SC* (*DBWE* 1):143, editorial note 40, and Holl, *Luther*, 235.

bound to Jesus Christ alone. This means completely breaking through anything preprogrammed, idealistic, or legalistic. No further content is possible because Jesus is the only content. There is no other content besides Jesus. He himself is it.

So the call to discipleship is a commitment solely to the person of Jesus Christ, a breaking through of all legalisms by the grace of him who calls. It is a gracious call, a gracious commandment. It is beyond enmity between law and gospel. Christ calls; the disciple follows. That is grace and commandment in one. "I walk joyfully, for I seek your commands" (Ps. 119:45).[5]

Discipleship is commitment to Christ. Because Christ exists, he must be followed. An idea about Christ, a doctrinal system, a general religious recognition of grace or forgiveness of sins does not require discipleship. In truth, it even excludes discipleship; it is inimical to it. One enters into a relationship with an idea by way of knowledge, enthusiasm, perhaps even by carrying it out, but never by personal obedient discipleship. Christianity without the living Jesus Christ remains necessarily a Christianity without discipleship; and a Christianity without discipleship is always a Christianity without Jesus Christ. It is an idea, a myth.[6] A Christianity in which there is only God the Father, but not Christ as a living Son actually cancels discipleship. In that case there will be trust in God, but not discipleship. God's Son became human, he is the *mediator*—that is why discipleship is the right relation to him. Discipleship is bound to the mediator, and wherever discipleship is rightly spoken of, there the mediator, Jesus Christ, the Son of God, is intended. Only the mediator, the God-human,[7] can call to discipleship.

Discipleship without Jesus Christ is choosing one's own path. It could be an ideal path or a martyr's path, but it is without the promise. Jesus will reject it.

48

[5.] The NRSV reads: "I shall walk at liberty, for I have sought your precepts."

[6.] Kierkegaard, *The Journals of Søren Kierkegaard:* "'Discipleship' . . . really provides the guarantee that Christianity does not become poetry, mythology, and abstract idea" (2:348 [trans. altered]; in the Kierkegaard text Bonhoeffer is using, this passage has underlining and "!!" in the margin.). On the following, cf. ibid.: ". . . that it is 'the mediator' himself who makes things difficult. For if I have only God to deal with, no 'imitation' [Efterfølgelse] is required" (2:347–48).

[7.] In Bonhoeffer's 1936 draft of a catechism for a confirmation lesson plan he writes with 1 Tim. 2:5 in mind: "Jesus Christ is entirely God and entirely human in one person. Therefore, he is the mediator between God and me and my savior" (*DBW* 14:804 [*GS* 3:352]); see also *CC* 44–45 (*DBW* 12:294–95 [*GS* 3:180]).

"Then they went on to another village. As they were going along the road, someone said to him, 'I will follow you wherever you go.' And Jesus said to him, 'Foxes have holes, and birds of the air have nests; but the Son of Man has nowhere to lay his head.' To another he said, 'Follow me.' But he said, 'Lord, first let me go and bury my father.' But Jesus said to him, 'Let the dead bury their own dead; but as for you, go and proclaim the kingdom of God.' Another said, 'I will follow you, Lord; but let me first say farewell to those at my home.' Jesus said to him, 'No one who puts a hand to the plow and looks back is fit for the kingdom of God' " (Luke 9:57-62).[8]

The *first* disciple took the initiative to follow Jesus. He was not called, and Jesus' answer shows the enthusiastic man that he does not know what he is doing. He cannot know at all. That is the meaning of the answer which shows the disciple the reality of life with Jesus. The answer is spoken by the one who is going to the cross, whose whole life is described in the Apostles' Creed with the one word "suffered." None can want that by their own choice. None can call themselves, says Jesus; and his word receives no reply. The gap between the free offer of discipleship and real discipleship remains wide open.

When Jesus himself calls, however, he overcomes the widest gap. The *second* disciple wants to bury his father before he follows Jesus. The law obliges him.[9] He knows what he wants to do and has to do. First he has to fulfill the law; then he will follow. Here a clear command of the law stands between the one called and Jesus. Jesus' call forcefully challenges this gap. Under no circumstances is anything permitted to come between Jesus and the one called, even that which is greatest and holiest, even the law. Just at that point, for the sake of Jesus, the law which tries to get in the way has to be broken through, because it no longer had any right to interpose itself between Jesus and the one called. So Jesus here opposes the law and bids the man follow him. Only Christ speaks that way. He has the last word. The other person cannot contradict. This call, this grace, is irresistible.[10]

49

[8.] The NRSV has this passage begin at verse 56, not 57 as in the Luther Bible being used by Bonhoeffer. On this passage see Bonhoeffer's sermon on Psalm 129 in *DBW* 9:513–32; see also his "Devotional Writing for the New Year" in *DBW* 13:344–46 (*GS* 4:171–74), and his letter to Henry L. Henriod, April 7, 1934, in *DBW* 13:120–21 (*GS* 6:351).

[9.] See the fourth of the Ten Commandments in Exod. 20:12: "Honor your father and your mother."

[10.] Bethge's and Zimmermann's notes from Bonhoeffer's lecture here contain the Latin phrase "*gratia irresistibilis*," instead of "*unwiderstehliche Gnade*" (irresistible grace). *NL*

The *third* one called, like the first, understands discipleship as an offer made only by him, as his own self-chosen program for life. But in contrast to the first, he thinks he is justified in setting his own conditions. Doing so entangles him in a complete contradiction. He wants to join Jesus, but at the same time he himself puts something in the way between himself and Jesus: "Let me first." He wants to follow, but he wants to set his own conditions for following. Discipleship is a possibility for him, whose implementation requires fulfilling conditions and prerequisites.[11] This makes discipleship something humanly reasonable and comprehensible. First one does the one thing, and then the other. Everything has its own rights and its own time. The disciple makes himself available, but retains the right to set his own conditions. It is obvious that, at that moment, discipleship stops being discipleship. It becomes a human program,[12] which I can organize according to my own judgment and can justify rationally and ethically. This third one wants to follow [Christ], but already in the very act of declaring his willingness to do so, he no longer wants to follow him. He eliminates discipleship by his offer, because discipleship does not tolerate any conditions that could come between Jesus and obedience. Hence, this third one gets caught in a contradiction, not only with Jesus, but with himself. He does not want what Jesus wants; he does not even want what he himself wants. He likewise does not want what he thinks he wants. He judges himself; he causes his own downfall, all by [his request], "Let me first." Jesus' answer graphically attests to this person's inner conflict, which rules out discipleship. "No one who puts a hand to the plow and looks back is fit for the kingdom of God."

50

Following Christ means taking certain steps. The first step, which responds to the call, separates the followers from their previous exis-

B 8 (4) and *NL* B 9, 5 (43). Bonhoeffer translated the Latin phrase for the book. See Seeberg, *Lehrbuch der Dogmengeschichte*, 2:234. Seeberg traces the phrase to Augustine, declaring that it would correctly render Augustine's understanding of this concept even though the phrase is not found in his writings. Seeberg then cites passages from Augustine to support his assertion. This section was eliminated in the revised, amended English translation of Seeberg. [JG/GK]

[11.] In *Creation and Fall*, Bonhoeffer uses the same expression, "Let me first . . . ," to characterize a potential disciple's fleeing into a mere possibility of following Jesus. He writes, "In other words, in this question what is possible is played off against reality [Wirklichkeit], and what is possible undermines what is reality. In the relation of human beings to God, however, there are no possibilities: there is only reality" (*CF* [*DBWE* 3]:108–9).

[12.] In a 1932 sermon Bonhoeffer contrasts 2 Chron. 20:12: "We do not know what to do, but our eyes are on you" with "Christian programmatic speech" in which "prayers become programs and petitions become orders" (*DBW* 11:417 [*GS* 1:134]).

tence. A call to discipleship thus immediately creates a new situation.[13] Staying in the old situation and following Christ mutually exclude each other. At first, that was quite visibly the case. The tax collector had to leave his booth and Peter his nets to follow Jesus.[14] According to our understanding, even back then things could have been quite different. Jesus could have given the tax collector new knowledge of God and left him in his old situation. If Jesus had not been God's Son become human, then that would have been possible. But because Jesus is the Christ, it has to be made clear from the beginning that his word is not a doctrine. Instead, it creates existence anew. The point was to really walk with Jesus. It was made clear to those he called that they only had one possibility of believing in Jesus, that of leaving everything and going with the incarnate Son of God.

The first step puts the follower into the situation of being able to believe. If people do not follow, they remain behind, then they do not learn to believe. Those called must get out of their situations, in which they cannot believe, into a situation in which faith can begin. This step has no intrinsic worth of its own; it is justified only by the community with Jesus Christ that is attained. As long as Levi sits in the tax collector's booth and Peter at his nets, they would do their work honestly and loyally, they would have old or new knowledge about God. But if they want to learn to believe in God, they have to follow the Son of God incarnate and walk with him.

Things used to be different. Then they could live quietly in the country, unnoticed in their work, keep the law, and wait for the Messiah. But now he was there; now his call came. Now faith no longer meant keeping quiet and waiting, but going in discipleship with him. Now his call to discipleship dissolved all ties for the sake of the unique commitment to Jesus Christ. Now all bridges had to be burned and the step taken to enter into endless insecurity, in order to know what Jesus demands and what Jesus gives. Levi at his taxes could have had Jesus as a helper for all kinds of needs, but he would not have recognized him as the one Lord, into whose hand he should entrust his whole life. He would not have learned to have faith. The situation has to be initiated which will

---

[13.] Cf. Kierkegaard, *The Journals of Søren Kierkegaard:* "*Imitation* in the direction of decisive action whereby the situation for becoming a Christian comes into existence" (2:352; Bonhoeffer's copy of Kierkegaard has markings at this point).

[14.] Mark 2:14 and 1:16-18.

enable faith in Jesus, the incarnate God. This is the impossible situation, in which everything is based on only one thing, the word of Jesus. Peter has to get out of the boat into the waves,[15] in order to experience his own powerlessness and the almighty power of his Lord. If he had not gotten out, he would not have learned to believe. His situation on the tempestuous sea is completely impossible and, ethically, simply irresponsible, but it has to happen for him to believe. The road to faith passes through obedience to Christ's call. The step is required; otherwise Jesus' call dissipates into nothing. Any intended discipleship without this step to which Jesus calls becomes deceptive enthusiasts' illusion.

There is a great danger in telling the difference between a situation where faith is possible and where it is not. It is clear that there is nothing in the situation as such to indicate which kind it is. Only the call of Jesus Christ qualifies it as a situation where faith is possible. Second, a situation where faith is possible is never made by humans. Discipleship is not   52
a human offer. The call alone creates the situation. Third, the value of the situation is never in itself. The call alone justifies it. Finally and most of all, the situation which enables faith can itself happen only in faith.

The concept of a situation in which faith is possible is only a description of the reality contained in the following two statements, both of which are equally true: *only the believers obey,* and *only the obedient believe.*[16]

It is really unfaithfulness to the Bible to have the first statement without the second. Only the believer obeys—we think we can understand that. Of course, obedience follows faith, the way good fruit comes from a good tree,[17] we say. First there is faith, then obedience. If this meant only that faith alone justifies us and not deeds of obedience, then it is a firm and necessary precondition for everything else. But if it meant a chronological sequence, that faith would have to come first, to be later followed by obedience, then faith and obedience are torn apart, and the very

---

[15.] Matt. 14:29.

[16.] These two sentences are first found in Wolf-Dieter Zimmermann's 1936 notes from Bonhoeffer's lectures, in connection with the story of the rich young man: "Only the believers are obedient (do not generalize). Only the obedient person believes" (*NL* B 9, 5 [43]). In Bonhoeffer's lectures on contemporary theology from 1932–33, in the section dealing with Emil Brunner's book *The Divine Imperative,* Ferenc Lehel noted: "*Faith and obedience are one*" (*NL* Appendix 9 [Cf. *DBW* 12:174]). Brunner had written: "The first commandment is a promise, and grace consists in this, that we are commanded to believe in this promise. Hence faith is obedience, just as obedience is only genuine when it is faith" (*The Divine Imperative,* 81). Bonhoeffer marked this passage in his own copy of the book.

[17.] Cf. Matt. 7:17.

practical question remains open: when does obedience start? Obedience remains separated from faith. Because we are justified by faith, faith and obedience have to be distinguished. But their division must never destroy their unity, which lies in the reality that faith exists only in obedience, is

53   never without obedience. Faith is only faith in deeds of obedience.

Because talk about obedience as a consequence of faith is unseemly, due to the indissoluble unity between faith and obedience, the statement "only the believers obey" has to be paired with the other one, "only the obedient believe." In the first, faith is the precondition of obedience; in the second, obedience is the precondition of faith. In exactly the same way that obedience is called a consequence of faith, it is also called a prerequisite of faith.

Only the obedient believe. A concrete commandment has to be obeyed, in order to come to believe. A first step of obedience has to be taken, so that faith does not become pious self-deception, cheap grace. The first step is crucial. It is qualitatively different from all others that follow. The first step of obedience has to lead Peter away from his nets and out of the boat; it has to lead the young man away from his wealth.[18] Faith is possible only in this new state of existence created by obedience.

This first step should, to begin with, be viewed as an external deed which exchanges one mode of existence for another. Anyone can take that step. People are free to do that. It is a deed within the *iustitia civilis* [civil justice],[19] within which people are free. Peter cannot convert himself, but he can leave his nets. In the Gospels that first step consists of a deed which affects all of one's life. The Roman church required such a step only for the exceptional alternative of monasticism. For the other faithful it was enough to be willing to subject themselves unconditionally

54   to the church and its commands. In the Lutheran confessions the importance of a first step is recognized in a significant way: after they thoroughly removed the danger of a synergistic misunderstanding,[20] space could be kept and had to be kept for that first external deed required to

---

[18.] Mark 1:16-18; Matt. 14:29; and Matt. 19:21.

[19.] "Civil justice" (in contrast to faith-justice). The term is often used in Lutheran confessional writings for external justice that people can accomplish with their natural powers—reason and free will—while *iustitia spiritualis* ("spiritual justice") is only granted by the Holy Spirit. See "Apology of the Augsburg Confession" (*The Book of Concord*, 226, art. 18, par. 9, *et passim*).

[20.] The reformers rejected as a misunderstanding the notion that human "co-working" (σύν—ἔργον) for grace to happen could count as a human merit and could contribute to salvation. Cf. *DBW* 14:428–29.

enable faith—the step, in this case, to the church, where the word of salvation is preached. This step can be taken in full freedom. Come to the church! You can do that on the strength of your human freedom. You can leave your house on Sunday and go to hear the preaching. If you do not do it, then you willfully exclude yourself from the place where faith is possible. In this the Lutheran confessions show that they know there is a situation which enables faith and one in which faith is not possible. To be sure, this knowledge is very hidden here, almost as if they were ashamed of it, but it is present as one and the same knowledge of the significance of the first step as an external deed.[21]

Once this knowledge is ascertained, then something else must be acknowledged, namely, that this first step as an external deed is and remains a dead work of the law, which can by itself never lead to Christ. As an external deed, the new existence just remains the old existence. At best, a new law of life, a new lifestyle, is reached, which has nothing to do with the new life in Christ. The alcoholic who gives up alcohol or the rich man who gives away his money are truly freed from alcohol and money, but not from themselves. They remain as their old selves, maybe even more so than before. Subject to the demand for works, they remain in the death of their old lives. The works do have to be done, but by themselves they do not lead out of death, disobedience, and godlessness. If we ourselves understand our first step as a precondition for grace, for faith, then we are judged by our works and completely cut off from grace. Everything we call convictions or good intentions is included in those external deeds, everything which the Roman church calls *facere quod in se est* [to do what is in oneself, i.e., to act according to one's own abilities].[22] If we take the first step with the intention of putting ourselves into the situation of being able to believe, then even this ability to believe is itself nothing but works. It is but a new possibility for living within our old existence and thereby a complete misunderstanding. We remain in unbelief.

55

[21.] See Bethge's 1935 notes from Bonhoeffer's lectures on the visible church in the New Testament, found in *NL* B 18 (3) [see *DBW* 14:426, n. 20], indicate that Bonhoeffer refers to the Formula of Concord, Solid Declaration, article 2: "On Free Will" (*The Book of Concord*, 531, par. 53). This passage is marked by Bonhoeffer. Cf. the student notes found in *NL* Anh. B 2, 3 (47f.), which refer to the "*practice of attending church*, approaching word and sacrament. Being able to receive, being able to be told something, being still in the realm of the church" (*DBW* 12:198).

[22.] See Holl, *Luther*, 31–32, note 2. On this concept, see the article on "Facienti quod in se est," in Höfer and Rahner, *Lexikon für Theologie und Kirche*, 1336–37.

But the external works have to take place; we have to get into the situation of being able to believe. We have to take the step. What does that mean? It means that we take this step in the right way only when we do not look to the necessity of our works, but solely with a view to the word of Jesus Christ, which calls us to take the step. Peter knows that he cannot climb out of the boat by his own power. His first step would already be his downfall, so he calls, "Command me to come to you on the water." Christ answers, "Come."[23] Christ has to have called; the step can be taken only at his word. This call is his grace, which calls us out of death into the new life of obedience. But now that Christ has called, Peter has to get out of the boat to come to Christ. So it is, indeed, the case that the first step of obedience is itself an act of faith in Christ's word. But it would completely misrepresent the essence of faith to conclude that that step is no longer necessary, because in that step there had already been faith. To the contrary, we must venture to state that the step of obedience must be done first, before there can be faith. The disobedient cannot have faith.

You complain that you cannot believe? No one should be surprised that they cannot come to believe so long as, in deliberate disobedience,
56   they flee or reject some aspect of Jesus' commandment. You do not want to subject some sinful passion, an enmity, a hope, your life plans, or your reason to Jesus' commandment? Do not be surprised that you do not receive the Holy Spirit, that you cannot pray, that your prayer for faith remains empty! Instead, go and be reconciled with your sister or brother;[24] let go of the sin which keeps you captive; and you will be able to believe again! If you reject God's commanding word, you will not receive God's gracious word. How would you expect to find community while you intentionally withdraw from it at some point? The disobedient cannot believe; only the obedient believe.

Here the gracious call of Jesus Christ to discipleship becomes a strict law: Do this! Stop that! Come out of the boat to Jesus! Jesus says to anyone who uses their faith or lack of faith to excuse their acts of disobedience to his call: First obey, do the external works, let go of what binds you, give up what is separating you from God's will! Do not say, I do not have the faith for that. You will not have it so long as you remain disobedient, so long as you will not take that first step. Do not say, I have faith, so I do not have to take the first step. You do not have faith,

---

[23.] Matthew 14:28f.
[24.] Matthew 5:24.

because and so long as you will not take that first step. Instead, you have hardened yourself in disbelief under the appearance of humble faith. It is an evil excuse to point from inadequate obedience to inadequate faith, and from inadequate faith to inadequate obedience. It is the disobedience of the "faithful" if they confess their unbelief where their obedience is required and if they play games with that confession (Mark 9:24). You believe—so take the first step! It leads to Jesus Christ. You do not believe—take the same step; it is commanded of you! The question of your belief or unbelief is not yours to ask. The works of obedience are required and must be done immediately. The situation is given in which faith becomes possible and really exists.

Actually, it is not *the works* which create faith. Instead, you are given a situation in which you can have faith. The point is to get into such a situation, so that faith is true faith and not self-deception. Because the only goal is to have true faith in Jesus Christ, because faith alone is and remains the goal ("out of faith into faith,"[25] Rom. 1:17), this is an indispensable situation. Anyone who protests too quickly and in too Protestant a manner should be asked whether or not they are defending cheap grace. In fact the two statements, if they remain juxtaposed, will not offend true faith, but if each is taken alone it would cause serious offense. Only the believers obey—that is said to the obedient person inside the believer. Only the obedient person believes; this is what is said to the believer in his obedience. If the first statement remains alone, the believer is prey to cheap grace, that is, damnation. If the second statement remains alone, the believers are prey to their works, that is, damnation.

At this point let us now take a look at Christian pastoral care.[26] It is particularly important for pastors giving care to speak from knowledge of both of these statements. They need to know that sorrow over a lack of faith repeatedly comes from disobedience, which may be intentional or even no longer noticed, and that such sorrow all too often corresponds to the comfort of cheap grace. But the disobedience remains unbroken, and words of grace become a consolation which the disobedient grant to themselves and a forgiveness of sins they accord themselves. But for such people, the Christian message becomes empty; they no longer hear it.

57

[25.] This follows Luther's translation of ἐκ πίστεως εἰς πίστιν, that is, righteousness, which comes *from* faith and leads *to* faith. The NRSV reads: "[T]he righteousness of God is revealed through faith for faith."

[26.] According to his students' notes, this section corresponds largely to Bonhoeffer's lectures on pastoral care from 1935 to 1939 (*DBW* 14:559–71 [*GS* 5:367–79]).

Even though they forgive themselves a thousand times over, they are incapable of believing in true forgiveness, because in truth, it has not been granted them. Unbelief feeds on cheap grace, because it clings to disobedience. This is a common situation in today's pastoral care. What then happens is that people get so stubborn in their disobedience through their self-granted forgiveness that they claim they can no longer discern what is good and what is God's command. They claim it is ambiguous and permits various interpretations. At first they know clearly that they were disobedient, but their knowledge is gradually dimmed until they become unapproachable. Then the disobedient have entangled themselves so badly that they simply are no longer *able* to hear the word. Then they can no longer have faith. Something like the following conversation will take place between the obstinate disbeliever and the pastor: "I can believe no longer."—"Listen to the Word, it is being proclaimed to you!"—"I hear it, but it doesn't say anything to me. It seems empty to me; it is beyond me."—"You don't want to hear."—"Yes, I do." With that, they reach the point where most pastoral conversations break off, because the pastors do not know what is going on. They only know the one statement: only the believer obeys. With this statement, they are no longer able to help the obstinate unbeliever, who does not and cannot have this kind of faith. Pastors think they are standing here before an ultimate puzzle, that God gives faith to some and denies it to others. With this one statement, they surrender their efforts. The obstinate persons remain alone and continue to bewail their predicament. But this is the turning point in the conversation. The change is a complete one. There is no longer any sense in arguing; the questions and worries of the other person are no longer taken so seriously. Instead the person hiding behind them is taken all the more seriously. The pastor breaks through the walls such a person has built with the statement, "Only the obedient have faith." So the conversation is interrupted, and the pastor's next sentence is, "You are disobedient; you refuse to obey Christ; you desire to keep a piece of autonomy for yourself. You cannot hear Christ, because you are disobedient; you cannot believe in grace, because you do not want to obey. You have hardened some corner of your heart against Christ's call. Your trouble is your sin." At this point Christ reappears on the scene; he attacks the devil in the other person, who until then had been hiding behind cheap grace. At that point everything depends on the pastor having both statements ready: only the obedient believe, and only the believer obeys. In the name of Jesus, the pastor must call the other to obedience, to a deed, to a first step. Leave what binds you and follow him! At that moment everything depends on that step. The position taken by the disobedient person must be broken through, for in it Christ can no longer be heard. Fugitives must leave the hiding places they built for themselves. Only when they get out of them can they again see, hear, and believe freely. Indeed, as far as Christ is concerned, doing the deed itself gains nothing; it remains a dead work. But in spite of that, Peter has to step out onto the rolling sea,[27] so that he can believe.

In short, the situation is that people have poisoned themselves with cheap grace by the statement that only the believer obeys. They remain disobedient and console themselves with a forgiveness that they grant themselves, and in doing so, they close themselves off from the word of God. The fortress walls around them cannot be broken through, so long as all they hear is the statement they are hiding behind being repeated. A change has to come about by calling people to obedience: only the obedient have faith!

Will people thus be led down the fatal path of belief in their own works? No, they will learn instead that their faith is not faith; they will be liberated from their entanglement with themselves. They have to get out in the fresh air of a decision. In that way Jesus' call to faith and discipleship is made audible anew.

This brings us already to the middle of the story of the rich young man.

"Then someone came to him and said, 'Teacher, what good deed must I do to have eternal life?' And he said to him, 'Why do you ask me about what is good? There is only one who is good. If you wish to enter into life, keep the commandments.' He said to him, 'Which ones?' And Jesus said, 'You shall not murder; You shall not commit adultery; You shall not steal; You shall not bear false witness; Honor your father and mother; also, You shall love your neighbor as yourself.' The young man said to him, 'I have kept all these, what do I still lack?' Jesus said to him, 'If you wish to be perfect, go, sell your possessions, and give the money to the poor, and you will have treasure in heaven; then come, follow me.' When the young man heard this word, he went away grieving, for he had many possessions" (Matt. 19:16-22).[28]

60

[27.] Matt. 14:29.

[28.] On the "rich young man," cf. Kierkegaard, *The Journals of Søren Kierkegaard:* "Take an example, the rich young ruler. What did Christ require as the preliminary act? He

The young man's question about eternal life is the question of salvation. It is the only really serious question there is. But it is not easy to ask it in the right way. This is made evident by the way the young man, who obviously intends to ask this question, actually asks a quite different one. He even avoids the real question. He addresses his question to the "good master." He wants to hear the opinion, advice, the judgment of the good master, the great teacher, on the matter. In doing so he reveals two points: First, the question is really important to him, and Jesus should have a meaningful answer to offer. Second, however, he is expecting from the good master and great teacher a significant response, but not a divine order with unconditional authority. For the young man, the question of eternal life is one which he desires to speak of and discuss with a "good master." But right away Jesus' answer trips him up. "Why do you ask me about what is good? No one is good except the one God."[29] The question had already betrayed what was in his heart. He wanted to talk about eternal life with a good rabbi, but what he got to hear was that with his question he was in truth not standing before a good master, but before none other than God. He will not get an answer from the Son of God that would do anything else but clearly refer him to the commandment of the one God. He will not get an answer of a "good master," who

61 would add his own opinion to the revealed will of God. Jesus directs attention away from himself to the God who alone is good, and in doing so proves himself to be the fully obedient Son of God. But if the questioner is standing directly before God, then he is exposed as one who was fleeing from God's revealed commandment, which he himself already knew. The young man knew the commandments. But his situation is that he is not satisfied with them; he wants to move beyond them. His question is unmasked as a question of a self-invented and self-chosen piety. Why is the revealed commandment not enough for the young man? Why does he act as if he did not already know the answer to his question? Why does he want to accuse God of leaving him in ignorance in this most decisive question of life? So the young man is already caught and brought to judgment. He is called back from the nonbinding question of salvation to simple obedience to the revealed commandments.

---

required action that would shoot the rich young ruler out into the infinite. The requirement is that you must venture out [like Peter], out into water 70,000 fathoms deep. This is the situation. Now there can be a question of having faith, or of despairing. But there will be nothing meritorious about it, for you will be so thoroughly shaken that you will learn to let meritoriousness go" (2:20, marked in Bonhoeffer's copy of Kierkegaard).

[29.] The NRSV reads: "There is only one who is good."

He tries a second attempt to flee. The young man answers with a second question: "Which ones?"[30] Satan himself is hiding in that question. This was the only possible way out for someone who felt himself trapped. Of course the young man knew the commandments, but who should know which commandment is meant just for him, just for right then, out of the full number of commandments? The revelation of the commandment is ambiguous and unclear, says the young man. He is not looking at the commandments. He is instead looking at himself again, his problems, his conflicts. He retreats from God's clear commandment back to the interesting, indisputably human situation of "ethical conflict."[31] It is not wrong that he knows about such a conflict, but it is wrong that the conflict is played off against God's commandments. The commandments are actually given in order to bring ethical conflicts to an end. Ethical conflict is the primordial ethical phenomenon for human beings after the fall. It is the human revolt against God. The serpent in paradise put this conflict into the heart of the first human. "Did God say?"[32] People are torn away from the clear commandment and from simple childlike obedience by ethical doubt, by asserting that the commandment still needs interpretation and explanation. "Did God say?" People are made to decide by the power of their own knowledge of good and evil, by the power of their conscience to know what is good. The commandment is ambiguous; God intends for people to interpret it and decide about it freely.

62

Even thinking this way is already a refusal to obey the commandment. Double-minded thinking has replaced the simple act. The person of free conscience boasts of being superior to the child of obedience. To invoke ethical conflict is to terminate obedience. It is a retreat from God's reality to human possibility, from faith to doubt. So the unexpected now happens. The same question with which the young man tried to hide his disobedience now unmasks him for who he is, namely, a person in sin. Jesus' answer does this. God's revealed commandments are named. By naming them, Jesus confirms anew that they are, indeed, God's commandments. The young man is once again caught. He hoped to evade once more and reenter into a nonbinding conversation about eternal

---

[30.] Matthew 19:18; this is not in the parallel passage in Mark. Cf. Mark 10:17ff.

[31.] This phrase is found on a piece of paper apparently written by Bonhoeffer in 1937, entitled "Rich Young Man."

[32.] Genesis 3:1.

questions. He hoped Jesus would offer him a solution to his ethical conflict. But Jesus lays hold, not of the question, but of the person himself. The only answer to the predicament of ethical conflict is God's commandment itself, which is the demand to stop discussing and start obeying. Only the devil has a solution to offer to ethical conflicts. It is this: keep asking questions, so that you are free from having to obey. Jesus takes aim at the young man himself instead of his problem. The young man took his ethical conflict deadly seriously, but Jesus does not take it seriously at all. He is serious about only one thing, that the young man finally hears and obeys God's command. When ethical conflict is taken so seriously that it tortures and subjugates people because it hinders their doing the liberating act of obedience, then it is revealed in its full godlessness as complete disobedience in all its insincerity. Only the obedient deed is to be taken seriously. It ends and destroys the conflict and frees us to become children of God. That is the divine diagnosis the young man receives.

63

The young man is subjected to the truth of God's word twice. He can no longer avoid God's commandment. Yes, the commandment is clear and has to be obeyed. But it is not enough! "I have kept all these from my youth, what do I still lack?" With this answer the young man will still be just as convinced of the sincerity of his concern as he was previously. That is precisely what makes him defiant against Jesus. He knows the commandment; he has kept it, but he thinks that it could not be the whole will of God.[33] Something else has to be added, something extraordinary, unique. He desires to do that. God's revealed commandment is incomplete, the young man says in his final flight away from the true commandment, in his last attempt to retain his autonomy and to decide good and evil on his own. He affirms the commandment, and launches a frontal attack against it at the same time. "I have kept all these, what do I still lack?" Mark adds at this point: "Jesus, looking at him, loved him" (Mark 10:21). Jesus recognizes how hopelessly the young man has closed himself off from God's living word, how his whole being is raging against the living commandment, against simple obedience. He wants to help the young man; he loved him. That is why he gave him one final answer: "If you wish to be perfect, go, sell your possessions, and give the money to the poor, and you will have treasure in heaven; then come, follow me!"

[33.] Bonhoeffer's note on the "Rich Young Man" says at this point: "These simple things will not make me a Christian."

¶Three points should be noted in these words to the young man: *First,* it is now Jesus himself who is commanding. Jesus had just referred the young man away from the good master to God who alone is good. Now Jesus claims authority to say to him the last word and commandment. The young man has to recognize that the Son of God himself is standing before him. Jesus' reality as the Son of God was hidden from the young man when Jesus pointed away from himself toward the Father. Yet this　64 pointing away from himself united him completely with his Father. It is this unity which now enables Jesus to speak his Father's commandment. That must have become unmistakably clear to the young man when he heard Jesus' call to follow him. This call is the sum of all commandments the young man is called to live in community with Christ. Christ is the fulfillment of the commandments.[34] This is the Christ who is standing before him and calling him. He cannot flee any longer into the untruth of ethical conflict. The commandment is clear: follow me.

¶The *second* point is this: Even this call to discipleship needs clarification so it will not be misunderstood. Jesus has to make it impossible for the young man to misunderstand following him as an ethical adventure, an unusual, interesting, but potentially revocable path and lifestyle. Discipleship would also be misunderstood if the young man were to view it as a final conclusion of his previous deeds and questions, as a summary of what went before, as a supplement, completion, or perfection of his past. In order to eliminate all ambiguity, a situation has to be created in which the person cannot retreat, in other words, an irrevocable situation. At the same time it must be clear that it is not just a complement to life before the call. Jesus' challenging the young man to voluntary poverty creates the situation that is called for. This is the existential, pastoral side of the matter. It is intended to help the young man finally to understand and to obey in the right way. It arises from Jesus' love for the young man. It is only the intermediate link between the young man's previous life and discipleship. But notice that it is not identical with discipleship itself. It is not even the first step of discipleship. Rather, it is the obedience within which discipleship can then become real. *First* the young man must go

---

[34.] Luther translates Rom. 10:4, which speaks about Christ, as the τέλος (νόμου) [fulfillment or perfection] as "the end of the law." Bonhoeffer, however, sides with Karl Barth in translating this word as "goal" [*Ziel*] that is, fulfillment (of the law) (see *Der Römerbrief,* 358). Also see *DBW* 6:231, 235 and *DBW* 14:807. [Despite this, the English translation of *Römerbrief* translates Barth's phrase "denn das *Ziel* des Gesetzes ist der Christus" as "For Christ is the *end* of the Law" (*The Epistle to the Romans,* 374).] [JG/GK]

and sell everything and give to the poor, and *then* come and follow Jesus.

65　The goal is following Jesus, and the way in this case is voluntary poverty.

¶The *third* point is that Jesus accepts the young man's question about what he is still lacking: "If you want to be perfect . . ." That really could give the impression that Jesus is talking about adding something on to the young man's previous life. It really is an addition, but one whose content abolishes everything of one's past. The young man has not been perfect so far, for he has wrongly understood and obeyed the commandment. Now he can rightly understand and obey in discipleship, but even then only because Jesus Christ has called him to it. By accepting the young man's question, Jesus has wrested it from him.[35] The young man asked about his path to eternal life. Jesus answered: I am calling you, that is all.

The young man seeks an answer to his question. The answer is: Jesus Christ. The young man wanted to hear the word of a good master, but now he has to recognize that this Word is actually the man himself whom he is questioning. The young man is standing before Jesus, the Son of God. The full encounter is present. The only choices are yes or no, obedience or disobedience. The young man's answer is no. He went away sadly; he was disappointed and had lost his hope, but he still could not abandon his past. He had a lot of property. The call to discipleship here has no other content than Jesus Christ himself, being bound to him, community with him. But the existence of a disciple does not consist in enthusiastic respect for a good master. Instead, it is obedience toward the Son of God.

This story of the rich young man has a direct correspondence with the story framing the parable of the Good Samaritan. "Just then a scribe stood up to test Jesus. 'Teacher,' he said, 'what must I do to inherit eter-

66　nal life?' He said to him, 'What is written in the law? What do you read there?'[36] He answered, 'You shall love the Lord your God with all your heart, and with all your soul, and with all your strength, and with all your mind; and your neighbor as yourself.'[37] And he said to him, 'You have

---

[35.] See Bethge's notes *NL* B 8 (7): "Do you want to be perfect? (In Matthew) not a second stage. This only repeats the young man's question again (against Catholicism)." [Bonhoeffer expresses here a long-held Lutheran suspicion that a typical Catholic exegesis of this passage at that time emphasized a 'perfection' attained not by faith alone, but by doing those good works that thereby accord perfection to the believer.] [JG/GK]

[36.] Bonhoeffer noted at this point in his Greek New Testament: "Micah 6:8." The NRSV says "lawyer" rather than "scribe."

[37.] The scribe quoted Deut. 6:5 and Lev. 19:18.

given the right answer; do this, and you will live.' But wanting to justify himself, he asked Jesus, 'And who is my neighbor?' " (Luke 10:25-29).

The scribe's question is the same as the young man's. Only here it is clear from the outset that the question is intended as a temptation. The tempter's solution is already set. It is intended to dead-end in the aporia [perplexity] of ethical conflict. Jesus' answer fully resembles his answer to the young man. The questioner basically knows the answer to his question. But by asking it, even though he already knows the answer, he is shirking obedience to God's commandment. The only thing left for him is the advice: do what you know; then you will live.

This takes his first position away from him. There follows, again like the young man's, the scribe's flight into ethical conflict: "Who is my neighbor?" Since then, this question of the tempting scribe has been asked countless times in good faith and ignorance. It has the good reputation of being a serious and reasonable question from an inquiring person. But people doing so have not carefully read the context. The whole story of the Good Samaritan is Jesus' singular rejection and destruction of this question as satanic. It is a question without end, without answer. It springs from "those who are depraved in mind and bereft of the truth," who are "conceited, understanding nothing, and [have] a morbid craving for controversy and for disputes about words." From them flow "envy, dissension, slander, base suspicions, and wrangling" (1 Tim. 6:4f.). It is a question from the pompous, "who are always being instructed and can never arrive at a knowledge of the truth," who are "holding to the outward form of godliness but denying its power" (2 Tim. 3:5ff.).[38] They are unqualified to have faith. They ask questions like this because their "consciences are seared with a hot iron" (1 Tim. 4:2), because they do not want to obey God's word. Who is my neighbor? Is there an answer to this, whether it is my biological brother, my compatriot, my brother in the church, or my enemy? Could we not assert or deny the one just as rightly as any other? Is the end of this question not division and disobedience? Yes, this question is rebellion against God's commandment itself. I want to be obedient, but God will not tell me how I can be so. God's commandment is ambiguous; it leaves me in perpetual conflict. The question What should I do? was the first betrayal. The answer is: do the

67

[38.] The citation should more precisely read 2 Tim. 3:5, 7. On the Timothy passages in *Discipleship*, see "The Servant in the House of God," in the Bible study on the Letters to Timothy, October 20, 1936 (*DBW* 14:954–69).

commandment that you know. You should not ask; you should act. The question Who is my neighbor? is the final question of despair or hubris, in which disobedience justifies itself. The answer is: You yourself are the neighbor. Go and be obedient in acts of love. Being a neighbor is not a qualification of someone else; it is their claim on me, nothing else. At every moment, in every situation I am the one required to act, to be obedient. There is literally no time left to ask about someone else's qualification. I must act and must obey; I must be a neighbor to the other person. If you anxiously ask again whether or not I should know and consider ahead of time how to act, there is only the advice that I cannot know or think about it except by already acting, by already knowing myself to be challenged to act. I can only learn what obedience is by obeying, not by asking questions. I can recognize truth only by obeying. Jesus' call to the simplicity of obedience pulls us out of the dichotomy of conscience and sin. The rich young man was called by Jesus into the grace of discipleship, but the tempting scribe is shoved back to the commandment.

Chapter Three

Simple Obedience

When Jesus demanded voluntary poverty of the rich young man, the   69
young man knew that his only choices were obedience or disobedience.
When Levi was called from tax collecting and Peter from his nets, there
was no doubt that Jesus was serious about those calls. They were supposed to leave everything and follow him. When Peter was called to step
out onto the stormy sea, he had to get up and risk taking the step.[1]
Only one thing was demanded in each of these cases. That was their
entrusting themselves to the word of Jesus Christ, believing it to be a
stronger foundation than all the securities of the world. The forces that
wanted to get between the word of Jesus and obedience were just as great
back then as they are today. Reason objected; Conscience, responsibility,
piety, even the law and the principle of Scripture intervened to inhibit
this most extreme, this lawless "enthusiasm."[2] Jesus' call broke through
all of this and mandated obedience. It was God's own word. Simple obedience was required.[3]

[1.] Matthew 19:21; Mark 2:14; 1:16f.; Matt. 14:29.

[2.] Here Bonhoeffer objects to the way that simple obedience was labeled a "heresy"
against the Reformation, an accusation that some Lutherans liked to make; for example,
see Althaus, *Der Geist der lutherischen Ethik im Augsburgischen Bekenntnis*, 45: "Even among us
today, what the reformers called enthusiasm is a powerful element" in the form of "Chris-
tian-pacifist and other irrational opinions."

[3.] The formulation "simple obedience" appears (together with "Christian conscientious objection") in the 1936 Finkenwalde notes by Zimmermann found in *NL* B 9, 5 (51)
(*DBW* 14:621–22). See Kierkegaard, *The Journals of Søren Kierkegaard:* "If the gospel demands
that we renounce this world . . . , then the simple thing to do is: do it" (3:93–95). See also
below, page 161.

If Jesus Christ were to speak this way to one of us today through the
Holy Scripture, then we would probably argue thus: Jesus is making a
specific commandment; that's true. But when Jesus commands, then I
should know that he never demands legalistic obedience. Instead, he has
only one expectation of me, namely, that I believe. My faith, however, is
not tied to poverty or wealth or some such thing. On the contrary, in faith
70 I can be both—rich and poor. The main concern is not whether or not
I have any worldly goods, but that I should possess goods as if I did not
possess them, and inwardly I should be free of them. I should not set my
heart on my possessions.[4] Thus, Jesus says, "Sell your possessions!" But
what he intends is that it is not important if you actually do this literally,
outwardly. You are free to keep your possessions, but have them as if you
did not have them. Do not set your heart on your possessions. Our obedience to Jesus' word would then consist in our rejecting simple obedience
as legalistic obedience, in order to be obedient "in faith."[5] This is the
difference between us and the rich young man. In his sadness, he is not
able to calm himself by saying to himself, "In spite of Jesus' word, I want
to remain rich, but I will become inwardly free from my riches and comfort my inadequacy with the forgiveness of sins and be in communion
with Jesus by faith." Instead, he went away sadly[6] and, in rejecting obedience, lost his chance to have faith. The young man was sincere in going
away. He parted from Jesus, and this sincerity surely had more promise
than a false communion with Jesus based on disobedience. Apparently
Jesus thought that the young man was unable to free himself inwardly
from his wealth. Probably the young man, as a serious and ambitious
person, had tried to do it himself a thousand times. The fact that at the
decisive moment he was unable to obey the word of Jesus shows that he
failed. The young man was sincere in parting from Jesus. By the way
we argue, we distance ourselves fundamentally from a biblical hearer
of Jesus' word. If Jesus said: leave everything else behind and follow
me, leave your profession, your family, your people, and your father's

---

[4.] Bonhoeffer rejects interpretations like Tholuck's (*Commentary on the Sermon on
the Mount,* 373), who wrote about Matt. 6:19 ("Do not collect treasure"): "The words are
intended to convey no other meaning than that expressed in 1 Cor. 7:30-31: 'They that
possess as though they possessed not.' That is apparent from Matt. 6:21: what the Saviour
there warns against, is having one's *heart* in the treasures."

[5.] See, for example, Brunner, *The Divine Imperative,* 150, concerning "the ethical
pathos lies in faith."

[6.] Matthew 19:22.

house,[7] then the biblical hearer knew that the only answer to this call   71
is simple obedience, because the promise of community with Jesus is
given to this obedience. But we would say: Jesus' call is to be taken "absolutely seriously," but true obedience to it consists of my staying in my
profession and in my family and serving him there, in true inner freedom. Thus, Jesus would call: come out!—but we would understand that
he actually meant: stay in!—of course, as one who has inwardly come
out.[8] Or Jesus would say, do not worry;[9] but we would understand:
of course we should worry and work for our families and ourselves.[10]
Anything else would be irresponsible. But inwardly we should be free of
such worry. Jesus would say: if anyone strikes you on the right cheek, turn
the other also.[11] But we would understand: it is precisely in fighting, in
striking back, that genuine fraternal love grows large. Jesus would say:
strive first for the kingdom of God.[12] We would understand: of course,
we should first strive for all sorts of other things. How else should we
survive? What he really meant was that final inner willingness to invest
everything for the kingdom of God. Everywhere it is the same—the deliberate avoidance of simple, literal obedience.

How is such a reversal possible? What has happened that the word of
Jesus has to endure this game? That it is so vulnerable to the scorn of the
world?[13] Anywhere else in the world where commands are given, the
situation is clear. A father says to his child: go to bed! The child knows
exactly what to do. But a child drilled in pseudotheology would have to   72
argue thus: Father says go to bed. He means you are tired; he does not
want me to be tired. But I can also overcome my tiredness by going to
play. So, although father says go to bed, what he really means is go play.
With this kind of argumentation, a child with its father or a citizen with

---

[7.] Bethge's notes from the summer course of 1935 cite Matt. 4:18-22. In Bonhoeffer's
Greek New Testament the words καὶ τὸν πατέρα (those called by Jesus left the boat "and
their father") in verse 22 are underlined.

[8.] In 1932–33, in lectures on Brunner's *The Divine Imperative*, Bonhoeffer stated: "If
one asks, 'What should I do?' the answer is 'Stay in your vocation!' . . . In your vocation you
are allowed to have a clear conscience" (*DBW* 12:175 [*GS* 5:337]). Cf. also Brunner, *The
Mediator*, 419: "The ethics of the gospel are impossible, precisely because they are serious."

[9.] Matthew 6:25.

[10.] The understanding Bonhoeffer is arguing against—that worrying is proper
human conduct—may be found, for example, in Hegel's *The Christian Religion*, 196.

[11.] Matthew 5:39.

[12.] Matthew 6:33.

[13.] Cf. Mark 15:20; such scorn was a part of Christ's crucifixion.

the authorities would run into an unmistakable response, namely, punishment. The situation is supposed to be different only with respect to Jesus' command. In that case simple obedience is supposed to be wrong, or even to constitute disobedience.[14] How is this possible?

It is possible, because there is actually something quite right at the basis of this wrong argumentation. Jesus' command to the rich young man or his call into a situation that enables faith really has only the one goal of calling a person to faith in him, calling into his community. Nothing finally depends on any human deed at all; instead, everything depends on faith in Jesus as the Son of God and the mediator. Nothing finally depends on poverty or riches, marriage or the single state, having or leaving a profession. Rather, everything depends on faith. To this extent, we really are right that it is possible to believe in Christ while we have wealth and possess the goods of this world, so that we have them as if we did not have them.[15] But this is a last possible form of Christian existence, a possibility of living in the world, only in light of the serious expectation that Christ would return in the immediate future. It is not the first and simplest possibility. A paradoxical[16] understanding of the commandments has a Christian right to it, but it must never lead to the annulment of a simple understanding of the commandments. Rather, it is justified and possible only for those who have already taken simple obedience seriously at some point in their lives, and so already stand in community with Jesus, in discipleship, in expectation of the end. Understanding Jesus' call paradoxically is the infinitely more difficult

73

[14.] Bonhoeffer is worried about people drilled in pseudotheology being incited to disobedience by arguments such as that in Tholuck, *Commentary on the Sermon on the Mount*: "[T]he commands are to be regarded as only concrete illustrations of the state of mind and heart required" (269). See below, page 136, editorial note 7. Theologians had given special effort to reinterpreting the issue of war; for example, see Herrmann, *Die sittlichen Weisungen Jesu*, 65: "[If we have only] understood the state of mind to which Jesus is trying to win us over," then, as Christians, we will have *endorsed* something that "contradicts [the Sermon on the Mount] as fiercely as armaments and their bold use." In contrast, Bonhoeffer argued in Fanø, Denmark, in 1934: "There are two ways of reacting to this command from God: the unconditional blind obedience of action, or the hypocritical question of the Serpent: 'Did God say?' . . . 'Did God say you should not protect your own people? . . .' Who among us can say they know what it might mean for the world if one nation should meet the aggressor—not with weapons in hand—but praying, defenseless . . . ?" (*DBW* 13:302–4 [*GS* 1:216–18]).

[15.] 1 Corinthians 7:29f.

[16.] This is an expression used frequently, often with reference to Kierkegaard, in Barth, *The Epistle to the Romans*, for example, 123. See Althaus, *Religiöser Sozialismus*, 27 and 84; see also the reference to "paradox" in *DBW* 10:344 (*GS* 5:178).

possibility. In human terms it is an impossible possibility, and because it is, it is always in extreme danger of being turned over into its opposite and made into a comfortable excuse for fleeing from concrete obedience. Anyone who does not know that it would be the infinitely easier way to understand Jesus' commandment simply and obey it literally— for example, to actually give away one's possessions at Jesus' command instead of keeping them—has no right to a paradoxical understanding of Jesus' word. It is therefore necessary always to include a literal understanding of Jesus' commandment in every paradoxical interpretation.

Jesus' concrete call and simple obedience have their own irrevocable meaning. Jesus calls us into a concrete situation in which we can believe in him. That is why he calls in such a concrete way and wants to be so understood, because he knows that people will become free for faith only in concrete obedience.[17]

Wherever simple obedience is fundamentally eliminated, there again the costly grace of Jesus' call has become the cheap grace of self-justification. But this too constructs a false law, which deafens people to the concrete call of Christ. This false law is the law of the world, matched by an opposing law of grace. The world here is not that world which has been won over by Christ and is daily to be won over anew in his community. Rather, it is the world which has become a rigid, inescapable law of principles. But in that case grace is also no longer the gift of the living God, rescuing us from the world for obedience to Christ. Rather, it becomes a general divine law, a divine principle, whose only use is its application to special cases. The principle of struggle against the "legalism" of simple obedience[18] itself erects the most dangerous law of all, the law of the world and the law of grace. The struggle based on principle against legalism is itself the most legalistic attitude. It is overcome only by genuine obedience to Jesus' gracious call to follow him. The law is fulfilled and done away with by Jesus himself for those who follow.

74

[17.] Cf. Zimmermann's 1936 *NL* B 9, 5 (50) (*DBW* 14:620): One must not use the lack of content in the call to discipleship "to relativize the Sermon on the Mount. . . . There are concrete Christian ethics. The New Testament is concerned with works, deeds, fulfilling the commandments. Commandments are not symbols and mirrors of sins. The rich young man receives the commandment in order to do it (sell!)."

[18.] According to Brunner, *The Divine Imperative*, "[T]he main accent of biblical ethics lies . . . in the *struggle against legalism*" (marked in the margin of Bonhoeffer's copy) (72). Cf. Bethge's 1935 *NL* B 8 (4): "Allegiance to Christ and remaining in the real *iustitia civilis* does not work. In that case legalism is better. In legalism at least I do not bother Jesus the person."

Fundamentally eliminating simple obedience introduces a principle of scripture foreign to the Gospel.[19] According to it, in order to understand scripture, one first must have a key to interpreting it. But that key would not be the living Christ himself in judgment and grace, and using the key would not be according to the will of the living Holy Spirit alone. Rather, the key to scripture would be a general doctrine of grace, and we ourselves would decide its use. The problem of following Christ shows itself here to be a hermeneutical problem. But it should be clear to a Gospel-oriented hermeneutic that we cannot simply identify ourselves directly with those called by Jesus. Instead, those who are called in scripture themselves belong to the word of God and thus to the proclamation of the word. In preaching we hear not only Jesus' answer to a disciple's question, which could also be our own question. Rather, question and answer together must be proclaimed as the word of scripture. Simple obedience would be misunderstood hermeneutically if we were to act and follow as if we were contemporaries of the biblical disciples. But the Christ proclaimed to us in scripture is, through every word he says, the one whose gift of faith is granted only to the obedient, faith to the obedient alone. We cannot and may not go behind the word of scripture to the actual events. Instead, we are called to follow Christ by the entire word of scripture, simply because we do not intend to wish to violate scripture by legalistically applying a principle to it, even that of a doctrine of faith.[20]

This shows that a paradoxical understanding of Jesus' commandments must include a simple understanding, precisely because we do not intend

---

[19.] Bonhoeffer felt that this subject was so important that he added an entry on "principle of scripture and discipleship" to his subject index for the 1937 edition of *Discipleship*. See also Bonhoeffer's 1925 term paper, "Is There a Difference between Historical and Pneumatic Interpretation of Scripture, and What Is the Point of View of Dogmatics?" (*DBW* 9:305–23).

[20.] Tholuck preceded his interpretation of the so-called antitheses, Matt. 5:21-48, with "two hermeneutic canons" (i.e., rules of interpretation), "through neglect of which misunderstandings of a radical and practical nature have been occasioned. 1. In this section, as indeed everywhere, not the *literal*, but the *spiritual*, interpretation is the true one" (*Commentary*, 163). "2. Our Lord's mode of address is that of the popular orator; . . . hence, we have no right to take the letter of what He says in a strict literal sense, and to press it unduly" (165). Both places are marked in Bonhoeffer's copy. Bonhoeffer was thinking of such rules for "dealing with" the Sermon on the Mount (cf. below, page 181) when he wrote on October 24, 1936: "I hope to finish my book [*Discipleship*], and would really like to start writing a hermeneutics volume. It seems to me there is a huge deficit there" (*DBW* 14:257 [*GS* 1:47]).

to set up a law, but to proclaim Christ. That nearly takes care of the suspicion that simple obedience might mean some sort of meritorious human achievement, a facere quod in se est [to do what is in oneself],[21] and a precondition one would have to fulfill for faith. Obedience to Jesus' call is never an autonomous human deed. Thus, not even something like actually giving away one's wealth is the obedience required. It could be that such a step would not be obedience to Jesus at all, but instead, a free choice of one's own lifestyle. It could be a Christian ideal, a Franciscan ideal of poverty.[22] It could be that by giving away wealth, people affirm themselves and an ideal, and not Jesus' command. It could be that they do not become free from themselves, but even more trapped in themselves. The step into the situation is not something people offer Jesus; it is always Jesus' gracious offer to people. It is legitimate only when it is done that way, but then it is no longer a free human possibility.[23]

76

"Then Jesus said to his disciples, 'Truly I tell you, it will be hard for a rich person to enter the kingdom of heaven. Again I tell you, it is easier for a camel to go through the eye of a needle than for someone who is rich to enter the kingdom of God.' When the disciples heard this, they were greatly astounded and said, 'Then who can be saved?' But Jesus looked at them and said, 'For mortals it is impossible, for God all things are possible' " (Matt. 19:23-26).[24]

It can be inferred from the perplexity of the disciples about Jesus' word and from their question—"Who, then, can be saved?"—that they believe that the case of the rich young man is not an individual case, but the most general case possible. They do not ask, "Which rich person?" Instead, they ask the general question, "Who, then, can be saved?" This is because everyone, even the disciples, forms part of those rich people, for whom it is so difficult to enter heaven. Jesus' answer confirms this interpretation of his words by his disciples. Being saved by discipleship is not a human possibility, but for God all things are possible.

[21.] Cf. above, page 65.

[22.] See the article "Franziskaner" in Gunkel et al., *Religion in Geschichte und Gegenwart*, II:686–87. On the same theme, see von Balthasar, *Die grossen Ordensregeln* (*Lectio Spiritualis* 12), 263–321.

[23.] Cf. Martin Luther's theological understanding of unfree will in *The Bondage of the Will* (*LW* 33:3-295 [*WA* 18:600–787]).

[24.] These verses immediately follow the story of the "rich young man" discussed above, pages 77f.

CHAPTER FOUR

DISCIPLESHIP AND THE CROSS

77 "THEN HE BEGAN to teach them that the Son of Man must undergo great suffering, and be rejected by the elders, the chief priests, and the scribes, and be killed, and after three days rise again. He said all this quite openly. And Peter took him aside and began to rebuke him. But turning and looking at his disciples, he rebuked Peter and said, 'Get behind me, Satan! For you are setting your mind not on divine things but on human things.'

¶ "He called the crowd with his disciples, and said to them, 'If any want to become my followers, let them deny themselves and take up their cross and follow me. For those who want to save their life will lose it, and those who lose their life for my sake, and for the sake of the gospel, will save it. For what will it profit them to gain the whole world and forfeit their life? Indeed, what can they give in return for their life? Those who are ashamed of me and of my words in this adulterous and sinful genera-tion, of them the Son of Man will also be ashamed when he comes in the glory of his Father with the holy angels'" (Mark 8:31-38).[1]

The call to discipleship is connected here with the proclamation of Jesus' suffering. Jesus Christ has to suffer and be rejected. God's promise requires this, so that scripture may be fulfilled.[2] Suffering and being rejected are not the same. Even in his suffering Jesus could have been the

---

[1.] Bonhoeffer based his 1935 and 1936 lectures on Matt.16:13, 21-28, and used the par-allels in Mark and Luke in his exegesis. The phrase "being rejected" (Mark 8:31), so impor-tant to Bonhoeffer, is not found in Matthew. In translating Mark 8:36–37, Bonhoeffer, like Luther, renders the Greek translated in the NRSV as "life" by the German word for "soul."

[2.] The phrase "may be fulfilled" appears often in Matthew, for example, in Matt. 1:22. Bonhoeffer uses it to explain "God's requirement" in the prophesies of suffering, to which Mark 8:31 belongs.

celebrated Christ. Indeed, the entire compassion and admiration of the world could focus on the suffering. Looked upon as something tragic, the suffering could in itself convey its own value, its own honor and dignity. But Jesus is the Christ who was rejected in his suffering. Rejection removed all dignity and honor from his suffering. It had to be dishonorable suffering. Suffering and rejection express in summary form the cross of Jesus. Death on the cross means to suffer and die as one rejected and cast out. It was by divine necessity that Jesus had to suffer and be rejected. Any attempt to hinder what is necessary is satanic. Even, or especially, if such an attempt comes from the circle of disciples, because it intends to prevent Christ from being Christ. The fact that it is Peter, the rock of the church, who makes himself guilty doing this just after he has confessed Jesus to be the Christ and has been commissioned by Christ,[3] shows that from its very beginning the church has taken offense at the suffering Christ. It does not want that kind of Lord, and as Christ's church it does not want to be forced to accept the law of suffering from its Lord. Peter's objection is his aversion to submit himself to suffering. That is a way for Satan to enter the church. Satan is trying to pull the church away from the cross of its Lord.

So Jesus has to make it clear and unmistakable to his disciples that the need to suffer now applies to them, too. Just as Christ is only Christ as one who suffers and is rejected, so a disciple is a disciple only in suffering and being rejected, thereby participating in crucifixion.[4] Discipleship as allegiance to the person of Jesus Christ places the follower under the law of Christ, that is, under the cross.[5]

When Jesus communicates this inalienable truth to his disciples, he begins remarkably by setting them entirely free once more. "*If* any want to become my followers,"[6] Jesus says. Following him is not something

---

[3.] Matthew 16:22-23.

[4.] See Paul's account in Rom. 6:6. In 1936 Bonhoeffer used the example: "Today cold martyrdom (Russia) . . . Even unknown rejection is included in the promise" (Zimmermann's notes in *NL* B 9, 5 [46]). At the time, Stalinism ruled in the Soviet Union, which prevented martyrdoms from becoming known. This is an indirect reference to the German National Socialist regime.

[5.] See Bethge's notes in *NL* B 8 (9). In the first course the phrase "law of Christ" was added to the title of this chapter, "Discipleship and the Cross." On this "inalienable truth" (cf. the following sentence), see Bonhoeffer's London sermon on Jer. 20:7 from January 21, 1934, *DBW* 13:347–50 (*GS* 5:505–9), and *DB-ER* 346.

[6.] Luther translated this according to a textual variant as "Those who . . ." instead of "If any. . . ."

79 that is self-evident, even among the disciples. No one can be forced, no one can even be expected to follow him. Rather, "if any" intend to follow him, despite any other offers they may get. Once again everything depends on a decision. While the disciples are already engaged in discipleship, everything is broken off once again, everything is left open, nothing is expected, nothing is forced. What he is going to say next is that decisive. Therefore, once again, before the law of discipleship is proclaimed, even the disciples must accept being set free.

"If any want to follow me, they must deny themselves." Just as in denying Christ Peter said, "I do not know the man,"[7] those who follow Christ must say that to themselves. Self-denial can never result in ever so many single acts of self-martyrdom or ascetic exercises. It does not mean suicide, because even suicide could be the expression of the human person's own will. Self-denial means knowing only Christ, no longer knowing oneself. It means no longer seeing oneself, only him who is going ahead, no longer seeing the way which is too difficult for us. Self-denial says only: he is going ahead; hold fast to him.

". . . and take up their cross." The grace of Jesus is evident in his preparing his disciples for this word by speaking first of self-denial. Only when we have really forgotten ourselves completely, when we really no longer know ourselves, only then are we ready to take up the cross for his sake. When we know only him, then we also no longer know the pain of our own cross. Then we see only him. If Jesus had not been so gracious in preparing us for this word, then we could not bear it. But this way he has made us capable of hearing this hard word as grace. It meets us in the joy of discipleship, and confirms us in it.

The cross is neither misfortune nor harsh fate. Instead, it is that suffering which comes from our allegiance to Jesus Christ alone. The cross is not random suffering, but necessary suffering. The cross is not suffering that stems from natural existence; it is suffering that comes from being Christian. The essence of the cross is not suffering alone; it is suf-

80 fering and being rejected. Strictly speaking, it is being rejected for the sake of Jesus Christ, not for the sake of any other[8] attitude or confession. A Christianity that no longer took discipleship seriously remade the gospel into only the solace of cheap grace. Moreover, it drew no line

---

[7.] Matthew 26:74.
[8.] Bethge's notes in *NL* B 8 (11) adds: "[not for the sake of another] political ideological human [attitude] . . ."

between natural and Christian existence. Such a Christianity had to understand the cross as one's daily misfortune, as the predicament and anxiety of our natural life. Here it has been forgotten that the cross always also means being rejected, that the cross includes the shame of suffering. Being shunned, despised, and deserted by people, as in the psalmist's unending lament,[9] is an essential feature of the suffering of the cross, which cannot be comprehended by a Christianity that is unable to differentiate between a citizen's ordinary existence and Christian existence. The cross is suffering with Christ. Indeed, it is Christ-suffering. Only one who is bound to Christ as this occurs in discipleship stands in seriousness under the cross.

". . . let them take up their cross . . ." From the beginning, it lies there ready. They need only take it up. But so that no one presumes to seek out some cross or arbitrarily search for some suffering, Jesus says, they each have *their* own cross ready, assigned by God and measured to fit.[10] They must all bear the suffering and rejection measured out to each of them. Everyone gets a different amount. God honors some with great suffering and grants them the grace of martyrdom, while others are not tempted beyond their strength. But in every case, it is the one cross.

It is laid on every Christian. The first Christ-suffering that everyone has to experience is the call which summons us away from our attachments to this world. It is the death of the old self in the encounter with Jesus 81
Christ. Those who enter into discipleship enter into Jesus' death. They turn their living into dying; such has been the case from the very beginning. The cross is not the terrible end of a pious, happy life. Instead, it stands at the beginning of community with Jesus Christ. Whenever Christ calls us, his call leads us to death.[11] Whether we, like the first disciples, must leave house and vocation to follow him, or whether, with Luther, we leave the monastery for a secular vocation, in both cases the

---

[9.] See the psalms of lamentation, for example, Ps. 69:7-8: ". . . shame has covered my face. I have become a stranger to my kindred. . . ." Bonhoeffer marked verse 22 of that psalm in his copy of Luther's Bible (NRSV, v. 21): "poison to eat and vinegar to drink." It suggests the crucifixion narrative of Matt. 27:34, 48.

[10.] In his Greek New Testament Bonhoeffer underlined the word αὐτοῦ, "their [cross]," in Matt. 16:24 and wrote in the margin, "δεῖ predest[inatio]!"—"Must—predestination!"

[11.] In the earlier English version of *The Cost of Discipleship*, Fuller translated this famous aphorism as: "When Christ calls a man, he bids him come and die." The austere German text reads: "Jeder Ruf Christi führt in den Tod." Literally, that says, "Every call of Christ leads into death." [JG/GK]

same death awaits us, namely, death in Jesus Christ, the death of our old self caused by the call of Jesus. Because Jesus' call brings death to the rich young man, who can only follow Jesus after his own will has died, because Jesus' every command calls us to die with all our wishes and desires, and because we cannot want our own death, therefore Jesus Christ in his word has to be our death and our life. The call to follow Jesus, baptism in the name of Jesus Christ,[12] is death and life. The call of Christ and baptism leads Christians into a daily struggle against sin and Satan. Thus, each day, with its temptations by the flesh and the world, brings Jesus Christ's suffering anew to his disciples. The wounds inflicted this way and the scars a Christian carries away from the struggle are living signs of the community of the cross with Jesus. But there is another suffering and another indignity from which no Christian can be spared. To be sure, Christ's own suffering is the only suffering that brings reconciliation. But because Christ has suffered for the sin of the world, because the whole burden of guilt fell on him, and because Jesus Christ passes on the fruit of his suffering to those who follow him, temptation and sin fall also onto his disciples. Sin covers the disciples with shame and expels them from the gates of the city like a scapegoat.[13] So Christians become bearers of sin and guilt for other people. Christians would be broken by the weight if they were not themselves carried by

82   him who bore all sins. Instead, by the power of Christ's suffering they can overcome the sins they must bear by forgiving them. A Christian becomes a burden-bearer—bear one another's burdens, and in this way you will fulfill the law of Christ (Gal. 6:2). As Christ bears our burdens, so we are to bear the burden of our sisters and brothers. The law of Christ, which must be fulfilled, is to bear the cross. The burden of a sister or brother, which I have to bear, is not only his or her external fate, manner, and temperament; rather, it is in the deepest sense his or her sin. I cannot bear it except by forgiving it, by the power of Christ's cross, which I have come to share. In this way Jesus' call to bear the cross places all who follow him in the community of forgiveness of sins. [14] Forgiving sins is the Christ-suffering required of his disciples. It is required of all Christians.

[12.] It is the *call* to discipleship in the Synoptic Gospels and *baptism* in Paul.

[13.] Hebrews 13:12-13; cf. Lev. 16:10, 21-22.

[14.] This refers to Luke 23:34. Jesus on the cross cries out: "Father, forgive them . . ."

But how should disciples know what their cross is? They will receive it when they begin to follow the suffering Lord. They will recognize their cross in communion with Jesus.

Thus, suffering becomes the identifying mark of a follower of Christ. The disciple is not above the teacher.[15] Discipleship is passio passiva [passive suffering], having to suffer.[16] That is why Luther could count suffering among the marks of the true church.[17] A preparatory document for the Augsburg Confession defined the church as the community of those "who are persecuted and martyred on account of the gospel."[18] Those who do not want to take up their cross, who do not want to give their lives in suffering and being rejected by people, lose their community with Christ. They are not disciples. But those who lose their lives in discipleship, in bearing the cross, will find life again in following in the community of the cross with Christ. The opposite of discipleship is being ashamed of Christ, being ashamed of the cross, being scandalized by the cross.

Discipleship is being bound to the suffering Christ. That is why Christian suffering is not disconcerting. Instead, it is nothing but grace and joy. The acts of the church's first martyrs give witness that Christ transfigures the moment of greatest suffering for his followers through the indescribable certainty of his nearness and communion.[19] In the middle of the most terrible torment that the disciples bore for their Lord's sake, they experienced the greatest joy and blessedness of his community. Bearing the cross proved to be for them the only way to overcome suffering. But this is true for all who follow Christ, because it was true for Christ himself.

83

[15.] Matthew 10:24.

[16.] Using "passiva" shows that suffering is obligatory (as opposed to self-chosen).

[17.] Martin Luther, "On the Councils and the Church," 1539 (*LW* 41:164–65 [*WA* 50:641, 35—642, 32]); see "The Seventh Signum [Mark]," and also "Against Hans Worst: Ninth Proof," 1541 (*LW* 41:202 [*WA* 51:484]).

[18.] See the Twelfth Schwabach Article, 1529, in *Die Bekenntnisschriften der evangelisch-lutherischen Kirche* (1930 ed., 1:59, 19; 1952 ed., 61; this is also in *WA* 30/3: 181, 25–32). The text of this article reads: "Such a church of those who believe in Christ, who . . . because of this are persecuted and martyred in the world." Bonhoeffer appears to have changed "because of this" to "on account of the gospel." [JG/GK]

[19.] Records (and legends) of the first Christian martyrs were edited in 1689 in Paris by Ruinart in *Acta primorum martyrum;* see Krüger, *Ausgewälte Märtyrerakten.* Also see the report of Stephen's martyrdom in Acts 7:54-60.

"And going a little farther, [Jesus] threw himself on the ground and prayed, 'My Father, if it is possible, let this cup pass from me; yet not what I want but what you want.' . . . Again he went away for the second time and prayed, 'My Father, if this cannot pass unless I drink it, your will be done'" (Matt. 26:39, 42).

Jesus prays to the Father that the cup pass from him, and the Father hears the son's prayer. The cup of suffering will pass from Jesus, but *only by his drinking it*. When Jesus kneels in Gethsemane the second time, he knows that the cup will pass by his accepting the suffering. Only by bearing the suffering will he overcome and conquer it. His cross is the triumph over suffering.

Suffering is distance from God. That is why someone who is in communion with God cannot suffer. Jesus affirmed this Old Testament testimony.[20] That is why he takes the suffering of the whole world onto himself and overcomes it. He bears the whole distance from God. Drinking the cup is what makes it pass from him. In order to overcome the suffering of the world Jesus must drink it to the dregs. Indeed, suffering remains distance from God, but in community with the suffering of Jesus Christ, suffering is overcome by suffering. Communion with God is granted precisely in suffering.

Suffering must be borne in order for it to pass. Either the world must bear it and be crushed by it, or it falls on Christ and is overcome in him. That is how Christ suffers as vicarious representative for the world. [21] Only his suffering brings salvation. But the church-community itself knows now that the world's suffering seeks a bearer. So in following Christ, this suffering falls upon it, and it bears the suffering while being borne by Christ. The community of Jesus Christ vicariously represents the world before God by following Christ under the cross.

God is a God who bears. The Son of God bore our flesh. He therefore bore the cross. He bore all our sins and attained reconciliation by his bearing. That is why disciples are called to bear what is put on them.

84

[20.] The same emphasis is found in Bethge's notes from 1935 in *NL* B 8 (15): "In the Old Testament there are the equations suffering = distance from God, and piety = happiness. That is why there is a rebellion against suffering, and in this rebellion there is included and intended a rebellion against distance from God. The problem of suffering, thus, remains unsolved in the Old Testament." In Matt. 27:46, Jesus on the cross quotes Ps. 22:1: "My God, my God, why have you forsaken me?"

[21.] On the concept of "*Stellvertretung*," or "vicarious representative action," see *SC* (*DBWE* 1):155 *et passim*.

Bearing constitutes being a Christian. Just as Christ maintains his communion with the Father by bearing according to the Father's will, so the disciples' bearing constitutes their community with Christ. People can shake off the burdens laid on them. But doing so does not free them at all from their burdens. Instead, it loads them with a heavier, more unbearable burden. They bear the self-chosen yoke of their own selves. Jesus called all who are laden with various sufferings and burdens to throw off their yokes and to take his yoke upon themselves. His yoke is easy, and his burden is light.[22] His yoke and his burden is the cross. Bearing the cross does not bring misery and despair. Rather, it provides refreshment and peace for our souls; it is our greatest joy. Here we are no longer laden with self-made laws and burdens, but with the yoke of him who knows us and who himself goes with us under the same yoke. Under his yoke we are assured of his nearness and communion. It is he himself whom disciples find when they take up their cross.

"Things must go, not according to your understanding but above your understanding. Submerge yourself in a lack of understanding, and I will give you My understanding. Lack of understanding is real understanding; not knowing where you are going is really knowing where you are going. My understanding makes you without understanding. Thus Abraham went out from his homeland and did not know where he was going (Gen. 12:1ff.). He yielded to My knowledge and abandoned his own knowledge; and by the right way he reached the right goal. Behold, that is the way of the cross. You cannot find it, but I must lead you like a blind man. Therefore not you, not a man, not a creature, but I, through My Spirit and the Word, will teach you the way you must go. You must not follow the work which you choose, not the suffering which you devise, but that which comes to you against your choice, thoughts, and desires. There I call; there you must be a pupil; there it is the time; there your Master has come" (Luther).[23]

85

[22.] Matthew 11:30.

[23.] Bonhoeffer took this quotation from Witte's *Nun freut euch lieben Christen gemein*, 243–44. Bonhoeffer's copy is marked at this place. Witte, in turn, quoted from Luther's second edition of "The Seven Penitential Psalms," 1525 (*LW* 14:152 [*WA* 18:489, 15–27]).

CHAPTER FIVE

DISCIPLESHIP
AND THE INDIVIDUAL

87   "WHOEVER COMES TO ME and does not hate father and mother, wife and
children, brothers and sisters, yes, and even life itself, cannot be my disciple" (Luke 14:26).[1]

Jesus' call to discipleship makes the disciple into a single individual.
Whether disciples want to or not, they have to make a decision; each
has to decide alone. It is not their own choice to desire to be single
individuals. Instead, Christ makes everyone he calls into an individual.
Each is called alone. Each must follow alone. Out of fear of such alone-
ness, a human being seeks safety in the people and things around them.
Individuals suddenly discover all their responsibilities and cling to them.
Under their cover, they want to make their decision, but they do not
want to stand up alone in front of Jesus, to have to decide with only Jesus
in view. But at that moment neither father nor mother, neither spouse
nor child, neither nation nor history cover a person being called. Christ
intends to make the human being lonely. As individuals they should see
nothing except him who called them.[2]

[1.] Bonhoeffer referred to this verse at the ecumenical assembly in Fanø on August 28,
1934 (*DBW* 12:299 [*GS* 1:217]).

[2.] Bonhoeffer's insight that someone following Jesus will inevitably become an individual agrees with Barth's reference to Kierkegaard in *The Epistle to the Romans*, 116. See
Kierkegaard, *The Journals of Søren Kierkegaard*: ". . . for Christianity is accessible to all, to
be sure, but—note well—this occurs through and only through each one's becoming an
individual, the single individual" (2:398). Kierkegaard adds: "If 'discipleship' is not applied
at least minimally in order dialectically to maintain justice and to set the relationship in
order—namely, that Christianity involved the single individual, every single individual, who
must relate himself to the ideal, even though it only means humbly to admit how infinitely
far behind it he is—then the 'race' has taken over. Then Christianity is only mythology,
poetry, and the preaching of Christianity is theatrical, for the guarantee of distinction

Jesus' call itself already breaks the ties with the naturally given sur-
roundings in which a person lives. It is not the disciple who breaks them;
Christ himself broke them as soon as he called. Christ has untied the
person's immediate connections with the world and bound the person
immediately to himself. No one can follow Christ without recognizing
and affirming that that break is already complete. Not the caprice of a   88
self-willed life, but Christ himself leads the disciple to such a break.[3]

Why must that be so? Why can there not be an unbroken growth, a
series of slow sanctifying steps out of the natural orders into the community of Christ? What sort of annoying power comes here between
human persons and the God-given orders of their natural lives?[4] Is not
such a break legalistic "methodism"? Is it not the same as that unhappy
contempt for God's good gifts, which has nothing in common with the
"freedom of the Christian"?[5] It is true, there is something which comes
between persons called by Christ and the given circumstances of their
natural lives. But it is not someone unhappily contemptuous of life; it is
not some law of piety. Instead, it is life and the gospel itself; it is Christ
himself. In becoming human, he put himself between me and the given
circumstances of the world. I cannot go back. He is in the middle. He has
deprived those whom he has called of every immediate connection to
those given realities. He wants to be the medium; everything should happen only through him. He stands not only between me and God, he also
stands between me and the world, between me and other people and

---

between theater and Church is 'discipleship,' its earnestness, and the sobriety involved
in making men into single individuals, so that every single individual relates himself, is
obliged to relate himself, to the ideal" (2:348 [trans. altered]). National Socialism used the
phenomenon of mass hysteria (e.g., the torchlight parade when Hitler seized power January 30, 1933, or party congresses in Nuremberg). As early as his dissertation, Bonhoeffer
recognized the seductive power of such "experiences of unity" (*SC* [*DBWE* 1]:94). From
March 1933 see his lecture "The Leader and the Individual in the Young Generation"
(*DBW* 12:259 [*GS* 2:37]).

[3.] Bonhoeffer is opposing interpretations such as that of Althaus, *Kirche und Volkskampf:* "The New Testament speaks of the serious *possibility* that we can obey Jesus only
when we have broken with our natural community. But we certainly may not make that
exception into the *rule*" (31).

[4.] Cf. the formulation by Althaus, *Der Geist der lutherischen Ethik*, 43, which refers to the
language of the Augsburg Confession, art. 16: "true orders of God" (*Book of Concord*, 37).
Ever since his time as a university lecturer in Berlin, Bonhoeffer had disputed the theology
of orders of creation, especially as held by the Lutherans. See *DBW* 11:312 (*GS* 5:291–94),
as well as *DB-ER* 459.

[5.] Reference to Luther's 1520 essay "On the Freedom of a Christian" (*LW* 31:333–77
[*WA* 7:49–73]).

things. *He is the mediator,* not only between God and human persons, but also between person and person, and between person and reality.[6] Because the whole world was created by him and for him (John 1:3; 1

89 Cor. 8:6; Heb. 1:2), he is the sole mediator in the world. Since Christ there has been no more unmediated relationship for the human person, neither to God nor to the world. Christ intends to be the mediator. To be sure, there are plenty of other gods which offer immediate access and, in fact, the world tries by all means to relate to persons immediately. But herein lies precisely its hostility to Christ, the mediator. Other gods and the world want to tear away from Christ what he deprived them of, namely, the ability to relate immediately to human persons.

This breaking with the immediacy [Unmittelbarkeit] of the world is nothing other than recognizing Christ as the Son of God, the mediator. It is never an arbitrary act, in which a person loosens his or her ties to the world for the sake of some ideal, exchanging a lesser ideal for a greater one. That would again be enthusiasm, high-handedness, even a return immediacy to the world. Only the disciples' recognition that the deed is done, namely, that Christ is the mediator, separates them from the world of people and things. Jesus' call, to the extent that it is understood not as an ideal, but as the word of the mediator, brings about this accomplished break with the world in me. If it were only a matter of weighing ideals against each other, then by all means a balance should be sought, which then could turn to the advantage of a Christian ideal, but this should never be one-sided. From the point of view of idealism, or from the perspective of "responsibilities" of life, it would be inexcusable to radically debase the natural orders of life by confronting them with a Christian ideal of life. Instead, much would have to be said on behalf of the contrary evaluation—especially from the point of view of a Christian idealism, a Christian ethic of responsibility or ethic of conscience! But the issue here is not at all about ideals, values, responsibilities. Instead, it is about accomplished facts and recognizing them, and therefore about the person of the mediator himself, who has come to stand between us and the world. That is why there must be a break with the immediacies of life; that is why a person called must become an individual before the mediator.

So people called by Jesus learn that they had lived an illusion in
90 their relationship to the world. The illusion is immediacy.[7] It has

---

[6.] See Brunner, *The Mediator:* "Only through faith in Christ, the mediator, does man gain a really ethical relation to historical reality" (613).

[7.] In contrast to Gogarten, *Politische Ethik,* for whom "the immediate" natural bonds of authority are really "the genuine ones" (14f.), see Bonhoeffer's presentation for his 1932–33 lectures on "Recent Theology" (*DBW* 12:162).

blocked faith and obedience. Now they know that there can be no unmediated relationships, even in the most intimate ties of their lives, in the blood ties to father and mother, to children, brothers and sisters, in marital love, in historical responsibilities. Ever since Jesus called, there are no longer natural, historical, or experiential unmediated relationships for his disciples. Christ the mediator stands between son and father, between husband and wife, between individual and nation, whether they can recognize him or not. There is no way from us to others than the path through Christ, his word, and our following him. Immediacy is a delusion.

But because any delusion which hides truth from us must be hated, immediacy to the natural given things in life must also be hated, for the sake of Jesus Christ, the mediator. Anytime a community hinders us from coming before Christ as a single individual, anytime a community lays claim to immediacy, it must be hated for Christ's sake. For every unmediated natural relationship, knowingly or unknowingly, is an expression of hatred toward Christ, the mediator, especially if this relationship wants to assume a Christian identity.

Theology makes a serious mistake whenever it uses Jesus' mediation between God and human persons to justify immediate relationships in life. This mistake says, "If Christ is the mediator, then by being so he bore the sins of all our unmediated relationships to the world and justified us in them. Jesus is our mediator with God, so that with a clean conscience we can again relate directly to the world, to the world which crucified Christ." That brings love of God and love of the world down to a common denominator. The break with the given circumstances of the world is presented here as a "legalistic" misunderstanding of God's grace, which is said to spare us from precisely such a break. Jesus' words on 91
hatred toward what is unmediated now are twisted into an obvious, joyful Yes to the "God-given realities" of this world.[8] The justification of the sinner again[9] turns into the justification of the sin.

For a disciple of Jesus, "God-given realities" exist only through Jesus Christ. Anything not given me through Christ, the incarnate one, was not given to me by God. Anything not given me for the sake of Christ does

---

[8.] The key words in this paragraph all point to dangers which Bonhoeffer sees, for example, in Emil Brunner's theology.

[9.] See above, page 50, where Bonhoeffer mentions that Luther's followers repeated the master's teaching literally but without Luther's emphasis on discipleship. [JG/GK]

not come from God. Our gratitude for the gifts of creation is offered through Jesus Christ, and our request for the merciful preservation of this life is made for Christ's sake. Anytime I cannot be grateful for something for the sake of Christ, I may not be grateful for it at all lest it becomes my sin. Even the way to the "God-given reality" of that other person, with whom I live, must go through Christ, or it is a wrong way. All our attempts to bridge the chasm that separates us from others, or to overcome the unbridgeable distance, the otherness or strangeness of another person, by means of natural or psychic connections are doomed to fail. No human way leads from person to person. The most loving sensitivity, the most thoughtful psychology, the most natural openness do not really reach the other person—there are no psychic immediacies.[10] Christ stands between them. The way to one's neighbor leads only through Christ. That is why intercession is the most promising way to another person, and common prayer in Christ's name is the most genuine community.

There is no true knowledge of God's gifts without knowledge of the mediator, for whose sake alone they are given to us. There is no genuine gratitude for nation, family, history, and nature without a deep repentance that honors Christ alone above all these gifts. There is no genuine tie to the given realities of the created world; there are no genuine responsibilities in the world without recognition of the break, which already separates us from the world. There is no genuine love for the world except the love with which God has loved the world in Jesus Christ. "Do not love the world" (1 John 2:15). But "God so loved the world that he gave his only Son, so that everyone who believes in him may not perish but may have eternal life" (John 3:16).

Breaking with immediate relationships is inevitable. There is no ultimate difference whether it takes place externally in a break with one's family or nation, whether one is called to visibly bear Christ's shame, to accept the reproach of hatred for humans (odium generis humani [hatred of the human race]),[11] or whether the break must be borne

---

[10.] In 1938 in his report of the community life in Finkenwalde, Bonhoeffer emphasized that "*Christian community is a spiritual [pneumatische] and not a psychic [psychische] reality*" (*LT* [*DBWE* 5]:35).

[11.] See Harnack, *The Mission and Expansion of Christianity*, 1/2:338 and note 2. The phrase is found in Tacitus, *Annales* XV, 44; cf. Tertullian, *Apologeticus* 35. Also see Kierkegaard, *The Journals of Søren Kierkegaard* (with Bonhoeffer's marking): "Once the

hidden, known by the individual alone, who, however, is prepared to make it visible at any time. Abraham has become a role model for both possibilities. He had to leave his friends and his father's house.[12] Christ came between him and his relatives. In that case the break had to become visible. Abraham became a stranger for the sake of the promised land. That was his first call. Later Abraham was called by God to sacrifice his son, Isaac. Christ steps between the father of faith and the son of the promise.[13] Not only natural immediate relationships are broken, but even unmediated spiritual relationships are broken here. Abraham had to learn that the promise did not depend on Isaac, but only on God. No one hears about that call from God, not even the servants who accompany Abraham to the site of the sacrifice. Abraham remains completely alone. He is again completely the single individual, just as he was long ago, when he left his father's house. He receives the call as it is given. He does not try to interpret it, nor does he spiritualize it. He takes God at God's word and is prepared to obey. Against every natural immediacy,   93 against every ethical immediacy, against every religious immediacy, he obeys God's word. He brings his son to be sacrificed. He is prepared to make the secret break visible, for the sake of the mediator. At the same time, everything that he had given up is restored to him. Abraham receives his son back. God shows him a better sacrifice, which is to take Isaac's place. It is a turnaround of 360 degrees.[14] Abraham received Isaac back, but he has him in a different way than before. He has him through the mediator and for the sake of the mediator. As the one who was prepared to hear and obey God's command literally, he is permitted to have Isaac as though he did not have him; he is permitted to have him through Jesus Christ. No one else knows about it. Abraham comes down from the mountain with Isaac, just as he went up, but everything has changed. Christ came between the father and the son. Abraham had left everything and had followed Christ, and while he was following Christ,

---

objection against Christianity (and this was right at the time when it was most evident what Christianity is and the objection was made by the genuinely keen-eyed pagans) was that it was antihuman—and now Christianity has become humanity" (4:182 [trans. altered]).

[12.] Genesis 12:1.

[13.] See Gen. 15:5 and 22:1-19.

[14.] See Barth, *The Epistle to the Romans:* "When such a Church embarks upon moral exhortation, its exhortation can be naught else but a criticism of all human behavior, a criticism which moves through every one of the 360 degrees of the circle of our ambiguous life" (428). Bonhoeffer uses the image of a complete rotation as an interpretation of "having" ὡ̣ζ μή ("as though one did not have") in 1 Cor. 7:29ff.

he was permitted to go back to live in the same world he had lived in before. Externally everything remained the same. But the old has passed away; see, everything has become new.[15] Everything had to go through Christ.

This is the second possibility for being a single individual, namely, to be a follower of Christ in the midst of the community, in nation and family, in land and property. But it is Abraham who is called to that existence, Abraham, who earlier had gone through the visible break, whose faith became the role model for the New Testament.[16] It is all too tempting for us to generalize this possibility that Abraham had and to understand it as a matter of law, namely, by applying it directly to ourselves. Then we would say that this, too, is our Christian existence, to follow Christ while possessing the goods of this world, and in this way, to be a single individual. But it is certain that the path of being led into an external break is easier for a Christian than that of bearing in hiddenness and faith a secret break. Those who do not know this, that is, those who do not know it from scripture and from their own experience, are surely deceiving themselves along the other path. They will fall back into immediate relationships and lose Christ.

It is not in our power to choose one or the other possibility. According to the will of Jesus, we are called one way or the other out of immediate relationships, and we must become single individuals, visibly or secretly.

But it is precisely this same mediator who makes us into individuals, who becomes the basis for entirely *new community*.[17] He stands in the center between the other person and me. He separates, but he also unites. He cuts off every direct path to someone else, but he guides everyone following him to the new and sole true way to the other person via the mediator.

"Peter began to say to him, 'Look, we have left everything and followed you.' Jesus said, 'Truly I tell you, there is no one who has left house or

---

[15.] 2 Corinthians 5:17.

[16.] See Heb. 11:8, 17 (both passages are marked in Bonhoeffer's Luther Bible), and Romans 4 (Gen. 15:5 is quoted in verse 18).

[17.] In Bethge's notes in *NL* B 8 (18) at this point there is a note, "Invocavit sermons." In *SC* (*DBWE* 1) Bonhoeffer quoted *both* Luther's "The First Sermon: Invocavit Sunday" (March 9, 1522), which says, "Every one of us must be prepared for the time of death" (*LW* 51:70 [*WA* 10/3:1], quoted in *SC* (*DBWE* 1):181, *and* the sermon of Luther that Bonhoeffer so frequently quotes, "The Blessed Sacrament of the Holy and True Body of Christ, and the Brotherhoods" (1519), that says, "If I should die [in the faith-community], I am not alone in death, if I suffer, they suffer with me" (*LW* 35/1:54 [*WA* 2:745], quoted in *SC* [*DBWE* 1]:180–81).

brothers or sisters or father or mother or spouse or children or fields, for my sake and for the sake of the good news, who will not receive a hundred-fold now in this age—houses, brothers and sisters, mothers and children, and fields with persecutions—and in the age to come eternal life. But many who are first will be last, and the last will be first'" (Mark 10:28-31).[18]

Jesus is speaking here to people who became single individuals for his sake, who left everything when he called, who can say of themselves: 95 behold, we left everything and followed you. The promise of new community is given to them. Jesus says that already in this life they are to receive a hundredfold of what they left behind. Jesus is speaking here of his faith-community, those who have come together in him. Those who left their fathers for Jesus' sake will surely find new fathers in the community, they will find brothers and sisters; there are even fields and houses prepared for them. Everyone enters discipleship alone, but no one remains alone in discipleship. Those who dare to become single individuals trusting in the word are given the gift of church-community. They find themselves again in a visible community of faith, which replaces a hundredfold what they lost. A hundredfold? Yes, in the mere fact that they now have everything solely through Jesus, that they have it through the mediator. Of course, that includes "persecutions." "A hundredfold"—"with persecutions": that is the grace of the community which follows its Lord under the cross. The promise for those who follow Christ is that they will become members of the community of the cross, they will be people of the mediator, people under the cross.

"They were on the road, going up to Jerusalem, and Jesus was walking ahead of them; they were amazed, and those who followed were afraid. He took the twelve aside again and began to tell them what was to happen to him" (Mark 10:32). As if to confirm the seriousness of his call to discipleship, and at the same time the impossibility of discipleship based on human strength, and to confirm the promise of belonging to him in times of persecution,[19] Jesus then goes ahead to Jerusalem to the cross, and those following him are overcome with amazement and fear at the way to which he has called them.

[18.] In the story of the rich young man, this passage follows the part Bonhoeffer quoted above, pages 77ff., according to the version in Matthew.

[19.] In Bethge's notes in *NL* B 8 (5–8), the three parts of Bonhoeffer's exegesis of the passage on the rich young man are headed "The Call into the Situation," "On the Possibility of Discipleship" (see Matt. 19:26), and "On the Promise of Discipleship."

CHAPTER SIX

THE SERMON ON THE MOUNT

MATTHEW 5:
ON THE "EXTRAORDINARY" OF CHRISTIAN LIFE

The Beatitudes

99 JESUS ON THE MOUNTAIN, the crowd, the disciples. *The crowd sees:* There is Jesus with his disciples, who have joined him. The disciples—not so long before, they themselves were fully part of the crowd. They were just like all the others. Then Jesus' call came. So they left everything behind and followed him. Since then they have belonged to Jesus—completely. Now they go with him, live with him, follow him wherever he leads them. Something has happened to them which has not happened to the others. This is an extremely unsettling and offensive fact, which is visibly evident to the crowd. *The disciples see:* this is the people from whom they have come, the lost sheep of the house of Israel.[1] It is the chosen community of God. It is the people as church [Volkskirche].[2] When the disciples were called by Jesus from out of the people, they did the most obvious and natural thing lost sheep of the house of Israel could do: they followed the voice of the good shepherd, because they knew his voice.[3] They belong to this people, indeed, especially because of the path on which they were led. They will live among this people, they will go into it and preach Jesus' call and the splendor

---

[1.] Matthew 10:6. See below, chap. 9, "The Messengers," page 187.

[2.] "Here and here alone church and nation are one." This applies to Israel. See Zimmerman's notes in *NL* B 8 (34) on Matt. 5:38. In contrast, in the "Lutheran" milieu, in which Bonhoeffer is writing, according to his judgment "*Volkskirche* = false understanding of grace" (see Bethge's notes in *NL* B 9, 5 [51] [*DBW* 14:622]; see above, page 53).

[3.] John 10:4, 11.

of discipleship. But how will it all end? *Jesus sees:* his disciples are over there. They have visibly left the people to join him. He has called each individual one. They have given up everything in response to his call. Now they are living in renunciation and want; they are the poorest of the poor, the most tempted of the tempted, the hungriest of the hungry. They have only him. Yes, and with him they have nothing in   100 the world, nothing at all, but everything, everything with God. So far, he has found only a small community, but it is a great community he is looking for, when he looks at the people. Disciples and the people belong together. The disciples will be his messengers; they will find listeners and believers here and there. Nevertheless, there will be enmity between the disciples and the people until the end.[4] Everyone's rage at God and God's word will fall on his disciples, and they will be rejected with him. The cross comes into view. Christ, the disciples, the people—one can already see the whole history of the suffering of Jesus and his community.[1]

Therefore, "Blessed!" Jesus is speaking to the disciples (cf. Luke 6:20ff.). He is speaking to those who are already under the power of his call. That call has made them poor, tempted, and hungry. He calls them blessed, not because of their want or renunciation. Neither want nor renunciation are in themselves any reason to be called blessed. The only adequate reason is the call and the promise, for whose sake those following him live in want and renunciation. The observation that some of the Beatitudes speak of want and others of the disciples' intentional renunciation or special virtues[6] has no special meaning. Objective want

---

1. The exegetical basis of this interpretation lies in the ανίγειν τὸ στόμα, which even the early church heavily emphasized in its exegesis. Before Jesus speaks, there are moments of silence.[5]

[4.] See the passage on Matt. 10:16-25 in chap. 9, "The Messengers."

[5.] Luther translated the Greek expression in Matt. 5:2 as "And he opened his mouth." Tholuck, *Commentary on the Sermon on the Mount*, says about this, referring to Chrysostom (fourth century) and Euthymius (twelfth century), "From ancient times, a peculiar significance has been found in the expression . . ." (57).

[6.] Tholuck observes: "These eight beatitudes are arranged in an ethical order. The first four are of a negative character. . . . The three following . . . set forth what attributes of character are required in the members of that kingdom" (*Commentary*, 64).

and personal renunciation have their joint basis in Christ's call and
promise. Neither of them has any value or claim in itself.[2]

101

Jesus calls his disciples blessed. The people hear it and are dismayed
at witnessing what happens. That which belongs to the whole people of
Israel, according to God's promise, is now being awarded to the small
community of disciples chosen by Jesus: "Theirs is the kingdom of heaven." But the disciples and the people are one in that they are all the
community called by God. Jesus' blessing should lead to decisions and
salvation for *all* of them. All are called to be what they truly are. The
disciples are blessed because of Jesus' call that they followed. The entire
people of God is blessed because of the promise which pertains to them.
But will God's people, in faith in Jesus Christ and his word, now in fact
seize the promise or will they, in unfaith, depart from Christ and his
community? That remains the issue.

"Blessed are the poor in spirit, for theirs is the kingdom of heaven."
The disciples are needy in every way. They are simply "poor" (Luke 6:20).
They have no security, no property to call their own, no piece of earth
they could call their home, no earthly community to which they might

---

2. There is no basis in scripture for constructing a contrast between Matthew and Luke. Matthew is not interested in spiritualizing the original Beatitude
(Luke's form), nor is Luke interested in politicizing any original Beatitudes (Matthew's form) referring only to "state of mind."[7] Need is not the basis of blessedness in Luke, nor is renunciation the basis in Matthew. Rather, in both, need
or renunciation, spiritual or political matters are justified only by the call and
promise of Jesus, who alone makes the Beatitudes into what they are, and who
alone is the basis of calling those matters blessed. Catholic exegesis, starting with
the letters of Clement,[8] wanted to have the virtue of poverty declared blessed,
thinking on the one hand of the *paupertas voluntaria* [voluntary poverty][9]
of the monks, on the other hand of any voluntary poverty for Christ's sake. In
both cases the mistake in interpretation lies in seeking to make some human
behavior the basis for blessedness, and not solely Jesus' call and promise.

[7.] In this entire note, Bonhoeffer is responding to Tholuck's scholarly deliberations.
Cf. Tholuck, *Commentary*, on spiritual versus political interpretations of the text (59–62).
Tholuck himself sides with "spirit"; see especially his comment on Matt. 5:38 (270).

[8.] Tholuck, *Commentary*, mentions writings of Jewish-Christian origin, which were
wrongly attributed (probably in the third century) to Bishop Clement of Rome (first century), alleged to be a student of the apostles (60). See Hennecke and Schneemelcher, *New
Testament Apocrypha*, 2:532-70. For further information on Pseudo-Clementine literature,
see Elliott, *The Apocryphal New Testament*, 431–38.

[9.] Regarding "on the one hand, on the other hand," see Tholuck, *Commentary*, 68ff.

fully belong. But they also have neither spiritual power of their own, nor experience or knowledge they can refer to and which could comfort them. For his sake they have lost all that. When they followed him, they lost themselves and everything else which could have made them rich. Now they are so poor, so inexperienced, so foolish that they cannot hope for anything except him who called them. Jesus also knows those others, the representatives and preachers of the national religion, those powerful, respected people, who stand firmly on the earth inseparably rooted in the national way of life, the spirit of the times, the popular piety [Volksfrömmigkeit].[10] But Jesus does not speak to them; he speaks only to his disciples when he says, blessed—for theirs is the kingdom of heaven. The kingdom of heaven will come to those who live thoroughly in *renunciation and want* for Jesus' sake. In the depths of their poverty, they inherit the kingdom of heaven. They have their treasure well hidden, they have it at the cross. The kingdom of heaven is promised them in visible majesty, and it is already given them in the complete poverty of the cross.

Here Jesus' blessing is totally different from its caricature in the form of a political-social program.[11] The Antichrist also declares the poor to be blessed, but he does it not for the sake of the cross, in which all poverty is embraced and blessed. Rather, he does it with political-social ideology precisely in order to fend off the cross. He may call this ideology Christian, but in doing so he becomes Christ's enemy.[12]

"Blessed are those who mourn, for they will be comforted." Every additional Beatitude deepens the breach between the disciples and the people. The disciples' call becomes more and more visible. Those who mourn are those who are prepared to renounce and live without everything the world calls *happiness*[13] *and peace.* They are those who cannot be brought into accord with the world, who cannot conform to the world.[14] They mourn over the world, its guilt, its fate, and its happiness. The world celebrates, and they stand apart. The world shrieks "Enjoy life,"[15]

margin note: 102

margin note: 103

[10.] The terms used in this sentence refer to National Socialism, to which large parts of the church had adjusted. The calendar page from October 1936 (enclosed Bethge's notes in *NL* B 8) notes here: "the church of children and old women: scorn."

[11.] See Althaus, *Religiöser Sozialismus*, 11, 27.

[12.] The party program of the National Socialists proclaimed in article 24: "The party as such represents the point of view of a positive Christianity."

[13.] See "giv[ing] up happiness" in *SC* (*DBWE* 1):184.

[14.] See Rom. 12:2.

[15.] This is the beginning of the refrain of a popular party song of the time.

and they grieve. They see that the ship, on which there are festive cheers and celebrating, is already leaking.[16] While the world imagines progress, strength, and a grand future, the disciples know about the end, judgment, and the arrival of the kingdom of heaven, for which the world is not at all ready [geschickt].[17] That is why the disciples are rejected as strangers in the world, bothersome guests, disturbers of the peace. Why must Jesus' community of faith stay closed out from so many celebrations of the people among whom they live? Does the community of faith perhaps no longer understand its fellow human beings? Has it perhaps succumbed to hating and despising people? No one understands people better than Jesus' community. No one loves people more than Jesus' disciples—that is why they stand apart, why they mourn. It is meaningful and lovely that Luther translates the Greek word for what is blessed with "to bear suffering."[18] The important part is the bearing. The community of disciples does not shake off suffering, as if they had nothing to do with it. Instead, they bear it. In doing so, they give witness to their connection with the people around them. At the same time, this indicates that they do not arbitrarily seek suffering, that they do not withdraw into willful contempt for the world. Instead, they bear what is laid upon them, and what happens to them in discipleship for the sake of Jesus Christ.[19] Finally, disciples will not be weakened by suffering, worn down, and embittered, until they are broken. Instead, they bear suffering by the power of him who supports them. The disciples bear the suffering laid on them only by the power of him who bears all suffering on the cross. As bearers of suffering, they stand in communion with the Crucified. They stand as strangers in the power of him who was so alien to the world that it crucified him. This is their comfort, or rather, he is their comfort, their comforter (cf. Luke 2:25).[20] This alien community is

---

[16.] This is a reference to the British steamer *Titanic*, which sank on its first voyage after hitting an iceberg in 1912. Simultaneously, there is a veiled reference in the phrase "festive cheers," which were grandly staged in Germany at the 1936 Olympics. The National Socialist recreation organization, "Strength through Joy," organized ship tours.

[17.] Bonhoeffer uses the archaic meaning of the word *geschickt*, which Luther used to translate εὔθετος in Luke 9:62: "No one who puts a hand to the plow and looks back is *fit* for the kingdom of God." [JG/GK]

[18.] See Luther's 1522 translation of *Das Neue Testament* (*WA Deutsche Bibel* 6:26): "those who bear suffering."

[19.] Bethge's note in *NL* B 8 (19f.) reads: "Christians are the *forbearing* people! Not the questioning people (Johannes Müller)."

[20.] Cf. also John 16:7 and *passim*.

comforted by the cross. It is comforted in that it is thrust out to the place where the comforter of Israel is waiting. Thus it finds its true home with the crucified Lord, here and in eternity.

"Blessed are the meek, for they will inherit the earth." No rights they might claim protect this community of strangers in the world. Nor do they claim any such rights, for they are the meek, who *renounce all rights of their own* for the sake of Jesus Christ. When they are berated, they are quiet. When violence is done to them, they endure it. When they are cast out, they yield.[21] They do not sue for their rights; they do not make a scene when injustice is done them. They do not want rights of their own. They want to leave all justice to God; non cupidi vindictae [not desirous of vengeance][22] is the interpretation of the early church. What is right for their Lord should be right for them. Only that. In every word, in every gesture, it is revealed that they do not belong on this earth. Let them have heaven, the world says sympathetically, that is where they belong.[3] But Jesus says, they will inherit the earth. The earth belongs to these who are without rights and power. Those who now possess the earth with violence and injustice will lose it, and those who renounced it here, who were meek unto the cross, will rule over the new earth. We should not think here of God's punishing justice in this world (Calvin).[24] Rather, when the realm of heaven will descend,[25] then the form of the earth will be renewed, and it will be the earth of the community of Jesus. God does not abandon the earth. God created it. God sent God's Son to earth. God built a community on earth. Thus, the beginning is already made in this world's time. A sign is given. Already here the powerless are given a piece of the earth; they have the church, their community, their

---

3. The emperor Julian wrote sarcastically in his forty-third letter that he was confiscating the property of Christians just so that they would enter the kingdom of heaven poor.[23]

[21.] Bethge's note in *NL* B 8 (20f.) says here "the serene ones."

[22.] Tholuck, *Commentary,* quotes the phrase (82). Cf. Tertullian, *De patientia* 10.6, and Cyprian, *De bono patientiae* 21.

[23.] Tholuck, *Commentary,* makes this observation on the blessing of the poor, Matt. 5:3 (67–68). For Julian's letter, see Hertlein, *Iulian imperatoris quae supersunt praeter reliquias apud Cyrillum omnia,* 547.

[24.] Tholuck, *Commentary,* wrote that "Calvin, also, calls attention to that Divine justice manifesting itself throughout the whole course of the world's history, to which the humble Christian may safely entrust his cause" (85, marked in margin).

[25.] See Rev. 21:2.

property, their brothers and sisters—in the midst of persecution even unto the cross. But Golgotha, too, is a piece of the earth. From Golgotha, where the meekest died, the earth will be made new. When the realm of God comes, then the meek will inherit the earth.

"Blessed are those who hunger and thirst for righteousness, for they will be filled." Disciples live with not only renouncing their own rights, but even *renouncing their own righteousness.* They get no credit themselves for what they do and sacrifice. The only righteousness they can have is in hungering and thirsting for it. They will have neither their own righteousness nor God's righteousness on earth. At all times they look forward to God's future righteousness, but they cannot bring it about by themselves. Those who follow Jesus will be hungry and thirsty along the way. They are filled with longing for forgiveness of all sins and for complete renewal; they long for the renewal of the earth and for God's perfect justice. But the curse upon the world still conceals God's justice, the sin of the world still falls on it. The one they are following must die accursed on the cross. His last cry is his desperate longing for justice; "My God, my God, why have you forsaken me?"[26] But a disciple is not above the master.[27] They follow him. They are blessed in doing so, for they have been promised that they will be filled. They shall receive righteousness, not only by hearing,[28] but righteousness will physically feed their bodies' hunger. They will eat the bread of true life at the future heavenly Supper with their Lord.[29] They are blessed because of this future bread, since they already have it in the present. He who is the bread of life is among them even in all their hunger. This is the blessedness of sinners.

106

"Blessed are the merciful, for they will receive mercy." These people without possessions, these strangers, these powerless, these sinners, these followers of Jesus live with him now also in the *renunciation of their own dignity,* for they are merciful. As if their own need and lack were not enough, they share in other people's need, debasement, and guilt. They have an irresistible love for the lowly, the sick, for those who are in misery, for those who are demeaned and abused, for those who suffer injustice and are rejected, for everyone in pain and anxiety. They seek out all those who have fallen into sin and guilt. No need is too great, no sin is

---

[26.] Matthew 27:46.
[27.] Matthew 10:24.
[28.] The 1936 calendar page in Bethge's notes *NL* B 8 explains that they receive righteousness not only by hearing the "word of forgiveness."
[29.] John 6:35 and Luke 14:15.

too dreadful for mercy to reach. The merciful give their own honor to those who have fallen into shame and take that shame unto themselves. They may be found in the company of tax collectors and sinners and willingly bear the shame of their fellowship.[30] Disciples give away anyone's greatest possession, their own dignity and honor, and show mercy. They know only *one* dignity and honor, the mercy of their Lord, which is their only source of life. He was not ashamed of his disciples.[31] He became a brother to the people; he bore their shame all the way to death on the cross.[32] This is the mercy of Jesus, from which those who follow him wish to live, the mercy of the crucified one. This mercy lets them all forget their own honor and dignity and seek only the company of sinners. If shame now falls on them, they still are blessed. For they shall receive mercy. Some day God will bend down low to them and take on their sin and shame. God will give them God's own honor and take away their dishonor. It will be God's honor to bear the shame of the sinners and to clothe them with God's honor. Blessed are the merciful, for they have the merciful one as their Lord.

"Blessed are the pure in heart, for they will see God." Who is pure in heart? Only those who have completely given their hearts to Jesus, so that he alone rules in them. Only those who do not stain their hearts with their own evil, but also not with their own good. A pure heart is the simple heart of a child, who does not know about good and evil, the heart of Adam before the fall, the heart in which the will of Jesus rules instead of one's own conscience.[33] Those who *renounce their own good and evil,* their own heart, who are contrite[34] and depend solely on Jesus, have purity of heart through the word of Jesus. Purity of heart here stands in contrast to all external purity, which includes even purity of a well-meaning state of mind. A pure heart is pure of good and evil; it belongs entirely and undivided to Christ; it looks only to him, who goes on ahead.[35] Those alone

---

[30.] Matthew 9:9-13.

[31.] Hebrews 2:11; verse 17 calls this "merciful."

[32.] Philippians 2:8.

[33.] Zimmermann's notes in *NL* B 9, 5 (55) equate "child = obeying the father." See *AB* (*DBWE* 2):157–61, and *CF* (*DBWE* 3):87–88 and 128.

[34.] Zimmermann's notes in *NL* B 9, 5 say, with reference to Ps. 51:12 (Ps. 51:10 in the NRSV): "Create in me a clean heart, O God." "Contrition = the path of the heart, in order to stand on the other side of good and evil, through receiving the gospel" (55).

[35.] "For, in order to find Christ, as long as I still reflect on myself, Christ is not present. If Christ is truly present, I see only Christ" (*AB* [*DBWE* 2]:142).

will see God [36] who in this life have looked only to Jesus Christ, the Son of God. Their hearts are free of defiling images; they are not pulled back and forth by the various wishes and intentions of their own. Their hearts are fully absorbed in seeing God. They will see God whose hearts mirror the image of Jesus Christ.[37]

"Blessed are the peacemakers, for they will be called children of God." Jesus' followers are called to peace. When Jesus called them, they found their peace. Jesus is their peace. Now they are not only to have peace, but

108 they are to make peace.⁴ To do this they *renounce violence and strife.* Those things never help the cause of Christ. Christ's kingdom is a realm of peace, and those in Christ's community greet each other with a greeting of peace. Jesus' disciples maintain peace by choosing to suffer instead of causing others to suffer. They preserve community when others destroy it. They renounce self-assertion and are silent in the face of hatred and injustice. That is how they overcome evil with good.[41] That is how they are makers of divine peace in a world of hatred and war. But their peace will never be greater than when they encounter evil people in peace and are willing to suffer from them. Peacemakers will bear the cross with their Lord, for peace was made at the cross.[42] Because they are drawn into Christ's work of peace and called to the work of the Son of God, they themselves will be called children of God.

"Blessed are those who are persecuted for righteousness' sake, for theirs is the kingdom of heaven." This does not refer to God's righteous-

---

4. εἰρηνοποιοί [38] has a double meaning: even "peaceful" according to Luther's own commentary[39] should be understood to be more than only passive. The English translation, "peacemaker," is one-sided and has caused various forms of misguided Christian activism.[40]

[36.] Bethge's notes in *NL* B 8 (22) refer here to "1 Corinthians 13" (verse 12).

[37.] 2 Corinthians 3:18, which is mentioned in Tholuck, *Die Bergpredigt,* 97.

[38.] Literally, "those who make peace"; the Greek word is heavily marked in red in Bonhoeffer's Greek New Testament.

[39.] Tholuck, *Commentary,* refers to Luther's explanation "in the margin" (98). See *WA Deutsche Bibel* 6:26, which gives the following commentary on Matt. 5:9: "those who make, further, and preserve peace among people, as Christ has made peace for us with God. And they are more than the peaceable."

[40.] In 1934 Bonhoeffer warned in Fanø that "organization tends to hide the seriousness of the evil powers and of the struggle with them. (Not against flesh and blood . . . Eph. 6:12.)" (*DBW* 13:279 [*GS* 1:446]).

[41.] Romans 12:21.

[42.] Ephesians 2:14-16.

ness, but to suffering for the sake of a righteous cause,[5] suffering because of the righteous judgment and action of Jesus' disciples. In judgment and action those who follow Jesus will be different from the world in renouncing property, happiness, rights, righteousness, honor, and violence.[43] They will be offensive to the world. That is why the disciples will be persecuted for righteousness' sake. Not recognition, but rejection, will be their reward from the world for their word and deed. It is important that Jesus calls his disciples blessed, not only when they directly confess his name, but also when they suffer for a just cause.[44] They are given the same promise as the poor. As those who are persecuted, they are equal to the poor.

Here at the end of the Beatitudes the question arises as to where in this world such a faith-community actually finds a place.[45] It has become clear that there is only one place for them, namely, the place where the poorest, the most tempted, the meekest of all may be found, at the cross on Golgotha. The faith-community of the blessed is the community of the Crucified. With him they lost everything, and with him they found everything. Now the word comes down from the cross: blessed, blessed. Now Jesus is speaking only to those who can understand it, to the disciples. That is why he uses a direct form of address: "Blessed are you when people revile you and persecute you and utter all kinds of evil against you falsely on my account. Rejoice and be glad, for your reward is great in heaven, for in the same way they persecuted the prophets who were before you." "On my account"—the disciples are reviled, but it actually hurts Jesus. Everything falls on him, for they are reviled on his account. He bears the guilt. The reviling word, the deadly persecution, and the evil slander seal the blessedness of the disciples in their communion with Jesus. Things cannot go any other way than that the world unleashes its fury in word, violence, and defamation at those meek strangers. The voice of these poor and meek is too threatening, too loud. Their

109

5. Note that there is no article before "righteousness"!

[43.] Bethge's notes in *NL* B 8 say that "everything is renunciation; nothing is Christian doctrine of virtue. Difference between 'active and passive' (making ethical distinction) is invalid" (22). As early as lectures of 1935 and 1935–36, Bonhoeffer sees the Beatitudes summarized in Matt. 5:10f.

[44.] See *E* 60 (*DBW* 6:349).

[45.] Bethge's calendar page 1936 in *NL* B 8 says here: ". . . this rootless band." The terms "rootless" or "nationless" were used as defamations by the National Socialist regime.

suffering is too patient and quiet. In their poverty and suffering, this group of Jesus' followers gives too strong a witness to the injustice of the world. That is fatal. While Jesus calls, "blessed, blessed," the world shrieks, "Away, away with them!" Yes, away! But where will they go? Into the kingdom of heaven. Rejoice and be glad, for your reward is great in heaven. The poor will stand there in the joyous assembly.[46] God's hand will wipe away the tears of estrangement from the eyes of the weeping.[47] God feeds the hungry with the Lord's own Supper.[48] Wounded and martyred bodies shall be transformed, and instead of the clothing of sin and penitence, they will wear the white robe[49] of eternal righteousness. From that eternal joy there comes a call to the community of disciples here under the cross, the call of Jesus, "blessed, blessed."

110

The Visible Church-Community

"You are the salt of the earth; but if salt has lost its taste, how can its saltiness be restored? It is no longer good for anything, but is thrown out and trampled under foot.

¶ "You are the light of the world. A city built on a hill cannot be hid. No one after lighting a lamp puts it under the bushel basket, but on the lampstand, and it gives light to all in the house. In the same way, let your light shine before others, so that they may see your good works and give glory to your Father in heaven" (Matt. 5:13-16).

Those being spoken to are those called in the Beatitudes into the grace of following the crucified one.[50] So far the blessed have appeared as people worthy of the kingdom of heaven, but obviously at the same time as people unworthy of living,[51] superfluous for this earth. Now they

---

[46.] Bonhoeffer here uses an image from the last stanza of the hymn by Johann Matthäus Meyfart (1590–1642), "Jerusalem, Thou City Fair and High," which is based on Rev. 21:1-3 (Winkworth, *Lyra Germanica: The Christian Life*, 220; also in *Chorale Book for England*, hymn no. 193).

[47.] The same hymn includes the line, "I was so far away in my land of tears." Cf. Rev. 7:17.

[48.] Revelation 7:16 and 3:20.

[49.] Revelation 7:13f.

[50.] Bethge's notes in *NL* B 8 reads: "Because the call is already present, the indicative [verb form] is used" (23).

[51.] "Unworthy of living" was Nazi jargon, as used in the "Law to Prevent Transmission of Genetic Diseases" of June 15, 1933. Starting in 1939 the law was used to cover "euthanasia" actions in the Third Reich, in which thousands of people with disabilities were murdered. See Lifton, *The Nazi Doctors*.

are described using the image of the most indispensable commodity on earth. They are the salt of the earth. They are the noblest asset, the highest value the world possesses. Without them the earth can no longer survive. The earth is preserved by salt; the world lives because of these poor, ignoble, and weak people, whom the world rejects. It destroys its own life by driving out the disciples, and—O wonder!—the earth may continue to live because of those outcasts. This "divine salt" (Homer)[52] proves itself by its effectiveness. It penetrates the entire earth. It is the earth's substance. Thus, the disciples are focused not only on heaven, but are reminded of their mission on earth. As those bound to Jesus alone are they sent to the earth, whose salt they are. When Jesus calls his disciples "the salt," instead of himself, this transfers his efficacy on the earth to them. He brings them into his work. He remains in the people of Israel, but he consigns the whole world to the disciples.[53] Only when salt remains salty is the cleansing, flavoring power of salt preserved and the earth preserved by salt. Salt must remain salty for its own sake, as well as for the sake of the earth. The community of disciples must remain what Christ's call has made them. That will be their true efficacy on earth and their preserving strength. Salt does not decay; it is, therefore, a lasting power for cleansing. That is why salt is used in the Old Testament for offerings, that is why in the Catholic baptism ritual salt is put into the child's mouth (Exod. 30:35; Ezek. 16:4).[54] The fact that salt will not decay guarantees that the community will last.

"You *are* the salt"—not "you should be the salt"! The disciples are given no choice whether they want to be salt or not. No appeal is made to them to become salt of the earth. Rather they just are salt, whether they want to be or not, by the power of the call which has reached them. You *are* the salt—not, "you have the salt." It would diminish the meaning to equate the disciples' message with salt, as the reformers did.[55] What is

111

[52.] The reference to Homer is found in Tholuck, *Die Bergpredigt*, 106, marked in the margin by Bonhoeffer.

[53.] Matthew 15:24 and the Great Commission in Matt. 28:18-20.

[54.] References to both passages are mentioned in the article on ἅλας in Kittel, *Theological Dictionary of the New Testament*, 1:228. Tholuck, *Commentary*, mentions regarding Ezek. 16:4 the custom "of putting salt into the mouth of the baptized child" (*Commentary*, 108). This custom (no longer practiced in Catholic liturgy) was carried over from catechumen rites to infant baptism. According to *NL* B 12, 2 (1), Bonhoeffer mentioned "datio salis" (gift of salt) in the context of the ancient church's catechumenate (see *DBW* 14:548).

[55.] Tholuck, *Commentary*, quotes Luther: "By the word '*salt*,' as we have said, He points out what their [those being addressed] office is to be" (112, quoting *LW* 21:54 [*WA* 32:343]).

meant is their whole existence, to the extent that it is newly grounded in
Christ's call to discipleship, that existence of which the Beatitudes speak.
All those who follow Jesus' call to discipleship are made by that call to be
the salt of the earth in their whole existence.

The other possibility, of course, is that salt loses its taste, that it stops
being salt. It ceases to be effective. Then it really is no longer good for
anything except to be thrown away. That is the special distinction of salt.
Everything has to be salted. But salt that has lost its taste can never again
be salty. Everything, even the most spoiled stuff, can be saved by salt.
Only salt which has lost its saltiness is hopelessly spoiled.[56] That is the
other reality of salt. That is the threatening judgment which hangs over
the disciples' community. The earth is supposed to be saved by the community. But the community that has stopped being what it is will be
hopelessly lost. The call of Jesus Christ means being salt of the earth or
being destroyed. It means following Christ or—the call itself will destroy
the one called. There is no second opportunity to be saved. There cannot be such a salvation.

Jesus' call promises the community of disciples not only the invisible
efficacy of salt, but the visible shine of light. "You *are* the light"—again,
not: "you should be the light"! The call itself has made them light. It
cannot be any other way. They are a light which is seen. If it were different, then the call would not be revealed in them. What an impossible,
senseless goal it would be for Jesus' disciples, for *these* disciples, to want to
become the light of the world! They have already been made into light by
the call, in discipleship. Again, not "you *have* the light," but "you are it!"
The light is not something given to you as for example your preaching,
but you yourselves are it. He who speaks directly of himself by saying, "I
am the Light,"[57] says directly to his disciples, "You are the light in your
whole lives, as long as you remain faithful to the call. Because you are
the light, you can stay hidden no longer, even if you wanted to. Light
shines, and the city on the hill cannot be hidden."[58] It simply cannot.
It is visible far into the countryside, no matter whether it is a strong city,
a guarded fortress, or a crumbling ruin.[59] This city on the hill—what

---

[56.] Cf. Luther, "Wochenpredigten über Matthäus 5–7": "Thus there is no greater
injury or decay in Christendom than when the salt, which should season and salt everything
else, has itself lost its taste" (*LW* 21:57).

[57.] John 8:12.

[58.] Bethge's notes in *NL* B 8 (24) refer here to Isa. 2:2-4 and the parallel, Mic. 4:1-3.

[59.] The word "ruin" does not appear in 1935, but it does appear in Zimmermann's
notes in *NL* B 9, 5 (57). The sad decline of the church in National Socialist Germany had
become more obvious.

Israelite would not be reminded of Jerusalem, the city built on high![60]—
is the community of disciples. With all this, the followers of Jesus are no   113
longer faced with a decision. The only decision possible for them has
already been made. Now they have to be what they are, or they are not
following Jesus. The followers are the visible community of faith; their
discipleship is a visible act which separates them from the world—or it
is not discipleship. And discipleship is as visible as light in the night, as a
mountain in the flatland.

To flee into invisibility is to deny the call. Any community of Jesus
which wants to be invisible is no longer a community that follows him.
"No one after lighting a lamp puts it under the bushel basket, but on the
lampstand"—there is that other possibility, that the light will be shaded
intentionally, that it is extinguished under the basket, that the call is
denied. The bushel basket, under which the visible community hides its
light, can be fear of human beings just as much as it can be intentional
conformity with the world for some arbitrary purposes, whether it be
missionary purposes or whether it arises from misguided love for people!
But it may also be—and that is even more dangerous—a so-called Reformation theology, which even dares to call itself theologia crucis [theol-
ogy of the cross][61] and whose signature is that it prefers a "humble"
invisibility in the form of total conformity to the world over "Pharisaic"
visibility.[62] In that case the identifying mark of the community ceases
to be an extraordinary visibility. Instead, it is identified by its fitness to
function within the justitia civilis.[63] Here the criterion for Christianity is
considered to be that the light should *not* shine. But Jesus says, "Let your
light shine before the Gentiles."[64] In any case, it is the light of Jesus' call
which is shining. But what sort of a light is it in which those followers of   114
Jesus, those disciples of the Beatitudes, are to shine? What sort of light

---

[60.] "Jerusalem, Thou City Fair and High" (see above, page 110, editorial note 46).
The first stanza was part of worship at Bonhoeffer's seminary in Zingst on June 2, 1935 (*TF*
256; DBW 14:856).

[61.] The Latin expression became generally known through von Loewenich's book
Luthers Theologia crucis (Luther's Theology of the Cross).

[62.] Bonhoeffer is debating opinions such as those of Brunner, *The Divine Imperative:*
"Here alone the worst enemy of true community, the Pharisaism of 'wishing to be better',
is rooted out [there on the cross]" (57).

[63.] The Latin term means "arena of civil justice." Brunner honors the *iustitia civilis*
in *The Divine Imperative* under the heading "The Better Righteousness" (180, marked in
Bonhoeffer's copy). See Bonhoeffer, *DBW* 12:175 [*GS* 5:337].

[64.] The NRSV in Matt. 5:16 has "before others."

should come from that place, to which only the disciples have a claim? What do the invisibility and hiddenness of Jesus' cross, under which the disciples stand, have in common with the light which is to shine? Shouldn't it follow from the hiddenness of the cross that the disciples should likewise be hidden, and not stand in the light? It is an evil sophistry which uses the cross of Jesus to derive from it the church's call to conformation to the world. Does not a simple listener recognize quite clearly that precisely at the cross something extraordinary has become visible? Or is that all nothing but justitia civilis? Is the cross conformation to the world? To the shock of everyone else, is the cross not something which became outrageously visible in the complete darkness? Is it not visible enough that Christ is rejected and must suffer, that his life ends outside the city gates on the hill of shame?[65] Is that invisibility?

The good works of the disciples should be seen in *this* light. "Not you, but your good works should be seen," says Jesus. What are these good works which can be seen in this light? They can be no other works than those Jesus himself created in the disciples when he called them, when he made them the light of the world under his cross—poverty, being strangers, meekness, peacemaking, and finally being persecuted and rejected, and in all of them the one work: bearing the cross of Jesus Christ. The cross is that strange light which shines there, by which alone all these good works of the disciples can be seen. Nowhere does it say that God becomes visible, but that the "good works" will be seen, and that the people will praise God for these works. The cross becomes visible, and the works of the cross become visible. The want and renunciation of the blessed become visible. But human beings can never be praised for the cross and for such a faith-community, only God can be praised. If the good works were all sorts of human virtues, then the disciples, not the Father, would be praised for them. As it is, there is nothing to praise in the disciple who bears the cross, or in the faith-community whose light so shines, which stands visibly on the mountain—only the Father in heaven can be praised for their "good works." That is why they *see* the cross and the community of the cross, and have faith in God. There, then, shines the light of the resurrection.

115

[65.] Hebrews 13:12f. In July 1936, Willi Brandenburg wrote on this passage from prison: "What should still prevent us—especially at this time—from going out to Him from the camp . . . to be thrown out of the civil or national community" ("Circular letter from Finkenwalde," enclosure [*DBW* 14:202 (*GS* 2:497)]).

The Righteousness of Christ

"Do not think that I have come to abolish the law or the prophets; I have come not to abolish but to fulfill. For truly I tell you, until heaven and earth pass away, not one letter, not one stroke of a letter,[66] will pass from the law until all is accomplished. Therefore, whoever breaks one of the least of these commandments, and teaches others to do the same, will be called least in the kingdom of heaven; but whoever does them and teaches them will be called great in the kingdom of heaven. For I tell you, unless your righteousness exceeds that of the scribes and Pharisees, you will never enter the kingdom of heaven" (Matt. 5:17-20).

It is not surprising that the disciples supposed that the end of the law[67] was coming with such promises they received from their Lord, in which everything was devalued which had value in the eyes of the people, and everything was called blessed which had no value. They were, indeed, addressed and set apart as people to whom simply everything had been given by God's free grace, as the certain heirs of the kingdom of heaven,[68] as those who now possessed everything. They had full and personal communion with Christ, who made everything new. They were the salt, the light, the city on the hill. Thus everything old had passed away and been replaced.[69] It was too easy to assume that Jesus would   116 draw a line of final separation between himself and what went before, that he would declare the law of the Old Covenant to be repealed and declare his independence from it in his freedom as the Son, that he would abolish it for his community. After everything that had been said before, the disciples could easily think like Marcion, who, complaining of Judaizing forgery, undertook the following text revision: "Do you think I came to fulfill the law or the prophets? I came to abolish them, and not to fulfill them."[70] Countless others since Marcion have read and

---

[66.] Literally, "not one 'iota' of the law." The Greek letter "iota" is used to mean something minuscule. Bonhoeffer leaves out the other word in Matt. 5:18, "tittle," from κεραία ("little horn," "little hook").

[67.] Bonhoeffer alludes here to Luther's translation of τέλος in Rom. 10:4 in using "end."

[68.] See the first and eighth Beatitudes in Matt. 5:3, 10.

[69.] 2 Corinthians 5:17 (and Heb. 8:13).

[70.] Tholuck wrote in his *Commentary* that "it was natural that it should prove a stumbling block to Marcion: he accused the Catholic Judaizers of altering the text, and thus conformed it himself . . ." (118). Tholuck then follows this with the citation written in Greek, which Bonhoeffer renders in German. According to Harnack's book on Marcion, it was not he but Marcion's *pupils* who inverted Matt. 5:17 (*Marcion*, 55).

interpreted Jesus' words in that way. But Jesus says, "Do not think that I have come to abolish the law or the prophets . . ." Christ puts the law of the Old Covenant into force.

How are we to understand that? We know that the disciples are addressed, they who are bound to Jesus Christ alone. No law was allowed to hinder the communion between Jesus and his disciples. That became clear in the commentary on Luke 9:57ff.[71] Discipleship is allegiance to Jesus Christ alone and is unmediated. Nevertheless, now an entirely unexpected step follows: the disciples are bound to the Old Testament law. In doing so, Jesus says two things to his disciples: allegiance to the law by itself is not yet discipleship; nor may allegiance to this person of Jesus Christ without the law be called discipleship. He refers those to whom he had just given his full promise and complete communion back to the law. Because it is he whom the disciples are following who does it, the law remains binding for them. The question must then arise, What is valid, Christ or the law? To which do I owe allegiance? To him alone, or back to the law? Christ had said that no law must come between him and his disciples. Now he says that abolishing the law would mean separation from him. What does that mean?

The law is the law of the Old Covenant, not a new law, but the one old law, to which the rich young man and the tempting scribe were referred as the revealed will of God.[72] It becomes a new commandment only because Christ binds his disciples to the law. His concern is not for a "better law" than that of the Pharisees. It is one and the same, it is the law which must remain and be carried out in every letter until the end of the world, which must be fulfilled to the letter. His concern really is for a "better righteousness." Those who do not have this better righteousness will not enter the kingdom of heaven. This will be because they have dispensed themselves from following Jesus, who referred them back to the law. But no one is able to achieve this better righteousness except those addressed here, those called by Christ. Christ's call, Christ himself, is required for that better righteousness.

Thus, it makes sense that at this point in the Sermon on the Mount, Christ speaks of himself for the first time. He himself stands between better righteousness and the disciples, from whom he demands that better

---

[71.] Cf. above, page 60, on the second of the three disciples.

[72.] Cf. above, pages 69–76, where Bonhoeffer comments on Matt. 19:16-22 and Luke 10:25-29.

righteousness. He has come to fulfill the law of the Old Covenant. That is the presupposition of everything else. Jesus shows his complete unity with God's will in the Old Testament, in the law and the prophets. Indeed, he has nothing to add to the commandments of God.[73] He keeps them—that is the only thing he adds. He fulfills the law; that is what he says about himself. Therefore it is true. He fulfills it to the last letter. By his fulfilling it, "everything is done" which is needed for the fulfillment of the law. Jesus will do what the law requires; therefore, he will have to suffer death. For he alone understands the law as God's law. That means that the law itself is not God; nor is God the law, as if the law had replaced God. That is how Israel misunderstood the law.[74] Idolizing the law and legalizing God were Israel's sins. Inverted, removing divinity from the law, and separating God from God's law would be the sinful misunderstanding of the disciples. In both cases, God and the law would be separated from each other, or identified with each other, which is basically the same thing. When the Jews equated God and the law, they did it in order to get God into their power with the law. God was dissolved into the law and was no longer Lord over the law. If the disciples supposed they might separate God from the law, they did it in order to get God into their power in the salvation they possessed. Both times the gift and the giver were switched; God was denied either by way of the law or by way of the promise of salvation.

118

Against both misunderstandings, Jesus validates anew the law as God's law. God is the giver and Lord of the law, and it is fulfilled only in personal communion with God. There is no fulfillment of the law without communion with God; there is also no communion with God without fulfillment of the law. The first refers to the Jews; the second refers to the misunderstanding that threatened the disciples.

Jesus, the Son of God, who alone stands in full communion with God, renews the validity of the law by coming to fulfill the law of the Old Covenant. Because he was the only One who did that, he alone could truly teach the law and how it is fulfilled. The disciples would know and understand this when he told it to them, because they knew who he was. The Jews could not understand it as long as they did not believe him.

[73.] Bethge's notes (*NL* B 8 [27]) refers here to "Matthew 19" (cf. verse 17).

[74.] A central thesis of Noth, *Das System der zwölf Stämme Israels*, was that in Israel the law had taken the place of a relationship to God (see 129ff.).

That was why they had to reject his teaching of the law as blasphemy against God[75] or, rather, against God's law. Thus, for the sake of God's true law, Jesus had to suffer at the hands of the advocates of the false law. Jesus died on the cross as a blasphemer, as a transgressor of the law, because he put into force the true law against the misunderstood, false law.

119   The fulfillment of the law, about which Jesus speaks, could therefore come about only through his being nailed to the cross as a sinner. He himself, as the crucified one, is the perfect fulfillment of the law.[76]

This means that Jesus Christ and only he fulfills the law, because he alone lives in perfect communion with God. He himself steps between his disciples and the law, but the law does not come between him and his disciples. The disciples' path to the law leads through the cross of Christ. Because Jesus points the disciples to the law, which he alone fulfills, he thus binds them anew to himself. He had to reject lawless allegiance apart from God's law, because this would be enthusiasm, and, therefore, would mean a disrupture of all bonds instead of being bound to him. The disciples' anxiety, however, that being bound to the law might separate them from Jesus was dispelled. Such anxiety could only arise from misunderstanding the law, which did, in fact, cut the Jews off from God. Instead of this, it became clear that true adherence to Jesus is granted only together with adherence to God's law.

But if Jesus stands between his disciples and the law, it is not to release them from fulfilling the law. Instead, it is to enforce his demand that the law be fulfilled. The disciples' adherence to him requires the same obedience of them. Also, fulfilling the law to the iota does not cancel that iota for the disciples from then on. It is fulfilled; that is all. But that fulfillment is precisely what really makes the law valid, so that now anyone who does and teaches these commandments will be called great in the kingdom of heaven. "*Do* and teach"—it would be possible to think of a teaching of the law which dispenses with doing it by explaining that the purpose of the law would be merely to let us know that its fulfillment is impossible.[77] Such a teaching cannot claim to be based on Jesus. The

---

[75.] Matthew 26:65 (during Jesus' trial).

[76.] See Bonhoeffer's notes from the winter semester of 1935–36, where we read: "The law of Christ is [crossed out: "his cross"] he himself as the crucified one. He is the law, because he is the fulfillment of the law." *DBW* 14:462.

[77.] The point of view Bonhoeffer rejects here was represented by Brunner, *The Mediator* (419; cf. above, page 79, editorial note 8, and page 126, editorial note 99).

law demands to be done, just as surely as he himself did it. Those who in discipleship follow Jesus, who fulfilled the law, do and teach the law in their following. Only those who do the law can remain in the community of Jesus.

It is not the law which distinguishes the disciples from the Jews. Instead, it is 'better righteousness'. The righteousness of the disciples "towers over" the scribes. It surpasses them; it is something extraordinary and distinctive. This is the first time that the concept of περισσεύειν[78] appears, which will assume so much importance in verse 47. We must ask, what did the righteousness of the Pharisees consist of? What does the righteousness of the disciples consist of? The Pharisees certainly never succumbed to the antiscriptural fallacy of believing that the law should be taught, but not done. The Pharisees intended to be doers of the law. Their righteousness consisted of their immediate, literal obedience to what was commanded in the law. Their righteousness was their action. The goal of their righteousness was complete conformity of their action to what was commanded in the law. Nonetheless, a remnant always remained, which had to be covered by forgiveness. Their righteousness always remained incomplete. The righteousness of the disciples could also consist solely of their doing the law. No one who did not keep the law could be called righteous. But the disciples' action surpasses that of the Pharisees in that it really is perfect righteousness, as opposed to the imperfect righteousness of the Pharisees. How can this be? The superiority of the disciples' righteousness is that Jesus stands between them and the law—he, who has completely fulfilled the law,[79] and in whose community they live. Instead of a law not yet fulfilled, the disciples confronted a law which had already been fulfilled. Before they even began to obey the law, it was already fulfilled; its demands were already satisfied. The righteousness required by the law is already there; it is the righteousness of Jesus, who went to the cross for the sake of the law. But because that righteousness is not only a good deed to be performed, but complete, true, and personal communion with God, Jesus not only *has* righteousness, he *is* righteousness personified. He is the disciples' righ-

120

121

[78.] "overshoot." Luther translated the verb in Matt. 5:20 with "[being] better than," while Bonhoeffer uses "tower over." Cf. below, page 144, on: περισσόν.

[79.] See the quote Bonhoeffer underlined in his copy of Tholuck, *Commentary* (120, on Matt. 5:17), from Ritschl's *Die Entstehung der altkatholischen Kirche*: "... *the perfect righteousness which, in opposition to the Pharisees, Jesus required as the condition of entrance into the kingdom of heaven was represented as a reality in Himself*" (44).

teousness. In calling his disciples, Jesus granted them participation in himself; he gave them community with him; he let them participate in his own righteousness; he granted them his own righteousness. The disciples' righteousness is the righteousness of Christ. Jesus begins his talk about 'better righteousness' by referring to his fulfillment of the law in order to make this point. The righteousness of Christ is really also the disciples' righteousness. In a strict sense, it remains righteousness freely granted, granted through the call to discipleship. It is that righteousness which consists precisely in following him. It is that righteousness which received the promise of the kingdom of heaven in the Beatitudes. The disciples' righteousness is righteousness under the cross. It is the righteousness of the poor, the mournful, the hungry, the meek, the peacemakers, and the persecuted—for the sake of the call of Jesus. It is the visible righteousness of those who in following him become the light of the world and the city on a hill—for the sake of the call of Jesus. The disciples' righteousness is "better" than that of the Pharisees in that it rests solely on the call into the community of Jesus, who alone has fulfilled the law. The disciples' righteousness really is righteousness, because they themselves now truly do the will of God and fulfill the law. The righteousness of Christ should not just be taught, but *done*. Otherwise, it is no better than the law which is merely taught, but not obeyed. Everything which will be said next should be understood in light of this doing of the righteousness of Christ by the disciples. In a word, this means to follow him. It is genuine, simple obedience in faith in the righteousness of Christ. The righteousness of Christ is the new law, the law of Christ.[80]

Kindred

"You have heard that it was said to those of ancient times, 'You shall not murder'; and 'whoever murders shall be liable to judgment.' But I say to you that if you are angry with a brother or sister, you will be liable to judgment; and if you insult a brother or sister, you will be liable to the council; and if you say, 'You fool,' you will be liable to the hell of fire. So when you are offering your gift at the altar, if you remember that your brother or sister has something against you, leave your gift there before the altar and go; first be reconciled to your brother or sister, and then come and

122

[80.] Gal. 6:2 (heavily marked in Bonhoeffer's Luther Bible).

offer your gift. Come to terms quickly with your accuser while you are on the way to court with him, or your accuser may hand you over to the judge, and the judge to the guard, and you will be thrown into prison. Truly I tell you, you will never get out until you have paid the last penny" [Matt. 5:21-26].

"But I say to you"—this is the way Jesus summarized everything he said about the law. After his previous words, it is obvious that Jesus is not to be understood here as a revolutionary.[81] Nor should we assume an exchange of opinion versus opinion in the manner of rabbis.[82] Instead, Jesus expresses, continuing what he has said thus far, his unity with the law of the Mosaic covenant. But precisely in his true unity with the law of God he makes clear that he, the Son of God, is the Lord and Giver of the law. Only those who perceive the law to be the word of Christ can fulfill it. He rejected the sinful misunderstanding in which the Pharisees were caught. True knowledge of the law lies solely in knowing Christ to be the Lord and the fulfiller of the law. Christ has laid his hand on the law and claimed it. In doing so, he did what the law truly intended. But in this unity with the law he is considered an enemy by the false understanding of the law. By honoring the law, he gives himself up to the false zealots of the law.[83]

The commandment to which Jesus first refers his disciples forbids murder and entrusts the disciples with the well-being of their brothers or sisters.[84] The life of one's brothers and sisters was granted by God and is | 123 in God's hand. Only God has power over life and death. There is no place in the faith-community of God for a murderer. Murderers are liable to the judgment they themselves exercise. The protection of God's command extends not only to brothers and sisters who belong to the church-community but beyond.[85] This is clearly shown by the fact that the

---

[81.] As argued by Hegel, *The Christian Religion*, 188, and *Lectures on the Philosophy of Religion*, 3:117–21.

[82.] Tholuck, *Commentary*, refers to the Talmud, in which "one teacher [of the law] so frequently [confronts] another" (173).

[83.] See Gal. 1:13f., where Paul wrote of his earlier life in Jerusalem, "I was far more zealous for the traditions of my ancestors." The German Bible translates "traditions" with "law."

[84.] See Bethge's notes in *NL* B 8 (29) on this point, where Bonhoeffer says "not a general law of reverence for life." This was intended to be critical of Albert Schweitzer, especially his book *Culture and Ethics*.

[85.] According to Bonhoeffer's 1934 sermon in London on 1 Cor. 13:13, Matt. 5:24 includes the "godless, racially different, despised, rejected brother [or sister]" (*DBW* 13:399 [*GS* 5:556]). The context implied for "the other person's identity" in the following sentence is the increasing Nazi mistreatment and murder of Jews.

actions of a follower of Jesus do not depend on the other person's identity, but only on him whom the disciple follows in obedience. Jesus' followers are forbidden to commit murder under penalty of divine judgment. The life of a brother or sister is a boundary for Jesus' followers which may not be crossed. But anger already crosses that boundary. It is crossed even more by words bursting out of us in haste (Racha [insults]), and it is crossed finally when we intentionally deride someone else (you fool). Every anger attacks the life of the other person; it begrudges others their lives; it craves the other's destruction. There is no distinction between so-called just anger and unjust anger.[6] The disciples should not even know what anger is, because anger is an assault on God and the other person. The angry words bursting out of us, which we take so lightly, reveal that we do not respect the other person, that we view ourselves to be superior, and that we thus value our own lives more than the other's. Such words are an injury to a sister or brother, a thrust to the heart. They are intended to strike, wound, and destroy. But intentional words of derision rob sisters and brothers of their dignity in public. They intend to make other people despise them, as well. They aim in hatred to destroy another's internal and external existence. I pass judgment on another. That is murder. A murderer is handed over to judgment.

124

---

6. Adding εἰκῇ [without cause] [86] in the text variant h[r][87] is the first cautious limitation of the sting of Jesus' words.

[86.] Tholuck, *Commentary*, translates it as "blindly" (174).

[87.] On this assertion Bethge penciled into his 1937 copy of *Discipleship* the word "wrong!" Bonhoeffer was referring to a note in his edition of Nestle's Greek New Testament, marked "h[r]," meaning a text variant Nestle noted and rejected, namely, the inclusion of εἰκῇ. Nestle based his decision on one of his sources, the small version of *The New Testament in the Original Greek*, edited by B. F. Westcott and F. J. A. Hort. Westcott-Hort classify εἰκῇ as a "noteworthy rejected reading."

In the postwar editions of *Discipleship* until 1958, Bonhoeffer's reference to "h[r]" was replaced by a note that the Koine or Byzantine group of manuscripts as well as manuscript *D*, the Codex Bezae Cantabrigiensis (the Beza text located in Cambridge), from the sixth century, contain the word εἰκῇ. From 1961 on, the German note was adjusted to conform to that of the English translation by Reginald Fuller: "The addition εἰκῇ in the majority of MSS. (though not in ℵ and *B*) is the first attempt to mitigate the harshness of this saying." Fuller called the reader's attention to the fact that the manuscripts ℵ (Sinaiticus) and *B* (Vaticanus), dating from the fourth century, present the text without εἰκῇ. Nestle took over this reading as the most reliable text. Bethge inked Fuller's revision of Bonhoeffer's note into his 1937 copy of *Discipleship*.

Anyone who is angry toward a sister or brother, who aims harsh words at them, who scorns or slanders another in public, has, as a murderer, no place before God. Alienating oneself from another person causes alienation from God. Such alienated persons no longer have access to God. Their offerings, their worship, their prayers cannot please God. For the followers of Jesus, unlike the rabbis, service to God in worship can never be separated from service to sisters and brothers.[88] Contempt for others makes worship dishonest and deprives it of any divine promise. Individuals as well as church communities who intend to enter God's presence with contemptuous or unreconciled hearts are playing games with an idol. As long as we withhold service and love from a sister or brother, as long as he or she remains a target of our contempt, as long as a sister or brother has something against me or Jesus' community, our offerings will remain unaccepted. It is not just my own anger which gets between me and God, but even the fact that a brother or sister exists whom I have abused, humiliated, and dishonored, and who "has something against me." So the community of Jesus' disciples ought to examine itself as to whether it is here and there at fault toward sisters and brothers, and whether, for the sake of the world, it has participated in hating, despising, and humiliating others. To do these things is to be guilty of their murder.[89] Jesus' community today ought to examine whether at the moment it enters God's presence for prayer and worship many accusing voices rise up between it and God and hinder its prayers. Jesus' community ought to examine whether it has given a sign of Jesus' love, which preserves, supports, and protects lives, to those whom the world has despised and dishonored. Otherwise the most correct form of worship, the most pious prayer, and the bravest confession will not help, but will give witness against it, because it has ceased following Jesus. We are not allowed to separate God from our sister or brother. God does not want to be honored if a sister or brother is dishonored. God is the Father. Yes, God is the Father of Jesus Christ, who came to be brother to us all.[90]

125

[88.] See Bonhoeffer's reputed oral remark, probably from late 1935, that "only those who cry out for the Jews may sing Gregorian chants" (Bethge, "Dietrich Bonhoeffer and the Jews," 71). The Babylonian *Talmud* (Yoma 8, 9) contains a parallel to Matt. 5:23f.

[89.] Bonhoeffer was thinking about how public agitation goaded people into participating in throwing the "enemies of the people" out of the "people's community" (Nazi jargon for persecution of Jews).

[90.] See Heb. 2:17.

That is the ultimate reason why God refuses to be separated from our sister or brother. God's own Son was dishonored and humiliated in order to honor the Father. But the Father, refusing to be separated from his Son, will likewise not be separated from those whose humanity the Son assumed as an equal and for whose sake the Son bore his humiliation.[91] Because the Son of God became a human being, service to God in worship can no longer be detached from service to sisters and brothers. Those who say that they love God and yet hate their brothers or sisters are liars.[92]

Thus there remains only one path for those who in following Jesus want to truly serve God in worship, and that is the path of reconciliation with their sisters and brothers. Anyone who comes to the word and sacrament with an unreconciled heart stands judged by doing so. Such a person is a murderer in God's sight. That is why you must "first be reconciled to your brother or sister, and then come and offer your gift." It is a difficult path Jesus imposes on his disciples. It includes much humiliation and dishonor for the disciples themselves. But it is the path to him, our crucified brother, and thus, it is a path full of grace. In Jesus, service to the least brother or sister and service to God became one. He went and was reconciled to his human kindred and then he came and offered himself, the one true sacrifice, to his Father.[93]

This is still a time of grace, for brothers and sisters are still given to us and we are still "on the way with them." The day of judgment lies before us. There is still time to offer satisfaction to a sister or brother; there is still time to pay what we owe to those to whom we are indebted. The hour is coming in which we shall be handed over to the judge. Then it will be too late; then righteousness and punishment shall rule until the last debt is paid. Can we understand that our sisters and brothers are not given to Jesus' disciples as an expression of the law, but of grace? It is grace to be permitted to satisfy our sisters and brothers, and to help them attain their rights. It is grace that we may be reconciled with our sisters and brothers. They are our grace before the day of judgment.

The only one who can speak to us like that is the one who himself, as our brother, became our grace, our reconciliation, our salvation

126

[91.] Hebrews 13:12 f.
[92.] 1 John 4:20.
[93.] Hebrews 9:14.

from judgment. The grace of sisters and brothers is granted to us in the humanity of the Son of God. Might the disciples of Jesus seriously contemplate that!

Service to sisters and brothers which satisfies them and respects their rights and life is the path of self-denial, the path to the cross. No one has greater love that those who lay down their lives for their friends.[94] That is the love of the crucified one. Thus, this commandment is fulfilled solely in the cross of Jesus.

Woman

"You have heard that it was said, 'You shall not commit adultery.' But I say to you that everyone who looks at a woman with lust has already committed adultery with her in his heart. If your right eye causes you to sin, tear it out and throw it away; it is better for you to lose one of your members than for your whole body to be thrown into hell. And if your right hand causes you to sin, cut it off and throw it away; it is better for you to lose one of your members than for your whole body to go into hell. It was also said, 'Whoever divorces his wife, let him give her a certificate of divorce.' But I say to you that anyone who divorces his wife, except on the ground of infidelity,[95] causes her to commit adultery; and whoever marries a divorced woman commits adultery" (Matt. 5:27-32).

Our bond to Jesus Christ permits no desire without love. Instead, such desire is forbidden the disciple. Because discipleship is self-denial and a complete bond with Jesus, at no point may the disciple's own desire-driven will take over. Such lust, and even if it were only in a single look, disconnects us from discipleship and brings the whole body into hell. It causes human beings to sell their heavenly birthright for a bowl of porridge.[96] They do not believe him, who can grant joy a hundredfold[97] to make up for desire denied. They do not trust what is invisible, but seize only the visible fruit of desire. They fall away from the path of discipleship and become separated from Jesus. Lack of faith is what makes lust

127

[94.] John 15:13. When Protestantism was something like a civil religion in Germany after the First World War, and earlier, this Bible verse was usually applied to soldiers killed in the war.

[95.] The NRSV has "unchastity."

[96.] Hebrews 12:16 (Gen. 25:33, 34).

[97.] Mark 10:30.

impure. That is the only reason it is to be condemned. No sacrifice that the disciples make to be free of that desire which separates them from Jesus is too great. The eye is less than Christ, and the hand is less than Christ. If the eye and the hand serve lust and hinder the whole body from the purity of discipleship, then they, rather than Jesus Christ, should be sacrificed. The benefits of desire are small compared to the harm it does—you gain the desire of your eye or your hand for a moment, and you lose your whole body for eternity. Your eye, when it is serving impure desire, cannot see God.[98]

At this point, must we not decisively face the question of whether Jesus intended his command to be taken literally or merely figuratively? Must not our whole life depend on a clear answer to this question? Must not the disciples' attitude already determine the answer? Our own will advises us to flee from this decision, which appears to be so deadly serious. But the question itself is wrong and evil. It cannot be answered. If we were to say that, of course, the command is not meant to be taken literally, then we would already have dodged the seriousness of the command. But if we were to say, of course, it should be taken literally, this would only show that Christian existence is absurd on principle, and the command would 128　lose its authority.[99] It is precisely the fact that, for us, this basic question is not answered that binds us completely to Jesus' command. Neither option offers us an escape. We are trapped and must obey. Jesus does not force his disciples into an inhuman constraint; he does not forbid them to look. But he guides the disciples to look to himself knowing that here the disciples' view will remain pure, even when they look at a woman. In this way he does not impose on his disciples an unbearable yoke of the law, but mercifully helps them by way of the gospel.

Jesus does not demand that his followers get married. But he sanctifies marriage according to the law by declaring it to be unbreakable. Even in cases where one party divorces the other because of infidelity, he prohibits the other from remarrying.[100] With this commandment Jesus liberates marriage from selfish evil desire and intends for it to be conducted as a service of love, as is possible only in following him. Jesus does not disapprove of the body and its natural desires. But he rejects

---

[98.] See Matt. 5:8.

[99.] See the argument in Brunner, *The Mediator:* "It is impossible to do the Divine Will," because "this historical existence is a sinful existence. Therefore the commandments of the Sermon on the Mount do not fit into it" (419).

[100.] Bethge's notes (*NL* B 8 [31]) refers to "1 Corinthians 7:10f.!!"

the lack of faith that is concealed in it. Thus he does not dissolve marriage, but strengthens and sanctifies it by faith. Those who follow him maintain their sole allegiance to Christ even in their marriage by practicing discipline and self-denial. Christ is Lord even of the followers' marriage. This causes the marriage of disciples to be something different than civil marriage, but, again, this is not contempt for marriage, but precisely its sanctification.

It appears that Jesus contradicts Old Testament law by demanding that marriage be indissoluble. But he explains his conformity with Mosaic law (Matt. 19:8). "Because of the hardness of their hearts" the Israelites were permitted to divorce. That means it was permitted only to keep their hearts from even greater wantonness. But the intent of Old Testament law agrees with Jesus in that its main concern is the purity of marriage, marriage conducted in faith in God. This purity, that is, chastity,[101] is preserved in community with Jesus, in discipleship.

Because Jesus is solely concerned with the complete purity, that is, the chastity, of his disciples, he must also praise complete renunciation of marriage for the sake of God's realm.[102] Jesus does not make either marriage or celibacy into a required program. Instead, he frees his disciples from πορνεία, infidelity within and outside of marriage, which is a sin not only against one's own body, but a sin against the very body of Christ (1 Cor. 6:13-15). Even the body of the disciple belongs to Christ and discipleship; our bodies are members of his body. Because Jesus, the Son of God, assumed a human body, and because we are in communion with his body, that is why infidelity is a sin against Jesus' own body.

Jesus' body was crucified. The apostle says of those who belong to Christ that they have crucified the flesh with its passions and desires (Gal. 5:24). Thus, the fulfillment of even this Old Testament commandment becomes true only in the crucified, martyred body of Jesus Christ. The sight of that body, which was given for us,[103] and our communion with it provide the disciples with the strength for the chastity which Jesus commands.

129

[101.] Luther uses "chastity" to translate ἐγκράτεια, for example, in Gal. 5:22 ("self-denial"). Luther also uses "chastity" (and "discipline") in his interpretation of the Sixth Commandment in his Small Catechism (*The Book of Concord*, 343).

[102.] Matthew 19:11f. is discussed by Bonhoeffer together with Luke 14:26 in Bethge's notes in *NL* B 8 (17) and Zimmermann's notes in *NL* B 9, 5 (49). During his time in Finkenwalde, Bonhoeffer himself was prepared to renounce marriage (see *DB-ER* 468–69).

[103.] These are the words of institution from the Lord's Supper, according to 1 Cor. 11:24.

Truthfulness[104]

"Again, you have heard that it was said to those of ancient times, 'You shall not swear falsely, but carry out the vows you have made to the Lord.' But I say to you, Do not swear at all, either by heaven, for it is the throne of God, or by the earth, for it is God's footstool, or by Jerusalem, for it is the city of the great King. And do not swear by your head, for you cannot make one hair white or black. Let your word be 'Yes, Yes' or 'No, No'; anything more than this comes from the evil one" (Matt. 5:33-37).

130   The interpretation of these verses in the Christian church has been extraordinarily uncertain, even up until today.[105] Ever since the early church, interpreters have differed widely, from the rigorous rejection of any oath as a sin, to the milder rejection of frivolous oaths and perjury. In the early church the interpretation most widely recognized was that oaths were forbidden for "perfect" Christians, but permitted within certain limits for weaker ones. Augustine, among others, was of this opinion.[106] In his evaluation of oath-taking, he was in agreement with secular philosophers such as Plato, the Pythagoreans, Epictetus, and Marcus Aurelius. They considered oaths to be unworthy of a noble man. In their confessional writings the Reformation churches took it for granted that Jesus' words did not apply to the oaths required by secular authorities. [107] From the beginning the main arguments have been that oaths were required in the Old Testament,[108] Jesus himself swore before the court, and the apostle Paul used formulations similar to oaths several times.[109] For the reformers, in addition to the immediate proofs from

---

[104.] Schlatter, *Der Evangelist Matthäus,* gives Matt. 5:33-37 the heading "Unlimited Truthfulness." The NRSV gives it the heading "Concerning Oaths."

[105.] This paragraph and the following make extensive use of Tholuck, *Commentary,* 246–65.

[106.] St. Augustine, *Commentary on the Lord's Sermon on the Mount with Seventeen Related Sermons,* 11:73–77.

[107.] Augsburg Confession 16 (*The Book of Concord,* 37–38).

[108.] Tholuck, *Commentary,* cites Exod. 22:10; Deut. 6:13; 10:20 (250).

[109.] Tholuck, *Commentary,* cites "Christ *taking* an oath of the authorities, Matt. 26:63," and "2 Cor. 1:23, Rom. 1:9, Phil. 1:8, 1 Cor. 15:31" (253). [This is a controversial interpretation of Matt. 26:63. A contrary interpretation holds that Matthew is using language reminiscent of Peter's confession of faith in Matt. 16:16, language that represents the confession of faith of Matthew's community. In this passage Jesus is "placed under oath" and charged with claiming to be the Messiah, the Son of God. By answering clearly but indirectly, Jesus shows that he is practicing his own precept in chapter 5 by avoiding the use of an oath to confirm his word. To emphasize this, Matthew changes Mark's "I am" to "you say so." Jesus' reply is noncommittal and evasive.] [JG/GK]

scripture, their own distinction between the spiritual and secular realms was especially significant.

What is an oath? It is the public calling for God to be witness for a statement I make about something past, present, or future. God, the all-knowing One, shall avenge untruthfulness. How can Jesus call this oath sin, indeed, even say that it comes ἐκ τοῦ πονηροῦ [from the evil one], that it is "satanic"?[110] Because Jesus is concerned with complete truthfulness.

The oath is proof of the existence of lies in the world. If human beings could not lie, oaths would not be necessary. Thus an oath is a barrier against lying. But in providing this, it also encourages lying, for whenever an oath claims final truthfulness for itself, then at the same time room is also given for lying to take place; a certain right to existence is granted to the lie. Old Testament law uses oaths to reject lying. But Jesus rejects lying by prohibiting oaths. Both are concerned with the same thing, namely, destroying untruthfulness in the life of faithful persons. The oath the Old Testament employs to hinder lying was taken up and put into service by the lie itself. Thus, by means of the oath, the lie was able to establish itself securely as rightful. That is why Jesus had to attack the lie where it had sought refuge, in the oath. That is why the oath had to fall, because it had become the protector of the lie.

The assault of the lie on the oath could take place in two ways: either by asserting itself under oath (perjury), or by slipping into the form of the oath itself. In this case the lie used the oath not to call upon the living God, but to call upon some sort of secular or divine power. Once the lie had penetrated so deeply into the oath, then complete truthfulness could be warranted only by abolishing oaths altogether.

"Let your word be 'Yes, Yes' or 'No, No.'" This does not release the disciple's word from responsibility before the all-knowing God. Rather, precisely because the name of God is no longer explicitly called on, everything the disciple says is simply placed in the unquestionable presence of the all-knowing God. Thus disciples of Jesus should not swear, because there is no such thing as speech not spoken before God. All of their words should be nothing but truth, so that nothing requires veri-

131

[110.] Tholuck, *Commentary*, discusses this expression from Matt. 5:37 (248–65); on his copy of Tholuck's book, on page 264, Bonhoeffer wrote: ". . . ἐκ τοῦ πονηροῦ," and underlined it several times. Tholuck considers whether "the evil one" (not abstract "evil") could be meant, but thinks it would be "very strange" if Jesus "had declared that the oath, the act of the most intense religious self-determination, was of the *devil*" (264–65, marked in the margin by Bonhoeffer).

fication by oath. An oath consigns all other statements to the darkness of doubt. That is why it is "from the evil one." But in all their words the disciples are supposed to be full of light.

If the oath is thus prohibited, then it is also clear that the only goal is that of truthfulness. It is obvious that Jesus' command permits no exceptions, regardless of the forum demanding an oath. But we should also note that refusing to take an oath must not serve the purpose of concealing the truth. No generalized decision can be made as to when this is the case, that is, when an oath has to be taken for the sake of truthfulness. Instead, each case must be decided on its own by the person of whom an oath is demanded. The Reformation churches believe that every oath required by secular authority constitutes such a case.[111] It must remain questionable whether this general decision is possible.

But it is certain that, whenever such a case arises, an oath is to be taken only when, first, it is completely clear and transparent what content is included in the oath; and second, when the distinction has been made between oaths which refer to past or present circumstances which are known to us, and those which have the character of a vow. Since Christians can never be completely free of errors with respect to knowledge of the past, for them to call upon the all-knowing God serves the purity of their knowledge and consciences; it does not assert statements that may be subject to error. But because Christians never control their future, a solemn promise under oath, as, for example, loyalty oaths,[112] is fraught with greatest danger for them. For Christians control neither their own future, nor, what is more, the future of those to whom they are bound after the loyalty is sworn. Thus, for the sake of truthfulness and following Jesus, it is impossible to swear such an oath without the reservation of submitting it to the will of God. For Christians, there is no such thing as absolute earthly allegiance. A loyalty oath which intends to bind a Christian absolutely is a lie that comes "from the evil one." Calling upon the name of God in such an oath can never function as a confirmation of a solemn promise. Instead, it functions solely as witness to the fact that, in following Jesus, we are bound solely to the will of God, and that any other allegiance must be

[111.] See the Augsburg Confession, 16 (*Book of Concord*, 37–38).

[112.] On August 9, 1934, the German Evangelical National Synod under the German Christian bishop Ludwig Müller had passed a resolution requiring an oath for pastors and church officials, saying that they would be "faithful and obedient to the *Führer* of the German people and state, Adolf Hitler" (Schmidt, *Die Bekenntnisse und grundsätzlichen Äußerungen zur Kirchenfrage*, 2:128).

subject to this condition for the sake of Jesus. If in doubtful cases this limitation is not expressly spoken, or if it is not recognized, then an oath may not be sworn, because my taking such an oath misleads those who are demanding it of me. "Let your word be 'Yes, Yes' or 'No, No.' "

The command of complete truthfulness is only another way of expressing the total claim of discipleship. Only those who are bound to Jesus in discipleship stand in complete truthfulness. They have nothing to conceal from their Lord. They live unveiled before him.[113] Jesus knows them and places them into the truth. They are revealed as sinners before Jesus. They did not reveal themselves to Jesus, but as soon as Jesus revealed himself to them in his call, they knew themselves revealed in their sinfulness. Complete truthfulness emerges only from sin that is unveiled and forgiven by Jesus. Only those who stand in the truth by confessing their sins before Jesus are not ashamed of the truth, whenever it must be told. The truthfulness which Jesus requires of his disciples lies in the self-denial which does not conceal sin. Everything is revealed and illumined.

Because the first and last concern of truthfulness is the revealing of persons in their whole being, in their evilness before God, such truthfulness is resisted by the sinner. That is why it is persecuted and crucified. The truthfulness of the disciples has its sole basis in following Jesus, in which he reveals our sins to us on the cross. Only the cross as God's truth about us makes us truthful. Those who know the cross no longer shy away from any truth. Those who live under the cross can do without the oath as a commandment establishing truthfulness, for they exist in the perfect truth of God.

There is no truth toward Jesus without truth toward other people. Lying destroys community. But truth rends false community[114] and founds genuine fellowship. There is no following Jesus without living in the truth unveiled before God and other people.

134

Retribution

"You have heard that it was said, 'An eye for an eye and a tooth for a tooth.'[115] But I say to you, Do not resist an evildoer. But if anyone strikes

---

[113.] See 2 Cor. 3:18: "with unveiled faces."

[114.] In 1932 at Ciernohorské Kúpele, Bonhoeffer said, "A community of peace can only exist when it is not based on *lies* and on *injustice*" (*DBW* 11:339).

[115.] Leviticus 24:20. This rule states a criterion for *legally* ordered behavior, instead of totally uninhibited retaliation.

you on the right cheek, turn the other also; and if anyone wants to sue you and take your coat, give your cloak as well; and if anyone forces you to go one mile, go also the second mile. Give to everyone who begs from you, and do not refuse anyone who wants to borrow from you" (Matt. 5:38-42).

At this point Jesus is placing the rule "an eye for an eye, a tooth for a tooth" parallel to the other Old Testament commandments he has already quoted, for example, to the prohibition against killing in the Decalogue. He thus recognizes the rule as a valid commandment of God, just as much as that prohibition. As in that case, it is not to be abolished, but fulfilled completely. Jesus does not elevate the Ten Commandments above other Old Testament commandments as we once did. For him the commandment of the Old Testament is one, and he directs his disciples to obey it.

Jesus' followers renounce their own rights for his sake. He blesses them as the meek. If, after they had given up everything else for the sake of his community, they desired to hold fast to this one possession, they would have abandoned discipleship. Therefore, this is nothing more than an expansion of the Beatitude.[116]

The Old Testament law puts the claim to rights, or justice, under the divine protection of retribution. Nothing evil may happen without its being retaliated. Its concern is to construct a just community, to overcome and identify evil, and to eradicate evil from the community of God's people. That is the purpose of justice, which is enforced by retribution.

135   Jesus takes up this will of God and affirms the power of retribution to convict and overcome evil, and to ensure the community of disciples as the true Israel. Just retribution should do away with injustice and give proof to the disciples' following Jesus.

According to Jesus' words, such just retribution takes place only in not resisting it.

With this statement, Jesus releases his community from the political and legal order, from the national form of the people of Israel, and makes it into what it truly is, namely, the community of the faithful that is not bound by political or national ties. God's chosen people of Israel did exist in a political form in which, according to the divine will, retribution consisted of returning a blow for a blow. For the community of disciples, which makes no national or legal claims for itself, retribution

---

[116.] Matthew 5:5.

means patiently bearing the blow, so that evil is not added to evil. That is the only way community can be established and preserved.

Here it has become clear that the followers of Jesus who experience injustice do not cling to their own rights as if they were possessions to be defended at all costs. Instead, they are completely free of such possessions and are bound to Jesus Christ alone. Indeed, in giving witness to their sole allegiance to Jesus, they create the only solid foundation for community and place sinners into the hands of Jesus.

The overcoming of others now occurs by allowing their evil to run its course. The evil does not find what it is seeking, namely, resistance and, therewith, new evil which will inflame it even more. Evil will become powerless when it finds no opposing object, no resistance, but, instead, is willingly borne and suffered.[117] Evil meets an opponent for which it is not a match. Of course, this happens only when the last remnant of resistance is removed, when the urge to retaliate evil with evil is completely renounced. Then evil cannot achieve its goal of creating more evil; it remains alone.   136

Suffering passes when it is borne.[118] The evil comes to an end when we permit it to pass over us, without defense. Humiliation and debasement are revealed as sin when the disciple does not commit them, but bears them, without defense. Assault is condemned by not being met with violence. The unjust claim on my coat is answered by my giving up my cloak as well.[119] The exploitation of my service becomes obvious as exploitation when I set no limit on it. Our willingness to yield up everything when we are bidden to do so is our willingness to have enough in Jesus Christ alone, to desire to follow him alone. Our voluntary renunciation of counterviolence confirms and proclaims our unconditional allegiance to Jesus as his followers, our freedom, our detachment from our own egos. And it is only in the exclusivity of this adherence that evil can be overcome.

[117.] See Bethge's notes in *NL* B 8 (37) and Zimmermann's notes in *NL* B 9, 5 (64). These two sets of notes from different years are literally almost identical at this point. Bonhoeffer was explaining the power of bearing with evil done by one's enemies: "passio; bearing." Evil "falls on Jesus and burns up in the fire of forgiveness." "One who follows Christ on this way of unconditional passio. Here he retaliates against evil with his love." [See below, page 136, editorial note 127.] [JG/GK]

[118.] See above, page 90, on Matt. 26:39, 42.

[119.] In Bethge's notes in *NL* B 8 (37f.) Bonhoeffer is recorded to have said: "Verse 40 is apparently intended to apply to a legal offense. Even there is passio."

Our concern here is not only with evil, it is with the person who is evil. Jesus calls the evil person evil. My behavior should not give excuses and justification for those who indulge in violence or who oppress me. Nor do I intend to express my understanding for the rights of an evil person by my patient suffering. Jesus has nothing to do with such sentimental considerations. The humiliating blow, the violent deed, and the act of exploitation all remain evil. Disciples are to know this and to give witness to it just as Jesus did, because otherwise the evil person will not be engaged and overcome. A disciple should not resist when challenged by evil that cannot be justified at all. Instead, by suffering, the disciple will bring evil to its end and thus will overcome the evil person. Suffering willingly endured is stronger than evil; it is the death of evil.

137

There is no thinkable deed in which evil is so large and strong that it would require a different response from a Christian. The more terrible the evil, the more willing the disciple should be to suffer. Evil persons must be delivered to the hands of Jesus. Not I but Jesus must deal with them.

At this point, the Reformation interpretation introduced a decisively new concept, namely, that we should differentiate between harm done to me personally, and harm done to me as bearer of my office, that is, in the responsibility given me by God.[120] In the former case I am to act as Jesus commands, but in the latter case I am released from doing so. Indeed, for the sake of true love, I am even obligated to behave in the opposite way, to answer violence with violence in order to resist the inroads of evil.[121] This is what justifies the Reformation position on war, and on any use of public legal means to repel evil.[122] But this distinction between private person and bearer of an office as normative for my

---

[120.] [Cf. Luther's interpretation in 1530 of this passage of the Sermon on the Mount. Luther states that "a Christian should not resist any evil; but within the limits of his office, a secular person should oppose every evil" ("The Sermon on the Mount [Sermons] and the Magnificat," *LW* 21:113 [*WA* 32:393]).] [JG/GK] Althaus, *Religiöser Sozialismus*, states that "Luther even calls the responsibility of a mother to protect her child an 'office' . . ." (81).

[121.] Althaus emphasizes this distinction in *Der Geist der lutherischen Ethik im Augsburgischen Bekenntnis:* "In turning to the orders, the same love is retained which is the law of God's realm. The service-character of the orders includes those acts which superficially seem to be the exact opposite of what is commanded by the gospel, for example, the use of violence in office" (41).

[122.] See the Augsburg Confession, 16 (*The Book of Concord*, 137–38). In *The Social Teaching of the Christian Churches*, Troeltsch applied this Reformation legal distinction between person and office to "Christian ethics in the general state of sin" (2:499f.).

behavior is foreign to Jesus. He does not say a word about it. He addresses his disciples as people who have left everything behind[123] to follow him. "Private" and "official" spheres are all completely subject to Jesus' command. The word of Jesus claimed them undividedly. He demands undivided obedience. In fact, the distinction between private and official is vulnerable to an insoluble dilemma. Where in real life am I really only a private person and where only the bearer of my office? Wherever I am attacked, am I not simultaneously the father of my children, the pastor of my congregation, the statesman of my people? For this reason, am I not required to fight back against any attack, just because of my responsibility for my office?[124] Am I not always myself in my office, too, who stands alone before Jesus? Should this distinction cause us to forget that followers of Jesus are always completely alone, single individuals who can act and make decisions finally only by themselves, and that the most serious responsibility for those entrusted to me takes place precisely in *these* acts?

138

But how can Jesus' statement be justified in light of our experience that evil seeks out the weak and rampages most wildly among the most defenseless? Isn't Jesus' statement just an ideology which does not take into account the realities of the world, let us say the sin of the world? Perhaps this statement could be valid within a Christian community. But in confrontation with the world it seems to be an enthusiast's ignoring of sin. Because we live in the world and the world is evil, therefore this statement cannot be valid.

But Jesus says: because you live in the world and because the world is evil, that is why the statement is valid: do not resist evil. It would be difficult to accuse Jesus of not knowing the power of evil, Jesus, who battled with the devil from the first day of his life onward.[125] Jesus calls evil evil and that is just why he speaks to his disciples in this way. How is this possible?

Indeed, what Jesus says to his disciples would all be pure enthusiasm if

---

[123.] Mark 10:28.

[124.] On the deferment of obedience to the commandment which thus becomes possible, see Barth's dictum in *The Epistle to the Romans:* "the reservation which Lutherans made when in their distress they proclaimed a 'moratorium for the Sermon on the Mount'" (470). The National Socialist regime had corrupted many "offices" in government and society, and reference to obedience in office could serve to excuse one's own participation in evil acts.

[125.] See the story of Jesus' temptation in Matt. 4:1-11.

we were to understand these statements to be a general ethical program, if we were to interpret the statement that evil will only be conquered by good[126] as general secular wisdom for life in the world. That really would

139   be an irresponsible imagining of laws which the world would never obey. Nonresistance as a principle for secular life is godless destruction of the order of the world which God graciously preserves. But it is not a programmatic thinker who is speaking here. Rather, the one speaking here about overcoming evil with suffering is he who himself was overcome by evil on the cross and who emerged from that defeat as the conqueror and victor. There is no other justification for this commandment of Jesus than his own cross. Only those who there, in the cross of Jesus, find faith in the victory over evil can obey his command, and that is the only kind of obedience which has the promise. Which promise? The promise of community with the cross of Jesus and of community with his victory.

The passion of Jesus[127] as the overcoming of evil by divine love is the only solid foundation for the disciples' obedience. With his command Jesus calls disciples again into communion with his passion. How will our preaching of the passion of Jesus Christ become visible and credible to the world if the disciples avoid this passion for themselves, if they despise it in their own bodies? Through his cross Jesus himself fulfilled the law

---

7. It is evil thoughtlessness to state, referring to John 18:23, that Jesus did not literally fulfill his own command and, therefore, we are excused from obedience to it. Jesus calls evil evil, but he suffers[128] without resistance, even to death on the cross.[129]

[126.] Romans 12:21.

[127.] According to two sets of notes from Bonhoeffer's New Testament lectures, here and in the following sentences Bonhoeffer uses the Latin expression *passio*, incorporating the Latin phrase into his published text toward the end of the chapter: "This deed will prove to be what is 'special' by leading Christians to the passio of Christ. This deed itself is continuous suffering. In it Christ's suffering is borne by his disciples." See Bethge's notes in *NL* B 8 and Zimmermann's notes in *NL* B 9, 5. [JG/GK]

[128.] See Tholuck, *Commentary*, on Matt. 5:38: "In St. John 18:23, we have a case where the Saviour had an opportunity of literally fulfilling the command of v. 39 and has not done it." Christ only intended to condemn "the spirit of revenge. . . . The man who is capable of literally fulfilling these injunctions is also morally capacitated to leave them externally unfulfilled" (270).

[129.] In the 1961 German edition of *Nachfolge*, the word "it" (*es*) was added to the verb "suffers" (*erleidet*), hence "he suffers it." [See above, page 90, where Bonhoeffer uses the infinitive "to suffer/suffering" (*erleiden*) as a noun in the sense of the *passio Christi* or passion of Christ, in order to conclude that this suffering or passion is not anything merely passive.] [JG/GK]

he gives us,[7] and in his commandment he graciously keeps his disciples in communion with his cross. In the cross alone is it true and real that suffering love is the retribution for and the overcoming of evil. Participation in the cross is given to the disciples by the call into discipleship. They are blessed in this visible community.

The Enemy—the "Extraordinary"

"You have heard that it was said, 'You shall love your neighbor and hate your enemy.' But I say to you, Love your enemies; bless those who curse you, do good to those who hate you, and pray for those who abuse and persecute you, so that you may be children of your Father in heaven; for he makes his sun rise on the evil and on the good, and sends rain on the righteous and on the unrighteous. For if you love those who love you, what reward do you have? Do not even the tax collectors do the same? And if you greet only your brothers and sisters, what more are you doing than others? Do not even the Gentiles do the same? Be perfect, therefore, as your heavenly Father is perfect" (Matt. 5:43-48).[130]

This is the point in the Sermon on the Mount where we encounter for the first time the word which summarizes everything in it: love. Immediately it is put into the clear-cut context of love for our enemies. Loving one's kindred is a commandment that could be misunderstood. Loving enemies makes unmistakably clear what Jesus intends.

"Enemy" was no empty concept for the disciples. They knew it well. They met enemies daily. There were those who cursed them as destroyers of the faith and lawbreakers; there were those who hated them because they had left everything for Jesus' sake and did not highly value anything but communion with him; there were those who insulted and scorned them for their weakness and humility; there were those who persecuted them, who feared a growing revolutionary danger in the group of disciples and were intent on destroying them.[131] One kind of enemy were

---

[130.] The words "bless those who curse you, do good to those who hate you" come from the Lucan parallel to Matthew 5 (Luke 6:28-29). They were contained in the critical apparatus of Bonhoeffer's Greek New Testament.

[131.] See Kierkegaard, *Søren Kierkegaard's Journals and Papers*, referring to early Christian persecutions: "Once the objection against Christianity (and this was right at the time when it was most evident what Christianity is) was that it was unpatriotic, a danger to the state, revolutionary . . ." (4:182, with Bonhoeffer's marking).

141   the representatives of a people's piety, who could not tolerate Jesus' claim to exclusive and complete loyalty.[132] They were armed with power and respect. Another enemy, which would be apparent to every Jew, was the political enemy in Rome. The Jews experienced powerful oppression from that enemy.[133] In addition to these two inimical groups, there was all the personal enmity which anyone encounters who does not participate in the norms of the majority: daily defamation, humiliation, and threats.

To be sure, nowhere in the Old Testament is there a statement which commands us to hate our enemies. On the contrary, we find the commandment to love our enemies (Exod. 23:4f.; Prov. 25:21f.; Gen. 45:1ff.; 1 Sam. 24:7; 2 Kings 6:22; and elsewhere).[134] But Jesus is speaking here, not of natural enmity, but of the enmity of God's people against the world. Israel's wars were the only "holy" wars[135] the world has ever known. They were God's wars against the world of idols. Jesus does not condemn that enmity, otherwise he would have to condemn God's entire history with God's own people. Instead, Jesus affirms the Old Covenant. His only concern is to overcome enemies, to achieve victory for God's community. But in this command, once again[136] he released his community of disciples from the political form of the people of Israel. As a result, there will be no more wars of faith. God promised that we would gain victory over our enemies precisely by loving them.

Loving one's enemies is not only an unbearable offense to the natural person. It demands more than the strength a natural person can muster, and it offends the natural concept of good and evil. But even more important, loving one's enemies appears to people living according to the law to be a sin against God's law itself. Separation from enemies and

---

[132.] In the Barmen Theological Declaration of 1934 Christ was confessed as the only Lord in all areas of life—"solus [alone] Christus"—a refutation of the German Christians' allegiance to the people and its traditional way of life.

[133.] "Every Jew" also had plenty of reasons to be reminded of political enemies in National Socialist Germany. The Confessing Church refused to adapt itself to the people's demands. For example, it rejected the National Socialist "non-Aryan" racial laws being applied to the church. For this it was forced into illegality by government rulings (see *DB-ER* 496f.).

[134.] Bonhoeffer includes a number of the passages mentioned by Tholuck on Matt. 5:43 (*Commentary*, 279–81).

[135.] On this topic, see von Rad, *Der Heilge Krieg im alten Israel*.

[136.] See above, page 132.

[137.] Bornhäuser refers to the Ten Commandments and Ps. 139:21 (Tholuck, *Commentary*, 127; in Bonhoeffer's copy this passage is marked up to page 130).

condemning them is what the law demands.[137] But Jesus takes God's law into his hands and interprets it. To overcome enemies by loving them—that is God's will which is contained in the law.

142

In the New Testament, the enemy is always the one who hates me. Jesus does not even consider the possibility that there could be someone whom the disciple hates. Enemies should receive what sisters and brothers receive, namely, love from Jesus' followers. The actions of the disciples should not be determined by the human actions they encounter, but by Jesus acting in them. The only source of the disciples' action is the will of Jesus.

Jesus speaks of enemies, that is, of those who will remain our enemies, unmoved by our love; those who do not forgive us anything when we forgive them everything; those who hate us when we love them; those who insult us all the more, the more we serve them. "In return for my love they accuse me, even while I make prayer for them" (Ps. 109:4). But love must not ask if it is being returned. Instead, it seeks those who need it. But who needs love more than they who live in hate without any love? Who, therefore, is more worthy of my love than my foe? Where is love praised more splendidly than amidst love's enemies?[138]

This love knows no difference among diverse kinds of enemies, except that the more animosity the enemy has, the more my love is required. No matter whether it is a political or religious enemy, they can all expect only undivided love from Jesus' followers. This love recognizes no inner conflict within myself, even between my being a private person and my being an officeholder.[139] In both cases I can be only one who follows Jesus, or I am no follower of Jesus at all. I am asked, how does this love act? Jesus says: bless them, do good to them, pray for them without condition, without regard for who they are.

"Love your enemies." While the previous command spoke only of defenseless suffering from evil, Jesus here goes much further. We should not only bear evil and the evil person passively, not only refuse to answer a blow with a blow, but in sincere love we should be fond of our enemies. Unhypocritically and purely we are to serve and help our enemies in all things. No offering which a lover would bring to a beloved can be too great and too valuable for our enemies. If, because of love for our kindred, we are obliged to offer our goods, our honor, and our life, then in

143

[138.] Reference to Ps. 110:2.
[139.] See above, pages 134f.

the same way we are obliged to offer them for our enemies. Does this, then, make us participants in the evildoing of our enemies? No, for how should that love which is born not of weakness but of strength,[140] which comes not from fear but from the truth,[141] become guilty of the hatred of another? And to whom must such love be given, if not to those whose hearts are suffocating in hate?

"Bless those who curse you." If our enemies curse us because they cannot bear our presence, then we should lift our hands to bless them: "You, our enemies, be blessed by God; your curse cannot harm us, but may your poverty be filled by the riches of God, by the blessing of God, against whom you rail in vain. We shall willingly bear your curse, if only God's blessing comes over you."

"Do good to those who hate you." Words and thoughts are not enough. Doing good involves all the things of daily life. "If your enemies are hungry, feed them; if they are thirsty, give them something to drink" (Rom. 12:20).[142] In the same way that brothers and sisters stand by each other in times of need, bind up each other's wounds, ease each other's pain, love of the enemy should do good to the enemy. Where in the world is there greater need, where are deeper wounds and pain than those of our enemies? Where is doing good more necessary and more blessed than for our enemies? "It is more blessed to give than to receive."[143]

"Pray for those who abuse and persecute you." That is the most extreme. In prayer we go to our enemies, to stand at their side. We are with them, near them, for them before God. Jesus does not promise us that the enemy we love, we bless, to whom we do good, will not abuse and persecute us. They will do so. But even in doing so, they cannot harm and conquer us if we take this last step to them in intercessory prayer. Now we are taking up their neediness and poverty, their being guilty and lost, and interceding for them before God. We are doing for them in vicarious representative action what they cannot do for themselves.[144] Every insult from our enemy will only bind us closer to God and to our enemy. Every persecution can only serve to bring the enemy

144

[140.] 2 Timothy 1:7.
[141.] 1 John 4:18 and 3:18.
[142.] Romans 12:20 cites Prov. 24:21; Tholuck points this out (*Commentary*, 279).
[143.] Quoted in Acts 20:35 as "words of the Lord Jesus."
[144.] On intercession and vicarious representative action, see *SC* (*DBWE* 1):185ff.

closer to reconciliation with God, to make love more unconquerable.

How does love become unconquerable? By never asking what the enemy is doing to it, and only asking what Jesus has done. Loving one's enemies leads disciples to the way of the cross and into communion with the crucified one. But the more the disciples are certain to have been forced onto this path, the greater the certainty that their love remains unconquered, that love overcomes the hatred of the enemy; for it is not their own love. It is solely the love of Jesus Christ, who went to the cross for his enemies and prayed on the cross for them. Faced with the way of the cross of Jesus Christ, however, the disciples themselves recognize that they were among the enemies of Jesus who have been conquered by his love. This love makes the disciples able to see, so that they can recognize an enemy as a sister or brother and behave toward that person as they would toward a sister or brother. Why? Because they live only from the love of him who behaved toward them as toward brothers and sisters, who accepted them when they were his enemies and brought them into communion with him as his neighbors. That is how love makes disciples able to see, so that they can see the enemies included in God's love, that they can see the enemies under the cross of Jesus Christ. God did not ask me about good and evil, because before God even my good was godless.[145] God's love seeks the enemy who needs it, whom God considers to be worthy of it. In the enemy, God magnifies divine love. Disciples know that. They have participated in that love through Jesus. For God lets the sun shine and the rain fall on the righteous and the unrighteous. It is not only the earth's sun and earthly rain which descend on good and evil, but it is also the "sun of righteousness,"[146] Jesus Christ himself, and the rain of God's word, which reveal the grace of his Father in heaven toward sinners. Undivided, perfect love is the act of the Father; it is also the act of the children of their

145

[145.] Barth comments on Rom. 1:18: "God's anger is revealed over the people's godlessness in evil *and* over their godlessness in good, over my enemy *and* over me, if I intend to be my enemy's enemy" (*The Epistle to the Romans,* 473). In Bonhoeffer's lectures in 1931–32 on "Systematic Theology of the Twentieth Century," he picked up Barth's use of godlessness (*DBW* 11:210 [*GS* 5:225]).

[146.] Bonhoeffer cites these words "Sun of Rightcousness" (*Sonne der Gerechtigkeit*), which is the title of hymn 263 in the *Evangelisches Gesangbuch.* The lyrics of this hymn were written in 1741 by Christian David, cofounder of the Herrenhuter Community of the Brethren. It is not found in the *Evangelisches Gesangbuch für Brandenburg und Pommern,* but it was incorporated as hymn 129 in *Ein neues Lied,* the hymnal of the German Protestant youth; the second edition was published in Berlin in 1933, just prior to the Third Reich. This hymnal was very popular among the seminarians. See *DBWE* 5:123–24. [JG/GK]

[147.] The following quotation is included according to a page from the twenty-third circular letter from Finkenwalde of August 26, 1937, which reports that the manuscript for

Father in heaven, just as it was the deed of God's only begotten Son.[147]

"The prayers of neighborly love and of nonrevenge will be especially important in the struggle fought by God toward which we are moving, and in which to some extent we have already been engaged for years. On one side, hatred is fighting, and on the other, love. Every Christian soul must seriously prepare for this. The time is coming in which everyone who confesses the *living* God will become, *for the sake of that confession*, not only an object of hatred and fury. Indeed, already we are nearly that far along now.[148] The time is coming when Christians, for the sake of their confession, will be excluded from 'human society,' as it is called, hounded from place to place, subjected to physical attack, abused, and under some circumstances even killed. *The time of a widespread persecution of Christians is coming*, and that is actually the real meaning of all the movements and struggles of our time. Those opponents intent upon destroying the Christian church and Christian faith cannot live together with us, because they see in all of our words and all of our actions that their own words and deeds are condemned, even if ours are not directed against them. And they are not wrong in seeing this and feeling that we are indifferent to their condemnation of us. They have to admit that their condemnation is completely powerless and negligible. They sense that we do not relate to them at all, as would be quite all right with them, on the basis of mutual blaming and quarreling. And how are we supposed to fight this fight? The time is approaching when we—no longer as isolated individuals, but *together* as congregations, as the church—shall lift our hands in prayer. The time is coming when we—as crowds of people, even if they are relatively small crowds among the many thousands-times-thousands of people who have fallen away—will loudly confess and praise the crucified and resurrected Lord, and his coming again. And what

---

the book *Discipleship* is finally complete. On this page Bonhoeffer crossed out the heading from the circular letter, "A. F. C. *Vilmar* on *Matt. 5:48*," and noted instead "page 60a." This page was found in the copy which Eberhard Bethge received from Bonhoeffer on the first Sunday of Advent 1937. The text comes from the 1850 essay "Haß und Liebe" [Hate and love] in Vilmar's *Zur neuesten Kulturgeschichte Deutschlands* and contains parts of pages 353 and 357. (This was probably a text which was already edited and copied for the circular letter; cf. below, pages 267f., the Kohlbrügge quotation from a book of devotions.) The beginning of the quotation expands the line in Vilmar: "Whenever, on one side, hatred is fighting, and on the other, love, it is a struggle fought by God" (353).

[148.] Vilmar in *Zur neuesten Kulturgeschichte Deutschlands* wrote: "We have already come this far in the last two years" (354), meaning since the revolution of 1848.

prayer, what confession, what song of praise is this? It is a prayer *of most intimate love for those who are lost,* who stand around us and glare at us with eyes rolling with hatred, some of whom have already even conspired to kill us. It is a prayer for peace for these distraught and shaken, disturbed and destroyed souls, a prayer for the same love and peace that we ourselves enjoy. It is a prayer which will penetrate deeply into their souls and will tug at their hearts with a much stronger grip than they can manage to tug at our hearts, despite their strongest efforts to hate. Yes, the church which is truly waiting for its Lord, which really grasps the signs of the time of final separation, such a church must fling itself into *this prayer of love,* using all the powers of its soul and the total powers of its holy life" (A. F. C. Vilmar, 1880).[149]

What is undivided love? Love which does not show special favor to those who return our love with their own. In loving those who love us, our kindred, our people, our friends, yes, even our Christian community, we are no different than the Gentiles and the tax collectors. That kind of love is self-evident, regular, natural, but not distinctly Christian. Yes, in this case it really is "the same"[150] thing that non-Christians[151] and Christians do. Loving those who belong to me through blood,[152] history, or friendship is the same for non-Christians and Christians. Jesus does not have a lot to say about that kind of love. People know all by themselves what it is. He does not need to light its flame, to emphasize it or exalt it. Natural circumstances alone force it to be recognized, for non-Christians and for Christians. Jesus does not need to say that people should love their sisters and brothers, their people, their friends. That goes without saying. But by simply acknowledging that and not wasting any further words on it, and, in contrast to all that, commanding only love for enemies, he shows what he means by love and what they are to think about the other sort of love.

147

How are disciples different from nonbelievers? What does "being Christian" consist of? At this point the word appears toward which the whole fifth chapter is pointed, in which everything already said is sum-

---

[149.] This is Bonhoeffer's addendum to the page of the twenty-third circular letter from Finkenwalde.

[150.] This is the way Luther translates τὸ αὐτό in Matt. 5:46.

[151.] Even the "New Gentiles" in the Third Reich respected the people's community.

[152.] When National Socialist ideology spoke of "blood," it was understood to speak of race, far more than the common use of "blood" as a metaphor for relationship.

marized: what is Christian is what is *"peculiar,"* περισσόν, the extraordinary, irregular, not self-evident.[153] This is the "better righteousness" which "outdoes" that of the Pharisees, towers over them, that which is more, beyond all else. What is natural is τὸ αὐτὸ (one and the same) for non-Christians and Christians. What is distinctly Christian begins with the περισσόν, and that is what finally places what is natural in the proper light. When this specialness, this extraordinariness, is absent, then what is Christian is absent. What is Christian does not take place in naturally given circumstances, but in stepping beyond them. The περισσόν never dissolves into τὸ αὐτό. It is the great mistake of a false Protestant ethic to assume that loving Christ can be the same as loving one's native country, or friendship or profession, that the better righteousness and justitia civilis are the same.[154] Jesus does not talk that way. What is Christian depends on the "extraordinary." That is why Christians cannot conform to the world, because their concern is the περισσόν.

148

What does the περισσόν, the extraordinary, consist of? It is the existence of those blessed in the Beatitudes, the life of the disciples. It is the shining light, the city on the hill. It is the way of self-denial, perfect love, perfect purity, perfect truthfulness, perfect nonviolence. Here is undivided love for one's enemies, loving those who love no one and whom no one loves. It is love for one's religious, political, or personal enemy. In all of this it is the way which found its fulfillment in the cross of Jesus Christ. What is the περισσόν? It is the love of Jesus Christ himself, who goes to the cross in suffering and obedience. It is the cross. What is unique in Christianity is the cross, which allows Christians to step beyond the world in order to receive victory over the world. The passio

---

[153.] "Something strange" or *Sonderliches* is Luther's translation of the Greek word in Matt. 5:47. On the related verb περισσεύειν, see above, page 119. In a New Testament lecture Bonhoeffer explained: "The περισσόν is the cross, which places Christians outside of the ordinary orders of things" (Bethge's notes in *NL* B 8, 40). The word "extraordinary," which Bonhoeffer chose as a heading for Matthew 5 in the printed version, is used frequently by Kierkegaard, for example: "'The apostle' is not the extraordinary [Overordentlige] because of his voluntary poverty and the like. No, this is what is required, and in so doing he is a Christian. But he is the extraordinary through his immediate God-relationship. Only in this sense can Christianity admit to extraordinary Christians" (*Søren Kierkegaard's Journals and Papers* 2:356). But Kierkegaard omits the inference of "orders," which is important to Bonhoeffer (see above, especially pages 93ff., for his defense against a theology of "natural" orders of creation).

[154.] Bonhoeffer is criticizing explanations of *justitia civilis*, such as that in Brunner's book *The Divine Imperative*, 179–80 (see above, page 113).

in the love of the crucified one—that is the "extraordinary" mark of Christian existence.

The extraordinary is doubtless that which is visible, which magnifies the Father in heaven. It cannot remain hidden. The people have to see it. The community of Jesus' disciples, the community of better righteousness, is the visible community, that took the step beyond the orders of the world. It has left everything behind to gain the cross of Christ.

What are you *doing* that is special? The extraordinary—and that is what is most offensive—is a *deed* the disciples do. It has to be done—like the better righteousness—and done visibly! Not in ethical rigor, not in the eccentricity of Christian ways of life, but in the simplicity of Christian obedience to the will of Jesus. This deed will prove to be what is "special"   149 by leading Christians to the passio of Christ. Such action itself is continuous suffering.[155] In this action Christ is his disciples' passio. If it is not that, then *this* is not the deed which Jesus intends.

The περισσόν is, thus, the fulfillment of the law, the keeping of the commandments. In Christ the Crucified and his community, the "extraordinary" occurs.

Here are those who are perfect, perfect in undivided love, just as their Father in heaven is. It was the undivided, perfect love of the Father which gave the divine Son up to die on the cross for us. Likewise, the passio of the communion with this cross is the perfection of the followers of Jesus. [156] The perfect are none other than those who, in the Beatitudes, are called blessed.

[155.] Cf. Bethge's notes in *NL* B 8 (40): "ποιεῖτε is itself passio." The Greek verb is found in Matt. 5:47 ("what are you doing"). Bonhoeffer uses the Latin word *passio* to express a meaning which does not dissolve into passivity, but includes activity.

[156.] Bonhoeffer, according to Bethge's notes in *NL* B 8 (39f.), comments about the Greek word for "perfect" in verse 48 (τέλειος): ". . . not ethical. Not Ritschl . . . Like Jesus, undivided for all." Ritschl (1822–89) speaks of "the feeling of religious-ethical perfection" (*Instruction in the Christian Religion*, sec. 47).

150

MATTHEW 6:
ON THE HIDDEN NATURE
OF THE CHRISTIAN LIFE

Hidden Righteousness

"BEWARE OF PRACTICING your righteousness[157] before others in order to be seen by them; for then you have no reward from your Father in heaven.

¶ "So whenever you give alms, do not sound a trumpet before you, as the hypocrites do in the synagogues and in the streets, so that they may be praised by others. Truly I tell you, they have received their reward. But when you give alms, do not let your left hand know what your right hand is doing, so that your alms may be done in secret; and your Father who sees in secret will reward you" (Matt. 6:1-4).[158]

The fifth chapter spoke of the visibility of the disciples' community and culminated in the περισσόν, requiring us to understand that what is characteristically Christian is that which steps away from the world, rises above the world, is extraordinary. Then the next chapter links up with this περισσόν and reveals its ambiguity. The danger is great that the disciples will completely misunderstand this as a command to start building a heavenly kingdom on earth, despising and destroying the world order. The danger is great that in enthusiasts'[159] indifference to this age they will think it their duty now to achieve and make visible the extraordinariness of this new world, separating themselves from the world radically and with no willingness to compromise, in order to force into being what is Christian, what is appropriate to discipleship, what is extraordinary. It was too easy to mistake this for the preaching of another pious style

151

[157.] This variation from Luther's translation ("Beware of your almsgiving, that you do not give . . .") is appropriate to the Greek words δικαιοσύνη (righteousness) and ποιεῖν [to do/doing] in the main text of Nestle's Greek New Testament used by Bonhoeffer. The word Luther translates with "almsgiving" is listed in Nestle's notes as a variant. Schlatter, *Der Evangelist Matthäus,* explains that "the Palestinians used the word 'righteousness' as a name for charity."

[158.] Here, as well as in verses 6 and 18, Bonhoeffer follows Luther's text and not the reading in Nestle's main text, which excludes εν τω φανερω ("in public").

[159.] Bonhoeffer agreed with Althaus's warning against the human willfulness of "chiliastic-revolutionary" enthusiasm (*Der Geist der lutherischen Ethik,* 43).

and way of life, even if it was a free, new, inspiring one.[160] And one's pious flesh would be so willing to accept this extraordinariness, poverty, truthfulness, suffering, or even to seek it out, if only doing so would satisfy the heart's longing to actually see something with one's own eyes[161] and not merely to believe. One would surely be willing to nudge the boundaries of a pious lifestyle and obedience to the word, until they move more closely together, and are finally no longer distinguishable from each other. It would only be for the one goal of finally achieving the extraordinary.

On the other hand, those would gather on the battlefield who had only been waiting for Jesus to speak about the extraordinary so that they could attack him with even more rage. Proclaiming the extraordinary unmasked Jesus as an enthusiast,[162] a revolutionary extremist who wanted to turn the world upside down, who instructs his disciples to leave the world and build a new world. Is that still obedience to Old Testament scripture? Is it not a thoroughly self-selected personal righteousness that is being proposed here?[163] Doesn't Jesus know about the sin of the world that will wreck anything he commands? Doesn't he know anything about God's revealed commandments, which are given to ward off sin? Isn't this extraordinariness he is demanding proof of a spiritual arrogance, which is the beginning of all enthusiasm?[164] No, not the extraordinary, but rather the completely ordinary, everyday, regular, unobtrusive 152 behavior is the sign of genuine obedience and genuine humility. If Jesus had sent his disciples to their people, to their vocations, their responsibilities, their obedience to the law as the scribes interpreted it to the

---

[160.] See Zimmermann's notes in *NL* B 9, 5 (41) (*DBW* 14:619): "Christian lifestyle (= to contemplate oneself), one's own joy in one's own form." Bonhoeffer warns against this, in agreement with Barth's reservations against "realization in a specifically human sphere," expressed in Bonhoeffer's letter of October 14, 1936 (*WF* 120 [*DBW* 14:251]).

[161.] See Bonhoeffer's letter of October 18, 1931 (*DBW* 11:33 [*GS* 1:61]): "This invisibility is ruining us."

[162.] Here, as above, page 77, and in other places Bonhoeffer rejects the criticism that obedience in discipleship is enthusiasm.

[163.] The phrase "self-selected personal righteousness" can be found in Gogarten, *Politische Ethik*, 166 (with reference to Luther); this was reviewed by Bonhoeffer during 1932–33 (*DBW* 12:162 [*GS* 5:321]).

[164.] Brunner wrote that "Christian enthusiasm" is dangerous by its "spirit of Pharisaism[,] which makes such people consider themselves far above all who—in their own terms—'do not take the gospel seriously'" (*The Divine Imperative*, 479).

people, then he would have shown himself to be pious, truly humble, and obedient. He would have inspired people to more serious piety and stricter obedience. He would have taught what the scribes already knew, but what they liked to hear preached again with emphasis, that true piety and righteousness consist of not only the external deed, but also of one's heartfelt intentions, and not only of intentions, but also of the deed. That would really be "better righteousness" the way the people needed it, the way no one could have avoided it. But now all of that was shattered. Instead of the humble teacher of the law, they recognized an arrogant enthusiast. Of course, in all ages the preaching of enthusiasts has been able to inspire the human heart, indeed, even the noble human heart. But didn't the teachers of the law know that the voice of the flesh was speaking from this heart in all its goodness and nobility? Didn't they themselves know the power the pious flesh had over people? Jesus sacrificed the best sons of the country, the honorably pious ones useless in a struggle for a chimera. The extraordinary—that was the works of a pious person, done quite voluntarily, springing from one's own heart. It was the triumphant insistence on human freedom against simple obedience to God's commandment. It was forbidden human self-righteousness, which the law never permitted. It was lawless self-sanctification, which had to be rejected by the law. It was the free works which established themselves in opposition to unfree obedience.[165] It was the destruction of God's community, the denial of faith; it was blasphemy against the law, blasphemy against God. Assessed by the law, the extraordinariness Jesus taught was deserving of the death penalty.

153   What does Jesus say about all that? He says: "Beware of practicing your righteousness before others in order to be seen by them." The call to be extraordinary is the great, inevitable danger of discipleship. Therefore, beware of this extraordinariness, of the way that discipleship becomes visible. Jesus calls a halt to our thoughtless, unbroken, simple joy in what is visible. He gives a sting to the extraordinary. Jesus calls us to reflection.

The disciples should have this extraordinariness only by way of reflection. They should heed it, watch out for it. The extraordinary is not supposed to happen in order to be seen. This means that the extraordinary

---

[165.] Bonhoeffer is protesting against the misuse of Luther's theological insight in *De Servo Arbitrio* on the bondage of will (*LW* 33:3-295 [*WA* 18:600-787]). Cf. above, page 83, editorial note 23.

deed should not be done for the sake of its being extraordinary. And it should not be seen just for the sake of being seen. The better righteousness of the disciples should not be an end in itself. Of course, what is extraordinary does have to become visible, it does have to happen, but— beware that you do not do it *in order* for it to become visible. Although the visibility of discipleship docs have a necessary reason, which is the call of Jesus Christ, it is never a goal in itself. If it were, then the focus would no longer be on discipleship itself; then a moment of repose would occur, our following would be interrupted, and we would not be able to take it up again at the point where we had stopped to rest. We would immediately be sent back to begin all over again. We would have to take note that we are no longer disciples.[166] So something has to become visible, but—paradoxically: beware that it does not happen for the sake of being seen by people. "Let your light shine before the people . . ." (5:16), but: pay attention to the hiddenness! Chapters 5 and 6 collide hard against each other. What is visible should be hidden at the same time; at the same time both visible and not to be seen. The reflection we have mentioned, thus, needs to be guided so that we do not stray into reflection about our extraordinariness. Our paying attention to our righteousness is supposed to support our not paying attention to our righteousness. Otherwise extraordinariness is no longer the extraordinariness of discipleship, but the extraordinariness of our own will and desire.

154

How are we to understand this contradiction? *First,* we ask:[167] from whom should the visibility of discipleship be hidden? Not from the other people, for they are to see the light of Jesus' disciples shining. Rather it should be hidden to those doing the visible deed of discipleship. They should keep on following Jesus, and should keep looking forward to him who is going before them, but not at themselves and what they are doing. The righteousness of the disciples is hidden from themselves. Of course, they, too, can see the extraordinariness, but not themselves in it; they remain hidden from themselves. They see the extraordinary only when

---

[166.] See Bethge's notes in *NL* B 8 (18), saying that "because discipleship takes place only step by step. Therefore every step is a new entry into discipleship."

[167.] Here and in the following two paragraphs, Bonhoeffer retained a numerical outline, as he used when lecturing on this material to his seminary students in 1935 and 1936. Ever since *Creation and Fall* Bonhoeffer had usually omitted outline numbers in manuscripts to be printed.

they look at Jesus, and in him they do not see it as extraordinary, but as something obvious and normal. So what is visible really is hidden from them, in *obedience* to the word of Jesus. If the extraordinariness were important to them because it is extraordinary, then they would act like enthusiasts, out of their own power, out of the flesh. But because Jesus' disciples act in simple obedience to their Lord, they view the extraordinary as only the normal act of obedience. According to Jesus' word, the disciples can do nothing else but be the light that shines. They do not do anything to accomplish this; they are the light while following Christ, looking only to their Lord. Precisely because what is Christian is *necessarily* extraordinary, that is, in the *indicative* form ["you are"],[168] it is at the same time normal and *hidden*. Otherwise it is not Christian, it is not obedience to the will of Jesus Christ.

Second, we ask: what in the content of the act of following Christ constitutes the union of the visible and the hidden? How can the same thing be simultaneously visible and hidden? To answer we need only to turn back to the result of chapter 5. What is extraordinary and visible is the cross of Christ, beneath which the disciples stand. The cross is at once what is necessary and hidden, and what is visible and extraordinary.

Third, we ask: how can the paradox between the fifth and sixth chapters be resolved? The concept of discipleship itself provides the resolution. It is exclusive allegiance to Jesus Christ. Disciples always look only to their Lord and follow him. If they were to see the extraordinariness itself, then they would no longer stand in discipleship. In simple obedience disciples do the will of the Lord who bids them do something extraordinary, and they know in everything only that they can do nothing else, that they are, therefore, doing what is simply a matter of course.

The only required reflection for disciples is to be completely oblivious, completely unreflective in obedience, in discipleship, in love.[169] If you do good, do not let your left hand know what your right hand is doing. You should not know your own goodness.[170] Otherwise it will really be

---

[168.] See Matt. 5:13, 14: "You are . . ." (not: "You should be . . .").

[169.] See Bonhoeffer's distinction between *actus reflexus* and *actus directus* in *Act and Being.* He describes "direct action" using Luther's terms: "Here [in the community of faith] even the *agere* [believing] is *pati* [being borne]" (*AB* [*DBWE* 2]:121). He makes the same interconnection between 'deed' and 'suffering' later on page 145. [On the distinction between *actus directus* and *actus reflexus,* see Feil, *The Theology of Dietrich Bonhoeffer,* 48–49, and Kelly, *Liberating Faith,* 54–56.] [JG/GK]

[170.] Bethge's notes in *NL* B 8 (43) say: "Do not know about your own good!! That is the only way it will remain God's good."

your goodness, and not the goodness of Christ. The goodness of Christ, the goodness of discipleship takes place without awareness. The genuine deed of love is always a deed hidden to myself.[171] Pay heed that you do not know it. Only in this way is it the goodness of God. If I want to know my own goodness and my own love, then it is no longer love. Even the extraordinary love of enemies remains hidden to disciples. When they love their enemies, then they no longer view them as enemies. This blindness of the disciples, or rather this vision enlightened by Christ, is what makes them certain. The hiddenness of their lives from themselves is their promise.

The other side of hiddenness is its being in the open. There is nothing hidden which will not be revealed.[172] That is how God made things   156
to be, before whom everything hidden is already revealed. God wants to show us what is hidden. God will make it visible. Being revealed in public is the reward ordained by God for hiddenness. The question is only where and from whom people receive this reward of public recognition. If they long for it to be in sight of other people, then they will have had their reward as soon as they get such publicity. There is no difference whether they seek it in the cruder form, in the presence of others, or in the more subtle form, in the presence of themselves. Whenever the left hand knows what the right is doing, whenever I myself become aware of my own hidden goodness, whenever I want to know about my own goodness, then I have already prepared for myself the public reward which God intended to store up for me. I am the one who revealed my own hiddenness to myself. I do not wait for God to show it to me. So I have gotten my reward. But those who remain hidden even from themselves until the end[173] will receive from God the reward of being revealed. But who can live in such a way as to do the extraordinary in secret? Who can prevent the left hand from knowing what the right hand is doing? What sort of love is that which does not know of itself, but can remain hidden from itself until the last day? It is clear that because it is hidden love, it cannot be a visible virtue, a human habitus [attitude]. Beware—it says—that you

[171.] See especially Bonhoeffer's 1934 sermon on 1 Cor. 13:8-12, where he says that the love in which "God acts through us" goes its way "with the surefootedness of the sleepwalker" (*DBW* 13:394 [*GS* 5:550]).

[172.] Matthew 10:26.

[173.] Matthew 24:13.

do not mistake genuine love for the virtue of kindness or for a human "quality"![174] It is self-forgetting love in the most genuine sense of the word. In this self-forgetting love, however, the old self must die with all its virtues and qualities. The old Adam dies in the disciples' love, which is oblivious of the self and bound solely to Christ. The death of the old Adam is proclaimed in the sentence. "Let not your left hand know what your right is doing." Once again, who can live so that chapters 5 and 6 are one? None except those whose old self has died in Christ and who have found a new life in Christ's community of discipleship.[175] Love as

157   the deed of simple obedience is death to the old self and the self's discovery to exist now in the righteousness of Christ and in one's brothers and sisters. Then the old self is no longer alive, but Christ is alive in the person.[176] The love of Christ the Crucified, who leads the old self in us to death, is what lives in Christ's follower. Disciples find themselves only in Christ and in their brothers and sisters.

The Hiddenness of Prayer

"And whenever you pray, do not be like the hypocrites; for they love to stand and pray in the synagogues and at the street corners, so that they may be seen by others. Truly I tell you, they have received their reward. But whenever you pray, go into your room and shut the door and pray to your Father who is in secret; and your Father who sees in secret will reward you in public. When you are praying, do not heap up empty phrases as the Gentiles do; for they think that they will be heard because of their many words. Do not be like them, for your Father knows what you need before you ask him" (Matt. 6:5-8).

Jesus teaches his disciples to pray. What does that mean? We should not take for granted that we are allowed to pray. Of course, prayer is a natural need of the human heart, but that does not mean that human beings have a right to pray before God. Even when it is done with firm discipline and practice, it can be fruitless and without promise. The disciples may pray because it is Jesus who tells them to do so, and he truly

---

[174.] In *NL* B 8 (44) Bethge notes: "This [love] which does not know itself is not a 'glued-in quality' (Luther was against gratia infusa [grace poured in]), it is not a human quality at all."

[175.] Reference to Rom. 6:6 and 6:4 on baptism.

[176.] Galatians 2:20.

knows the Father. He promises them that God will listen to them. So the disciples may pray only because they are in the community of Jesus, because they follow him. Anyone who is bound to Jesus in discipleship has access to the Father through him. Thus, every true prayer is mediated prayer. There is no such thing as unmediated praying. Even in prayer there is no unmediated access to the Father. Only through Jesus Christ may we find the Father in prayer. Faith, adherence to Christ, is the presupposition of prayer. He is the only mediator of our prayer. We pray trusting in his word. So our prayer is always prayer bound to his word.

We pray to God, in whom we believe through Christ. Therefore our 158 prayer can never be a pleading with God. We do not need to pose before God. We may trust that God knows what we need before we ask for it.[177] This gives our prayer greatest confidence and joyous certainty. It is not the formulation, not the number of words, but faith which reaches God's fatherly heart that has known us so long.

Genuine prayer is not a deed, an exercise, a pious attitude. Rather it is the request of the child to the heart of the Father. That is why prayer is never demonstrative, neither before God nor before ourselves, nor before others. If God did not know what I need, then I would have to think about *how* I should tell God, *what* I should tell God, *whether* I should tell God. But the faith out of which I am praying prevents such reflecting or demonstrating.

Prayer is necessarily hidden. It is the opposite of a public act in every way. When people pray, they no longer know themselves; they know only God, to whom they are calling. Because prayer does not reach out into the world, but is directed solely to God, it is the least demonstrative act there is.

Of course, even prayer can be distorted into a demonstrative act, which brings what is hidden into the light. This happens not only in public prayer, which degenerates into empty phrases. These days that will rarely happen.[178] But it is no better; indeed, it is even more harmful when I make myself the observer of my own prayer, when I pray before myself. It does not matter whether I am enjoying watching myself at

---

[177.] In *NL* B 8 (46) Bethge notes that "not only does this sentence ['your Father knows'] *not* invalidate prayer, no, instead, only *because* of *this* sentence can there be such a thing as Christian prayer."

[178.] In Germany under the Nazis Christians had to be aware of the danger that any public prayer, even a table grace in a restaurant, would attract unfavorable attention.

prayer, or whether I catch myself feeling irritated or ashamed at prayer. The public nature of life in the street is only a more naive form of the public display I construct by myself. Even in my little room I can produce quite a remarkable public demonstration. That is how far we can distort

159   Jesus' word. The public display I construct by myself consists of my being simultaneously the one who is praying and the one who is listening. I listen to myself; I hear myself. Because I do not want to wait for God to listen to me, because I do not want to wait for God to show me someday that my prayer was heard, I construct my own hearing of my prayer. I observe that I prayed piously, and this observation provides the satisfaction of being heard. My prayer is heard. I have received my reward. Because I have heard myself, God will not hear me. Because I have given myself the reward of public acclaim, God will give me no further reward.

What is the room into which I should go, of which Jesus speaks, if I am not even safe from myself? How can I lock it so tightly that no observer ruins the hiddenness of prayer and steals from me the reward of hidden prayer? How can I protect myself from myself? From my own reflections? How does my reflection kill reflection? The word "kill" must be spoken. My own will to have my own way by means of my prayer must die, must be killed. My will has died when Jesus' will alone reigns in me and all of my will has been drawn into his. It has died in community with Jesus, in discipleship. Then I can pray that the will of God, who knows what I need before I ask for it, be done. The only way my prayer is sure, strong, and pure is when it comes from the will of Jesus. Then prayer really is *supplication*. The child entreats the *Father* whom it knows. General adoration[179] is not the essence of Christian prayer; supplication is. The right and proper attitude of a human being before God is to entreat God with outstretched hands, knowing that God has the heart of a loving parent.

Although genuine prayer is hidden prayer, that does not exclude the possibility of community prayer, provided that it has become clear how great are the dangers of common prayer. Ultimately, it does not matter whether prayer is on the street or in one's room, whether it is short or

160   long, whether it is in the litany of church prayer or in the sighs of those who do not know how they should pray,[180] whether it is done by an individual or a community. The only thing that matters is knowing that your

---

[179.] In *NL* B 8 (47) Bethge notes: "Adoration is a great, titanic human possibility."
[180.] See Rom. 8:26.

Father knows what you need. That is what directs our prayer solely to God. That liberates the disciples from false belief in works.[181]

"Pray then in this way: Our Father in heaven, hallowed be your name. Your kingdom come. Your will be done, on earth as it is in heaven. Give us this day our daily bread. And forgive us our debts, as we also have forgiven our debtors. And do not lead us into temptation, but rescuc us from evil. For yours is the kingdom and the power and the glory, forever. Amen. For if you forgive others their trespasses, your heavenly Father will also forgive you; but if you do not forgive others, neither will your Father forgive your trespasses" (Matt. 6:9-15).

Jesus told his disciples not only *how* they should pray, but *what* they should pray. The Lord's Prayer is not an example for the prayer of the disciples. Rather, it is what *should* be prayed as Jesus taught them. God will hear them praying this. That is certain. The Lord's Prayer is the essence of prayer. The essence and limit of all the disciples' praying may be found in it. Here again, Jesus does not abandon his disciples to uncertainty. Instead, with the Lord's Prayer he leads them to complete clarity in prayer.

"Our Father in heaven"—together the disciples call upon their heavenly Father, who already knows what God's dear children need. They have been made into sisters and brothers by the call of Jesus, who binds them together. In Jesus they have come to know the kindliness of the Father. In the name of the Son of God they may call God their Father. They are on earth and their Father is in heaven.[182] The Father looks down on them, and they lift their eyes up to the Father.

"Hallowed be your name." God's fatherly name, as it has been   161 revealed to the disciples in Jesus Christ, should be kept holy among them, for the entire gospel is contained in this name. May God keep the

---

[181.] Bonhoeffer never spoke about the Lord's Prayer (Matt. 6:9-13) in any of his lectures. See the remark in Johannes Mickley's notes: "Warning against preaching about the Lord's Prayer. It should not be interpreted too much (not even when catechizing in the classroom!)" (*NL* B 9, 3 [22]). [While this is true of his Finkenwalde lectures, nonetheless, Bonhoeffer made a conscious effort to associate the Psalms with the Lord's Prayer in his 1940 book, *The Prayerbook of the Bible: An Introduction to the Psalms.* He even quotes Luther on this connection: "It [the Psalter] runs through the Lord's Prayer and the Lord's Prayer runs through it, so that it is possible to understand one on the basis of the other and to bring them into joyful harmony" (*DBWE* 5:157–58).][JG/GK]

[182.] Karl Barth cites Eccles. 5:1 [5:1 Hebrew text, 5:2 in NRSV], "God is in heaven, and you upon earth," in *The Epistle to the Romans,* 10.

holy gospel from being tarnished and spoiled by false teaching and an unholy life. May God reveal in Jesus Christ God's holy name to the disciples forevermore. May God lead all preachers to pure proclamation of the gospel which makes people blessed. May God turn back the tempters and convert the enemies of God's name.[183]

"Your kingdom come." In Jesus Christ the disciples have experienced the inbreaking of God's kingdom on earth. This is where Satan is overcome, the power of the world, sin, and death broken. God's kingdom still is found in suffering and in struggle. The small community of those called forth will participate in such suffering and struggle. They stand under the rule of God in new righteousness, but also in enduring persecution.[184] May God grant that the kingdom of Jesus Christ on earth grow in his community. May God soon put an end to the kingdoms of this world and bring about God's own reign with power and glory.

"Your will be done on earth as in heaven." In the community of Jesus Christ, the disciples have completely surrendered their will to God's will. They pray, therefore, that God's will be done on the whole earth. No creature should obstruct it. But because the will of evil still lives even in the disciples trying to tear them out of their community with Jesus, they must also pray that the will of God rule in them more completely every day and break down their resistance. Ultimately, however, the whole world shall bend to the will of God and gratefully worship God in distress and in joy. Heaven and earth shall be subject to God.

Above all, Jesus' disciples should pray for God's name, God's kingdom, and God's will. Of course, God does not need these prayers, but through them the disciples themselves participate in the heavenly treasures for which they are praying. Also, such prayers may hasten the end of time.[185]

162

"Give us this day our daily bread." As long as the disciples are on earth, they should not be ashamed of asking their heavenly Father for the things they need for their bodily life. God who created human beings on earth intends to preserve and protect human bodies. God does not intend that God's own creation become disdained. Disciples pray for

---

[183.] Bonhoeffer interprets this petition in the language of prayer. He does the same for the second and fifth petitions.

[184.] Mark 10:30.

[185.] See Bonhoeffer's remark about ". . . 'waiting for and hastening' the second coming of Jesus (2 Peter 3:12)" (*DBW* 14:287 [*GS* 2:515]).

bread to be shared. None of them will be given it alone. They also pray that God give daily bread to all of God's children on the whole earth, for they are all sisters and brothers in the flesh. The disciples know that the bread which grows from the earth comes down from heaven[186] and is God's gift alone. That is why they do not simply take their bread; they ask for it. Because it is bread from God, it comes anew every day. The disciples do not pray for advance supplies, but for the daily gift from God today, which sustains their lives in the community of Jesus and for which they praise God's gentle goodness. This petition is proof of the disciples' faith in God's living action on earth doing what is best for them.

"Forgive us our sin, as we forgive those who sin against us." The disciples' daily sorrow is the recognition of their guilt. They, who could live without sin in community with Jesus, sin daily in all sorts of ways: they lack faith, are lethargic at prayer, lack bodily discipline, and give in to self-indulgence, envy, hatred, and ambition. So they must pray daily for God's forgiveness. But God will only hear their prayer when they forgive each other's guilt in a loving and willing way. Together, they bring their guilt before God and pray together for grace. May God forgive not only me my sins, but us our sins.

"Lead us not into temptation." The temptations of the disciples are various. Satan attacks them from all sides and tries to bring them down. False security and godless doubt tempt them severely. Knowing of their weakness, the disciples do not provoke their being tempted in order to prove the strength of their faith. They ask God not to tempt their weak faith and to protect them in the hour of temptation.

163

"But deliver us from evil." The disciples' final prayer is to be that someday they be delivered from this evil world[187] and inherit the kingdom of heaven. This petition is for a blessed end[188] and for the salvation of the Christian community at the last days of this world.

"For yours is the kingdom . . ." Daily the disciples receive this certainty anew from their communion with *Jesus Christ, who is the fulfillment of all*

[186.] See James 1:17.

[187.] In the Large Catechism, Luther explains the sense of the Greek text: "Deliver or keep us from the Evil One, or the Wicked One" (*The Book of Concord*, 435). Bonhoeffer here uses the archaic German word *Argen* that Luther used for "Evil One."

[188.] This is reminiscent of Luther's Small Catechism, which says "he may grant us a blessed end and graciously take us from this world of sorrow to himself in heaven" (*The Book of Concord*, 348).

their petitions. In him God's name is hallowed; in him God's kingdom comes; in him God's will is done. For his sake the bodily life of the disciples is preserved; for his sake they receive forgiveness for their sins. In his power they are protected from temptation; in his power they are saved unto eternal life. His is the kingdom and the power and the glory forever in communion with the Father. The disciples are certain of this.

As if to summarize the prayer, Jesus states once again that everything depends on receiving forgiveness, and that this forgiveness can only be received when living in the fellowship of other sinners.

The Hiddenness of Practicing Piety

"And whenever you fast, do not look dismal, like the hypocrites, for they disfigure their faces so as to show others that they are fasting. Truly I tell you, they have received their reward. But when you fast, put oil on your head and wash your face, so that your fasting may be seen not by others but by your Father who is in secret; and your Father who sees in secret[189] will reward you" (Matt. 6:16-18).

164   Jesus takes it for granted that disciples will keep the pious practice or exercise [Übung] of fasting. The life of a disciple requires the strict practice of austerity. The only purpose of such practices [exercitia] is to make disciples more willing and more joyous in following the designated path and doing the works required of them. The selfish and lethargic will, which resists being of service, is disciplined; the flesh is chastened and punished. The practice of austerity makes me feel the estrangement of my Christian life from the world. A life which remains without any ascetic discipline, which indulges in all the desires of the flesh as long as they are "permitted" by the justitia civilis [civil order], will find it difficult to enter the service of Christ. Satiated flesh is unwilling to pray and is unfit for self-sacrificing service.[190]

[189.] See Bethge's note in *NL* B 8 (47): "exegetical difficulty verse 18 ἐν τῷ κρυφαίῳ] could refer to God's hiddenness or our hiddenness. Ambiguous."

[190.] Bonhoeffer's support of these practices or exercises [Übungen] of piety is not a new idea with him. As early as his Barcelona sermon on Ps. 62:2, he had written that one's "relationship with God must be exercised in practice. . . . Religion is work (*DBW* 10:484)." He recommended to his congregants that they try to spend at least ten minutes each day in silent meditation. [JG/GK]

So a disciple's life requires strict external discipline. This is not to suggest that the will of the flesh can be broken by discipline. The daily death[191] of the old self cannot be achieved by anything other than faith in Jesus. But persons of faith, disciples whose will is already broken, whose old selves have died to Jesus Christ, do know precisely the rebellion and daily pride of their flesh. They know their lethargy and lack of discipline and know that to be the source of arrogance which must be conquered. This takes place in daily and extraordinary practice of discipline. The disciples are meant when it is said that the spirit is willing, but the flesh is weak. Therefore, "watch and pray."[192] The spirit knows the path of discipleship and is ready to follow it, but the flesh is too fearful; the path is too difficult for it, too uncertain, too arduous. So the spirit falls silent. The spirit affirms Jesus' commandment to love one's enemies unconditionally, but flesh and blood are too strong, so that the commandment does not become the deed. Thus in daily and extraordinary exercise and discipline, the flesh must learn to understand that it has no rights of its own. The daily, orderly exercise of prayer helps in this. So does daily meditation on the word of God,[193] as do all sorts of practices of physical discipline and austerity.

165

At first, the resistance of the flesh against these daily humiliations comes frontally; then later it comes hidden behind the word of the Spirit, that is, in the name of evangelical freedom. The flesh's resistance to the word of Jesus becomes evident whenever evangelical freedom from legalistic coercion, from self-martyrdom, and mortification is played off against legitimate evangelical use of discipline, exercises, and asceticism; whenever lack of discipline and disorder in prayer, in using scripture, or in one's physical life are justified in the name of Christian freedom. In such circumstances people have lost sight of the fact that daily life in discipleship is foreign to the world. They have also lost sight of the joy and the true freedom which genuine discipline gives to the life of disciples. Christians will have to attack the resistance of their flesh whenever they recognize that they have failed in their service, that their willingness has weakened, that they have become guilty influencing the lives of others or causing the guilt of others, that their joy in God is fading, that their

---

[191.] 1 Corinthians 15:31.

[192.] Matthew 26:41.

[193.] See Eberhard Bethge's account of Bonhoeffer's 1936 "Instructions in Daily Meditation," in Bonhoeffer's *Meditating on the Word*, 30–41 (*DBW* 14:945–50 [*GS* 2:478–82]). [JG/GK]

strength for prayer is no longer present. Christians who recognize that will try to get ready for better service through spiritual exercises, fasting, and prayer (Luke 2:37; 4:2; Mark 9:29; 1 Cor. 7:5).[194] The objection that Christians should take refuge in faith and scripture and forsake asceticism is without any merit. It is without mercy and has no power to help. What is a life of faith, if not an endless manifold struggle of the spirit against the flesh?[195] How can anyone live in faith whom prayer makes slothful, who is tired of scripture, or whose joy in God is stolen by sleeping, eating, or sexual desire?[196]

166   Asceticism is self-chosen suffering; it is passio activa, not passio passiva, and, therefore, most vulnerable.[197] Asceticism is constantly threatened by the godless, pious wish to make oneself equal to Christ through suffering. One's own claim to take the place of Christ's suffering, to complete the work of Christ in suffering, namely, killing off the old self in us, is also lurking dormant within asceticism. In this, asceticism usurps the bitter and ultimate seriousness of Christ's work of salvation. Here asceticism makes a dreadfully harsh show of itself. Voluntary suffering should serve only better ministry and deeper humility on the basis of Christ's suffering. But here it becomes a terrible distortion of the suffering of the Lord himself. It wants to be seen; it becomes a merciless living reproach to other people, for it has become the path to salvation. In such "public" ostentatiousness, its reward is really squandered, because it is sought from other people.

    "Put oil on your head and wash your face"[198] could likewise become an opportunity for subtle pleasure or self-praise. But that would misinterpret it as a disguise or mask. Jesus, however, says to his disciples that they should remain humble in the voluntary exercises of humility, that

---

[194.] At the latter verse, 1 Cor. 7:5, Bonhoeffer inserted the word νηστεια, fasting, from the Nestle critical apparatus, into the text of his edition of the Greek New Testament.

[195.] See, for example, Gal. 5:17 (marked in Bonhoeffer's Greek New Testament). See the appeal to the colleague pastors of the Confessing Church: ". . . Having started with the Spirit, are you now ending with the flesh?" (Gal. 3:3) (*DBW* 14:170–71 [*GS* 2:483]).

[196.] See *DBW* 14:211–13 (*GS* 2:501–2).

[197.] Bethge's notes in *NL* B 8 (48) say that "*passio activa* is suffering which I bring upon myself: the *terrible danger* in it: choosing one's own cross!" This is suggestive of some of Luther's formulations, for example in Luther, *Disputationes,* from 1535–45, which Bonhoeffer used in 1926 (see *DBWE* 9:355–410, esp. 367). Cf. above, page 89.

[198.] In the margin of *NL* B 8 (49) Bethge remarks, "Using oil and washing is daily routine, not something special!"

they should never burden others with such exercises, using them as a reproach or a law. Instead, they should become grateful and joyous that they are permitted to remain in service to their Lord. What is meant here is not the cheerful face of a disciple seen as a Christian stereotype, but the proper hiddenness of Christian deeds, the humility which does not know of itself, just as the eye does not see itself, but only others. Such hiddenness shall be revealed one day, but only by God, not by oneself.

The Simplicity of Carefree Life   167

"Do not store up for yourselves treasures on earth, where moth and rust consume and where thieves break in and steal; but store up for yourselves treasures in heaven, where neither moth nor rust consumes and where thieves do not break in and steal. For where your treasure is, there your heart will be also. The eye is the lamp of the body. So, if your eye is healthy, your whole body will be full of light; but if your eye is unhealthy, your whole body will be full of darkness. If then the light in you is darkness, how great is the darkness! No one can serve two masters; for a slave will either hate the one and love the other, or be devoted to the one and despise the other. You cannot serve God and wealth" (Matt. 6:19-24).

The life of those who follow proves to be on the right course when nothing comes between them and Christ, not the law, not their own piety, and not the world. The disciples always see only Christ. They do not see Christ *and* the law, Christ *and* piety, Christ *and* the world. They do not even begin to reflect that; they just follow Christ in everything. So their vision is simple. Its sole focus is on the light which comes from Christ. There is no darkness or ambiguity in their eyes. Just as the eye must remain simple, clear, and pure, so that the body may remain in the light, just as the foot and the hand have no other source of light except the eye, just as the foot stumbles and the hand gropes when the eye is clouded, just as the whole body is in darkness when the eye is blinded, so disciples are in the light only as long as they look simply to Christ and not to this or that. The disciples' hearts must simply be focused on Christ alone. If the eye sees something other than what is real, then the whole body is deceived. If the heart clings to the appearances of the world, to the creatures instead of the creator, then the disciple is lost.

It is the goods of the world which try to turn away the hearts of Jesus' disciples. What is it that attracts the heart of a disciple? That is the

question. Is it attracted by the goods of the world, or even by Christ *and*
the goods of the world? Or does it stand by Christ alone? The light for
the body is the eye, and the light for a disciple is the heart. If the eye is
dimmed, how dark the whole body must be. If the heart is darkened,
how dark it must be in the disciple. The heart becomes dark when it
clings to the goods of the world. Then Jesus' call, be it as urgent as can
be, nevertheless bounces off; it finds no entry in the person, because the
heart is closed. It belongs to another. Just as no light can enter the body
if the eye is evil, so the word of Jesus cannot enter the disciple if the heart
is shut. The word is choked off, just as the seed among thorns is choked
by the "cares, riches, and pleasures of this life" (Luke 8:14).

The simplicity of the eye and the heart is like the hiddenness in which
nothing except Christ's word and call is known and complete communion with Christ is all there is. How should disciples deal simply with the
goods of the earth?

Jesus does not forbid them to use the goods. Jesus was human. He ate
and drank just as his disciples did. In doing so, he purified the use of the
goods of the earth. Disciples should gratefully use the goods required
for their bodies' daily need and nutrition—goods which are consumed
in sustaining life.[199] "We're wandering Pilgrims day by endless days, /
ill-clothed and poor yet freed in fearless ways. / We need not gather,
hoard, nor trade, / lest our paths to God overburdened fade. / Who so
craves with greed's lethal eyes, / cannot along life's journey with us have
ties. / Few goods at hand, we live at peace, / with God our lot our needs
decrease."[200] Goods are given to us to be used, but not to be stored
away. Just as Israel in the desert received manna daily from God and did
not have to worry about food and drink, and just as the manna which
was stored from one day for another rotted,[201] so should Jesus' disciples
receive their share daily from God. But if they store it up as lasting treasure, they will spoil both the gift and themselves. The heart clings to collected treasure. Stored-up possessions get between me and God. Where

---

[199.] See Luther's commentary on article 1 of the Creed in the Small Catechism (*The
Book of Concord*, 345).

[200.] Bonhoeffer is citing verse 4 of the hymn "Kommt, Kinder, laßt uns gehen"
(Come children, let us go) by Gerhard Tersteegen [trans. GK]; see *Evangelisches Gesangbuch
für Brandenburg und Pommern*, 189, 4. The hymn is based on Matt. 7:13, 14. On the use of
this hymn for Evensong at Finkenwalde, see *DB-ER* 540.

[201.] See Exodus 16.

my treasure is, there is my trust, my security, my comfort, my God. Treasure means idolatry.[8]

But where is the boundary between the goods I am supposed to use and the treasure I am not supposed to have? If we turn the statement around and say, What your heart clings to is your treasure, then we have the answer. It can be a very modest treasure; it is not a question of size. Everything depends on the heart, on you. If I continue to ask how can I recognize what my heart clings to, again there is a clear and simple answer: everything which keeps you from loving God above all things,[203] everything which gets between you and your obedience to Jesus is the treasure to which your heart clings.

Because the human heart needs a treasure to cling to, it is Jesus' will that it should have a treasure,[9] but not on earth where it decays. Instead, the treasure is in heaven, where it is preserved. The "treasures" in heaven of which Jesus is speaking are apparently not the One Treasure, Jesus himself, but treasures really collected by his followers. A great promise is expressed in this, that disciples will acquire heavenly treasures by following Jesus, treasures which will not decay, which wait for them, with which they shall be united.[204] What other treasures could they be except that extraordinariness, that hiddenness of life as a disciple? What treasures could they be except the fruits of Christ's suffering, which the life of a disciple will bear?

If disciples have completely entrusted their hearts to God, then it is clear to them that they *cannot* serve two masters. They simply cannot. It is impossible in discipleship. It would be tempting to demonstrate one's Christian cleverness and experience by showing that one did know how to serve both masters, mammon [wealth] and God, by giving each their limited due. Why shouldn't we, who are God's children, also be joyous

169

170

---

8. It is no coincidence that in his catalogues of sins Paul always lists infidelity and greed next to each other and calls both idolatry.[202]

9. We should note that Jesus does not deprive the human heart of what it needs: treasure, honor, renown. But he gives the heart another object: honor that comes from God (John 5:44), the glory of the cross (Gal. 6:14), and treasure in heaven.

[202.] See below, page 264.

[203.] See Luther's commentary in the Small Catechism on the First Commandment (*The Book of Concord*, 342).

[204.] On this, see the text references cited in *NL* B 8 (50) where Bethge notes: "Eph. 2 [verse 10], 2 Timothy 1:12!!"

children of this world, who enjoy God's good gifts and receive their treasures as God's blessings? God and world, God and earthly goods are
against each other, because the world and its goods reach for our hearts.
Only when they have won our hearts are they really what they are. Without our hearts, earthly goods and the world mean nothing. They live
off our hearts. In that way they are against God. We can give our hearts
in complete love only to one object, we can cling only to one master.
Whatever opposes this love falls into hatred. According to Jesus' word,
there can be only love or hate toward God. If we do not love God, then
we hate God. There is no in-between. That is the way God is, and that is
what makes God be God, that we can only love or hate God. Only one or
the other option is possible. Either you love God or you love the goods
of the world. If you love the world, you hate God; if you love God, you
hate the world.[205] It does not matter at all whether you intend to do it
or whether you know what you are doing. Of course, you will not intend
to do so, and you will probably not know what you are doing. It is much
more likely that you do not *intend* what you do; you just *intend* to serve
both masters. You intend to love God and goods, so you will always view
it as an untruth that you hate God. You love God, you think. But by loving God and also the goods of the world, our love for God is actually
hate; our eye no longer views things simply, and our heart is no longer
in communion with Jesus. Whether it is your intention or not, it cannot
be otherwise. You cannot serve two masters, you who are following Jesus.

"Therefore I tell you, do not worry about your life, what you will eat
or what you will drink, or about your body, what you will wear. Is not life
more than food, and the body more than clothing? Look at the birds of
the air; they neither sow nor reap nor gather into barns, and yet your
heavenly Father feeds them. Are you not of more value than they? And
can any of you by worrying add a single hour to your span of life? And
why do you worry about clothing? Consider the lilies of the field, how
they grow; they neither toil nor spin, yet I tell you, even Solomon in all
his glory was not clothed like one of these. But if God so clothes the grass
of the field, which is alive today and tomorrow is thrown into the oven,
will he not much more clothe you—you of little faith? Therefore do not
worry, saying, 'What will we eat?' or 'What will we drink?' or 'What will we

171

[205.] See the student notes of Wolf-Dieter Zimmerman in *NL* B 9, 5 (73) with reference to 1 John 2:15 and John 3:16: "Our love for the world goes through God's love for the
world in Jesus Christ. Not flight from the world, but—love God."

wear?' For it is the Gentiles who strive for all these things; and indeed your heavenly Father knows that you need all these things. But strive first for the kingdom of God and righteousness, and all these things will be given to you as well. So do not worry about tomorrow, for tomorrow will bring worries of its own. Today's trouble is enough for today" (Matt. 6:25-34).

Do not worry! Earthly goods deceive the human heart into believing that they give it security and freedom from worry. But in truth, they are what cause anxiety. The heart which clings to goods receives with them the choking burden of worry. Worry collects treasures, and treasures produce more worries. We desire to secure our lives with earthly goods; we want our worrying to make us worry-free, but the truth is the opposite. The chains which bind us to earthly goods, the clutches which hold the goods tight, are themselves worries.

Abuse of earthly goods consists of using them as a security for the next day. Worry is always directed toward tomorrow. But the goods are intended only for today in the strictest sense. It is our securing things for tomorrow which makes us so insecure today. It is enough that each day should have its own troubles. Only those who put tomorrow completely into God's hand and receive fully today what they need for their lives are really secure. Receiving daily liberates me from tomorrow. The thought of tomorrow gives me endless worries. "Do not worry about tomorrow"— that is either cruel ridicule of the poor and suffering, whom Jesus is addressing, of all those who—in human perspective—will starve tomorrow if they do not worry today; it is either an intolerable law that people will reject and detest *or* it is the unique gospel proclamation of the freedom of God's children, who have a Father in heaven, who has given them the gift of his dear Son. Will he not with him also give us everything else?[206]

172

"Do not worry about tomorrow"—we should not understand that to be human wisdom or a law. The only way to understand it is as the gospel of Jesus Christ. Only those disciples who have recognized Jesus can receive from this word an affirmation of the love of the Father of Jesus Christ and liberation from all things. It is not worrying which makes disciples worry-free; it is faith in Jesus Christ. Now they know: we *cannot* worry (v. 27). The next day, the next hour is completely out of our hands' reach. It is meaningless to behave as if we could worry. We can change nothing about the conditions of the world. Only God can change the conditions, for example, a body's height, for God rules the world. Because we cannot

---

[206.] Romans 8:32.

worry, because we are so powerless, we *should* not worry. Worrying means taking God's rule onto ourselves.

Disciples know not only that they may not and cannot worry, but also that they need not worry. It is not worry, it is not even work which produces daily bread, but God the Father. The birds and the lilies do not work and spin, but they are fed and clothed; they receive their daily share without worry. They need the goods of the world only for daily life. They do not collect them. By not collecting they praise the creator, not by their industry, their work, their worry, but by receiving daily and simply the gifts God gives. That is how birds and lilies become examples for disciples. Jesus dissolves the connection between work and food, which is conceived in terms of cause and effect apart from God. He does not value daily bread as the reward for work. Instead, he speaks of the carefree simplicity of those who follow the ways of Jesus and receive everything from God.[207]

173

"Now no animal works for its living, but each has its own task to perform, after which it seeks and finds its food. The little birds fly about and warble, make nests, and hatch their young. That is their task. But they do not gain their living from it. Oxen plow, horses carry their riders and have a share in battle; sheep furnish wool, milk, cheese, and so on. That is their task. But they do not gain their living from it. It is the earth which produces grass and nourishes them through God's blessing. . . . Similarly, man must necessarily work and busy himself at something. At the same time, however, he must know that it is something other than his labor which furnishes him sustenance; it is the divine blessing. Because God gives him nothing unless he works, it may seem as if it is his labor which sustains him; just as the little birds neither sow nor reap, but they would certainly die of hunger if they did not fly about to seek their food. The fact that they find food, however, is not due to their own labor, but to God's goodness. For who placed their food there where they can find it? . . . For where God has not laid up a supply no one will find anything, even though they all work themselves to death searching." (Luther)[208]

[207.] See Zimmerman's notes in *NL* B 9, 5 (74): "God's call is different from worries and ethos of work." This contrasts with Tholuck's remark in *Commentary:* "Now, that God *can* support life even without work, is a statement which assumes that work is for man the appointed means by which life is to be supported" (386). "These animals cannot, like man, procure for themselves food by labour" (387).

[208.] This quote is taken from Witte, *Nun freut euch lieben Christen gemein,* which varies slightly from Luther's original, which is quoted here ("Exposition of Psalm 127, for the Christians at Riga in Livonia, 1524" [*LW* 45:326–27 (*WA* 15:367–68)]). Witte omits from

But if the creator sustains birds and lilies, won't the Father also feed his children, who daily ask him to do so? Shouldn't God give them what they need for their daily lives, God, to whom all the goods of the earth belong and who can distribute them according to God's own pleasure? "God give me every day as much as I need to live. He gives it to the birds on the roof, how should he not give it to me?" (Claudius).[209]

Worry is the concern of nonbelievers, who rely on their strength and work, but not on God. Nonbelievers are worriers, because they do not know that the Father knows what their needs are.[210] So they intend to get for themselves what they do not expect from God. But disciples are to "strive first for the kingdom of God and his righteousness, and all these things will be given to you as well." This makes clear that concern for food and clothing is not yet concern for the kingdom of God, as we would like to understand it. We would like to consider performing our work for our families and ourselves, our worrying for food and a place to live and sleep, to be the same thing as striving for the kingdom of God, as if striving for the kingdom took place only in the context of those concerns. The kingdom of God and God's righteousness are something entirely different from the gifts of the world that are to come to us. It is nothing other than the righteousness about which Matthew 5 and 6 have spoken, the righteousness of the cross of Christ and discipleship under the cross. Communion with Jesus and obedience to his commandment come *first;* then everything else follows. There is no blending of the two; one follows the other. Striving for the righteousness of Christ stands *ahead of* the cares of our lives for food and clothing, or for job and family. This is the most exacting summary of everything which has been said

174

---

his citation the *WA* lines 5–8 and 16–18 on page 368; he also emphasizes in the phrase "it is something other than its labor which furnishes him sustenance," the words *labor* and *sustenance.*

[209.] This is the final stanza of the poem "To Be Sung Daily" by Matthias Claudius (1740–1815), found in his *ASMUS omnia sua Secum portans oder Sämtliche Werke des Wandsbecker Boten* (Pantheon ed., 1:282 [reprint: 150]). It is correctly cited in Bonhoeffer's letter of December 4, 1935, thanking Martin Niemöller's congregation in Berlin for a contribution they sent (*DBW* 14:104 [*GS* 2:461]). On December 2 the National Socialist state had declared the activities and structures of the Confessing Church to be illegal, which meant that the financial situation and even the existence of the Finkenwalde Seminary became very precarious (see *DB-ER* 496–97). Bonhoeffer had learned the Claudius song from Gerhard Vibrans, who was at Finkenwalde in 1935. See his letter of March 4, 1942, to Gerhard Vibrans's father after his son's death in the war (Barbara Green, "Poore Foolische Friend," 197–98 [*DBW* 16:243 (*GS* 2:591)]).

[210.] Matthew 6:8.

before. This word of Jesus, like the commandment not to worry, is either an unbearable burden, an impossible destruction of human existence for the poor and suffering—or it is the gospel itself, which can make us completely free and completely joyous. Jesus is not speaking of what people should do but cannot do. Rather, he is speaking of what God has granted us and continues to promise us. If Christ has been given to us, if we are called to follow him, then everything, everything indeed is given us with him.[211] Everything else shall be given to us. Those who in following Jesus look only to his righteousness are in the care and protection 175 of Jesus Christ and his Father. Nothing can harm those who are thus in communion with the Father; they cannot doubt that the Father will feed his children and will not let them starve. God will help them at the right time. God knows what we need.

Jesus' disciples, even after having followed him for a long time, will be able to answer the question, "Were you ever in need?" with "Lord, never!"[212] How could they suffer need who in hunger and nakedness, persecution and danger are confident of their community with Jesus Christ?

[211.] See Rom. 8:32.

[212.] Luke 22:35, related to the Great Commission (also called the "Sending Forth of the Apostles").

MATTHEW 7:
THE COMMUNITY OF DISCIPLES IS SET APART

The Disciple and the Unbelievers[213]

"DO NOT JUDGE, so that you may not be judged. For with the judgment
you make you will be judged, and the measure you give will be the measure you get. Why do you see the speck in your neighbor's eye, but do
not notice the log in your own eye? Or how can you say to your neighbor,
'Let me take the speck out of your eye,' while the log is in your own eye?
You hypocrite, first take the log out of your own eye, and then you will
see clearly to take the speck out of your neighbor's eye.

¶ "Do not give what is holy to dogs; and do not throw your pearls before
swine, or they will trample them under foot and turn and maul you.

¶ "Ask, and it will be given you; search, and you will find; knock, and
the door will be opened for you. For everyone who asks receives, and
everyone who searches finds, and for everyone who knocks, the door will
be opened. Is there anyone among you who, if your child asks for bread,
will give a stone? Or if the child asks for a fish, will give a snake? If you
then, who are evil, know how to give good gifts to your children, how
much more will your Father in heaven give good things to those who ask
him! In everything do to others as you would have them do to you; for
this is the law and the prophets" (Matt. 7:1-12).

There is an essential connection that leads from chapters 5 and 6
to these verses and then to the great conclusion of the Sermon on the
Mount. The fifth chapter spoke of the extraordinariness of discipleship (περισσόν), while the sixth chapter spoke of the disciples' hidden, simple righteousness (ἁπλοῦς). In both aspects the disciples were
separated from the community to which they had previously belonged
and bound solely to Jesus. The boundary became clearly visible. This
raises the question of the relationship between disciples and the people
around them. Did their being set apart give them special rights of their
own? Did they receive special powers, measuring standards, or talents,
which enabled them to assume a special authority toward others? This
would have been most likely if Jesus' disciples had now separated themselves from their environment by sharp, divisive judgments. People

---

[213.] Until fall 1936 this heading read: "The Right Way to One's Neighbor."

could even have come to think that it was Jesus' will that such divisive
and condemnatory judgments were to be made in the disciples' daily
dealings with others. Thus Jesus must make clear that such misunderstandings seriously endanger discipleship. Disciples are not to judge. If
they do judge, then they themselves fall under God's judgment. They
themselves will perish by the sword with which they judge others.[214]
The gap which divides them from others, as the just from the unjust,
even divides them from Jesus.

Why is that so? Disciples live completely out of the bond connecting
them with Jesus Christ. Their righteousness depends only on that bond
and never apart from it. Therefore, it can never become a standard which
the disciples would own and might use in any way they please. What makes
them disciples is not a new standard for their lives, but Jesus Christ alone,
the mediator and Son of God himself. The disciples' own righteousness
is thus hidden from them in their communion with Jesus. They can no
longer see, observe, and judge themselves; they only see Jesus and are
seen, judged, and justified by grace by Jesus alone. No measuring standard for a righteous life stands between the disciples and other people;
but once again,[215] only Jesus Christ himself stands in their midst. The
disciples view other people only as those to whom Jesus comes. They
encounter other people only because they approach them together with
Jesus. Jesus goes ahead of them to other people, and the disciples follow
him. Thus an encounter between a disciple and another person is never
just a freely chosen encounter between two people, confronting each
other's views, standards, and judgments immediately. Disciples can
encounter other people only as those to whom Jesus himself comes.
Jesus' struggle for the other person, his call, his love, his grace, his judgment are all that matters. Thus the disciples do not stand in a position
from which the other person is attacked. Instead, in the truthfulness of
Jesus' love they approach the other person with an unconditional offer
of community.

When we judge, we encounter other people from the distance of
observation and reflection. But love does not allot time and space to do
that. For those who love, other people can never become an object for
spectators to observe. Instead, they are always a living claim on my love
and my service. But doesn't the evil in other people necessarily force me

178

[214.] Matthew 26:52.
[215.] Cf. above, page 95.

to pass judgment on them, just for their own sake and because of our love for them? We recognize how sharply the boundary is drawn. Love for a sinner, if misunderstood, is frightfully close to love for the sin. But Christ's love for the sinner is itself the condemnation of sin; it is the sharpest expression of hatred against sin. It is that unconditional love, in which Jesus' disciples should live in following him, that achieves what their own disunited love, offered according to their own discretion and conditions, could never achieve, namely, the radical condemnation of evil.[216]

If the disciples judge, then they are erecting standards to measure good and evil. But Jesus Christ is not a standard by which I can measure others. It is he who judges me and reveals what according to my own judgment is good to be thoroughly evil. This prohibits me from applying a standard to others which is not valid for me. When I judge, deciding what is good or evil, I affirm the evil in other persons, because they, too, judge according to good and evil.[217] But they do not know that what they consider good is evil. Instead, they justify themselves in it. If I judge their evil, that will affirm their good, which is never the good- 179 ness of Jesus Christ. They are withdrawn from Christ's judgment and subjected to human judgment. But I myself invoke God's judgment on myself, because I am no longer living out of the grace of Jesus Christ, but out of a knowledge of good and evil. I become subject to that judgment which I think valid. For all persons, God is a person's God in the way the person believes God to be.[218]

Judging is the forbidden evaluation of other persons. It corrodes simple love. Love does not prohibit my having my own thoughts about others or my perceiving their sin, but both thoughts and perceptions are liberated from evaluating them. They thereby become only an occasion for that forgiveness and unconditional love Jesus gives me. My refraining from judgment of others does not validate *tout comprendre c'est tout pardonner;*[219]

[216.] See Bethge's notes in *NL* B 8 (58f.): "By not judging, but loving, I overcome the other's understanding of good and evil. . . . They cannot withstand this love."

[217.] Cf. Bethge's notes in *NL* B 8 (57): "Judging is a godless situation before God. In it people want to invoke being sicut deus [like God]." See Genesis 3:5.

[218.] This is a reference to Luther's interpretation of the First Commandment in the Large Catechism (*The Book of Concord*, 365).

[219.] The quote appears in German translation in Zimmermann's notes in *NL* B 9, 5 (76): "'Understanding everything means pardoning everything' (Voltaire). This is not what is meant (i.e., excusing and explaining)." Büchmann cites Madame de Staël as the source (*Geflügelte Worte*, 212); in her book *Corinne*, she writes: "comprendre c'est pardonner."

it does not concede that the other person is somehow right after all. Neither I nor the other person is right. God alone, God's grace and judgment is proclaimed to be right.

Judging others makes us blind, but love gives us sight.[220] When I judge, I am blind to my own evil and to the grace granted the other person. But in the love of Christ, disciples know about every imaginable kind of guilt and sin, because they know of the suffering of Jesus Christ. At the same time, love recognizes the other person to be one who received forgiveness under the cross. Love sees the other person under the cross, and that is what enables it to have true sight. If my intent in passing judgment were really to destroy evil, then I would seek evil where it really threatens me, namely, in myself. But the fact that I seek evil in another person reveals that in such judgments I am really seeking to be 180 right myself, that I want to avoid punishment for my own evil by judging another person. All judging presupposes the most dangerous self-deception, namely, that the word of God applies differently to me than it does to my neighbor. I claim an exceptional right in that I say: forgiveness applies to me, but condemnation applies to the other person. Judgment as arrogation of false justice about one's neighbor is totally forbidden to the disciples. They did not receive special rights for themselves from Jesus, which they ought to claim before others. All they receive is communion with him.

But it is not only judging words which are forbidden to the disciples. Proclaiming salvific words of forgiveness to others also has its limits. Jesus' disciples do not have the power and the right to force them on anyone at any time. All our urging, running after people, proselytizing, every attempt to accomplish something in another person by our own power is in vain and dangerous. In vain—because swine do not recognize the pearls thrown before them; dangerous—because not only does this defile words of forgiveness, not only does it make the other person I am to serve into a sinner against holy gifts, but even the disciples who are preaching are in danger of being needlessly and pointlessly harmed by the blind fury of hardened and darkened hearts. Squandering cheap grace disgusts the world.[221] Then the world will turn violently on those who want to force on it what it does not desire. This signifies for the disciples a

---

[220.] See (on 1 Cor. 13:7): ". . . with seeing eyes love believes everything, or with blind eyes it sees the true future" (*DBW* 13:392 [*TF* 247]).

[221.] See *WF* 151 (*DBW* 14:832).

serious limitation on their work. It agrees with the directive in Matthew 10 to shake from their feet the dust of any place that does not hear the word of peace.[222] The driving restlessness of the group of disciples, who do not want to accept any limitation on their effectiveness, and their zeal, which does not respect resistance, confuses the word of the gospel with a conquering idea. An idea requires fanatics, who neither know nor respect resistance. The idea is strong. But the Word of God is so weak that it suffers to be despised and rejected by people. For the Word, there are such things as hardened hearts and locked doors. The Word accepts the resistance it encounters and bears it. It is a cruel insight: nothing is impossible for the idea, but for the gospel there are impossibilities. The Word is weaker than the idea. Likewise, the witnesses to the Word are weaker than the propagandists of an idea.[223] But this weakness liberates them from the sick restlessness of a fanatic; they suffer with the Word. Disciples may retreat, or even flee, as long as they are retreating and fleeing with the Word,[224] as long as their weakness is the weakness of the Word itself, as long as they do not abandon the Word in their flight. They are nothing but servants and tools of the Word, and should not want to be strong when the Word is weak. If they wanted to force the Word onto the world by all means, then they would make the living Word of God into an idea, and the world will justifiably fight back against an idea which cannot help it at all. But it is as weak witnesses that they do not flee, but remain—to be sure, only where the Word is. Disciples who would know nothing about this weakness of the Word would not have come to know the secret of God's lowliness. This weak Word, which suffers contradiction by sinners, is the only strong, merciful Word, that can make sinners repent from the bottom of their hearts. The Word's power is veiled in weakness. If the Word came in full, unveiled power, that would be the final judgment day.[225] The great task of recognizing the limits of their mission is given to the disciples. But when the Word is misused, it will turn against them.

What should the disciples do in the face of hardened hearts? When their approach to others is unsuccessful? They should recognize that

181

[222.] Matthew 10:13f.

[223.] Cf. the sinister way the Nazi regime forced propaganda on people. Joseph Goebbels was *Reichsminister* for the people's enlightenment and propaganda.

[224.] Matthew 10:23.

[225.] Matthew 10:14f.

they have no right or power over others at all, and that they have no sort of immediate access to others. The only way open to them is the way to the one in whose hand they themselves are kept, just like those others. This is what the following section is talking about. The disciples are called to prayer. They are told that no other way leads to their neighbor except prayer to God. Judgment and forgiveness remain in God's hand. God holds the key. Disciples are to request, seek, knock, and God will hear them. Disciples should know that their worry and concern about others must lead them to prayer. The promise given to their prayer is the greatest power they have.

The fact that disciples know what they are seeking distinguishes their searching from the nonbelievers' search for God. Only those who already know God can seek God. How could they seek what they do not know? How can they find, if they do not know what they are looking for? Thus disciples seek God, whom they have found[226] in the promise Jesus Christ gave them.

In summary, it has become clear that in dealing with other people, the disciples do not possess any special right or power of their own. They live completely out of the power of communion with Jesus Christ. Jesus gives the disciples a simple rule, by which even the most simpleminded can evaluate whether their dealings with others are right or wrong: they need only reverse the I and the You in the relationship. They need only put themselves in the other's place and the other in their own.[227] "Do unto others as you would have them do unto you." At that moment the disciples lose any claim of special rights toward other people. They cannot excuse in themselves what they condemn in others. Now they are as tough on the evil in themselves as they used to be on the evil in others, and as considerate of evil in others as they are of themselves. For our evil is no different than the evil in the others. There is *one* judgment, *one* law, *one* grace.[228] So disciples will always encounter other people only as those whose sins are forgiven

---

[226.] In his notes in *NL* B 8/18 (61) Bethge connects Augustine to this statement. In his *Christologie* lectures of 1933, Bonhoeffer attributes this thought to Pascal (*Christ the Center*, 32 [*DBW* 12:284, editorial note 9]). Also see *DBW* 9:314, editorial note 57: Pascal, *Pensées sur la religion*, frag. 736. Student notes mention that this thought may also be found in Augustine. Barth speaks of "the courage of that Augustinian word: you would not seek me if you had not already found me" (*The Word of God and the Word of Man*, 274).

[227.] See *NL* B 8/18 (62) where Bethge notes: "We can tolerate it when we talk about others. Intolerable when they talk about us." See *DB-ER* 349.

[228.] This is similar to the emphases in Eph. 4:4-6, possibly in contrast to the Nazi slogan, "One people [Volk], one nation [Reich], one leader [Führer]."

and who from now on live solely from God's love. "That is the law and the prophets"—for it is nothing other than the greatest commandment itself: love God above all things, and your neighbor as yourself.[229]

The Great Separation

"Enter through the narrow gate; for the gate is wide and the road is easy that leads to destruction, and there are many who take it. For the gate is narrow and the road is hard that leads to life, and there are few who find it.

¶ "Beware of false prophets, who come to you in sheep's clothing but inwardly are ravenous wolves. You will know them by their fruits. Are grapes gathered from thorns, or figs from thistles? In the same way, every good tree bears good fruit, but the bad tree bears bad fruit. A good tree cannot bear bad fruit, nor can a bad tree bear good fruit. Every tree that does not bear good fruit is cut down and thrown into the fire. Thus you will know them by their fruits.

¶ "Not everyone who says to me, 'Lord, Lord,' will enter the kingdom of heaven, but only the one who does the will of my Father in heaven. On that day many will say to me, 'Lord, Lord, did we not prophesy in your name, and cast out demons in your name, and do many deeds of power in your name?' Then I will declare to them, 'I never knew you; go away from me, you evil-doers'" (Matt. 7:13-23).

The faith-community of Jesus cannot arbitrarily separate itself from the community of those who do not hear Jesus' call. The faith-community is called to discipleship by their Lord's promise and commandment. That must suffice for them. They submit every judgment and separation to the one who has chosen them in predestination, not by the merits of their deeds, but by grace. It is not the faith community which separates itself from others, yet this separation necessarily takes place in the call by the Word.

The call separates a small group, those who follow, from the great mass of the people. The disciples are few and will always be only a few. [230] This word of Jesus cuts off any false hope of their effectiveness.

[229.] Matthew 22:36-40. Verse 40 reads: "On these two commandments hang all the law and the prophets." Matt. 7:12 is similar.

[230.] See *NL* B 8/18 (64f.) where Bethge notes: "Have courage to be a minority, courage to be completely alone. . . . Whoever does not have the courage to be solitary has

Disciples should never invest their trust in numbers. "There are few of them . . . ," but there are, and always will be, many others who go to their destruction. What can console disciples experiencing this, except the fact that life is promised to them, the eternal communion with Jesus?

The road of the disciples is narrow. It is easy to go past it; it is easy to miss it; it is easy to lose it, even for those who have already walked it. It is hard to find. The path is narrow indeed; there is a real danger of falling off on both sides. To be called to do the extraordinary, but not to see and to know that one is doing it—that is a narrow road. To give witness to and to confess the truth of Jesus, but to love the enemy of this truth, who is his enemy and our enemy, with the unconditional love of Jesus Christ— that is a narrow road. To believe in Jesus' promise that those who follow shall possess the earth, but to encounter the enemy unarmed, to prefer suffering injustice to doing ill—that is a narrow road. To perceive other people as being weak and wrong, but never to judge them; to proclaim the good news to them, but never to throw pearls before swine—that is a narrow road. It is an unbearable road. The danger of falling off threatens every minute. As long as I recognize this road as the one I am commanded to walk, and try to walk it in fear of myself, it is truly impossible. But if I see Jesus Christ walking ahead of me, step by step, if I look only at him and follow him, step by step, then I will be protected on this path. If I look at the danger in what I am doing, if I look at the path instead of at him who is walking ahead of me, then my foot is already slipping. He himself is the way.[231] He is the narrow road and the narrow gate. The only thing that matters is finding him. If we know that, then we will walk the narrow way to life through the narrow gate of the cross of Jesus Christ, then the narrowness of the way itself will reassure us. How could the road of the Son of God on earth, which we are to walk as citizens of two realms[232] at the boundary between the world and the kingdom of heaven, be a wide one? The narrow way has to be the right way.

185

Verses 15-20. The separation between community and world is complete. But now the word of Jesus presses into the faith-community itself, judging and separating. The separation has to take place again and again

---

not understood Jesus . . . Luke 12 [verse 32]. We should not seek the broadest possible basis for the church, but its only basis is the narrow road of Jesus' commandment."

[231.] John 14:6.

[232.] This is similar to the widely known book *Der Wanderer zwischen beiden Welten* by Walter Flex, who experienced World War I in the spirit of the hiking [Wandervogel] movement which preceded it. He was killed at the front in 1917.

among the disciples themselves. The disciples should not think that they could simply flee from the world and stay safely in the small group on the narrow path. False prophets will come among them, and the confusion will make their isolation even greater. Someone stands beside me, externally a member of the community. A prophet or preacher stands there, a Christian by appearances, words, and deeds. But internally dark motives are driving him to us. Internally he is a rampaging wolf; his words are lies and his deeds deceit. He knows how to guard his secret well, but under cover he works his evil deeds. He is among us, not because faith in Jesus Christ brought him to us, but because the devil drives him into the faith-community. Perhaps he is seeking power and influence, money, fame by his own thoughts and prophecies. He seeks the world, but not the Lord Christ. He hides his dark intent in the cloak of Christian piety [Christlichkeit] and knows that Christians are easy to fool. Because of his cloak of innocence, he is counting on not being unmasked. He knows well that Christians are prohibited from judging, and he will remind them of that at just the right moment! No one can see into another's heart. So he can deceive many a person to stray from the right way. Perhaps he does not even know all this, perhaps the devil who is driving him has concealed from him the truth about himself.[233]

186

Such an announcement by Jesus could drive great fear into his disciples. Who knows the other person? Who knows whether or not lies are hiding and deceptions lurking behind Christian appearances? Deep suspicion, cynical observation, and an anxious spirit of judgment could seep into the community. This word of Jesus could cause loveless condemnation to become the fate of every sister or brother who sins. But Jesus liberates his disciples from suspicions, which would tear apart the community. He says that a bad tree brings forth bad fruit. It will reveal itself in due time. We do not need to look into the heart of anyone else. We should wait until the tree bears its fruit. In due time you will know the trees by their fruits. Fruit cannot fail to come for long. Here this does not mean the difference between words and deeds of the false prophets, but the difference between appearance and reality. Jesus tells us that people cannot live for long under the cover of appearances. The time to bear fruit will come, the time of open difference will come. Sooner or later

---

[233.] See 2 Tim. 3:13: ". . . impostors will go from bad to worse, deceiving others and being deceived." During the Church Struggle, Bonhoeffer saw depressing examples of such theological teachers.

their situation will be revealed. Whether the tree intends not to bear fruit does not matter at all. Fruit comes by itself. Thus the decisive moment of distinguishing one tree from another, fruit-bearing time, will reveal everything. Whenever times of decision come, revealing the difference between the world and the church-community, and they can come any day, in quite small, mundane decisions, as well as in the big ones, then it will be revealed what is bad and what is good. Then only reality persists, not appearances.

187   Jesus expects from his disciples that at such moments they will distinguish clearly between appearances and reality, and see the difference between themselves and people who only appear to be Christian. That relieves them of all curious scrutinizing of other people, but it demands truthfulness and determination to recognize the decision God is making. It can happen at any moment that pseudo-Christians are torn out of our midst, or that we ourselves are revealed as pseudo-Christians. The disciples are called, therefore, to deeper communion [Gemeinschaft] with Jesus and to follow him more faithfully. The bad tree will be cut down and thrown into the fire. All its grandeur will not save it.

Verse 21. The separation caused by Jesus' call to discipleship goes even deeper. After the separation between world and community, between pseudo-Christians and true Christians, the next sorting out takes place within the confessing community of disciples. Paul says that no one can call Jesus Lord, except by the Holy Spirit (1 Cor. 12:3). No one can commit their life to Jesus and call him Lord out of their own reason, strength, and decision. But the possibility is considered here that someone could call Jesus Lord without the Holy Spirit, that is, without having heard Jesus' call. This is even less comprehensible in those times when it did not bring any earthly advantages to call Jesus Lord. Instead, it was a confession which led straight into gravest danger. "Not everyone who says to me, 'Lord, Lord,' will enter the kingdom of heaven. . . ." Saying "Lord, Lord" is the confession of the church-community. Not everyone who says it will enter the kingdom of heaven. The separation will even take place within the confessing community. The confession alone grants no claim on Jesus. On that day no persons can justify themselves on the basis of their confession. Being members of the church of the true confession[234] is

---

[234.] In 1934 the starting point for building the Confessing Church was the criticism by the Confessing congregations toward the German Evangelical Church as the national [Reich] church, that it was not a church of true confession.

nothing we can claim before God. Our confession will not save us. If we
think it will, then we commit Israel's sin of making the grace of our call- 188
ing into a right before God. This is sin against the grace of the one who
calls us. God will not ask us someday whether our confession was evangelical,[235] but whether we did God's will. God will ask that of everyone,
including us. The boundaries of the church are not the boundaries of
a privilege, but those of God's merciful selection and call. πᾶς ὁ λέων
and ἀλλ' ὁ ποιῶν [everyone who says . . . but who does]—"saying" and
"doing"—this does not necessarily mean the relationship between word
and deed. Instead, it is talking about two different kinds of human behavior before God. ὁ λέων κύριε—those who say "Lord, Lord" are those who
make claims based on their having said "yes." ὁ ποιῶν—"the doer[s]"
are those who are humble in their obedient deeds. The former justify
themselves by their confession; the latter, the doers, are the people who
obediently trust in God's grace. People's speech here is correlated with
their self-righteousness, and their deeds are correlated with that grace,
before which people cannot do anything else except humbly obey and
serve. Those who say "Lord, Lord" have called themselves to Jesus without the Holy Spirit, or they have made Jesus' call into a right of their
own. Those who do the will of God are called and forgiven by grace;
they obey and follow. They do not understand their call to be a right,
but to be judgment and pardon, and the will of God which alone they
intend to obey. The grace of Jesus calls the doers: their deeds become
genuine humility, genuine faith, genuine confession of the grace of the
One who calls.

Verse 22. Confessors and doers are separated from each other. Now
the separation is driven in as far as it can go. Here, finally, those speak
up who have survived the test up to now. They belong to the doers, but
now they make demands based upon their deeds instead of upon their
confession. They have done deeds in the name of Jesus. They know that
confession does not justify; hence, they went out to make the name of 189
Jesus great among the people by their deeds. Now they come before
Jesus and refer to those deeds.

Jesus reveals to his disciples here the possibility of a demonic faith,
which claims allegiance to him and which does wonderful deeds, to the

---

[235.] See Bonhoeffer's sermon on Rev. 14:6-13 from November 24, 1935: "God will
ask us solely about the everlasting gospel: Did you believe and obey the gospel? God won't
ask whether we were Germans or Jews, whether we were Nazis or not, not even whether we
belonged to the Confessing Church or not" (*TF* 265 [*DBW* 14:914 (*GS* 5:571)]).

point that they are indistinguishable from the deeds of true disciples of
Jesus. They do works of love, miracles, perhaps even sanctify themselves,
and yet deny Jesus and discipleship. It is just as Paul says in chapter 13
of the First Letter to the Corinthians about the possibility of preaching,
prophesying, having all knowledge, even all faith to remove mountains—
but without love, that is, without Christ, without the Holy Spirit.[236] Yes,
even more than this: Paul must even consider the possibility that the
works of Christian love themselves, giving away one's goods, even so far
as martyrdom, can be done—without love, without Christ, without the
Holy Spirit. Without love—that means that in all those actions the deed
of discipleship does not take place, that deed, whose doer is finally none
other than the one who calls us, Jesus Christ himself. That is the deepest,
least comprehensible possibility of the satanic within the congregation,
the ultimate separation, which, of course, does not take place until the
last judgment. But it will be a final one. Those following Jesus must ask
what is the ultimate standard of measure of who will be accepted by Jesus
and who will not. Who remains and who does not? Jesus' answer to those
who are rejected at the end says it all: "I never knew you." That is the
final secret, which has been kept from the beginning of the Sermon on
the Mount up until its end. That alone is the question, whether we were
190   known by Jesus or not.[237] To what should we hold fast, if we hear how
the word of Jesus draws the separation between the community and the
world, and then within the community until the last judgment? If nothing is left to us, neither our confession nor obedience? Then the only
thing left is his word: I have known you. This is his everlasting word, his
everlasting call. The end of the Sermon on the Mount connects here with
its beginning. His word at the last judgment—it is issued to us in his call
to discipleship. But from the beginning to the end, it remains his word,
his call. Those who in discipleship hold fast to nothing except this word

---

[236.] Bethge's notes in *NL* B 8/18 (70) give references to 1 Cor. 13:2f. and "First Corinthians 13:4ff. This love is really God, Christ."

[237.] Bonhoeffer's emphasis on "being known," which is not immediately obvious in
Matt. 7:23, relates his interpretation of the Sermon on the Mount to his sermon in London
on 1 Cor. 13:8-12: "That is the solution, 'as I have been known.' . . . I could not know Him,
if He did not know me" (*DBW* 13:398 [*GS* 5:554f.]). Also see Zimmermann's notes in *NL* B
9, 5 (85f.): "Whether we are known by Jesus (predestination). That is what matters." In the
1937 index of *Discipleship* prepared by Bonhoeffer himself this page is referenced to the
term "predestination." And see Barth's remark "that the man who selects God must make
way for the man who is selected by Him. This is the meaning of 'Double Predestination,'
the revelation of the *mystery* of God" (*Epistle to the Romans*, 415).

and let everything else go will be carried by this word through the last judgment. His word is his grace.

The Conclusion

"'Everyone then who hears these words of mine and acts on them will be like a wise man who built his house on rock. The rain fell, the floods came, and the winds blew and beat on that house, but it did not fall, because it had been founded on rock. And everyone who hears these words of mine and does not act on them will be like a foolish man who built his house on sand. The rain fell, and the floods came, and the winds blew and beat against that house, and it fell—and great was its fall!'

¶ "Now when Jesus had finished saying these things, the crowds were astonished at his teaching, for he taught them as one having authority, and not as their scribes" (Matt. 7:24-29).

We have heard the Sermon on the Mount; perhaps we have understood it. But who has heard it correctly? Jesus answers this question last. Jesus does not permit his listeners to simply walk away, making whatever they like of his discourse, extracting what seems to them to be useful in their lives, testing how this teaching compares to "reality."[238] Jesus does not deliver his word up to his listeners, so that it is misused in their rummaging hands. Instead, he gives it to them in a way that it alone retains power over them.[239] From the human point of view there are countless possibilities of understanding and interpreting the Sermon on the Mount. Jesus knows only one possibility: simply go and obey. Do not interpret or apply, but do it and obey. That is the only way Jesus' word is really heard. But again, doing something is not to be understood as an ideal possibility; instead, we are simply to begin acting.[240]

191

[238.] Bonhoeffer is opposing talk about 'reality', as in Hegel's *The Christian Religion*, 194 [trans. altered]. "When the community is established, when the Kingdom of God has attained its existence, its reality, then these teachings [of Jesus] will rather be defined differently, or be set aside."

[239.] See the comments at the end of Bonhoeffer's interpretation of the Sermon on the Mount according to Bethge's notes in *NL* B 8/18 (73): "Then the Sermon on the Mount is not a word you can handle at will: it doesn't work here, it doesn't work there, over there there are conflicts. Instead, it will carry you only when it is obeyed. It is not a free word to make use of, it is not to be taken along and thought about. Instead, it is a decisive word, a compelling one."

[240.] See 1 John 3:18, marked in Bonhoeffer's Luther Bible with a note in the margin: "!Blessed . . ." (see James 1:25: those who act "will be blessed in their deeds").

This word, which I accept as valid for myself; this word, which arises from "I have known you," which immediately draws me into acting, into obedience, is the rock on which I can build a house. This word of Jesus coming from eternity can only be answered by simply doing it. Jesus has spoken; the word is his; our part is to obey. The word of Jesus keeps its honor, its strength, and power among us only by our acting on it. Then a storm can sweep over the house, but it cannot tear apart the unity with Jesus created by his word.

The only thing which exists besides action is inaction. There is no such thing as intending to act and not doing it. Those who treat the word of Jesus any other way except by acting on it assert that Jesus is wrong; they say no to the Sermon on the Mount; they do not do his word. All our questions, complications, and interpretations are inaction. The rich young man and the scribe in Luke 10 are examples.[241] I can insist on my faith and my fundamental recognition of this word as much as I want; Jesus calls it inaction. The word that I do not want to do is no rock for me on which I can build a house. I have no unity with Jesus. He has never known me. Hence, when the storm comes, I will lose the word quickly and I will learn that in truth I never really had faith. I did not have the word of Christ. Instead, I had a word I wrested away from him and made my own by reflecting on it, but not doing it. Then my house falls down with a great fall, because it does not rest on the word of Christ.

"And the crowds were astonished . . ."[242] What had happened? The Son of God had spoken. He took the judgment of the world into his hands. And his disciples stood beside him.

192

[241.] Matthew 19:16-22 and Luke 10:25. In the latter the NRSV says "lawyer," not "scribe."

[242.] Bethge's notes in *NL* B 8/18 (73) say: "The crowds are told here: everything depends on this power." In *NL* B 9, 5 (88), Zimmermann's notes say: "Jesus calls and condemns. He is Lord over heaven and hell." This was the end of Bonhoeffer's New Testament lectures in 1935—on October 14—and also in 1936. On August 10, 1936, Bonhoeffer wrote to Bethge: the final lectures "make a remarkably strong impression on the brothers" (*DBW* 14:221 [*GS* 6:397]).

CHAPTER SEVEN

THE MESSENGERS

(AN INTERPRETATION OF MATTHEW 10)[1]

The Harvest

"THEN JESUS WENT ABOUT all the cities and villages, teaching in their   193
synagogues, and proclaiming the good news of the kingdom, and cur-
ing every disease and every sickness. When he saw the crowds,[2] he had
compassion for them, because they were ill-treated and helpless,[3] like
sheep without a shepherd. Then he said to his disciples, 'The harvest is
plentiful, but the laborers are few; therefore ask the Lord of the harvest
to send out laborers into his harvest'" (Matt. 9:35-38).

The gaze of the Savior falls in pity on his people, on God's people. It
could not be enough for him that only a few people heard his call and
followed him. He could not consider isolating himself aristocratically

---

[1.] The speech sending out the disciples is the second speech of Jesus in Matthew's
Gospel (after the Sermon on the Mount). Visits to church-communities in villages and
cities by groups of preachers were conducted in the Confessing Church; Bonhoeffer's
seminary in Finkenwalde participated in them. See Bonhoeffer's letter of June 26, 1936:
"We have made several attempts with the House of Brethren to do missionary work in the
neighborhood. Recently, with the leadership and help of the House of Brethren, the whole
seminary was in the villages for a week . . ." (*DBW* 14:176 [*GS* 6:377]).

[2.] In Bonhoeffer's Greek New Testament at this point τοὺς ὄχλους, "the crowds," and
Luther's translation, "the people [*Volk*]," are underlined. Bonhoeffer used Luther's trans-
lation "mass of people" above, page 100, as he did here (the beginnings of Matt. 5:1 and
Matt. 9:36 are the same). There are a number of other markings in Bonhoeffer's Greek
New Testament throughout this passage up to the end of Matthew 10.

[3.] Luther translates this as "parched with thirst and scattered." In the case of the first
word, Bonhoeffer deviated from the Greek text, whose meaning is "fatigued." In the Latin
text the word is *vexati*, "ill-treated" or "harassed." Concerning Bonhoeffer's choice of the
word "ill-treated" see *DB-ER* 540: "[In April 1936] W. Süssbach, a young pastor of Jewish
origin in the Church Province of Brandenburg, was attacked by a group of SA and badly
beaten up." Afterward he was invited into the Finkenwalde Seminary.

194 with his disciples and transmitting to them in the manner of great founders of religions the doctrines of higher knowledge and more perfect way of life separated from the mass of the people. Jesus had come; he worked, and he suffered on behalf of his entire people. And though the disciples wanted to have him all to themselves, and tried to keep distant from him the nuisance of the children who were brought to him[4] and of some poor beggars on the side of the road (Mark 10:48), they had to acknowledge that Jesus would not permit his ministry to be limited by them. His gospel of the kingdom of God and his power to save belonged to the poor and sick, wherever he found them among his people.

The view of the crowds, which perhaps prompted disgust, rage, or contempt in his disciples, filled Jesus' heart with deep pity and grief. No reproaches, no accusations! God's beloved people were lying ill-treated on the ground, and the guilt for this fell on those who were to serve them with God's ministry. It was not the Romans who had brought this about, but the misuse of the word of God by those called to be ministers of the Word.[5] There were no more shepherds there! Jesus found God's people to be a flock which was not led to fresh water, whose thirst remained unquenched[6]—sheep, whom no shepherd protects from the wolf,[7] battered and wounded, terrified and fearful under the hard staff of their shepherds, sheep lying on the ground. Questions, but no answer; need, but no help; consciences kept in fear, but no liberation; tears, but no consolation; sin, but no forgiveness! Where was the good shepherd this people needed? What did it help here that there were scribes, who drove the people into the synagogues by brute force? What did it matter that zealots of the law harshly condemned sinners without helping them? What did it matter that the most orthodox preachers and interpreters of

---

[4.] Mark 10:13f.

[5.] See above, pages 137f., on the two enemies: the political one, "Rome," and the representatives of "a people's piety." Piety connected with a certain people's way of life [*Volkstumsfrömmigkeit*] was represented by Reichsbishop Ludwig Müller. In 1936 he—one of the "called ministers of the Word"—published an adaptation of the Sermon on the Mount under the title *Deutsche Gottesworte.* In the preface of the book he says, "For you, my fellow Germans in the Third Reich [underlined by Bonhoeffer, in the margin: "not: congregation?"], I have not 'translated' the Sermon on the Mount, but 'Germanized' it" (7). There are further markings in Bonhoeffer's copy on the first pages. As early as 1929 the evangelical-religious writer (and founder of the meeting place Elmau Castle) Johannes Müller wrote in his book *Die Bergpredigt:* "We must transform Jesus' speeches *into German,* for they grew on Jewish ground and are addressed to Jews" (12).

[6.] See Ps. 23:2.

[7.] Matthew 7:15: the wolf is in the community in sheep's clothing.

the word of God were present, if they were not filled with all of the mercy and all of the grief over the abused and ill-treated people of God? What use are scholars of Scripture, pious followers of the law, preachers of the word, if the shepherds of the church-community themselves are missing? 195

¶The flock needs good shepherds, "pastors."[8] "Feed my lambs" is Jesus' last command to Peter.[9] Good shepherds[10] fight for their flock against the wolf and do not flee. Instead, they give their lives for the sheep. They know all their sheep by their names and love them. They know their needs and their weaknesses. They heal their wounds, giving drink to the thirsty and lifting up those who are in danger of falling. They feed them gently and not harshly. They lead them along the right path. They seek the single lost sheep and bring it back to the flock.[11] The evil shepherds, however, rule by violence; they forget their flock and tend to their own affairs. Jesus is looking for good shepherds, and behold, there are none to be found.

That saddens his heart. His divine pity embraces this lost flock, the mass of people around him. From the human point of view, it is a hopeless picture. But it is not hopeless for Jesus. Here, where God's people stand before him ill-treated, miserable, and poor, Jesus sees God's field ripe for harvest. "The harvest is great!" It is ripe to be brought into the barns. The hour has come that these poor and miserable people are brought home into the kingdom of God. Jesus sees God's promise dawning over the masses of people. The scribes and zealots of the law saw only a trampled, burned, battered field. Jesus sees the ripe, waving field of grain for the kingdom of God. The harvest is great! His mercy alone sees that!

Now there is no time to lose. Harvesting cannot be delayed. "But the laborers are few." Is it a miracle, since this merciful gaze of Jesus is given to so few? Who could enter into this work, besides those who have won a place in Jesus' heart, who have received from him eyes that can see?

Jesus is looking for help. He cannot do this work alone. Where are the workers to help him? God alone knows them and must give them to God's Son. Who would dare to take the initiative to offer to be Jesus' helper? Even the disciples do not dare to do so. They are to ask the Lord of the harvest to send workers at the right hour, for it is time. 196

[8.] The word "pastor" means "shepherd" in Latin.

[9.] John 21:15.

[10.] See John 10 and Ezekiel 34.

[11.] Luke 15:4-6.

The Apostles

"Then Jesus summoned his twelve disciples and gave them authority over unclean spirits, to cast them out, and to cure every disease and every sickness.[12] These are the names of the twelve apostles: first, Simon, also known as Peter, and his brother Andrew; James son of Zebedee, and his brother John; Philip and Bartholomew; Thomas and Matthew the tax collector; James son of Alphaeus, and Thaddaeus; Simon the Canaanaean, and Judas Iscariot, the one who betrayed him" (Matt. 10:1-4).

The prayer is heard. The Father has revealed God's own will to the Son. Jesus Christ calls his twelve disciples and sends them into the harvest. He makes them into "apostles,"[13] into his messengers and coworkers. "And he gave them power." This power is, indeed, what is at stake here. The disciples receive not only words or doctrine, but effective power. How should they do their work without this power? It has to be a power which is greater than the power of the one who rules on earth, the devil. The disciples know that the devil has power, although it is precisely the deception of the devil to deny his power and to make people believe that he does not exist. It is just this most dangerous expression of his power which must be confronted. The devil must be pulled into the light and defeated by the power of Christ. In this, the disciples come to stand by Jesus Christ himself. They are called to help him carry out his work. So Jesus does not deny them the highest gift possible to meet this task, namely, participating in his power over the unclean spirits and over the devil, who has taken hold of humanity. In this commission the apostles have become equal to Christ. They are doing the work of Christ.

The names of these first messengers will be preserved for the world until the Last Day. The people of God consisted of twelve tribes. There are twelve messengers, who are to complete the work of Christ among them. Twelve thrones will be standing ready for them as judges of Israel in the kingdom of God (Matt. 19:28). The heavenly Jerusalem will have twelve gates through which the holy people will come in. The names of the tribes will be inscribed on the gates. The wall of the city has twelve cornerstones and they will bear the names of the apostles (Rev. 21:12, 14).

The only thing which unites the twelve is the call of Jesus that selects

197

[12.] In Bonhoeffer's Greek New Testament beside Matt. 10:1 is written: "like Christ." The verse ends exactly like Matt. 9:35, which refers to Jesus.

[13.] The Greek word means "messenger."

them: Simon, the man of rock;[14] Matthew, the tax collector; Simon, the zealot, who struggles for justice and law against heathen oppression;[15] John, whom Jesus loved and who laid his head on Jesus' breast;[16] and the others, about whom we know only their names; and finally, Judas Iscariot, who betrayed him. Nothing in the world could have united these men to do the same work except the call of Jesus. It overcame all their previous divisions and founded a new, strong community in Jesus. The fact that even Judas went out to do the work of Christ remains for us an inscrutable dilemma and a terrible warning.

The Work

"These twelve Jesus sent out with the following instructions: 'Go nowhere among the Gentiles, and enter no town of the Samaritans, but go rather to the lost sheep of the house of Israel' " (Matt. 10:5-6).

As Jesus' helpers, the effectiveness of the disciples is grounded in the clear commandment of their Lord. It is not left up to them to decide how to undertake and understand their work. The work of Christ they are to do forces the messengers completely into the will of Jesus. Blessed are they who have such an authority given them for their office [Amt] and who are freed from their own discretion and calculations!

198

The very first word limits the messengers' work in a way which must have seemed strange and difficult to them. They were not allowed to choose where they were to work. What was decisive was not where their hearts led them, but where they were sent. This makes quite clear that they are not to do their own work, but God's work. Would it not have seemed obvious to go to the Gentiles and the Samaritans, because they had special need of the good news? That may be, but they were given no such commission. God's works cannot be done without God's commission; otherwise, they would be done without God's promise. But does this promise and commission to preach the gospel not apply everywhere?

[14.] *Petros* or Peter is the Greek word for "rock." See Matt. 16:18.

[15.] In explaining the surname "zealot" (Luke 6:15), Bonhoeffer emphasizes the struggle for justice and law. The background of that emphasis is the legal struggle of the Confessing Church in the Third Reich. Lawyers like Bonhoeffer's brother-in-law, Hans von Dohnanyi, and the legal counsel of the Confessing Church, Friedrich Justus Perels, were fighting for justice and law against the Nazi regime.

[16.] John 13:23; 21:20.

Both apply only where God has given the commission. But is it not precisely the love of Christ which urges us to proclaim the gospel without limits? The love of Christ differs from the enthusiasm and zeal of our own hearts in that it holds to the commission. We do not bring the salvation of the gospel to our sisters and brothers who belong to our own people[17] or to the Gentiles in foreign countries, for the sake of our own love for them, no matter how great that love is. Instead, we do it at the Lord's command, which he gave in the Great Commission.[18] Only the commission shows us the place on which God's promise rests. If Christ does not want me to preach the gospel here or there, then I should let everything go and obey Christ's will and word. So the apostles are bound to the word and to the commission. The apostles should be found only where the word of Christ, where the commission may be found. "Go nowhere among the Gentiles, and enter no town of the Samaritans, but go rather to the lost sheep of the house of Israel."

199   We, who came from the Gentiles, were once excluded from the good news. First, Israel had to hear and reject the message of Christ, so that it could be brought to the Gentiles, and so that a congregation of Gentile Christians could be built according to the commission of Jesus Christ. It is only after he is resurrected that Jesus gives the Great Commission. In this way the limitation of the commission, which the disciples surely could not understand, became an instrument of grace for the Gentiles, who received the good news of the crucified and risen one. That is God's way and wisdom. For us, only the commission remains.

"As you go, proclaim the good news, 'The kingdom of heaven has come near.'[19] Cure the sick, cleanse the lepers, raise the dead, cast out demons. You received without payment; give without payment" (Matt. 10:7-8). The message and the effectiveness of the messengers are exactly the same as Jesus Christ's own message and work. They participate in his power. Jesus commands that they proclaim the coming of the kingdom of heaven, and he commands the signs which authenticate the message.

[17.] This contrasts with the argument made by the German Christians that they were striving to win back "millions of our fellow Germans who are alienated from God," if necessary, by sacrificing the "thousand Jewish Christians." These expressions were included in Bonhoeffer's paper on the "Aryan Paragraph" in the church, written in August 1933 (*DBW* 12:411 [*GS* 2:65]).

[18.] Matthew 28:18-20.

[19.] A marginal note in Bonhoeffer's Greek New Testament reads: "like Christ" (the disciples are to preach the same thing Jesus preached, according to Matt. 4:17).

Jesus commands them to heal the sick, cleanse the lepers, raise the dead, and cast out demons! Proclamation becomes an event, and the event gives witness to the proclamation. The kingdom of God, Jesus Christ, forgiveness of sins, justification of the sinner by faith: all this is nothing other than the destruction of demonic power, healing, and raising the dead. As the word of the almighty God, it is deed, event, miracle. The *one* Jesus Christ goes out through the country in his twelve messengers and does his work. The royal[20] grace with which the disciples are equipped is the creative and redemptive word of God.

"Take no gold, or silver, or copper in your belts, no bag for your journey, or two tunics, or sandals, or a staff; for laborers deserve their food" (Matt. 10:9-10).[21] Because the command and the power of the messengers are given by the word of Jesus alone, nothing should be seen on Jesus' messengers which would make their royal mission unclear or incredible. In royal poverty the messengers are to witness to the riches of their Lord. What they have received from Jesus is no property of their own, with which they could bargain for other goods. "You received without payment!" Being a messenger of Jesus does not grant any personal rights; it does not entitle one to respect or power. That does not change even when the free messenger of Jesus has turned into an official pastor. The rights of a man with a university education and the privileges of social standing are no longer valid for anyone who has become a messenger of Jesus. "You received without payment!" Or was there something else which attracted us besides the call of Jesus which took us, who did not deserve it, into his service? "Give without payment." Let it become clear that with all the riches you have to give, you covet nothing for yourselves: no property, but also no respect or acknowledgment, not even gratitude! From where would you get such expectations? Any honors we claim for ourselves are stolen from him to whom they rightfully belong, the Lord who sent us out. The freedom of Jesus' messengers should show in their poverty. We cannot draw conclusions from the fact that Mark and Luke vary somewhat from Matthew in their lists of what

200

[20.] The literal translation of βασιλεία τῶν οὐρανῶν in verse 7 is: "kingdom of the heavens." Hence, Bonhoeffer chose the word "king-like."

[21.] In Bonhoeffer's Greek New Testament "the work" (the heading of this section) is written in the margin next to this sentence.

[22.] Matthew 10:9f.; cf. Mark 6:8f. and Luke 9:3. Tholuck draws the conclusions that "the injunction given in Matt. 10:9-10 is given in Mark 6:8-9 in a form so completely different, that, according to the letter, these verses express precisely the converse of St. Matthew's

the disciples are allowed or forbidden to take along.[22] Jesus prescribes poverty to those who set out in the authority of his word. We should not overlook the fact that this is a *commandment* of Jesus. The disciples' personal property is prescribed down to the smallest details. They should not be conspicuous as beggars with torn clothing and become burdensome parasites to other people. But they should go around in the working clothes of poverty. They should carry with them no more than a hiker in the country who is certain that at night he will find a house with friends who will shelter him and give him the food he needs. They are not to invest that kind of trust in people, but in him who sent them, and in their heavenly Father, who will take care of them.[23] In doing so they will give credibility to the message they proclaim, namely, the coming reign of God on earth. In the same freedom in which they do their ministry they should accept lodging and food, not as alms for beggars, but as the food laborers deserve. Jesus calls his messengers "laborers." Sloth, to be sure, does not deserve food.[24] But what is work, if not this struggle with the powers of Satan, this struggle for the hearts of the people, this renunciation of their own reputation, possessions, and joys of the world, for the sake of serving the poor, the mistreated, and the miserable? God was burdened and wearied by work for human beings (Isa. 43:24). The soul of Jesus worked until death on the cross for our salvation (Isa. 53:11). The messengers participate in this work: in proclamation, in overcoming Satan, and in intercessory prayer.[25] Anyone who does not acknowledge this work has not yet understood what the service of a faithful messenger of Jesus is like. They may receive their daily wages without shame, and without shame they should remain poor for the sake of their ministry.

"Whatever town or village you enter, find out who in it is worthy, and stay there until you leave. As you enter the house, greet it. If the house is worthy, let your peace come upon it; but if it is not worthy, let your peace return to you. If anyone will not welcome you or listen to your words, shake off the dust from your feet as you leave that house or town. Truly I tell you, it will be more tolerable for the land of Sodom and Gomorrah

---

words." This is "very instructive for the expositor of the Sermon on the Mount" (*Commentary on the Sermon on the Mount*, 166), namely, along the lines of the hermeneutical rule in Tholuck, "not the *literal*, but the *spiritual* interpretation is the true one" (163).

[23.] Like Matt. 6:26-32.

[24.] 2 Thessalonians 3:10: ". . . anyone who does not want to work does not deserve to eat."

[25.] See Isa. 53:12. In Bonhoeffer's Luther Bible there is a marginal note by "prayed for the evildoers" that reads: "intervened as mediator."

on the day of judgment than for that town" (Matt. 10:11-15). Work in the faith-community will start with the houses "which are worthy"[26] of lodging Jesus' messengers. God still has communities praying and wait-   202 ing everywhere. The disciples will be received there in the name of their Lord humbly and willingly. There their work will be assisted by prayer; there a small group exists, which stands in for the whole community. To prevent conflict in the community and false aspirations or concessions in the disciples, Jesus commands the apostles to remain in the same house as long as they are in the same town. The moment the messengers enter a house and a city, they get down to business. Time is valuable and short. Many are still waiting for the good news. Even the first word of greeting they speak, as their Lord does, "Peace be with this house!" (Luke 10:5),[27] is not an empty phrase. Instead, it immediately brings the power of God's peace to those "who are worthy." The messengers' proclamation is brief and clear. They proclaim the dawning of the reign of God; they call for repentance and for faith. They come in the authority of Jesus of Nazareth. A command is being delivered and an offer is being made under the highest authorization.[28] That took care of everything. Because everything has the utmost simplicity and clarity, and because the matter cannot be postponed, it needs no further preparation, discussion, or advertising. A king is standing outside the door; he can come at any minute: do you want to bow down and receive him humbly, or do you want him to destroy and kill you in his wrath? Those who are willing to hear now have heard all there is to say. They will not want to delay the messenger, who must go on to the next city. But for those who do not want to hear, the grace period is over. They have pronounced their own judgment. "Today, if you hear his voice, do not harden your hearts!" (Heb. 4:7).[29] That is gospel preaching. Is it unmerciful haste? Nothing is more unmerciful than pretending to the people that they still have a lot of time to repent. Nothing is more merciful; nothing is better news than the message to hurry, because the kingdom is very near. The messenger cannot wait until it is repeated over and over to everyone, and   203 repeated to everyone in his or her own language. God's language is clear enough. The messenger does not control who will hear and who will not.

[26.] This place in Bonhoeffer's Luther Bible is marked with "!".

[27.] At Matt. 10:12, the Greek New Testament cross-references Luke 10:5f. These are the only verses underlined in Luke 10.

[28.] The word ἐξουσία in Matt. 10:1 means "power," "authority."

[29.] Quote from Ps. 95:7f., which is marked in Bonhoeffer's Luther Bible.

God alone knows "who are worthy." They will hear the word, just as it is spoken by the disciples. Woe to the city and the house which does not receive the messenger of Jesus! It will undergo a terrible judgment. Sodom and Gomorrah, the cities of licentiousness and decadence,[30] may expect a more merciful judgment than the cities of Israel that reject the word of Jesus. Vices and sins can be forgiven by the word of Jesus, but those who reject the word of salvation itself cannot be saved. There is no worse sin than unbelief toward the gospel. Then there is nothing left for the messengers to do but leave that place. They go, because the word cannot remain there. In fear and astonishment they have to recognize the simultaneous power and weakness of the word of God. The disciples can only stay where the word of God stays,[31] because they cannot and should not force anything against the word or beyond the word. Their commission is not to wage a heroic struggle or fanatically enforce a great idea or a "good thing." If the word of God is rejected, then they are rejected with it. But they should shake the dust from their feet as a sign of the curse which will come to that place but will not harm them. The peace they brought to that place, however, will revert to them. "This is a consolation to the servants of the church, who think they are not accomplishing anything. You should not get upset; what other people do not want will become an even greater blessing for you yourselves. Thus says the Lord to them: They have despised it, so keep it for yourselves" (Bengel).[32]

204

The Suffering of the Messengers

"See, I am sending you out like sheep into the midst of wolves; so be wise as serpents and innocent as doves. Beware [the people], for they will hand you over to councils and flog you in their synagogues; and you will be dragged before governors and kings because of me, as a testimony to them and the Gentiles. When they hand you over, do not worry about how you are to speak or what you are to say; for what you are to say will

---

[30.] Genesis 18:20; 19:4f.

[31.] In 1936 Bonhoeffer advised the former Finkenwalde candidate Gerhard Vibrans and other pastors in uninterested parishes to write to their whole congregations in the sense of Matt. 10:13f. "that this may possibly be the last offer of the gospel they get" (*DBW* 14:195 [*GS* 2:490]).

[32.] Quoted, with slight deviations, from the commentary on Matt. 10:13 from the *Gnomen of the New Testament* (1:240) by Bengel.

be given to you at that time; for it is not you who speak, but the Spirit of
your Father speaking through you. Brother will betray brother to death,
and a father his child, and children will rise against parents and have
them put to death; and you will be hated by all because of my name. But
the one who endures to the end will be saved. When they persecute you
in one town, flee to the next; for truly I tell you, you will not have gone
through all the towns of Israel before the Son of Man comes.

¶ "A disciple is not above the teacher, nor a slave above the master; it
is enough for the disciple to be like the teacher, and the slave like the
master. If they have called the master of the house Beelzebul, how much
more will they malign those of his household!" (Matt. 10:16-25).

Lack of success and enmity cannot dissuade the messengers from
the fact that they are sent by Jesus. As a mighty strength and consolation, Jesus repeats: "Behold, I send you!" It is not their own way or
their own enterprise; they are sent. In this the Lord promises that he
will remain with his messengers when they will be like sheep among the
wolves, defenseless, powerless, fearful, and in great danger. Nothing
will happen to them that Jesus does not know. "Therefore be wise as
serpents and innocent as doves." How often the servants of Jesus have
misused this statement! How difficult it is even for the willing messenger
to understand this rightly and remain obedient! Who can always distinguish between spiritual wisdom and worldly cleverness? How tempting it
is, therefore, to renounce all "wisdom" and only be as simple as doves,   205
which, one-sided, is disobedience. Who tells us when we avoid suffering
out of fear and when we seek it out of recklessness? Who shows us the
hidden boundaries drawn here? It is the same disobedience, whether we
use the commandment to be wise against innocence, or the other way
around, whether we use innocence against wisdom. Because no human
heart can fully know itself, and because Jesus never called his disciples
to uncertainty, but always to greatest certainty, this warning by Jesus can
only call the disciples back to the word. Wherever the word is, that is
where the disciples are to be. That is their true wisdom and their true
innocence. If the word must retreat, because it is obviously being rejected, then the disciples should retreat with the word. If the word remains
in an open struggle, then the disciples should remain. They will have to
act wisely and simply at the same time. But the disciples should never set
out on a road out of "wisdom," when that road cannot be approved by
the word of Jesus. They should never justify with "spiritual wisdom" a way
which does not correspond to the word of Jesus. Only the truth of the

word will teach them to recognize what is wise. But it can never be "wise" to break off the smallest piece of the truth, for the sake of some human prospect or hope. Our own evaluation of our situation cannot make us see what is wise; only the truth of the word of God can do that. The only thing that is always wise is staying with the truth of God. Here alone is the place where of God's faithfulness and aid are promised. At all times it will prove to be the "wisest" for the disciples at this time and in the coming time to simply stand by the word of God.

The word will give the messengers true knowledge of the people. "Beware the people." The disciples should not show fear of the people, nor evil mistrust, least of all hatred toward human beings, nor should they show thoughtless trustfulness or faith in the good in all people. Instead, they should show true knowledge of the relationship of the word to the people and the people to the word. If they understand this soberly, then they will not be scared by Jesus' announcement that their path among the people will be a path of suffering. Rather, they will be able to endure it. A wonderful strength resides in the disciples' suffering. Criminals suffer their punishment in hiddenness. But the disciples' path of suffering will lead them before princes and kings, "for my sake, as a testimony to them and the Gentiles." The good news will be propagated by suffering. That is the plan of God and the will of Jesus; and that is why in the hour of accountability before courts and thrones the disciples will be given the power to give a good confession, to offer a fearless witness. The Holy Spirit itself will be with them. It will make them invincible. It will give them "a wisdom that none of your opponents will be able to withstand or contradict" (Luke 21:15). Because the disciples hold fast to the word in their suffering, the word will remain with them. Self-sought martyrdom would not have this promise. But the promise is absolutely certain for those who suffer with the word.

Hate toward the word of Jesus' messengers will remain until the end of time.[33] Hate will pronounce the disciples guilty of all the divisions which will come over cities and houses. Jesus and his disciples will be condemned by everyone as destroyers of the family, as forces leading the people astray, as crazy enthusiasts and troublemakers. Then the temp-

---

[33.] In the situation of 1936–37 these apocalyptic thoughts described current church events. For example, in 1936, Pastor Johannes Pecina, who refused to be driven from his church and manse, was put in prison. The vicar sent by the Council of Brethren of the Confessing Church to substitute for him, Willi Brandenburg, was also imprisoned (*DB-ER* 540).

tation to fall away will be very near to the disciples. But the end is also near. Until its coming they are to remain faithful, to endure, to stand fast. Only those who stand fast with Jesus and his word to the end will be blessed. But when the end comes, when the enmity toward Jesus and his disciples is revealed for all the world to see, then and only then should the disciples flee from one city to another, in order to proclaim the word where it will still be heard. Even in this flight, they are not separated from the word, but stand fast with it.

The promise of Jesus that he will come again soon[34] has been kept for us by the church-community in the belief that it is true. Its fulfillment is a mystery, and it is not a good thing to look for human ways to evade the issue. But what is clear, and the only thing important for us today, is the fact that the return of Jesus will come quickly. His coming is more certain than our being able to complete our work in his service. It is more certain than our death. Jesus' messengers can receive no greater consolation in all this than the certainty that in their suffering they will be like their Lord. Whatever happens to the master will happen to the disciple; whatever happens to the lord will also happen to the servant. If Jesus is called a devil, then that will happen even more to the servants of his house. So Jesus will be with them and they will be like Christ in everything.

207

The Decision

"So have no fear of them; for nothing is covered up that will not be uncovered, and nothing secret that will not become known. What I say to you in the dark, tell in the light; and what you hear whispered, proclaim from the housetops. Do not fear those who kill the body but cannot kill the soul; rather fear him who can destroy both soul and body in hell. Are not two sparrows sold for a penny? Yet not one of them will fall to the ground apart from your Father. And even the hairs of your head are all counted. So do not be afraid; you are of more value than many sparrows.

¶ "Everyone therefore who acknowledges me before others, I also will acknowledge before my Father in heaven; but whoever denies me before others, I also will deny before my Father in heaven.[35] Do not think that

---

[34.] Matthew 10:22f.

[35.] Beside this sentence in Bonhoeffer's Greek New Testament he wrote "The Decision," his heading for this section.

208 I have come to bring peace to the earth; I have not come to bring peace, but a sword. For I have come to set a man against his father, and a daughter against her mother, and a daughter-in-law against her mother-in-law; and one's foes will be members of one's own household. Whoever loves father or mother more than me is not worthy of me; and whoever loves son or daughter more than me is not worthy of me; and whoever does not take up the cross and follow me is not worthy of me. Those who find their life will lose it, and those who lose their life for my sake will find it" (Matt. 10:26-39).

The messenger stays with the word and the word stays with the messenger now and forever. Jesus encourages his messengers three times with the call "be not afraid!" Whatever happens to them now in secret will not remain in secret, but will be revealed before God and the people. The most secret suffering inflicted on them has the promise to be revealed as a judgment over the persecutors and as glory for the messengers. Likewise, the messengers' witness will not remain hidden, but become a public witness. The gospel should not become some sectarian affair.[36] Instead, it is meant to be preached in public. Today it may still have to live off in a corner here and there. But in the last days this preaching will fill the whole globe either for salvation or for condemnation. The Revelation of John prophesies: "Then I saw another angel flying in midheaven, with an eternal gospel to proclaim to those who live on the earth—to every nation and tribe and language and people" (14:6). Therefore, "be not afraid!"

Human beings should not be feared. They cannot do much to the disciples of Jesus. Their power stops with the disciples' physical death. The disciples are to overcome fear of death with fear of God. Disciples are in danger, not from human judgment, but from God's judgment, not from the decay of their bodies, but from the eternal decay of their bodies and souls. Anyone who is still afraid of people is not afraid of God. Anyone who fears God is no longer afraid of people. Daily reminders of this statement are valuable for preachers of the gospel.

The power which is given to people for a short time on this earth is not without God's knowledge and will. If we fall into human hands, if

[36.] See Bonhoeffer's sermon on Rev. 14:6–13 on the German Memorial Day, November 24, 1935: "No, in the face of God's terrible judgment on the world, let us not break out in the howling of a sectarian triumph" (*TF* 267 [*DBW* 14:917 (*GS* 5:574)]).

we suffer and die by human violence, we may be sure that everything 209
comes from God. God, who lets no sparrow fall to the ground without
the divine will and knowledge, will not permit anything to happen to
God's own people except what is good and useful for them and their
cause. We are in God's hands. Therefore, "be not afraid!"

Time is short. Eternity is long. It is the time of decision. Those who
remain faithful to the word and the confession here will find that Jesus
Christ will stand by them in the hour of judgment. He will know them
and stand with them when the accuser demands they be judged. The
whole world will be witnesses when Jesus names our name before his
heavenly Father. Those who have held on to Jesus in this life will find
that Jesus will hold on to them in eternity. But those who are ashamed
of this Lord and his name, those who deny him, will find that Jesus is
ashamed of them in eternity and will deny them.

This final separation has to commence here on earth. The peace of
Jesus Christ is the cross. The cross is God's sword on this earth. It creates division. The son against the father, the daughter against the mother, the household against its head, and all that for the sake of God's
kingdom and its peace—that is the work of Christ on earth! No wonder
the world accuses him, who brought the love of God to the people, of
hatred toward human beings! Who dares to speak about a father's love
and a mother's love to a son or daughter in such a way, if not either
the destroyer of all life or the creator of a new life? Who can claim the
people's love and sacrifice so exclusively, if not the enemy of humanity
or the savior of humanity? Who will carry the sword into their houses, if
not the devil or Christ, the Prince of Peace? God's love for the people
and human love for their own kind are utterly different. God's love for
the people brings the cross and discipleship, but these, in turn, mean
life and resurrection. "Anyone who loses his life for my sake will find it."
This affirmation is given by the one who has the power over death, the
Son of God, who goes to the cross and to resurrection and takes those
who are his with him.

The Fruit   210

"Whoever welcomes you welcomes me, and whoever welcomes me welcomes the one who sent me. Whoever welcomes a prophet in the name
of a prophet will receive a prophet's reward; and whoever welcomes
a righteous person in the name of a righteous person will receive the
reward of the righteous; and whoever gives even a cup of cold water to

one of these little ones in the name of a disciple—truly I tell you, none of these will lose their reward" (Matt. 10:40-42).[37]

Those who carry Jesus' word receive one last promise for their work. They have become Christ's coworkers and helpmates. They are to be like Christ in all things. Thus, for the people to whom they go, they are also to be "like Christ."[38] With them, Jesus Christ himself enters the house that takes them in. They are bearers of his presence. They bring the people the most valuable gift, Jesus Christ, and with him, God, the Father, and that means forgiveness, salvation, life, blessedness. That is the reward and the fruit of their work and their suffering. Every service done to them is done to Jesus Christ himself. In the same way, that is grace for both the community and the messengers. The community will be all the more willing to treat the messengers well, to honor them and serve them, for with them the Lord himself has entered their house. And the disciples may know that their entry into a house will not be in vain and empty, but that they bring an incomparable gift. It is a law in the realm of God that everyone comes to participate in the gift, when they willingly receive it as a gift from God. Those who take the prophets in, knowing what they are doing, shall come to participate in their cause, their gift, and their reward. Those who take in the righteous shall receive the reward of the righteous, for they have participated in their righteousness who give a cup of water to one of the least, the poorest, who bear no honorable name, to one of these messengers of Jesus Christ; they have served Jesus Christ himself and the reward of Jesus Christ shall be given them.

211

In this way, the final thought of the messengers is guided, not to their own way or their own suffering or their own reward, but to the purpose of their work: the salvation of the faith-community.

[37.] Bonhoeffer wrote in his Greek New Testament beside this line: "fruit."

[38.] *SC* (*DBWE* 1) where Bonhoeffer writes, ". . . act like Christ." Bonhoeffer's note adds a reference to Luther's "wonderful and profound thoughts on this question" (179).

PART TWO
THE CHURCH OF JESUS CHRIST AND DISCIPLESHIP

CHAPTER EIGHT

PRELIMINARY QUESTIONS

To HIS FIRST DISCIPLES Jesus was bodily present, speaking his word directly to them. But this Jesus died and is risen. How, then, does his call to discipleship [Ruf in die Nachfolge] reach us today? Jesus no longer walks past me in bodily form and calls, "Follow me,"[1] as he did to Levi, the tax collector. Even if I would be truly willing to listen, to leave everything behind, and to follow, what justification do I have for doing so? What for the first disciples was so entirely unambiguous is for me a decision that is highly problematic and fraught with uncertainty. What gives me the right, for example, to hear Jesus' call of the tax collector as being addressed to me? Did Jesus not say quite different things to others on other occasions? What about the paralytic to whom he extended forgiveness and healing?[2] And what about Lazarus whom he raised from the dead?[3] Did he love them any less than his disciples? And yet he did not call them to leave their profession and follow him, but left them at home with their families and their jobs. Who am I to recommend myself to do something unusual and extraordinary? Who is to judge whether I or others are not simply acting out of our own authority and religious enthusiasm? But that would definitely mean something other than discipleship!

There is something wrong with all of these questions. Every time we ask them, we place ourselves outside the living presence of the Christ. All of these questions refuse to take seriously that Jesus Christ is not dead but alive and still speaking to us today through the testimony of scripture. He

---

[1.] Mark 2:14.
[2.] Mark 2:5, 11f.
[3.] John 11.

is present with us today, in bodily form and with his word. If we want to hear his call to discipleship, we need to hear it where Christ himself is present. It is within the church that Jesus Christ calls through his word and sacrament.[4] The preaching and sacrament of the church is the place where Jesus Christ is present. To hear Jesus' call to discipleship, one needs no personal revelation. Listen to the preaching and receive the sacrament! Listen to the gospel of the crucified and risen Lord! Here he is, the whole Christ, the very same who encountered the disciples. Indeed, here he is already present as the glorified, the victorious, the living Christ. No one but Christ himself can call us to discipleship. Discipleship in essence never consists in a decision for this or that specific action; it is always a decision for or against Jesus Christ. And this is exactly why the situation was not any less ambiguous for the disciple or the tax collector who was called by him than it is for us today. The obedience of those who were first called constituted discipleship precisely in that they recognized Christ in the one who was calling them. For them, as for us, it is the hidden Christ who calls. The call as such is ambiguous. What counts is not the call as such, but the one who calls. But Christ can only be recognized in faith. That was true in the same way for the first disciples as it is for us. They saw the rabbi and the miracle worker, and believed in Christ. We hear the word and believe in Christ.

But did those first disciples not have an advantage over us in that, once they had recognized Christ, they received his unambiguous command from his very own lips and were told what to do? And are we not left to our own devices precisely at this crucial point of Christian obedience? Does not the same Christ speak differently to us than he spoke to them? If this were true, then we would indeed be in a hopeless situation. But it is far from true. Christ speaks to us exactly as he spoke to them. For the first disciples of Jesus it was also not as if they first recognized him as the Christ, and then received his command. Rather, it was only through his word and his command that they recognized him. They trusted in his word and his command, and thereby recognized him as the Christ.

[4.] The Augsburg Confession, article 7 (*The Book of Concord*, 32), and Calvin (*Institutes of the Christian Religion*, 103 [*Institutio* IV, 1, 9]) define the *notae ecclesiae*, or marks of the church, as the proper proclamation and hearing of the word, and the proper distribution and reception of the sacraments. These *notae ecclesiae* are signs by which the presence of the church is recognized. Regarding the significance of the sacrament in Bonhoeffer's thought, see *DBW* 11:310 (*GS* 5:290) and *DBW* 11:334 (*GS* 1:147).

There was no other way for the disciples to know Christ than through his clear word. Conversely, therefore, to recognize Jesus truly as the Christ necessarily included a recognition of his will. To recognize the person of Jesus Christ did not undermine the disciples' certainty about what to do, but on the contrary created that certainty. Indeed, there is no other way to recognize Christ. If Christ is the living Lord of my life, then I am addressed by his word whenever I encounter him; indeed, I do not really know him except through his clear word and command. There are those who object that this is precisely our dilemma: we would like to know Christ and have faith in him, and yet we are unable to recognize his will. This objection, however, springs from a vague and mistaken knowledge of Christ. To know Christ means to recognize him in his word as Lord and savior of my life. But that includes an understanding of his clear word spoken to me.

217

Suppose we say finally that, whereas the command the disciples received was unambiguous, we have to decide for ourselves which of his words is addressed to us. In that case, we have once again misunderstood not only the situation of the disciples, but also our own. Jesus' command always has a single purpose: it demands faith from an undivided heart, and love of God and neighbor with all our heart and soul.[5] This is the only aspect in which the command was unambiguous. Any attempt to carry out the command of Jesus, without also understanding it in this way, would again mean that we misinterpret and disobey Jesus' word. However, this does not mean that we would have no way of knowing the concrete command.[6] On the contrary, we hear it clearly in every word of proclamation in which we hear Christ, but we hear it knowing that it can only be fulfilled through faith in Jesus Christ. The gift Jesus gave to his disciples is thus fully available to us too. In fact, it is even more readily available to us now that Jesus has ascended, by our knowledge of his transfiguration, and by the Holy Spirit that has been sent.

All this makes it abundantly clear that we cannot play off the narrative of the calling of the disciples against other parts of the gospel account. It is never a question of our having or taking on the same identity as the disciples or other people in the New Testament. The only issue of importance is that Jesus Christ and his call are the same, then and now. His

---

[5.] See Luke 10:27.

[6.] Regarding Bonhoeffer's efforts to come to terms with this epistemological problem, see *DBW* 11:333–34 (*GS* 1:146f.). Also see *E* 286f. (*DBW* 6:392f.). [JG/GK]

word remains one and the same, whether it was spoken during his earthly life or today, whether it was addressed to the disciples or to the paralytic.[7] Then and now, it is the gracious call to enter his kingdom and to submit to his rule. The question whether I ought to compare myself with the disciple or with the paralytic poses a dangerous and false alternative. I need not compare myself with either of them. Instead, all I have to do is to listen and do Christ's word and will as I receive them in both of these biblical accounts. Scripture does not present us with a collection of Christian types[8] to be imitated according to our own choice. Rather, in every passage it proclaims to us the one Jesus Christ. It is him alone whom I ought to hear.[9] He is one and the same everywhere.

Thus, when we ask the question of where we can hear Jesus' call to discipleship today, there is no other answer than this: listen to the word that is preached, and receive the sacrament. In both of these listen to Christ himself. Then you will hear his call!

[7.] Mark 2:5.

[8.] In the notes taken during Bonhoeffer's New Testament lectures by Joachim Kanitz, we read: "God's creative glory and richness does not produce types" (*NL* B 10, 6 [47]).

[9.] See Matt. 17:5 where we read in the transfiguration narrative: ". . . listen to him!"

CHAPTER NINE

BAPTISM

IN THE SYNOPTIC GOSPELS the concept of discipleship can express 219 almost the full breadth and content of relations between the disciple and Jesus Christ. In the Pauline texts, however, this concept recedes almost completely into the background. Paul's primary concern is not to proclaim the story of the Lord's earthly life to us, but rather his presence as the risen and glorified Lord, and his work for us. This requires him to develop a new and distinctive terminology. Paul derives this new terminology from the special nature of his subject matter; its purpose is to capture what unites the proclamation of the one Lord who lived, died, and rose again. To express the full witness of Christ requires more than a single set of terms. Paul's terminology thus confirms that of the Synoptic Gospels, and vice versa. Neither terminology is intrinsically preferable to the other. After all, we do not "belong to Paul, or to Apollos, or to Cephas, or to Christ";[1] instead, our faith rests on the unity of the scriptural testimony to Christ. If we hold that the Christ Paul proclaims is still present to us in the same way, whereas the Synoptic Gospels testify to a presence of Christ which we no longer know, we break up the unity of scripture.[2] True, many regard the use of such language as reflecting thought that is grounded in history and in keeping with the Reformation.[3] But in fact, it is just the opposite, namely, religious enthusiasm of

---

[1.] 1 Corinthians 1:12. Cephas is another name of the apostle Peter.

[2.] Bonhoeffer thus considers it misleading to separate Paul from the Synoptics on the basis of 2 Cor. 5:16 ("even though we once knew Christ from a human point of view, we know him no longer in that way").

[3.] Rudolf Bultmann considered the earthly Jesus and his message as a renewal of the great prophetic tradition of the Old Testament, and thus part of the prehistory of the Christian kerygma. He distinguished this earthly Jesus from the kerygmatic Christ. The

220

the most dangerous kind. For how do we know that Christ is still present with us today in the way that Paul proclaims? How else, but from scripture itself? Or should this perhaps be the place to talk about an experience of Christ's presence and reality that would be free and independent of the word of scripture? But if it is indeed scripture alone that assures us of Christ's presence, then it must be scripture as a whole, the scripture which also testifies to the ongoing presence of the synoptic Jesus Christ. The synoptic Christ is neither more nor less distant from us than the Christ of Paul. The Christ who is present with us is the Christ to whom the whole of scripture testifies. He is the incarnate, crucified, risen, and glorified Christ; and he encounters us in his word. The different terminology with which the Synoptic Gospels and Paul communicate this message does not undermine the unity of the scriptural testimony.[10]

---

10. Mistaking the kerygmatic testimony for ontological propositions is what lies at the heart of all enthusiast spirituality [Schwarmgeisterei].[4] To take the statement that Christ is risen and present it as an ontological proposition would destroy the unity of scripture. For it would imply a proposition about a mode of existence of Jesus Christ which, for example, is different than that of the synoptic Jesus. To say that Christ is risen and present would then be understood as a generally valid proposition with an independent ontological status which could be set critically over against other ontological propositions. We would have turned it into a theological principle. Analogously, to give another example, every case of enthusiasts' perfectionism arises from a similar ontological misinterpretation of what scripture has to say about sanctification. Those holding this view take the statement that those who are in God do not sin,[5] for example, and make it into an ontological starting point of their inquiry. In that case the statement is no longer seen as being an integral part of scripture itself. Instead, it is being elevated to a self-sufficient truth and accessible through human experience. Such a view is in direct contradiction to the kerygmatic nature of the biblical testimony. The statement that Christ is risen and present must be taken strictly as a testimony of scripture, and is thus true only as word of scripture. It is on this word that my faith relies. Apart from this word, I can have no other conceivable access to this truth. But this word testifies equally to the presence of both the Pauline and the synoptic Christ. My nearness to the one or the other is

---

Christian faith which is relevant for us did not begin until Christ's resurrection into the kerygma, that is, into the preaching after Easter (Bultmann, *Jesus and the Word*, 25f. and 14f.). Hegel, in similar fashion, regarded "God's appearance in the flesh . . . to be a part of past history" (*The Christian Religion*, 213–14 [trans. altered]).

[4.] This note presumably is based on a discussion of the church as the "new human being"; see lecture notes by Johannes Mickley found in *NL* B 9, 3 (2f.).

[5.] 1 John 3:6 (underlined in Bonhoeffer's Bible).

What the Synoptics describe as hearing and following the call to discipleship, Paul expresses with the concept of *baptism*.[7]

Baptism is not something we offer to God.[8] It is, rather, something *Jesus Christ offers to us*. It is grounded solely in the will of Jesus Christ, as expressed in his gracious call. Baptism is essentially a paradoxically passive action; it means being baptized, suffering Christ's call.[9] In baptism we become Christ's possession. The name of Jesus Christ is spoken over baptismal candidates, they gain a share in that name; they are baptized "into Jesus Christ" (εἰζ,[10] Rom. 6:3; Gal. 3:27; Matt. 28:19). They now belong to Jesus Christ. Having been rescued from the rule of this world, they now have become Christ's own.

Baptism thus implies a *break*. Christ invades the realm of Satan and lays hold of those who belong to him, thereby creating his church-community [Gemeinde]. Past and present are thus torn asunder. The old has passed away, everything has become new.[11] The break does not come about by our breaking our chains out of an unquenchable thirst to see our life and all things ordered in a new and free way. Long ago, Christ himself had already brought about that break. In baptism this break now also takes effect in my own life. I am deprived of my immediate relationship

---

determined solely by the word, by the testimony of scripture. This is of course not to deny at all that the Pauline testimony differs from that of the Synoptics with regard to both subject matter and terminology, but both are understood strictly within the context of scripture as a whole.

All these statements are not merely truths derived a priori from a firm concept of the canon of scripture;[6] rather, each individual case must in turn also serve as proof for the legitimacy of this understanding of scripture. In what follows we thus have to show how Paul, albeit with a new terminology, adopts and further develops the concept of discipleship [Nachfolge].

[6.] The writings transmitted to us in the canon of the New Testament are in Bonhoeffer's view not per se, or a priori, of equal significance in every part.

[7.] See Bethge's notes in *NL* B 8 (3) on Mark 2:14: "By being called, Levi has become a 'baptized disciple.'"

[8.] See Luke 9:57.

[9.] In *NL* B 9, 5 (6) Zimmermann wrote: "Baptism is passio, not actio." See Klapproth's notes in *NL* B 9, 6 (6): "We are merely passive." See *DBW* 4:333–40. See Luther, "Resolutiones über [Luthers] Leipziger Disputationsthesen. 1519" (*WA* 2:421): "Liberum arbitrium est mere passivum in omni actu suo qui velle vocatur" ("in each act of willing, the free will is merely passive").

[10.] "into."

[11.] 2 Corinthians 5:17 reads: "So if anyone is in Christ, there is a new creation; everything old has passed away; see, everything has become new!"

to the given realities of the world, since Christ the mediator and Lord has stepped in between me and the world. Those who are baptized no longer belong to the world, no longer serve the world, and are no longer subject to it. They belong to Christ alone, and relate to the world only through Christ.

222 The break with the world is absolute. It requires and causes our *death*.[11] In baptism we die together with our old world. This death must be understood in the strictest sense as an event that is suffered. It is not as if we were asked to bring about this death ourselves through various kinds of sacrifice and renunciation. That would be an impossible attempt. Such a death would never be the death of the old self which Christ demands. The old self cannot kill itself. It cannot will its own death. We die in Christ alone; we die through Christ and with Christ. Christ is our death. It is for the sake of community with Christ, and only in that community, that we die. In baptism we receive both community with Christ and our death as a gift of grace.[12] This death is a gift of grace which we can never create for ourselves. True, in this death judgment is passed on the old self and its sin. But out of this judgment rises the new self which has died to the world and to sin.[14] This death is thus not the final, angry rejection of the creature by its creator but rather the gracious acceptance of the creature by the creator. This death taking place in baptism is the gracious death which is ours through the death of Christ. It is the death in the power and community of the cross of Christ. Those who become Christ's own must come under his cross. They must suffer and die with him. Those who are granted community with Christ must die the grace-filled death of baptism. That is the rule of the cross of Christ under which Jesus places his disciples. Christ's death and cross were cruel and hard; however, because of our community with him, the yoke of our cross is easy and light.[15] The cross of Christ is the gracious death, which we

---

11. Jesus already described his death as a baptism, and told his disciples that they too would undergo this baptism of death (Mark 10:39; Luke 12:50).[12]

12. Schlatter also considers 1 Cor. 15:29 as a reference to the baptism of martyrdom.[13]

[12.] The synoptic references correspond with Rom. 6:3: "Do you not know that all of us who have been baptized into Christ Jesus were baptized into his death?"

[13.] Schlatter, *Die Theologie der Apostel*, 518, note 1.

[14.] These are allusions to Romans 5 and 6.

[15.] Matthew 11:30 reads: "For my yoke is easy, and my burden is light."

die once and for all in our baptism; the cross to which we are called is our daily dying[16] in the power of the death accomplished by Christ. Baptism thus means to be received into the community of the cross of Jesus Christ   223 (Rom. 6:3ff.; Col. 2:12). The believer is placed under the cross of Christ.

The death of baptism means *justification away from sin.*[17] In order to be freed from their sin, sinners must die. Whoever has died is justified from sin (Rom. 6:7; Col. 2:20). Sin no longer has any claim on those who are dead; with death the claim has been met and has ceased to exist. Justification from (ἀπὸ)[18] sin can thus take place only through death. Forgiveness of sin does not mean that the sin is overlooked or forgotten; rather, it means that the sinner is really put to death and thus separated from (ἀπὸ) sin. However, the only reason the sinner's death means justification and not condemnation is that this death is suffered in communion [Gemeinschaft] with the death of Christ. Being baptized into the death of Christ is what brings forgiveness of sins and justification and a complete separation from sin. In calling his disciples into the community of the cross, Jesus gave them the gift of justification, of death and forgiveness of sins. The disciple who followed Jesus in the community of the cross received no other gift than the believer who was baptized according to Paul's teaching.

Although baptism requires a passive role on our human part, it must never be understood as a mechanical process. A look at the relation between *baptism* and *Spirit* makes this abundantly clear (Matt. 3:11; Acts 10:47; John 3:5; 1 Cor. 6:11; 12:13). The gift received in baptism is the Holy Spirit, and the Holy Spirit is Christ himself dwelling in the hearts of the believers (2 Cor. 3:17; Rom. 8:9-11, 14ff.; Eph. 3:16f.). Those baptized are the house in which the Holy Spirit dwells (οἰκεῖ). It is through the Holy Spirit that Jesus Christ remains present with us, and that we are in community with him. The Holy Spirit gives us a true understanding of Christ's nature (1 Cor. 2:10) and of his will; the Holy Spirit teaches us and reminds us of all that Christ has said to us (John 14:26); the Holy Spirit guides us into all truth (John 16:13), so that we may not be lacking in the

---

[16.] See 1 Cor. 15:31; also see, on baptism, Luther's Small Catechism (*The Book of Concord*, 348–49). Here Luther sees the dying of the old Adam taking place "through daily contrition and repentance."

[17.] See *NL A* 54, 12: "We are justified ἀπὸ τῆς ἁμαρτίας, away from our sin, not ἐν τῇ ἁμαρτία [in sin]. We have died to sin" (*DBW* 14:607).

[18.] "away from."

224   knowledge of Christ, and may understand the gifts bestowed on us by
God (1 Cor. 2:12; Eph. 1:9). The Holy Spirit does not create uncertainty in us, but certainty and clarity. We are thus enabled to walk in the
Spirit (Gal. 5:16, 18, 25; Rom. 8:1, 4), taking confident steps. After his
ascension, Jesus did not withdraw from those who belong to him that
measure of certainty which the disciples of Jesus enjoyed during their
earthly community with him. By sending the Holy Spirit into the hearts
of those who are baptized, the community with Jesus has in fact become
so intimate that the certainty of knowing him is not only preserved, but
increased and strengthened (Rom. 8:16; John 16:12f.).

In calling the disciples, Jesus demanded a *visible act of obedience*. To
follow Jesus was a public act. In just the same way baptism is a public act,
for in baptism we are incorporated into the visible church-community
[Gemeinde] of Jesus Christ (Gal. 3:27f.; 1 Cor. 12:13). The break with
the world which has taken place in Christ can no longer remain hidden;
it must become externally visible through active participation in the life
and worship[19] of the church-community. Christians who are actively
involved in the church-community take a step out of the world, their
work, and family; they visibly stand in the community with Jesus Christ.
They take this step on their own as individuals. But they regain what
they have given up—brothers, sisters, houses, fields.[20] Those who are
baptized live in the visible church-community of Jesus Christ. What that
means and entails must be examined in the following two chapters on
the "body of Christ" and the "visible church-community."

Baptism and the receiving of its gift take place only *once*.[21] No one
can be baptized twice with the baptism of Christ.[13] The fact that this
gracious act of God is unique and cannot be repeated is what the Letter
to the Hebrews is trying to express in that mysterious passage about the
impossibility of a second repentance after baptism and conversion (Heb.
225   6:4ff.). All those who are baptized are participating in Christ's death.
Through his death, they have received their death sentence and have

---

13. However, the baptism of John must be renewed through the baptism of
Christ (Acts 19:5).

[19.] See above, page 65. During the time of the Third Reich church attendance was
being frowned upon by the National Socialist regime, and thus became a political act.
[20.] Mark 10:30.
[21.] Romans 6:10 (and Heb. 9:11ff.): ἐφάπαξ ("once," "once and for all").

died. And just as Christ died once and for all (Rom. 6:10), and just as there can be no repetition of his sacrifice, so do those who are baptized suffer their death with Christ once and for all. Now they are dead. The daily dying of the Christian[22] is now merely a consequence of the one death that has already taken place in baptism, just as a tree dies whose roots have been cut off. Those who have been baptized live henceforth under the motto: "Consider yourselves dead to sin" (Rom. 6:11). They know themselves only as those who have already died, as those who have already undergone everything that is necessary for salvation. Those who have been baptized draw their life not from a real repetition of Christ's death, which would have to be accomplished ever anew as an act of grace. Instead, their life springs from looking back again and again, placing their faith in Christ's death as an act of grace which has already been fully accomplished in their baptism. They live out of the once-and-for-allness of Christ's death.

The fact that baptism can take place once and only once has important consequences with regard to infant baptism.[14] The question is not whether or not infant baptism is really baptism. But precisely because it is indeed baptism, that baptism that takes place only once and cannot be repeated, infant baptism requires certain restrictions in its use. True, it was certainly not a sign of a healthy church life when, in the second and third centuries, believing Christians postponed their baptism until they reached old age or were already on their deathbeds.[24] But this practice nonetheless speaks of a clear insight into the nature of baptismal grace, an insight which is widely lacking today. With regard to infant baptism this means

---

14. To the passages usually cited in support of the practice of infant baptism in New Testament times,[23] we may perhaps add 1 John 2:12ff. The fact that the same sequence—children, fathers, and young men—is used twice would seem to justify our taking τεκνία in verse 12 not as a general term for the church-community, but as a reference to children in the literal sense of the word.

[22.] This is an allusion to 1 Cor. 15:31, where the NRSV reads: "I die every day! That is as certain, brothers and sisters, as my boasting of you—a boast that I make in Christ Jesus our Lord."

[23.] In a critical report for the Brethren's Council in East Prussia, on the question of baptism, Bonhoeffer cites Acts 16:15, 16:33, and 18:8 as references (*DBW* 16:565 [*GS* 3:433]). In another instance, he leaves it open whether infant baptism "can be found in the New Testament or not" (*DBW* 14:834 [*GS* 3:372]).

[24.] See Harnack, *The Mission and Expansion of Christianity in the First Three Centuries* (1:481, note 1). Harnack's study covers only the first three centuries of Christianity. The postponement of baptism still represented a serious problem in the fourth and fifth centuries.

226 that the sacrament should be administered only where it is certain that the act of salvation already accomplished once and for all will be repeatedly remembered in faith. And that can only be the case in a living church-community. Infant baptism without the church-community is not only an abuse of the sacrament. It also betrays a reprehensible thoughtlessness in dealing with the children's spiritual welfare, for baptism can never be repeated.

For those who were called, Jesus' call was equally unique and unrepeatable. Whoever followed him had died to their previous life. This is why Jesus had to require his disciples to leave all they had.[25] Both the finality of their decision and the complete sufficiency of the gift they received from their Lord needed to be clearly expressed. "But if salt has lost its taste, how can its saltiness be restored?"[26] It could not be stated any more pointedly than this that Jesus' gift was offered and received once and once only. Having taken their life from them, he now sought to give them a life that was full and complete. And so he gave them his cross. That was the gift of baptism to the first disciples.

[25.] Mark 10:28.
[26.] Matthew 5:13.

CHAPTER TEN

THE BODY OF CHRIST

THE FIRST DISCIPLES lived in the bodily presence of and in community   227
with Jesus. What is the significance of this fact, and in what way does
this community still exist for us? Paul states that through baptism we
have become members of the body of Christ.[1] This statement sounds
very strange and incomprehensible to us, and thus requires a thorough
explanation.

It tells us that those who are baptized are still meant to live, even after
the Lord's death and resurrection, in the bodily presence of and community with Jesus. For those who belong to him, Jesus' departure does
not mean a loss but rather a new gift. For the first disciples the bodily
community with Jesus did not mean anything different or anything more
than what we have today. Indeed, for us this community is even more
definite, more complete, and more certain than it was for them, since
we live in full community with the bodily presence of the glorified Lord.
Our faith must become fully aware of the magnitude of this gift. The
body of Jesus Christ is the ground of our faith and the source of its certainty; the body of Jesus Christ is the one and perfect gift through which
we receive our salvation; the body of Jesus Christ is our new life. It is in
the body of Jesus Christ that we are accepted by God from eternity.

Since Adam's fall God sent the divine *word* to sinful humanity, in
order to seek and *accept* us.[2] This is why we have received God's word, to

---

[1.] 1 Corinthians 12:13: "For in the *one* Spirit we were all baptized into *one* body." Cf.
SC (*DBWE* 1):134–41.

[2.] See the Klapproth notes from the Finkenwalde homiletics lectures found in *NL* B
10, 5 (91): "The word that is preached seeks to accept human beings" (see *DBW* 14:503
[*GS* 4:241]).

reconcile our lost humanity with God. God's word came as promise and as law. For our sake God's word became weak and lowly. But human beings rejected this word, refusing to be accepted by God. They offered sacrifices; they performed good works which God was supposed to accept in their stead, thereby letting them go free.

Then the miracle of all miracles takes place. The Son of God becomes a human being. The Word became flesh.[3] The One who had dwelled from all eternity in the Father's glory, the One who was in the form of God, who in the beginning had been the mediator of creation so that the created world can only be known through him and in him,[4] the One who was very God (1 Cor. 8:6; 2 Cor. 8:9; Phil. 2:6ff.; Eph. 1:4; Col. 1:16; John 1:1ff.; Heb. 1:1ff.)—this One takes on humanity and comes to earth. He takes on humanity by taking on human qualities, human 'nature', "sinful flesh," human form (Rom. 8:3; Gal. 4:4; Phil. 2:6ff.). Now it is no longer only through the word of preaching that God accepts humanity, but also in the body of Christ. God's mercy sends the Son in the flesh, so that in his flesh he may shoulder and carry all of humanity. The Son of God accepts all of humanity in bodily form, the same humanity which in hate of God and pride of the flesh had rejected the incorporeal, invisible word of God. In the body of Jesus Christ humanity is now truly and bodily accepted; it is accepted as it is, out of God's mercy.

When contemplating this miracle, the early church fathers insisted passionately that while it was necessary to say that God had taken on human nature, it was wrong to say that God had chosen a single, perfect human being with whom God would then unite.[5] God became human. This means God took on the whole of our sick and sinful human nature, the whole of humanity which had fallen away from God. It does not mean, however, that God took on the individual human being Jesus. The entire gospel message can be understood properly only in light of this crucial distinction. The body of Jesus Christ, in which we together with all of humanity are accepted by God, has now become the foundation of our salvation.

The flesh borne by Christ was sinful flesh—yet borne without sin (2 Cor. 5:21; Heb. 4:15). Wherever his human body is, there all flesh is being accepted. "Surely he has borne our infirmities and carried our

[3.] John 1:14.

[4.] See above, pages 93–94.

[5.] In his 1933 Christology lectures, Bonhoeffer had dealt with the doctrine of the 'two natures' as elaborated in the early church and the Reformation (*DBW* 12:279–348 [*GS* 3:208–31). See also *The Book of Concord*, 600, 588, 594f. (sections underlined).

sorrows." Only by bearing all our infirmities and sorrows in his own body was Jesus able to heal the infirmities and sorrows of human nature (Matt. 8:15-17).[6] "He was wounded for our transgressions and crushed for our iniquities."[7] He bore our sin, and was therefore able to forgive sin; for in his body our sinful flesh had been "accepted." This is why Jesus accepted sinners (Luke 15:2): he bore them in his own body. In Jesus the "acceptable (δεκτόν) year of the Lord" had dawned (Luke 4:19).

229

The incarnate Son of God was thus both an individual self and the new humanity. Whatever he did was at the same time also done on behalf of the new humanity which he bore in his body. He is thus a second Adam, or the "last" Adam (1 Cor. 15:45). For Adam too was both an individual self and at the same time the whole of humanity. Adam also bore the whole of humanity in himself. In him all of humanity has fallen; in "Adam" (which in Hebrew means "human being"), humanity as such has fallen (Rom. 5:19). Christ is the second human being (1 Cor. 15:47) in whom the new humanity is created. He is the "new human being."

It is only with this perspective in mind that we are able to understand the nature of the bodily community which the disciples enjoyed with Jesus. The bond between Jesus and the disciples who followed him was a bodily bond. This was no accident but a necessary consequence of the incarnation. A prophet and teacher would not need followers, but only students and listeners. But the incarnate Son of God who took on human flesh does need a community of followers [Nachfolgegemeinde] who not only participate in his teaching but also in his body. It is thus in the body of Christ that the disciples have community. They live and suffer in bodily community with Jesus. By being in community with the body of Jesus they are placed under the burden of the cross. For in that body they are all borne and accepted.

The earthly body of Jesus is crucified and dies. In his death the new humanity is also crucified and dies with him. Since Christ had not taken on an individual human being, but rather human 'form', sinful flesh, human 'nature', all that he bore, therefore, suffers and dies with him. All our infirmities and all our sin he bears to the cross. It is we who are crucified with him and who die with him. True, Christ's earthly body dies,

---

[6.] Verse 17 quotes from Isa. 53:4: "Surely he has borne our infirmities and carried our diseases; yet we accounted him stricken, struck down by God, and afflicted." [JG/GK]

[7.] Isaiah 53:5: "But he was wounded for our transgressions, crushed for our iniquities; upon him was the punishment that made us whole, and by his bruises we are healed." [JG/GK]

but only to rise again from death as an incorruptible, transfigured body.
230　It is the same body—the tomb was, indeed, empty![8]—and yet it is a new
body. Jesus thus brings humanity not only into death with him, but also
into the resurrection. Thus even in his glorified body he still bears the
humanity which he had taken on during his days on earth.

How then do we come to participate in this body of Christ who did
all this for us? For this much is certain: there is no community with Jesus
Christ other than the community with his body! It is in this body alone
that we are accepted and able to find salvation! The way we do gain a
share in the community of the body of Christ is through the two sacraments of his body, that is, baptism and the Lord's Supper. In a very transparent allusion, John the Evangelist reports that from the crucified body
of Jesus Christ there issued water and blood, the elements of both sacraments (John 19:34, 35). This testimony is confirmed by Paul when he
ties membership in the body of Christ strictly to these two sacraments.[15]
The sacraments have their origin and goal in the body of Christ. Sacraments exist only because there is a body of Christ. There they begin and
end. The word of proclamation alone is not sufficient to bring us into
community with the body of Jesus Christ; the sacrament is necessary too.
Baptism incorporates us as members into the unity of the body of Christ.
The Lord's Supper keeps us in this community (κοινωνία) with Christ's
body.[9] Baptism makes us members of the body of Christ. We are "baptized into" Christ (Gal. 3:27; Rom. 6:3); we are "brought into one body
by baptism" (1 Cor. 12:13). In our death in baptism, the Holy Spirit thus
appropriates to us personally what Christ in his body has gained for the
whole of humanity. We receive the community of the body of Christ in
the same way the disciples and followers of Jesus received it in the early
days, and this means that we are now "with Christ" and "in Christ," and
that "Christ is in us."[10] Once the body of Christ is properly understood,
the meaning of these expressions becomes perfectly clear.

---

15. Eph. 3:6 also refers to the entire gift of salvation, namely, word, baptism,
and the Lord's Supper.

[8.] Luke 24:12; John 20:2-8.
[9.] Regarding the Lord's Supper and κοινωνία, "community," see 1 Cor. 10:16f. Also
see Otto Dudzus's notes in *NL* B 9, 4 (9): *"In baptism through one Spirit into one body. In the
Lord's Supper through one body into one Spirit"* (*DBW* 4:340).
[10.] See the article on ἀκολουθεῖν, "to follow," in Kittel, *Theological Dictionary of the New
Testament:* "In the letters of the New Testament, the term [*nachfolgen*] is replaced by other
expressions (σύν [with], ἐν [in])" (1:215).

It is true that all human beings as such are "with Christ" as a conse- 231
quence of the incarnation, since Jesus bears the whole of human nature.
His life, death, and resurrection are thus real events which involve all
human beings (Rom. 5:18ff.; 1 Cor. 15:22; 2 Cor. 5:14). Nevertheless,
Christians are "with Christ" in a special sense. What for the rest of humanity becomes a cause of death is for Christians a gift of grace. In baptism
they are assured that they have "died with Christ" (Rom. 6:8; Col. 2:20),
are "crucified with him" (Rom. 6:6), "buried with him" (Rom. 6:4; Col.
2:12), and "planted together [with him] in the likeness of his death"
(Rom. 6:5),[11] and that they will therefore also live with him (Rom. 6:8;
Eph. 2:5; Col. 2:12; 2 Tim. 2:11; 2 Cor. 7:3). The reason that "we are with
Christ" is that Christ is Immanuel,[12] "God with us." Only if we come to
know Christ in this way does our "being with Christ" become a gift of
grace. We are then "baptized into Christ" (εἰς), into the community of
his suffering. We become ourselves members of this body, and the community of those who are baptized becomes a body which is none other
than Christ's own body. They are thus "in Christ" (ἐν), and "Christ is in
them." They are no longer "under the law" (Rom. 2:12; 3:19), no longer
"in the flesh" (Rom. 7:5; 8:3, 8, 9; 2 Cor. 10:3), no longer "in Adam" (1
Cor. 15:22). With their entire existence and throughout all expressions
of their life they are henceforth "in Christ."

Paul can describe the miracle of Christ's incarnation in an almost
infinite variety of perspectives. Everything we have said thus far may be
summed up in the phrase: Christ is "for us," not only in his word and
his attitude toward us, but in his bodily life. Christ stands bodily before
God in the place that should be ours. He has stepped into our place. He
suffers and dies for us, and is able to do so because he bears our flesh (2
Cor. 5:21; Gal. 3:13; 1:4; Titus 2:14; 1 Thess. 5:10, etc.). The body of Jesus
Christ is "for us" in the strictest sense of the word—on the cross, in the
word, in baptism, and in the Lord's Supper. All bodily community with
Jesus Christ rests on this fact.

The body of Jesus Christ is identical with the new humanity which he
has assumed. The body of Christ is his church-community [Gemeinde].
Jesus Christ at the same time is himself and his church-community

---

[11.] The NRSV reads: "united with him in a death like his."
[12.] Isaiah 7:14.

232   (1 Cor. 12:12). Since Pentecost[13] Jesus Christ lives here on earth in the
form of his body, the church-community. Here is his body crucified and
risen, here is the humanity he assumed. To be baptized therefore means
to become a member of the church-community, a member of the body
of Christ (Gal. 3:28; 1 Cor. 12:13). To be in Christ means to be in the
church-community. But if we are in the church-community, then we are
also truly and bodily in Jesus Christ. This insight reveals the full richness
of meaning contained in the concept of the body of Christ.

Since the ascension, Jesus Christ's place on earth has been taken by
his body, the church [Kirche]. The church is the present Christ himself.
With this statement we are recovering an insight about the church which
has been almost totally forgotten. While we are used to thinking of the
church as an institution, we ought instead to think of it as a *person*[14] with
a body, although of course a person in a unique sense.

The church is one. All who are baptized are "one in Christ" (Gal. 3:28;
Rom. 12:5; 1 Cor. 10:17). The church is "the human being per se." It is
the *"new human being"* (καινὸς ἄνθρωπος).[15] As such, the church was
created through Christ's death on the cross. Here the hostility between
Jews and Gentiles which had torn humanity apart is abolished, "in order
that he might create in himself one new human being in place of the
two, thus making peace" (Eph. 2:15).[16] The "new human being" is one,
not many. Outside of the church, which is this new human being, there
is only the old, internally divided human being.

The "new human being," which is the church, is "created according
to the likeness of God in true righteousness and holiness and truth"
(Eph. 4:24).[17] The "new human being" is "being renewed in knowledge

---

[13.] See Acts 2:1-41 on the founding of the church through the coming of the Holy
Spirit. Bonhoeffer interpreted these verses at the beginning of the second course in Finkenwalde (see Bethge's notes in *NL* B 18 [3–6] [*DBW* 4:337; *DBW* 14:426–29]).

[14.] See *AB* (*DBWE* 2):105–6, 111–20.

[15.] Since 1935–36 such reflections on the "new human being" appeared in all the
New Testament lectures that were part of each course in Finkenwalde. In *The Epistle to the
Romans*, Karl Barth entitled the section on Rom. 5:1-11 "The New Human Being." Barth
states that this new human being [Mensch] ". . . lives from the *dying of Christ*" (125–41).

[16.] Bonhoeffer avoids here the antiquated German expression Luther used, "in ihm
selber," "in his self," by using "in sich selber," "in himself."

[17.] Following a variant listed in the critical apparatus of the Nestle Greek New
Testament (καὶ ἀληθείᾳ), Bonhoeffer added the words "and truth" to the Luther translation from which he quotes.

according to the image of its creator" (Col. 3:10). It is none other than
Christ himself who is described here as the image of God. Adam was
the first human being bearing the image of the creator. But he lost this
image when he fell. Now a "second human being," a "last Adam," is being
created in the image of God—Jesus Christ (1 Cor. 15:47).[18] The "new
human being" is thus at the same time Christ and the church. Christ is
the new humanity in the new human being. Christ is the church.

The relation of the individual believer to the "new human being" is
described in terms of "putting on"[19] the new human being.[16] The "new
human being" is like a garment made to cover the individual believers.
They are to put on the image[23] of God, that is, Christ and the church. In
baptism we are putting on Christ (Gal. 3:27), which means we are being
incorporated into his body, or into the one human being in whom there
is neither Greek nor Jew, neither free nor slave. Whoever is baptized is
being incorporated into the church-community. No one can become a
new human being except by being within the church, that is, through
the body of Christ. Whoever seeks to become a new human being individually cannot succeed. To become a new human being means to come
into the church, to become a member of Christ's body. The new human
being is not the single individual who has been justified and sanctified;
rather, the new human being is the church-community, the body of
Christ, or Christ himself.

---

16. The term ἐνδύσασθαι[20] somehow implies the spatial metaphor of being
housed or clothed. 2 Corinthians 5:1ff. might perhaps also be interpreted along
these lines. Here we find ἐνδύσασθαι associated with the heavenly οἰκητήριον.[21]
Without this οἰκητήριον human beings are γυμνός, naked, and afraid of God.
They are not covered, but long for a covering. That covering takes place when
they are clothed with the heavenly οἰκητήριον. Does it not make sense to say that
the "putting on" of the church in this world corresponds to a being clothed with
the heavenly church for which Paul longs? In both cases it is the one church with
which we are clothed, the tabernacle of God,[22] the place of the divine presence
and protection; in both cases it is the body of Christ which covers us.

[18.] It is verse 45 which speaks of the "last Adam."
[19.] Ephesians 4:24 (cited in the previous paragraph).
[20.] "To put on." See *SC* (*DBWE* 1):137, and 140; *AB* (*DBWE* 2):111.
[21.] "Dwelling" (v. 2).
[22.] "Tent" or "tabernacle" in verses 1 and 4. See Rev. 21:3: "The home of God is
among mortals."
[23.] Bonhoeffer follows Luther's translation here.

234   Through the Holy Spirit, the crucified and risen Christ exists as the
church-community [Gemeinde],[24] as the "new human being." For
Christ truly is and eternally remains the incarnate one, and the new
humanity truly is his body. Just as the fullness of the godhead became
incarnate in him and dwelled in him, so are Christian believers filled
with Christ (Col. 2:9; Eph. 3:19). Indeed, they themselves are that divine
fullness by being his body, and yet it is Christ alone who fills all in all.[25]
        The unity between Christ and his body, the church, demands that
we at the same time recognize Christ's lordship over his body. This is
why Paul, in developing further the concept of the body, calls Christ the
head of the body (Eph. 1:22; Col. 1:18; 2:19). The distinction is clearly
preserved; Christ is the Lord. There are two events in salvation history,
namely, Christ's ascension and his second coming, which make this distinction necessary; these events categorically rule out any idea of a mysti-
cal fusion between church-community and Christ.[26] The same Christ
who is present in his church-community will return from heaven. In both
cases it is the same Lord and it is the same church; in both cases it is the
very same body of the one who is present here and now, and the one who
will return in the clouds. However, it makes a serious difference whether
we are here or there. Thus, both the unity and the distinction are necessary aspects of the same truth.
        *The church is one; it is the body of Christ. At the same time it is the multiplicity
[Vielheit] and community [Gemeinschaft] of its members* (Rom. 12:5; 1 Cor.
12:12ff.).[27] The body has many members, and each member, whether
it be eye, hand, or foot, remains what it is. That is the very point of Paul's
analogy! A hand does not become an eye, nor does an eye change into an
ear. Each retains its own identity. Nevertheless, they all have an identity
of their own only as members of the one body, as a community that serves

---

[24.] This statement is an extension of the phrase "Christ existing as church-community" [Christus als Gemeinde existierend] in *SC* (*DBWE* 1):189 *et passim;* also see *AB* (*DBWE*
2):112.

[25.] Ephesians 1:23; Luther translates ἐν πᾶσιν as "in all [human beings]." Bonhoeffer
understands the Greek to mean "in all [that exists]."

[26.] See *SC* (*DBWE* 1):137, where Bonhoeffer refers to Eph. 5:32 and Traugott
Schmidt's study *Der Leib Christi.* In *NL* B 9, 4 (6), Dudzus's notes concerning Eph. 5:22-33,
"Heinrich Schlier, '[Christus und die] Kirche im Epheserbrief,'" is mentioned.

[27.] In his doctoral dissertation, Bonhoeffer similarly distinguished three forms in
which the church is being actualized. He speaks of "the plurality of spirit [Geistvielheit],"
"the community of spirit [Geistgemeinschaft]," and "the unity of spirit [Geisteinheit] of
the church-community" (*SC* [*DBWE* 1]:161–62, 165–66, 191–92).

in unity. The unity of the church-community gives identity and meaning 235
to each individual and to the community as a whole, just as Christ and
his body give identity and meaning to the church-community. It is at this
point that the office of the Holy Spirit is thrown into sharp relief.[28] It
is the Holy Spirit who brings Christ to the individuals (Eph. 3:17; 1 Cor.
12:3). It is the Spirit who builds up the church by gathering the individuals, even though in Christ the whole building is already complete
(Eph. 2:22; 4:12; Col. 2:7). The Holy Spirit creates the community (2
Cor. 13:13) of the members of the body (Rom. 15:30; 5:5; Col. 1:8; Eph.
4:3). The Lord is the Spirit (2 Cor. 3:17). The church of Christ is Christ
present through the Holy Spirit. The life of the body of Christ has thus
become our life. In Christ we no longer live our own lives, but Christ lives
his life in us. The life of believers in the church-community is truly *the
life of Jesus Christ in them* (Gal. 2:20; Rom. 8:10; 2 Cor. 13:5; 1 John 4:15).

In the community of the crucified and transfigured body of Jesus
Christ, we take part in Christ's suffering and glory. Christ's cross is laid
upon the body of the church-community. All sufferings under this cross
are Christ's sufferings. This suffering first takes the form of dying the
death upon the cross in baptism; it then is Christians' "daily dying" (1
Cor. 15:31) by virtue of their baptism. It is, in addition, a suffering that
bears an indescribable promise. True, it is only Christ's own suffering
which has atoning power; he suffered "for us" and won the victory "for
us." Yet to those who are not ashamed to belong to the community of
his body, Christ, in the power of his suffering, grants in turn the immeasurable grace to suffer "for him."[29] No greater glory could Christ have
granted to his own; no honor could be more astonishing for Christians
than to be granted the privilege of suffering "for Christ." What actually
takes place here runs totally counter to the law. For according to the
law, we are only capable of suffering the punishment for our own sins.
According to the law, we cannot do or suffer anything that would benefit
us,[30] let alone another, and least of all Christ! The body of Christ, which
was given for us,[31] which suffered the punishment for our sins, frees us 236

[28.] In the Large Catechism, Luther uses the expression "the Holy Spirit and his
office" (*The Book of Concord*, 415).

[29.] See Erich Klapproth's redaction of Bonhoeffer's comment in *NL* B 9, 6 (7): *"He is
so much in us that we are also able to be for him."*

[30.] Romans 7:14-18 presents a similar argument.

to exist "for Christ" in death and in suffering. Now we are able to work and suffer for Christ, for the sake of him who did everything for us! That is the miracle and grace we enjoy in the community of the body of Christ (Phil. 1:29; 2:17; Rom. 8:35ff.; 1 Cor. 4:10; 2 Cor. 4:10; 5:20; 13:9). Even though Jesus Christ has already accomplished all the vicarious suffering necessary for our redemption, his sufferings in this world are not finished yet. In his grace, he has left something unfinished (ὑστερήματα)[32] in his suffering, which his church-community is to complete in this last period before his second coming. This suffering will benefit the body of Christ, the church. Whether this suffering of Christians also has power to atone for sin (1 Peter 4:1) remains an open question. What is clear, however, is that those suffering in the power of the body of Christ suffer in a vicariously representative [stellvertretend] action "for" the church-community, "for" the body of Christ. They are permitted to bear what others are spared. "We always carry in the body the death of the Lord Jesus, so that the life of the Lord Jesus may also be made visible in our bodies. For while we live, we are always being given up to death for Jesus' sake, so that the life of Jesus may be made visible in our mortal flesh. So death is at work in us, but life in you" (2 Cor. 4:10-12; see also 1:5-7; 13:9; Phil. 2:17). There is a specific amount of suffering which has been allotted to the body of Christ. To one person God grants the grace to bear a special suffering on behalf of another person. The suffering must indeed be completed, borne, and overcome. Blessed are those to whom God grants the privilege of suffering for the body of Christ. Such suffering is joy (Col. 1:24; Phil. 2:17). In such suffering, believers may boast that they bear the dying of Jesus Christ and Christ's wounds on their bodies (2 Cor. 4:10; Gal. 6:17). Now a believer is privileged to become the means by which "Christ will be exalted in my body, whether by life or by death" (Phil. 1:20). Such vicariously representative action and suffering, which is carried out by the members of the body of Christ, is itself the very life of Christ who seeks to take shape in his members (Gal. 4:19).

In all this, we are in the community of the first disciples and followers of Jesus.

[31.] 1 Corinthians 11:24.
[32.] Luther translates this term in Col. 1:24 as "what is still lacking."

In concluding this chapter, we must now trace this testimony to the body of Christ throughout scripture as a whole. In so doing, we find that the body of Christ constitutes the fulfillment of the great Old Testament prophecy about the temple of God.

The concept of the body of Christ must be understood not in the context of the Hellenistic usage of this image,[33] but against the background of the Old Testament prophecy about the temple. David intends to build a temple for God. He consults the prophet, who conveys to him what God has to say about his plans: "Are you the one to build me a house to live in? . . . the Lord declares to you that the Lord will make you a house" (2 Sam. 7:5, 11). God's temple can only be built by God's own self. In peculiar contrast to what he has been told before, David is also given the promise that one of his offspring shall build the house for God, and that his rule will last in eternity (vv. 12, 13). "I will be his father, and he shall be my son" (v. 14). Solomon, the "son of peace"—meaning God's peace with the house of David[34]—claimed this promise for himself. He built the temple, and his action was approved by God. Nevertheless, this temple was not the fulfillment of the prophecy. For it was built by human hands, and thus doomed to destruction. The prophecy, still unfulfilled, remained valid. To this day, the Jewish people still wait for the temple built by the son of David whose kingdom shall endure forever. The temple in Jerusalem was destroyed more than once, a sign that it was not the temple of God's promise. Where, then, is the true temple to be found? Christ himself answers that question by applying the prophecy of the temple to his body. "The Jews then said: 'This temple has been under construction for forty-six years, and you will raise it up in three days?' But he was speaking of the temple of his body. After he was raised from the dead, his disciples remembered that he had said this; and they believed the scripture and the word that Jesus had spoken" (John 2:20ff.). The temple which the Jewish people expect is the body of Christ. The temple of the Old Testament is merely a shadow of the body of Christ (Col. 2:17;

238

[33.] See Klapproth's notes in *NL* B 9, 6 (1): "Speech by Agrippa." This is a reference to a fable by Menenius Agrippa, dated 494 B.C.E., according to which the members of the body join in a revolt against the belly but are forced to realize that they themselves depend on the stomach for nourishment; see Livius, *Ab urbe condita* 2.32; Dio Chrysostomus, *Orationes* 33.16. In his doctoral dissertation, *Sanctorum Communio*, Bonhoeffer had argued that "Paul takes the idea of organism from Greek tradition." Prior to 1930, Bonhoeffer had held that it is "misleading" to apply this concept to the church (*SC* [*DBWE* 1]:141).

[34.] This is an interpretation of the name Solomon; see also *DBW* 14:899f. (*GS* 4:315).

Heb. 10:1; 8:5). Jesus is speaking of his human body. He knows that the temple of his earthly body will be destroyed. But he will rise again, and the new, eternal temple will consist of his risen and transfigured body. This is the house built by God's own self for God's own Son; and yet it is also the house built by the Son for the Father. In this house God truly dwells, as does the new humanity, the church-community of Christ. The incarnate Christ himself is the temple which fulfills the prophecy. This corresponds to what the Revelation of John says about the new Jerusalem, namely, that it contains no temple, "for its temple is the Lord God the Almighty *and the Lamb*" (Rev. 21:22).

The temple is the place where God dwells and is graciously present among human beings. It is at the same time the place where the church-community is accepted by God. Both of these aspects have been fulfilled only in the incarnate Jesus Christ. Here is the place where God is truly and bodily present. It is also here that humanity is truly and bodily present, for Christ has accepted humanity in his own body. The body of Christ is thus the place of acceptance, the place of reconciliation and of peace between God and human beings. In the body of Christ God finds us, and in that same body of Christ we find ourselves being accepted by God. Christ's body is the spiritual temple (οἶκος πνευματικός)[35] built from living stones (1 Peter 2:5ff.). Christ is the sole foundation and cornerstone of this temple (Eph. 2:20; 1 Cor. 3:11); at the same time he himself is the temple (οἰκοδομή,[36] Eph. 2:21) in whom the Holy Spirit
239 dwells, filling and sanctifying the hearts of the believers (1 Cor. 3:16; 6:19).[37] The temple of God is the holy church-community in Jesus Christ. The body of Christ is the living temple of God and of the new humanity.

[35.] Luther translates this term in 1 Pet. 2:5 as "spiritual house."

[36.] Luther translates the word as "building."

[37.] See Klapproth's notes in *NL* B 9, 6 (2f.): "Verse 6:19 must be interpreted in light of 3:16: the bodily church-community is the body of Christ. Not a community of souls but rather: *the bodies of the church-community constitute the body of Christ.* . . . The concept of the *church-community* is what makes *fornication* especially significant." See below, pages 264–65.

CHAPTER ELEVEN

THE VISIBLE
CHURCH-COMMUNITY[1]

THE BODY OF CHRIST takes up physical space here on earth.[2] By   241
becoming human Christ claims a place among us human beings. He
came unto his own.[3] Yet when he was born he was given a stable,
"because there was no other place in the inn."[4] And when he died, they
cast him from their midst so that his body hung on the gibbet between
heaven and earth. Nevertheless, the incarnation does entail the claim to
space granted on earth, and anything that takes up space is visible. Thus
the body of Jesus Christ can only be a visible body, or else it is not a body
at all. Our human eyes see Jesus the human being; faith knows him as the
Son of God. Our human eyes see the body of Jesus; faith knows him as
the body of God incarnate. Our human eyes see Jesus in the flesh; faith
knows him as bearing our flesh. "To this human being you shall point
and say: 'Here is God'" (Luther).[5]

[1.] The section on Matt. 5:13-16 (see above, page 110) has the same title.

[2.] See *NL* A 57, 3 (1) (*DBW* 14:422–34 [*WF* 42–51 and *TF* 153–57]). The first New
Testament lecture for the second course at Finkenwalde (cf. above, page 25) was held on
November 11, 1935. Bonhoeffer's text for the first two lectures was sent out to the seminarians of the first course (summer course of 1935) in an insert to a circular letter. The text
begins: "The present situation in church and theology can be summed up in the form of
the following question: Does the church take up a space within the world, and if so, what
kind of space is it? That is basically the question around which the whole theological confrontation with the state revolves."

[3.] John 1:11.

[4.] Luke 2:7.

[5.] Bonhoeffer cites this phrase from Luther quite frequently in his Christology lectures; see *CC* 79 (*GS* 3:187) and (together with Franz Hildebrandt) *NRS* 146 (*DBW* 11:234).
See Hildebrandt's study *Est*, where he says: "I point to the human being and say: 'This is
God'" (82), in reference to Luther's *De captivitate Babylonica* 1520 (*LW* 36 [*WA* 6:511]).
There we read: "Hic homo est deus, hic deus est homo" ("This human being is God, this
God is human").

A truth, a doctrine, or a religion needs no space of its own. Such entities are bodyless.[6] They do not go beyond being heard, learned, and understood. But the incarnate Son of God needs not only ears or even hearts; he needs actual, living human beings who follow him. That is why he called his disciples into following him bodily. His community with them was something everyone could see. It was founded and held together by none other than Jesus Christ, the incarnate one himself. It was the Word made flesh[7] who had called them, who had created the visible, bodily community. Those who had been called could no longer remain hidden; they were the light which has to shine, the city on a hill which is bound to be seen.[8] Over their community stood visibly the cross and suffering of Jesus Christ. For the sake of community with him the disciples had to give up everything, they had to suffer and endure persecution; and yet, in the very midst of being persecuted together with him, they received back in visible form the very things they had lost—brothers and sisters, fields and houses.[9] The community of those who followed him was manifest to the eyes of the world. Here were bodies that acted, worked, and suffered in community with Jesus.

The body of the exalted Lord is likewise a visible body, taking the form of the church-community. How does this body become visible? First, in the *preaching of the word*. "They continued in the apostles' teaching" (Acts 2:42).[10] Every word in this sentence is significant. Preaching here is called teaching (διδαχή) in order to set it apart from all forms of religious speech. The term means communication of facts that have actually taken place. The content of what has to be said is already objectively determined. It simply needs to be conveyed through the 'teaching'. A communication of news is by definition confined to facts which are not

---

[6.] See Bonhoeffer's warning against an idealist ecclesiology in his 1935 lecture "Sichtbare Kirche im Neuen Testament." There he states emphatically that the "danger of an idealist-docetic ecclesiology [is that] a space in this world is denied," and the church would have "only apparent bodily existence." "Docetic" is derived from the Greek δοκεῖν, "to seem or appear," as opposed to reality (*TF* 153 [trans. altered] [*DBW* 14:423 (*GS* 3:325)]). In his 1933 Christology lectures Bonhoeffer rejected Hegel's view of the incarnation as the "most ingenious expression" of the docetic heresy. See *CC* 81 (*DBW* 12:321 [*GS* 3:211]).

[7.] John 1:14.

[8.] Matthew 5:13f.

[9.] Mark 10:28-31.

[10.] See *DBW* 14:429, 431: "Acts 2:42-47. The new community." The biblical translation here does not follow the NRSV, which reads, "They devoted themselves to the apostles' teaching."

yet known. Once these facts are known, it makes no sense to communicate them again. 'Teaching' thus aims by definition at making itself superfluous.[11] However, in strange contrast we read here that the earliest church-community "continued" listening to this teaching. This means that this teaching did not make itself superfluous, but, on the contrary, required precisely this continuing attention. There must, therefore, be some rational necessity for this particular 'teaching' to demand continued attention. This necessity lies in the fact that the teaching in question is "the teaching of the apostles." What does "teaching of the apostles" mean? Apostles are those chosen by God to witness to the facts of the revelation in Jesus Christ. They have lived in bodily community with Jesus. They have seen the one who became incarnate, was crucified, and is risen. They physically touched his body with their hands (1 John 1:1). They are the witnesses whom God the Holy Spirit uses as instruments to proclaim the Word. The apostles' preaching is the witness to the physical event of God's revelation in Jesus Christ. The apostles and prophets are the foundation of the church whose cornerstone is Jesus Christ (Eph. 2:20). Any subsequent preaching must itself be 'apostolic' in the sense of being based on the same foundation. Thus it is the word of the apostles which makes us one with the earliest church-community. But in what way does this apostolic teaching require ongoing and continual hearing? The word of the apostles is truly God's Word in human words (1 Thess. 2:13). It is thus a Word which seeks to accept human beings and which has the power to do so. The Word of God seeks out community in order to accept it. It exists mainly within the community. It moves on its own into the community. It has an inherent impulse toward community.[12] It is wrong to assume that on the one hand there is a word, or a truth, and on the other hand there is a community existing as two separate entities, and that it would then be the task of the preacher to take this word, to manipulate and enliven it, in order to bring it within and apply it to the community. Rather, the Word moves along this path of its own accord. The preacher should and can do nothing more than be a servant of this

243

[11.] Hegel considers "'teaching' as an external means by which I may acquire religion, but which I leave behind once I have faith" (*Lectures on the Philosophy of Religion*, 1:412 [trans. altered]). This sentence is highlighted by a line and a question mark (both showing disapproval) in the margin of Bonhoeffer's copy of the Lasson edition of Hegel.

[12.] See the Finkenwalde homiletics lectures found in *DBW* 14:478–530, especially 504. [See also the passage on the Word's relation to the church-community in the 1936 *Worldly Preaching*, 3ff.] [JG/GK]

movement inherent in the Word itself, and refrain from placing obstacles in its path. The Word goes forth to accept human beings. This is something the apostles knew. It is the very essence of their preaching. They had seen the Word of God with their own eyes, how it had come into the world and assumed human flesh, and with it the whole human race. Now they were compelled to bear witness to nothing else but the fact that God's Word had become flesh, and had come to accept sinners, to forgive their sins and sanctify them. It is this same Word which now enters the church-community. The Word made flesh, the Word which already bears the whole human race, the Word which can no longer exist in isolation from the humanity it has assumed—this same Word now comes to the church-community. And in this Word comes the Holy Spirit, revealing to the single individual and to the church-community the gifts they have already been given in Jesus Christ. The Holy Spirit bestows faith on the hearers, enabling them to believe that, in the word of preaching, Jesus Christ himself has come to be present in our midst in the power of his body. The Holy Spirit enables me to trust that Jesus Christ has come to tell me that he has accepted me and will do so again today.

244

The word of the apostles' preaching is the same Word which has borne in his body the sins of the whole world; it is Christ present in the Holy Spirit. Christ in his church-community is what sums up the "teaching of the apostles," the apostolic preaching. This teaching never makes itself superfluous. Rather, it creates by itself a church-community which remains constantly faithful to this teaching, a community that has been accepted by the Word, and is confirmed in this faith daily. This teaching creates by itself a visible church-community. Moreover, the body of Christ takes on visible form not only in the preaching of the word but also in *baptism and the Lord's Supper,* both of which emanate from the true humanity of our Lord Jesus Christ. In both, Christ encounters us bodily and makes us participants in the community of his body. Both sacraments must be accompanied by the proclamation of the Word. In baptism as well as in the Lord's Supper the content of that proclamation is the death of Christ for us (Rom. 6:3ff.; 1 Cor. 11:26). The gift we receive in both sacraments is the body of Christ. In baptism we are made members of Christ's body. In the Lord's Supper we receive the gift of bodily community (κοινωνία) with the body of the Lord, and through it bodily community with the members of this body. In receiving the gifts of Christ's body, we become, thereby, one body with him.[13] Neither the gift of baptism nor the gift of the Lord's Supper is fully understood if we interpret them only in terms of the forgiveness of sin. The gift of the body conferred in the sacraments presents us with the Lord in bodily form dwelling in his church-community.[14] Forgiveness of sin is indeed a part of this gift of the body of Christ as church-community. This explains why, in direct contrast to our contemporary practice, baptism and the Lord's Supper were originally not tied to the office of apostolic preaching, but were instead administered by the church-community itself (1 Cor. 1:1 and 14ff.; 11:17ff.). Baptism and the Lord's Supper belong solely to the community of the body of Christ. Whereas the word of proclamation is addressed to believers and unbelievers alike, the sacraments have been given solely to the church-community. The Christian community is thus essentially the community gathered to celebrate baptism and the Lord's Supper, and only then is it the community gathered to hear the word proclaimed.[15]

245

That the community of Jesus Christ claims a *space* in this world *for its proclamation* is now clear. The body of Christ becomes visible in the church-community that gathers around word and sacrament.

This community is a differentiated whole. The body of Christ as church-community includes both differentiation and a common order. These are characteristics essential to the body itself. A body lacking differentiation is in the process of decomposition. According to Paul's teaching, the form of the living body of Christ is that of differentiated members (Rom. 12:5; 1 Cor. 12:12ff.). In this case it is impossible to make a distinction between content and form, essence and appearance.[16] To make it would mean a denial of the body of Christ, that is, of the Christ

---

[13.] See Dudzus's notes in *NL* B 9, 4 (9), mentioning the "sermon of 1519." This refers to Luther's "The Blessed Sacrament of the Holy and True Body of Christ, 1519" (*LW* 35/1:45–73 [*WA* 2:742–58]). The same reference is found in *SC* (*DBWE* 1):244, and frequently throughout Bonhoeffer's writings.

[14.] See Klapproth's notes in *NL* B 9, 6 (10f.): "Regarding the power of the Lord's Supper, see an early apocryphal story, according to which, during the first Christians' celebration of the Lord's Supper, death and Satan are seen lamenting their lost power." See also Mickley's note in *NL* B 9, 3 (15): "'Who has robbed us of our power?' The Christians then spread out their hands, making the sign of the cross and proclaim, 'Here is Jesus Christ the crucified One'" (Cf. *DBW* 14:434, editorial note 54).

[15.] See *SC* (*DBWE* 1):237–47.

[16.] This "Protestant distinction" (see *SC* [*DBWE* 1]:210) was also proposed by Sohm in his *Kirchenrecht*. He revised this proposition later. See also Bonhoeffer's comment in *Sanctorum Communio* that "the 'essential' church can literally be seen in the empirical church" (*SC* [*DBWE* 1]:220).

who became flesh (1 John 4:3).[17] Thus the body of Christ, in claiming a *space for proclamation,* at the same time claims a *space for the order of the church-community.*

The order of the church-community is of divine origin and character, though it is, of course, intended to serve and not to rule. The offices of the church-community are "ministries" (διακονίαι) (1 Cor. 12:4). They

246   are appointed by God (1 Cor. 12:28), by Christ (Eph. 4·11), by the Holy Spirit (Acts 20:28)[18] *within* but not *by* the church-community. Even where the church-community itself assigns offices, it does so in complete submission to the guidance of the Holy Spirit (Acts 13:2 *et passim*). Both office and church-community have their origin in the triune God. The offices exist to serve the church-community; they can be justified spiritually only through this service. That is why different congregations require different offices or ministries. For example, the congregation in Jerusalem demanded different offices or ministries than those required in Paul's mission churches. To be sure, the ordering as such is given by God, but its specific form is open to change, and to be determined only by the spiritual judgment of the church-community itself as it appoints its members for service. Even the charisms[19] which the Holy Spirit confers upon individuals are in the same sense strictly subject to the discipline of serving the church-community, for God is not a God of disorder but of peace (1 Cor. 14:32f.). The Holy Spirit becomes visibly present (φανέρ-ωσις,[20] 1 Cor. 12:7) in the fact that everything is done for the benefit of the church-community. Apostles, prophets, teachers, overseers (bishops), deacons, elders, presiding officers, and leaders (1 Cor. 12:28ff.; Eph. 2:20 and 4:11) are all servants of the church-community, the body

---

[17.] In his copy of the Nestle edition of the New Testament, Bonhoeffer underlined the variant εν σαρκι εληλυδοτα (which the Luther Bible renders as "having come in the flesh"), which is not found in the main text.

[18.] In his position paper "Irrlehre in der bekennenden Kirche?" the three verses cited in this sentence, and other biblical verses, provide the basis for Bonhoeffer's argument from scripture: "The appointment to an office in the church by an authority outside the church is regarded as completely impossible in the New Testament" (*DBW* 14:703 [*GS* 2:266]).

[19.] In *NL* A 57, 3, Pt. III 6, Bonhoeffer gives the following definition: "*A charism is the subjective prerequisite, made possible by the Holy Spirit, to serve the church-community in an objective sense*"—that is, in a concrete way such as preaching, teaching, ministries of compassion and care (see *DBW* 14:454).

[20.] "disclosure." The 1937 German edition cited 1 Cor. 12:6 instead of verse 7 as reference. Erroneous references are relatively frequent throughout this chapter.

of Christ. Appointed to serve the church-community, their office is of divine origin and character. Only the church-community can release them from their service. Therefore, although the church-community is at liberty to modify the form of its order according to its needs, any tampering with the church's order from the outside is an infringement on the visible form of Christ's body itself.[21]

Of special importance among the offices of the church-community in every age is the untainted administration of word and sacrament. Here the following must be considered.[22] Proclamation will always vary and differ according to the commission and gifts of the preachers. However, whether it be the proclamation of Paul, or of Peter, or of Apollos, or of Christ, the one indivisible Christ must be recognized in them all (1 Cor. 1:11ff.). All are to work hand in hand (1 Cor. 3:6). The emergence of different schools of thought leads to divisive bickering, in which all involved promote their own self-interest (1 Tim. 6:5 and 6:20; 2 Tim. 2:16; 3:8; Titus 1:10). Here it is all too easy for 'godliness'[23] to be mistaken for earthly gain, whether it be gain in honor, power, or wealth. The tendency to pose problems for the sake of posing problems also will blossom and divert people from the clear and simple truth (2 Tim. 3:7). It will lure into self-centered intransigence and disobedience toward God's command. In contrast to this, genuine proclamation will always aim at a teaching which is sound[24] and salutary (2 Tim. 4:3; 1 Tim. 1:10; 4:16; 6:1; Titus 1:9 and 1:13; 2:1; 3:8), and for safeguarding proper church order and unity.

It is not always easy to recognize where a legitimate theological interpretation ends and heresy begins.[25] One congregation may still accept a particular teaching as legitimate, while another has already rejected it as heresy (Rev. 2:6 and 2:15ff.). However, once heresy has been identified, it must be rejected without compromise. The heretical teacher is

247

[21.] In the third thesis, the Theological Declaration of Barmen of 1934 emphasizes this purpose of the church's own order as a witness to the world (see Leith, *Creeds of the Churches*, 517ff.). [Here the subtle critique of Nazi attempts to interfere in and control church policies and practices is unmistakable.] [JG/GK]

[22.] Regarding the following passage, see *DBW* 14:842 (*GS* 3:380).

[23.] 2 Timothy 3:5: "holding to the outward form of godliness but denying its power."

[24.] In *NL* B 9, 4 (30) Dudzus writes: "The concept of *health* plays a strong role in the Pastoral Letters. There is unhealthy teaching which spreads like a cancer." See *DBW* 14:964 (*GS* 4:352), which makes reference to 2 Tim. 2:17.

[25.] See *DB-ER* 445. In 1934 Barth spoke of differences that generate schools of thought, *schulbildend*, and those that lead to schisms in the church, *kirchentrennend* (See also *DBW* 14:261–67).

cast out of the Christian community, and is excluded from any personal community with its members (Gal. 1:8; 1 Cor. 16:22; Titus 3:10; 2 John 10ff.). The word of authentic proclamation must therefore create both unity and separation in a visible way. It thus becomes clear that space *for proclamation and for the order* of the church-community are divinely ordained necessities.

We must now ask whether spaces of proclamation and order are already sufficient to describe the visible form of the community of the body of Christ, or whether this community claims yet another space in the world. The answer of the New Testament is unambiguous. It holds that the church-community claims a physical space here on earth not only for its worship and its order, but also for the daily life of its members. That is why we must now speak of the *living space* [Lebensraum] of the visible church-community.[26]

Jesus' community with his disciples was all-encompassing, extending to all areas of life. The individual's entire life was lived within this community of the disciples. And this community is a living witness to the bodily humanity of the Son of God. The bodily presence of the Son of God demands the bodily commitment to him and with him throughout one's daily life. With all our bodily living existence, we belong to him who took on a human body for our sake. In following him, the disciple is inseparably linked to the body of Jesus.

The first report about the young church-community in Acts (2:42ff.; 4:32ff.) testifies to this same fact: "They devoted themselves to the apostles' teaching and to the community, to the breaking of bread and the prayers."[27] "All who believed were together and had all things in common."[28] It is instructive to note that in this passage community (κοινωνία) finds its place between the word of proclamation and the

---

[26.] Bonhoeffer's index of the 1937 edition of *Nachfolge* refers to the following section under the subject "Incarnation." See 1935–36 *NLA* 57, 3 Pt. IV 1, where Bonhoeffer argues that the space of the church-community "includes the whole person in all areas of life and throughout all relationships. The reason for this is to be found in the *incarnation* of Jesus Christ. Since he became completely human in all relationships of life, he has a rightful claim on the human being as a whole. Christ's call to follow him is addressed to the entire person. Whoever seeks to belong to his church-community must totally belong to him. This space, which has its *foundation* in the presence of the incarnate Christ, is defined and delimited by *the commandments.* The proclamation of the whole incarnate Christ on one side, and the commandments on the other, are the perimeters within which the Christian lives" (see *DBW* 14:460).

[27.] Acts 2:42. The NRSV translates "to the community" as "[to the] fellowship."

[28.] Acts 2:44. Verse 43 ("many wonders and signs were being done") is omitted.

sacrament of the Lord's Supper. To define the nature of this community in such a way is not by accident, since this community springs ever anew from the word of proclamation, and continues to find its goal and fulfillment in the Lord's Supper. All Christian community exists between word and sacrament. It begins and ends in worship. It awaits the final banquet with the Lord in the kingdom of God. A community with such an origin and such a goal is a perfect community, in which even the material things and goods of this life are assigned their proper priority. Here a perfect community is established freely, joyfully, and by the power of the Holy Spirit, a community in which "there was not a needy person," in which possessions were distributed "as any had need," and in which "no one claimed private ownership of any possessions."[29] The fact that this practice was commonplace reveals the community's complete freedom, a freedom grounded in the gospel, and which requires no coercion. They were indeed "of one heart and soul."[30]

249

This young church-community was visible to all and, strangely enough, had "the goodwill of all the people" (Acts 2:47). Was this fact due to the blindness of the people of Israel, who no longer perceived the cross of Jesus as the foundation of this perfect communal bond? Or was it perhaps an anticipation of the day in which all the world shall honor God's people? Was it an expression of God's loving-kindness which, particularly in times of growth, serious struggle, or separation between believers and their enemies, will surround the church-community with ordinary human goodwill and concern for what happens to it?[31] Or was it simply that the church found favor with those who had cried "Hosanna" but not "crucify him"?[32] "And day by day the Lord added to their number those who were being saved." This visible church-community whose reality fully extends to all areas of life [Lebensgemeinschaft] invades the world and snatches its children. The daily growth of the church-community demonstrates the power of the Lord who dwells in its midst.

[29.] Acts 2:45; 4:32, 34f.; cf. Dudzus's notes, *NL* B 9, 6 (11) (*DBW* 14:722–23): "*Although still formally binding, even the holiest of rights,* the right of property, *loses its seriousness.*"

[30.] Acts 4:32; Acts 4:32-35 is a parallel to Acts 2:42-47.

[31.] Cf. *DBW* 14:934 (*GS* 4:325) and Dudzus's notes in *NL* B 9, 4 (3), which say that ". . . there is always this clement atmosphere whenever a young church comes into being. Cases in point are the first Christian congregation, the Jewish community in the exile, and also the period of the Reformation and the 'Confessional Community.'"

[32.] For "Hosanna," see Mark 11:9; for "crucify," see Mark 15:13f.

The first disciples are inseparable from their Lord: wherever he is, there they must also be, and wherever they will be, there their Lord will also be until the end of time.[33] Whatever the disciples do, they do it within the communal bond of the community of Jesus and as its members. Even the most secular act now takes place within the bounds of the church-community. This then is valid for the body of Christ: where one member is, there is also the whole body, and where the body is, there is also the member.[34] There is no area of life where the member would be allowed or would even want to be separated from the body. Wherever one member happens to be, whatever one member happens to do, it always takes place "within the body," within the church-community, "in Christ." Life as a whole is taken up "into Christ." Whether weak or strong, Christians are in Christ (Phil. 4:13; 2 Cor. 13:4). They work and toil or they rejoice "in the Lord" (Rom. 16:9, 12; 1 Cor. 15:58; Phil. 4:4); they speak and admonish in Christ (2 Cor. 2:17; Phil. 2:1), they show hospitality in Christ (Rom. 16:2), they marry in Christ (1 Cor. 7:39), they are imprisoned in the Lord (Phil. 1:13, 23), they are slaves in Christ (1 Cor. 7:22). The whole breadth of human relationships among Christians is encompassed by Christ, by the church-community.

The full life in Christ, in the church-community, is granted to every Christian through being baptized into the body of Christ. It is a terrible distortion of the New Testament view to reduce the gift of baptism to the right to participate in the sermon and the Lord's Supper, that is, in the means of grace, and in addition, perhaps, to the right to hold office and to share in the ministries of the church-community. Rather, any baptized person receives an unrestricted privilege to participate in all areas of the communal life of the members of the body of Christ. To allow other baptized Christians to participate in worship but to refuse to have community with them in everyday life, and to abuse them and treat them with contempt, is to become guilty against the body of Christ itself. To acknowledge that other baptized Christians have received the gifts of salvation, and then to deny them the provisions necessary for this earthly life, or to leave them knowingly in affliction and distress, is to make a mockery of the gift of salvation and to behave like a liar. When the Holy Spirit has spoken, but we still continue to listen to the voice of our race,[35]

[33.] Matthew 28:20.

[34.] Cf. 1 Cor. 12:12-26.

[35.] Bonhoeffer's catechetical lesson plan for confirmation from 1936 states that the church-community knows "that the Holy Spirit binds human beings closer together than

our nature, or our sympathies and antipathies, we are profaning the sacrament. Baptism into the body of Christ changes not only a person's 251 personal status with regard to salvation, but also their relationships throughout all of life.

The slave Onesimus had run away from his Christian master, Philemon, inflicting much harm on him. Now, after Onesimus has been baptized, Philemon is asked to "receive him back forever" (Philemon 15), "no longer as a slave but more than a slave, a beloved brother . . . both in the flesh and in the Lord" (Philemon 16).[36] In specifically calling Onesimus a brother "according to the flesh," Paul issues a warning against the dangerous misunderstanding of those "privileged"[37] Christians who think having community with Christians of lesser status and legal standing is acceptable in worship, but not to be practiced outside that context. Instead, Paul calls Onesimus Philemon's "brother according to the flesh"! And he instructs Philemon to receive his slave back like a brother, even as if he were Paul himself (v. 17), and in brotherly love to ignore the harm Onesimus inflicted on him (v. 18). Paul asks Philemon to do all this voluntarily, although, if need be, he would also not hesitate to issue it as a command (vv. 8-14). Besides, Paul is confident that Philemon will go beyond what is requested of him (v. 21). Onesimus is Philemon's "brother according to the flesh" because he is baptized. Even though Onesimus might remain a slave of his master Philemon, everything in their relationship with each other has radically changed. And the basis for that change? The free master and the slave have become members of the body of Christ. Their community with each other now embodies, like a small cell, the very life of the body of Christ, that is, the church-community. "As many of you as were baptized into Christ have clothed your-

race and history. Within the church-community there is neither . . . Jew nor German" (*DBW* 14:814 [*GS* 3:362]).

[36.] Dudzus's notes,1937 *NL* B 9, 4 (9) contains the note: "Philemon . . . (Steglitz Synod meeting: Our relationship to our Jewish brothers, i.e., to baptized Jews)" (*DBW* 14:823). Regarding the synod meeting of the Confessing Church within the Old Prussian Union Church in Berlin-Steglitz on September 23–26, 1935, see *DB-ER* 486f. The synod missed the opportunity to speak out clearly and unequivocally against the Nuremberg Laws, which had been enacted just a few days before on September 15, 1935. These laws inaugurated and officially sanctioned a new chapter in the persecution of Jews. In a letter dated October 5, 1935, and addressed to the parents of Gerhard Vibrans, Eberhard Bethge expressed outrage over "the sentence that was spoken at the Synod: 'Baptism does not confer any civil rights or claims to the Jew'" (Andersen et al., *So ist es gewesen*, 209).

[37.] Just as Philemon was "privileged" with regard to Onesimus, so were non-Jews with regard to Jews in the Third Reich.

selves with Christ. There is no longer Jew or Greek, there is no longer slave or free, there is no longer male and female; for all of you are one in Christ Jesus" (Gal. 3:27f.; Col. 3:11). Within the church-community, one no longer sees others as free or slave, as man or woman, but only as members of Christ's body. To be sure, this does not mean that a slave would no longer be a slave or a man cease to be a man. But this is a far cry from continuing to address everyone within the church-community with a view to their status as Jew or Greek, free or slave. This is precisely what should no longer happen. We see each other exclusively as members of the body of Christ, that is, as all being one in him. Jew and Greek, free and slave, man and woman now have community with each other because they are all part of the church-community of the body of Christ. They are in Christ wherever they live, speak, or interact with one another, and there the church-community is a reality. This fact determines and transforms their community with each other in a decisive way. The wife obeys her husband "in the Lord," slaves really serve God in serving their masters, and masters know that they too have a Lord in heaven (Col. 3:18—4:1).[38] But they are now all brothers and sisters, "both in the flesh and in the Lord."[39]

The church-community has, therefore, a very real impact on the life of the world. It gains space for Christ. For whatever is "in Christ" is no longer under the dominion of the world, of sin, or of the law. Within this newly created community, all the laws of this world have lost their binding force. This sphere in which brothers and sisters are loved with Christian love is subject to Christ; it is no longer subject to the world. The church-community can never consent to any restrictions of its service of love and compassion toward other human beings. For wherever there is a brother or sister, there Christ's own body is present; and wherever Christ's body is present, his church-community is also always present, which means I must also be present there.[40]

All who belong to the body of Christ have been freed from and called out of the world. They must become visible to the world not only through the communal bond evident in the church-community's order and worship, but also through the new communal life among brothers and sisters in Christ.

¶Where the world despises other members of the Christian family,

---

[38.] More accurately, Col. 3:18, 22f.; 4:1.

[39.] Philemon 16.

[40.] For a similar statement, see *Sanctorum Communio*, where Bonhoeffer speaks about Luther's sermon on the Lord's Supper from 1519 (*SC* [*DBWE* 1]:181).

Christians will love and serve them. If the world does violence to them, Christians will help them and provide them relief. Where the world subjects them to dishonor and insult, Christians will sacrifice their own honor in exchange for their disgrace. Where the world seeks gain, Christians will renounce it; where it exploits, they will let go; where it oppresses, they will stoop down and lift up the oppressed. Where the world denies justice, Christians will practice compassion; where it hides behind lies, they will speak out for those who cannot speak,[41] and testify for the truth. For the sake of brothers or sisters—be they Jew or Greek, slave or free,[42] strong or weak, of noble or of common birth[43]—Christians will renounce all community with the world, for they serve the community of the body of Jesus Christ. Being a part of this community, Christians cannot remain hidden from the world. They have been called out of the world and follow Christ.

However, "Let each of you remain in the condition [Beruf] in which you were called. Were you a slave when called? Do not be concerned about it. Even if you can gain your freedom, make use of your present condition now more than ever" (i.e., by remaining a slave![44]). "For whoever was called in the Lord as a slave is a freed person belonging to the Lord, just as whoever was free when called is a slave of Christ. You were bought with a price; do not become slaves of human masters. In whatever condition you were called, brothers and sisters, there remain with God" (1 Cor. 7:20-24). Does all this not sound very different from that first time Jesus called the disciples to follow him? Then the disciples had to leave everything behind[45] to follow Jesus. Now we are told: let

---

[41.] Proverbs 31:8 is heavily underlined in Bonhoeffer's Luther Bible. Cf. Bonhoeffer's statement in a letter to Erwin Sutz from September 11, 1934: "We also have to finally abandon our reluctance to speak out against the actions of the state. This reluctance is usually being justified on theological grounds, whereas in fact, of course, it simply is born out of fear. 'Speak out for those who have no voice' (Prov. 31:8)—who in the church today remembers that this is the least scripture demands from us in times such as these?" (*DBW* 13:204 [*GS* 1:42]). [This scriptural passage was frequently used by Bonhoeffer to reinforce his demand that the church speak up on behalf of the persecuted Jews. See Bethge, "Bonhoeffer and the Jews," 69–83, and Kelly, "Bonhoeffer and the Jews," 138–51.] [JG/GK]

[42.] Galatians 3:28.

[43.] 1 Corinthians 1:26-28.

[44.] Dudzus's notes, 1937 *NL* B 9,4(22) on 1 Cor. 7:21: μᾶλλον χρῆσαι [make use of your present condition now more than ever"], which was probably incorrectly translated by Luther as 'to use it to become free.' More correctly: stay in the state of slavery, bear it." See also Harnack, *The Mission and Expansion of Christianity* (1924), 192, editorial note 4. The list of situations "in Christ" includes those who are slaves; see above, 234f.

[45.] Mark 10:28.

each of you remain in the condition in which you were called! How are
we to reconcile the contradiction? Only by recognizing that the sole
point both in the call of Jesus and in the exhortation of the apostles is
to bring those that are called into the community of the body of Jesus
Christ. The first disciples had to come with Jesus in order to stay in
254   bodily community with him. But now, through word and sacrament,
the body of Christ is no longer confined to a single geographical location. The risen and exalted Christ has closed in on the world, in fact the
body of Christ—in the form of the church-community—has broken into
the very midst of the world itself. Those who are baptized are baptized
into the body of Christ. Christ has come to them, taken their life into
his own, and thus robbed the world of its possession. Those who are
baptized as slaves still remain slaves. But they are now already part of
the community of the body of Jesus Christ. As slaves they have already
been rescued from the world and become freed persons of Christ. Thus
slaves may remain slaves! As members of Christ's community they have
gained the kind of freedom which no rebellion or revolution[46] could
have brought them or could ever bring them. Paul's exhortation to
the slaves to remain slaves is most certainly not intended to tie them
closer to the world, to fasten their life to this world even further by
adding a "religious anchor," or to make them better and more loyal
citizens of this world! His statements are certainly not a justification or
a Christian apology for a shadowy social order.[47] The exhortation is
valid not because vocations in the world are so excellently ordered and
divinely instituted that this order must not be overturned. Rather, it is
valid because of the fact that Jesus Christ already has brought about an
upheaval of the whole world by liberating both slave and free. Would a
revolution which simply overturned the existing order of society[48] not
255   obscure the awareness of God's new ordering of all things through Jesus

---

[46] The National Socialists hailed Hitler's takeover in 1933 and the measures that
followed as a revolution.

[47.] On this point Bonhoeffer disagrees with Troeltsch's *The Social Teachings of the
Christian Churches*, which in citing "a study by Overbeck (*Studien zur Geschichte der alten
Kirche*, 1875) concerning 'the position of the ancient church toward slavery in the Roman
empire,'" speaks quite critically of the Christian point of view: ". . . Christianity considered
slavery as part and parcel of the traditional status quo, and actually provided it with additional underpinnings, as is evident by the fact that sometime later the church itself owned
slaves and even obeyed a law prohibiting their release" (132f.).

[48.] Barth considers Rom. 12:21—13:7 a warning against "the titanic mind-set behind
any revolution" (*The Epistle to the Romans*, 478), against the hubris of all revolutionaries.

Christ, and the establishment of his church-community? Moreover, would every such attempt not actually hinder and delay the abolition of the entire world order and the dawning of God's realm? The exhortation is also most certainly not based on the idea that the fulfillment of our secular vocation as such would already be identical with living the Christian life. Rather, by renouncing rebellion against the forms of order of this world, Christians express most convincingly that they expect nothing from the world but everything from Christ and his coming realm. That is why slaves are to remain slaves! Because this world is not in need of reform, but ripe to be demolished[49]—that is why slaves are to remain slaves! They have God's promise of something far better! Is it not both judgment enough on the world and comfort enough for slaves to know that the Son of God took "the form of a slave" (Phil. 2:5)[50] when he came to this earth? And Christians who were called as slaves—do they not, in their very existence as slaves in the world, already have enough distance from the world to naturally prevent them from loving, desiring, or even worrying about it? Therefore, slaves ought to suffer not as a consequence of being rebellious but as members of the church-community and the body of Christ! That is how the world is getting ripe for its demise.

"Do not become slaves of human masters!"[51] This would happen in two different ways. First, it may take place through a rebellion against and the overthrow of the established order. Second, it may come about by investing the current order with a religious significance.[52] "In whatever condition you were called, brothers and sisters, there remain with God." "With God"—and therefore "do not become slaves of human masters," neither by rebellion, nor by false submission. To remain

---

[49.] See Bonhoeffer's comments on 1 Cor. 13:13: ". . . the [eschatological] consummation in this world is the cross. . . . [This shows us] that this present world is ripe, in fact more than ripe, to be demolished" (*DBW* 13:403 [*GS* 5:559f.]). See also Barth's statement that "the last thing, the ἔσχατον, . . . is a radical break with everything that is next to the last" (*The Word of God and the Word of Man*, 324).

[50.] The quotation actually is from verse 7.

[51.] Bonhoeffer continues the exegesis of 1 Cor. 7:23.

[52.] See Dudzus's notes on 1 Cor. 7:23: "Paul is being misunderstood if this is considered an affirmation of the orders of creation" (*NL* B 9, 4 [24]). [On Bonhoeffer's criticism of the orders of creation and his use of the alternative term, orders of preservation, see *DB-ER* 214–15 and *TF* 96–101.] [JG/GK]

bound to God in one's calling or vocation in the midst of the world means to remain a member of the body of Christ within the visible church-community. It means to bear living testimony, through sharing in the church's worship and living the life of discipleship, that the world has been overcome.

256 Therefore, "let every person be subject to the governing authorities" (Rom. 13:1ff.). Christians must not be drawn upward, toward those who hold power and authority. Instead, their calling is to remain below. The authorities govern over (ὑπέρ) them, and they remain under (ὑπο) them. The world rules; Christians serve. In this, they have community with their Lord who became a slave. "So Jesus called them and said to them, 'You know that among the Gentiles those whom they recognize as their rulers lord it over them, and their great ones are tyrants over them. But it shall not be so[53] among you; but whoever wishes to become great among you must be your servant, and whoever wishes to be first among you must be slave of all. For the Son of Man came not to be served but to serve, and to give his life as a ransom for many'" (Mark 10:42-45). "For there is no authority except from God."[54] This statement is addressed to Christians, not the authorities! Paul wants Christians to know that their place to recognize and do God's will is precisely that subordinate place down below accorded them by the authorities. They are to take comfort from the fact that God will use the authorities as an instrument through which to work for their welfare, and that their God is Lord over the authorities. But this statement must be more than an abstract consideration and idea about the nature of authority (ἐξουσία—note the singular!)[55] in general. It must determine the attitudes of Christians to the actually existing authorities (αι δὲ οὖσαι . . .). Whoever resists them resists what God has decreed (διαταγῇ τοῦ θεοῦ), the God who intended for the world to exercise authority, and for Christ and the Christians belonging to him to gain victory through service.[56] Christians failing to recognize this fact would themselves become subject to judgment (v. 2), for they would once again no longer be any different from the world. Now what is it that

---

[53.] The NRSV reads "is not so."

[54.] Bonhoeffer continues the exegesis of Romans 13 with verse 1b.

[55.] The Greek text of Rom. 13:1a has the plural; verse 1b changes to the singular. Verse 1c will revert to the plural.

[56.] Cf. above, the citation from Mark 10:45.

so easily triggers the opposition of Christians against the authorities? It is the fact that they take offense at the mistakes and the injustice perpetrated by the authorities. But with considerations like these, Christians are already in grave danger of paying attention to something other than the will of God, which alone they are called to fulfill. They themselves ought to strive for the good in all things, and to practice it in the way God commands them. Then they need have "no fear" of authority, "for rulers are not a terror to good conduct [Werk],[57] but to bad [böse]" (v. 3). And what, indeed, would Christians have to fear if they stay with their masters and do good? "Do you wish to have no fear of the authority? Then do what is good"—do what is good! You do it. That is the only thing that counts. It is not important for you what others might do, but what you will do. Do what is good, fearlessly, unreservedly, and unconditionally. For how can you be in a position to criticize the authorities if you yourself fail to do what is good? Do you intend to pass judgment on others, you, who are submitted to judgment yourselves?[58] Do you wish to have no fear? Then do what is good! "And you will receive the approval of the authority; for it is God's servant for your good." It is not as if receiving approval could be the driving motive behind our doing what is good; it cannot even be our aim. Rather it is a bonus, indeed an inevitable bonus, if in fact all is well with the authority. Paul's thought is so exclusively focused on the Christian community that he is concerned only about its salvation and its conduct, that he feels bound to warn Christians not to commit any injustice and evil themselves. This exclusive focus prevents Paul from leveling any accusation against the authority. "But if you do what is wrong, you should be afraid, for the authority does not bear the sword in vain! It is the servant of God to execute wrath on the wrongdoer" (v. 4). It is absolutely paramount that no wrongdoing take place within the Christian community. It is once again Christians who are addressed here, not the authority. What is important to Paul is that Christians remain in a state of repentance and obedience wherever they may be and by whatever conflicts they may be threatened. To justify or condemn an authority of this world is irrelevant to him in this context! No authority can legitimately interpret Paul's words as a divine justification of its existence. If by chance there actually was a case in

257

[57.] Bonhoeffer's use of the singular follows the primary text of the Nestle Greek New Testament; Luther translates this as plural.

[58.] Romans 13:2; cf. Matt. 7:1.

258   which this statement would be heard by an authority, then it would also become a call to repentance for that authority, just as in this context it is in truth a call to repentance for the church-community. Those in authority (ἄρχων)[59] hearing this statement could never interpret it as a divine authorization of their conduct in office. Rather they would have to hear it as a call to be a servant of God by working for the good of the whole of Christianity, which does what is good. This mandate would inevitably lead them into repentance. Paul addresses Christians rather than the authorities, but he does this certainly not because the way this world is ordered is so good, but because its good or bad qualities are irrelevant compared to the only thing that is truly important, namely, that the church-community submit and live according to God's will. Paul does not intend to instruct the Christian community about the tasks of those in authority, but instead *only deals with the tasks of the Christian community toward authority.*

Christians deserve to receive approval from the authorities! If instead of receiving approval they are being subjected to punishment and persecution, what fault is that of theirs? After all, they were not seeking approval for doing what now turns out to be the reason for their punishment, nor did they do what is good for fear of being punished. Even if they now are being subjected to suffering instead of receiving approval, they remain free before God and free from fear, and have not brought any shame upon the church-community. They obey the authorities not in order to gain some advantage, but "because of [their] conscience" (v. 5).[60] The mistake of the authority cannot trouble the conscience of Christians. They remain free and without fear and, by submitting to suffering, even though they are innocent, they are still able to render the obedience they owe to the authorities. For they know that in the end it is God who rules, not the authorities, and that any authority is ultimately God's servant. Authority as the servant of God—here speaks the same

---

[59.] Luther, following the Greek text (ἄρχόντες), translates Rom. 13:3a as a plural; cf. NRSV, which reads: "rulers." [Here again Bonhoeffer contradicts the opinion widely held among German Christians that Hitler governs by some form of 'divine authorization' and that this 'justifies' the conduct of his government and the measures the Nazis take to enforce their law and order.] [JG/GK]

[60.] During his imprisonment, Bonhoeffer used this passage in 1943 as a cover in laying out his defense before the *Oberstkriegsgerichtsrat* or judge advocate, Manfred Roeder: "The appeal to subjection to the will and the demands of authority for the sake of the Christian conscience has probably seldom been expressed more strongly than there. That is my personal attitude to these questions!" (*LPP* 60–61 [*DBW* 16:417]). "Being imprisoned" is among the conditions "in Christ" listed above, page 234.

apostle who himself frequently had to suffer unjust imprisonment at the hands of this authority, who on three occasions received the cruel punishment of being flogged,[61] and who was aware of the edict by Emperor Claudius to banish all Jews from Rome (Acts 18:1ff.).[62] Authority as the servant of God—here speaks someone who knows that all powers and authorities of this world have already been stripped of their power, that Christ has already led them to the cross in triumphant victory,[63] and that it will be but a short while until all of this must become manifest.[64]

    259

The framework for all of what Paul has to say regarding authority is summed up in his introductory admonition: "Do not be overcome by evil, but overcome evil with good" (Rom. 12:21).[65] The passage on authority does not deal with the question whether a given authority is good or evil; its concern is that Christians should overcome all evil.

Whether or not to pay taxes to the emperor was a question that was truly full of temptation for the Jews, for they placed their hope in the destruction of the imperial Roman government and the establishment of their own rule. But for Jesus and his followers it is an uncomplicated question. "Give therefore to the emperor the things that are the emperor's" (Matt. 22:21), says Jesus. And "for the same reason you also pay taxes" (Rom. 13:6) is the way Paul concludes this passage. For Christians, this duty is fully in line with the command of Jesus, for they merely return to the emperor what belongs to him anyway. In fact, those who demand taxes from them and insist on their payment Christians ought to consider as "servants of God" (λειτουργοί)[66] (v. 6). Of course, this relationship is not reversible. Paul does not claim that Christians are engaged in worship [Gottesdienst] when they pay taxes, but only that those who levy taxes thereby do their service to God [Gottesdienst]![67] But this is not the kind

---

[61.] 2 Corinthians 11:23-25.

[62.] Acts 18:2. This is a clear, although exegetically concealed, allusion to the treatment of Jews in the Third Reich. [Bonhoeffer makes this even more explicit in a remarkable passage from his *Ethics:* "An expulsion of the Jews from the West must necessarily bring with it the expulsion of Christ. For Jesus Christ was a Jew" (89–90 [*DBW* 6:95]).][JG/GK]

[63.] Colossians 2:14f.

[64.] See Matt. 10:23, 26.

[65.] Barth takes this verse as the motto for the following passage, Rom. 13:1ff. (*The Epistle to the Romans*, 479). See also Matt. 5:39.

[66.] Bonhoeffer follows Luther in translating λειτουργοί (liturgy leaders, conducting established acts of worship) as "servant."

[67.] This argument hinges on the German term *Gottesdienst*, which literally means "God-service." Bonhoeffer's play on words cannot be adequately conveyed with the English term "worship."

of worship or service of God to which Paul summons Christians. He enjoins them, rather, to submit to authority and to owe no one anything that is due them (vv. 7-8). Every protest or resistance at this point would only be a sign that Christians confuse God's realm with a dominion of this world.

260   That is why slaves are to remain slaves; that is why Christians are to remain subject to the governing authorities, who have power over them; that is why Christians ought not to abandon this world (1 Cor. 5:10). But, of course, slaves ought to live as freed persons of Christ. As subjects of the authorities, Christians ought to do what is good. And in the world, they are called to live as members of the body of Christ, the new humanity.[68] All this they are to do in the midst of this world and without any reservation, in order to bear witness to the fact that the world is lost and the new creation has come about in the church-community. Christians ought to suffer for no other reason than for being members of the body of Christ.

Christians are to remain in the world, not because of the God-given goodness of the world, nor even because of their responsibility for the course the world takes. They are to remain in the world solely for the sake of the body of the Christ who became incarnate—for the sake of the church-community. They are to remain in the world in order to engage the world in a frontal assault.[69] Let them "live out their vocation in this world" in order that their "unworldliness" might become fully visible.[70] But this can take place only through visible membership in the church-community. The world must be contradicted within the world. That is why Christ became a human being and died in the midst of his enemies.[71] It is for this reason—and this reason alone!—that slaves are to remain slaves, and Christians are to remain subject to authority.

This is also entirely consistent with what Luther, in those decisive years after leaving the monastery, has to say about a secular vocation.[72] He

---

[68.] See above, page 218.

[69.] See above, pages 47–50, on Kierkegaard's comments on Luther's position.

[70.] See Weber, *The Protestant Ethic and the Spirit of Capitalism*, 79–92 (sec. 3: "Luther's Conception of the Calling"). Weber claims that the New Testament, and especially Paul, "had either an indifferent or a conservative view on practicing a vocation in this world. This position is grounded in the eschatological expectations held by those first generations of Christians" (84). Weber further maintains that Luther argues "in a highly unworldly fashion . . . by claiming that the division of labor forces everyone to work for *others*." Luther had a "pre-capitalist" perspective.

[71.] See Ps. 110:2.

[72.] See Luther, "De votis monasticis. 1521" (*LW* 44:243–400 [*WA* 8:573–669]). Weber refers to Luther's translation of Jesus Sirach 11:20f. (". . . remain in your vocation") (*The Protestant Ethic and the Spirit of Capitalism*, 79, 207).

did not repudiate the very lofty standards set by monastic life, but that 261
obedience to the command of Jesus was understood as an achievement
of individuals. Luther did not attack the "unworldliness" of monastic
life, but the fact that within the confines of the monastery this estrangement from the world had been turned into a new spiritual conformity
to this world. This, to Luther, was the most insidious perversion of the
gospel. The "unworldliness" of the Christian life is meant to take place
in the midst of this world. Its place is the church-community which must
practice it in its daily living. That is what Luther thought. And that is why
Christians ought to carry out their Christian life in the midst of their
secular vocation. That is why they ought to die to the world in the midst
of their worldly calling. The value of the secular vocation for Christians is
that it allows them to live in the world by God's goodness and to engage
more fervently in the fight against the things of this world. Luther did
not return to the world based on a "more positive assessment" of this
world, or even by abandoning the expectation of the earliest church that
Christ's return was imminent.[73] His return rather was meant as a protest and criticism of the secularization of Christianity within the monastic
life. By calling Christians back into the world, Luther in fact calls them
to become unworldly in the true sense. This actually proved to be his
own experience. Luther's call to return into the world always was a call
to become a part of the visible church-community of the incarnate Lord.
And the same is also true of Paul.

It is, therefore, also evident that in living out their secular vocations,
Christians come to experience very definite *limits,* and that in certain
cases the call into a secular vocation must of necessity be followed by the
call to leave that worldly vocation. This is entirely in keeping with both
Luther's and Paul's thinking on the matter. What defines these limits
is our very belonging to the visible community of Christ. The limits are
reached wherever there is a clash between the space the body of Christ
claims and occupies in this world for worship, offices, and the civic life of

---

[73.] Here Bonhoeffer critically discusses a notion that was held by Troeltsch, among
others, who argues that in the ancient church there was no "motivation for a positive
assessment of secular vocations." Troeltsch maintains that, "due to eschatological expectations and a focus on the transcendent, the same was true in the very earliest period of the
church, when most of its members were part of the lower middle class" (*Social Teaching,*
1:121). In similar fashion, Troeltsch asserts that secular vocation, as understood at that
time, did not include an "internal connection to religious values" (125). Note the phrase
"adding a 'religious anchor' " above, page 238.

its members, and the world's own claim for space. That this state of affairs has been reached becomes at the same time evident in two ways. First, it becomes necessary for members of the church-community to make a visible and public confession of faith in Christ. Second, it becomes necessary for the world either wisely to withdraw or to resort to violence. This is the point where Christians are drawn into public suffering. They who died with Christ in baptism and whose secret sufferings with Christ had thus far not been noticed by the world are now publicly dismissed from their profession in this world.[74] They join their Lord in a visible community of suffering [Leidensgemeinschaft]. They now need even more the full fellowship and support of brothers and sisters in the church-community.[75]

But it is not always the world which expels Christians from their professional life. Even as early as the first few centuries of the church, certain professions were considered incompatible with being a member of the Christian community.[76] Actors who had to portray pagan gods and heroes, teachers who were forced to teach pagan mythologies in pagan schools, gladiators who had to take human life for entertainment's sake, soldiers who carried the sword, police officers and judges—they all had to leave their pagan professions if they wanted to be baptized. Later the church—or rather the world!—managed to give Christians permission again to take up most of these professions.[77] Rejections

---

[74.] After 1935, the National Socialist regime increasingly emphasized that membership in the church and membership in the party were mutually incompatible. Many who refused to join the Nationalsozialistische Deutsche Arbeiterpartei, the German National Socialist Workers' Party, were forced from office, especially those in leading positions.

[75.] The members of the Pfarrernotbund, the "Pastors' Emergency League," which was founded in September of 1933, committed themselves to financially assist those who had suffered from new legal measures or outright violence. Initially this was primarily "a show of solidarity with 'non-Aryan' colleagues" (*DB-ER* 309).

[76.] See Troeltsch's statement that "it was not allowed for Christians to hold . . . any positions in federal and local governments, to be a judge or an officer, in fact, even [to] serve as a common soldier. . . . also prohibited was any participation in drama, the arts, or rhetoric. . . . Christians cannot serve as teachers in schools or in any scientific field since texts and other teaching materials in those arenas would also bring them in contact with idolatry" (*Social Teachings*, 123f.). Harnack refers to Tertullian's treatise *De idololatria* (Harnack, *The Mission and Expansion of Christianity*, 2:208). Bonhoeffer, in his 1936–37 lectures on the catechetical practices of the early church (*NL* B 12, 2 [1] [*DBW* 14:548]), apparently referred to Hippolytus's canons from the third century (see Harnack, *Mission and Expansion of Christianity*, 1:162) when discussing the list of prohibited occupations in the early church.

[77.] See Troeltsch, *Social Teaching*, 1:124f. (permission was granted again from the third century onward).

were from now on more and more enacted by the world rather than the church-community.

But the older this world grows, and the more sharply the struggle between Christ and Antichrist grows, the more thorough also become the world's efforts to rid itself of the Christians. To the first Christians the world still granted a space in which they were able to feed and clothe themselves from the fruits of their own labor. A world that has become entirely anti-Christian, however, can no longer grant Christians even this private sphere in which they pursue their professional work and earn their daily bread. It feels compelled to force Christians to deny their Lord in exchange for every piece of bread they want to eat. In the end, Christians are thus left with no other choices but to escape from the world or to go to prison. But when they have been deprived of their last inch of space here on earth, the end will be near.[78]

The body of Christ is thus deeply involved in all areas of life in this world. And yet there are certain points where the complete separation remains visible, and must become even more visible. However, whether in the world or separated from it, Christians in either case seek to obey the same word: "Do not be conformed to this world, but be transformed into a new form (μεταμορφοῦσθε)[79] by the renewing of your minds, so that you may discern what is the will of God" (Rom. 12:2). There is a way of living in conformity with this world while being in it, but there is also a way of creating for oneself the spiritual 'world' of the monastery.[80] There is an illegitimate way of remaining in the world, just as there is an illegitimate way of escaping from it. In either case we become conformed to the world. But the community of Christ has a 'form' that is different from that of the world. The community is called to be ever increasingly transformed into this form. It is, in fact, the form of Christ himself. He came into the world and in infinite mercy bore us and accepted us. And yet he did not become conformed to the world but was actually rejected and cast out by it. He was not of this world.[81] If it engages the world

263

[78.] See Matt. 10:22f. [These comments are a veiled reference to the same choices Christians in Nazi Germany had to face.] [JG/GK]

[79.] See *NL* A 57, 3, pt. IV 2 (*DBW* 14:462), which reads "μεταμορφοῦσδε—change into a new μορφή [form]—*church*," plus the additional comment that "this μορφή is solely determined by Christ himself. This is the basis for why Christians remain free from what happens in the world."

[80.] See above, pages 48–49.

[81.] See John 18:36.

properly, the visible church-community will always more closely assume the form of its suffering Lord.

264   Christians must therefore be aware that "the time has grown short. In addition, I hold that from now on, let even those who have wives be as though they had none; and those who mourn as though they were not mourning; and those who rejoice as though they were not rejoicing; and those who buy as though they had no possessions; and those who make use of this world take care not to misuse it. For what is of this world is passing away. I want you to be free from anxieties" (1 Cor. 7:29-32a).[82] This describes the life of Christ's community in the world. Christians live just like other people. They marry, they mourn and they rejoice, they buy and they make use of the world for their daily needs. But whatever they possess, they possess only through Christ, and in Christ, and for the sake of Christ, and are thus not bound by it. They possess it as though they did not possess it. They do not set their heart on their possessions, and thus they remain entirely free. This is why they are able to make use of the world and why they ought not to escape from it (1 Cor. 5:10). But since they are free, they are also able to abandon the world whenever it prevents them from following their Lord. They marry; the apostle, however, thinks it is more beneficial if they remain unmarried provided this can be done in faith (1 Cor. 7:7, 33-40). They buy and engage in commerce, but they do this only to provide for their daily needs. They do not store up treasures for themselves nor set their hearts on them.[83] Christians work since they are called not to be idle. But their work is, of course, for them not an end in itself. The idea of work simply for work's sake is foreign to the New Testament. Everyone ought to provide for themselves through their labor. And each ought to earn enough to be able to share something with other Christians (1 Thess. 4:11f.; 2 Thess. 3:11f.; Eph. 4:28). Christians ought to remain independent of "those on the outside," that is, the pagans (1 Thess. 4:12). In this they follow the example of Paul himself, who took special pride in earning his daily bread by the work of his own hands, and thus even maintaining his independence from the church communities he had founded (2 Thess. 3:8; 1 Cor. 9:15). Paul insists on this independence, hoping that it will prove that his preaching

---

[82.] NRSV [trans. altered]. See above, page 97: to possess it as though one did not own it (ὡζ μή)—this is how Abraham received back his son whom he was willing to sacrifice.

[83.] Matthew 6:19-21.

is not motivated by the desire for financial gain.[84] All work is done in service to the church-community. The commandment to work is accom- 265
panied by another commandment: "Do not worry about anything, but in everything by prayer and supplication with thanksgiving let your requests be made known to God" (Phil. 4:6).[85] Christians know: "Of course, there is great gain in godliness combined with contentment; for we brought nothing into the world, so that we can take nothing out of it; but if we have food and clothing, we will be content with these. But those who want to be rich fall into temptation and are trapped by many senseless and harmful desires" (1 Tim. 6:6-9). Christians make use of the things of this world as things "that perish with use" (Col. 2:22). And they do so with thanksgiving and prayer to the creator of all the goodness of creation (1 Tim. 4:4). But all the while they are nonetheless free. They can cope with being well fed and with going hungry, with having plenty and with being in need. "I can do all things through the one who empowers me, Christ" (Phil. 4:12f.).[86]

Christians are in the world and they need the world; they are fleshly; for the sake of their fleshly nature, Christ came into the world. They do worldly things. They marry, but their marriage will look different from that of the world. Their marriage will be "in the Lord" (1 Cor. 7:39). It will be sanctified through being in the service of the body of Christ, and it will be subject to the discipline of prayer and abstinence (1 Cor. 7:5). In this, Christian marriage will become a parable of Christ's self-sacrificial love for his church-community. Indeed, their marriage will itself be a part of the body of Christ. It will be church (Eph. 5:32).[87] Christians buy and sell, they are engaged in trade and commerce. But even this they will practice in a different way than the pagans. Not only will they refrain from taking unfair advantage of one another (1 Thess. 4:6), but they will

---

[84.] See Bethge's notes in *NL* B 18 (21) (*DBW* 4:337), which include a reference to Matt. 10:8 (Christ's work is to be done without asking for payment): "Paul works with his own hands . . . in order to distinguish his own mandate clearly from that of the false apostles."

[85.] Cf. Matt. 6:25.

[86.] In his Greek copy of the New Testament, Bonhoeffer, through a change in punctuation, creates a direct connection between "I can do all things . . ." (v. 13) and the things listed in verse 12b, that is, "being well fed . . . being in need."

[87.] See Bonhoeffer's comment on Gen. 2:24 with reference to Eph. 5:30-32 in *CF* (*DBWE* 3):101. Cf. Dudzus's notes in *NL* B 9, 4 (6) that "Ephesians 5 [vv. 22-32] in reality speaks of Christ and the church. . . . The Roman Catholic position is that the passage actually speaks of marriage, and of the relationship between Christ and the church only in a figurative sense."

even do what must seem incomprehensible to the world, namely, to prefer to be taken advantage of and to suffer injustice rather than to insist
on their rights before a pagan court of law over "things that are only of
temporary significance." If it is unavoidable, they will settle their disputes
within the church-community, before their own tribunals (1 Cor. 6:1-8).

The Christian community thus lives its own life in the midst of this
world, continually bearing witness in all it is and does that "the present form of this world is passing away" (1 Cor. 7:31), that the time has
grown short (1 Cor. 7:23),[88] and that the Lord is near (Phil. 4:5). That
prospect is cause for great joy to the church-community (Phil. 4:4). The
world becomes too confining; all its hopes and dreams are set on the
Lord's return. The community members still walk in the flesh. But their
eyes are turned to heaven, from whence shall return the one whom they
await. Here on earth, the church-community lives in a foreign land. It
is a colony of strangers far away from home, a community of foreigners
enjoying the hospitality of the host country in which they live, obeying its
laws, and honoring its authorities.[89] With gratitude it makes use of what
is needed to sustain the body and other areas of earthly life.[90] In all
things the church-community proves itself to be honorable, just, chaste,
gentle, quiet, and willing to serve.[91] It demonstrates the love of its Lord
to all people, but "especially for those of the family of faith" (Gal. 6:10;
2 Peter 1:7). In suffering it is patient and joyful, taking pride in its tribu-
lation.[92] It lives its own life subject to a foreign authority and foreign
justice. It prays for all earthly authority, thus rendering this authority the
best service it can offer (1 Tim. 2:1). But it is merely passing through its
host country. At any moment it may receive the signal to move on.[93]

[88.] The correct citation is 1 Cor. 7:29.

[89.] See *DBW* 14:814 (*GS* 3:362). Cf. Bonhoeffer's statement that the space occupied
by the church-community "is the living space of a colony of foreigners [Fremdlingen]. . . .
although they share the same earth and the same earthly laws of life, they have no sense of
ownership in this earth; at least they do not have it to the same degree as those who are its
true citizens" (*NL* A 57, 3, pt. IV 2 [*DBW* 14:461–62]). Bonhoeffer had served pastorates
within "colonies" of Germans in both Spain (1928–29 in Barcelona) and England (1933–35
in London). [Bonhoeffer uses the term "foreigners" in the sense of "transients."] [JG/GK]

[90.] 1 Corinthians 7:31.

[91.] See Phil. 4:8; 1 Thess. 4:11; 2 Thess. 3:12; Luther translates τὸ ἐπιεικές, "goodness," in Phil. 4:5 as "gentleness," *Sanftmut.*

[92.] Romans 12:12.

[93.] Bonhoeffer uses this image of marching, together with the image of Noah's ark, to illus-
trate the biblical concept of "being marked with a seal" [*Versiegelung*] (see below, page 260). For
example, see Klapproth's notes, *NL* B 9, 6 (15) (*DBW* 14:728): "Like a *marching column* in which

Then it will break camp, leaving behind all worldly friends and relatives,[94] and following only the voice of the one who has called it. It leaves the foreign country and moves onward toward its heavenly home.

Christians are poor and suffering, hungry and thirsty, gentle, compassionate and peaceable, persecuted and scorned by the world.[95] Yet it is for their sake alone that the world is still preserved. They shield the world from God's judgment of wrath. They suffer so that the world can still live under God's forbearance. They are strangers and sojourners on this earth (Heb. 11:13; 13:14; 1 Peter 1:1). They set their minds on things that are above, not on things that are of the earth (Col. 3:2). For their true life has not yet been revealed; it is still hidden with Christ in God (Col. 3:3). Here on earth, they only see the opposite of what they are to become. What is visible here is nothing but their dying—their hidden, daily dying to their old self,[96] and their public dying before the world. They are still hidden even from themselves. The left hand does not know what the right hand is doing.[97] As a visible church-community, their own identity remains completely invisible to them. They look only to their Lord. He is in heaven, and their life for which they are waiting is in him. But when Christ, their life, reveals himself, then they will also be revealed with him in glory (Col. 3:4).

> They wander this earth, but their life lies in heaven;
> powerless though they be, their weakness protects the world.
> While turmoil rages around them, they taste only peace;
> poor though they be, they possess what gives them joy.
> Suffer though they may, they remain joyful;
> They seem to have died to the natural senses,
> and instead live the internal life of faith.

---

one marches together with all the others; 'taking steps' (περιπατεῖν) [walking] jointly; being on a pilgrimage; walking on my own and yet being compelled to keep up with others, being carried along; the *goal: on the day of Jesus Christ* to stand before him in purity, which means as one who has not stepped outside the space (i.e., outside of the new human being, outside of the Christ, outside of the church-community)."

[94.] Genesis 12:1.

[95.] See Matt. 5:3-11.

[96.] See 1 Cor. 15:31, and Luther's comments on baptism in his Small Catechism (*The Book of Concord*, 348–49).

[97.] Matthew 6:3.

When Christ, their life, will be revealed,
when someday he will show himself in glory,
then together with him as princes of the earth,
they will appear in glory while the world gazes in wonder.
Then shall they reign in triumph with him,
as glorious lights adorn the heavens.
Openly then shall joy burst forth.

—Chr. Fr. Richter [98]

This is the community of those who have been called out of this world, the ecclesia, Christ's body on earth, the followers and disciples of Jesus.

[98.] This hymn by Christian Friedrich Richter is based on Col. 3:3-4 (*Evangelisches Gesangbuch für Brandenburg und Pommern*, no. 176, stanzas 5 and 6, in the section "Sanctification." Bethge's 1937 copy of *Nachfolge* contains a penciled note of the first line of the hymn, "The Christians' Inward Life Is Shining," and the number "176." In the editions following World War II, this line was cited together with the author's name Christian Friedrich Richter. At the conclusion of Bonhoeffer's reflections on the 'space' of the Christian community, and the transition to a section on the "actions of the Christian 'in Christ,'" Bonhoeffer is quoted in Klapproth's notes from his winter semester 1936 presentations on the subject of "the new commandment" as linking sanctification with the community's place in the world. See *NL* B 9, 6 (12) (*DBW* 14:725): "Everything that has to be said about sanctification, etc., takes place within *this* space, i.e., within the 'new human being.'"

CHAPTER TWELVE

THE SAINTS

THE 'EKKLESIA' OF CHRIST, the community of disciples, is no longer subject to the rule of this world. True, it still lives in the midst of the world. But it already has been made into one body. It is a territory with an authority of its own, a space set apart. It is the holy church (Eph. 5:27), the church-community of saints (1 Cor. 14:34). Its members are the saints called by God (Rom. 1:7), sanctified in Jesus Christ (1 Cor. 1:2), chosen and set apart before the foundation of the world (Eph. 1:4). The goal of their call to follow Jesus Christ, indeed, of their being chosen before the foundation of the world, was that they be holy and blameless (Eph. 1:4). This is the reason why Christ surrendered his body unto death, so as to present those who are his own as holy, blameless, and irreproachable before him (Col. 1:22). The fruit of being freed from sin by Christ's death is that those who once surrendered their bodies as instruments of unrighteousness are now able to use them in the service of righteousness, as instruments of their sanctification (Rom. 6:19-22).[1]

God alone is holy. God is holy, both in being completely set apart from the sinful world and in the foundation of a realm of holiness in the midst of the world. Thus, after the Egyptians have perished, Moses and the children of Israel sing a hymn of praise to the Lord who delivered God's people from the slavery of the world: "Who is like you, O Lord, among the gods? Who is like you, majestic in holiness, awesome in splendor, doing wonders? You stretched out your right hand, the earth swallowed them. In your steadfast mercy[2] you led the people whom you redeemed; you guided them by your strength to your holy abode. . . . You brought them in and planted them on the mountain of your own possession, the

---

[1.] Bonhoeffer's expressions echo phrases in the Pauline text, verse 19.
[2.] The NRSV reads "love."

place, O Lord, that you made your abode, the holy place,[3] O Lord, that your hands have established" (Exod. 15:11ff.).[4] God's holiness consists in establishing a divine dwelling place, God's realm of holiness in the midst of the world, as the source of both judgment and redemption (Psalm 99 et al.). It is in this realm of holiness that the holy one enters into a relationship with God's people. This takes place through reconciliation, which can be attained only in holiness (Lev. 16:16f.). God enters into a covenant with God's people. God sets them apart, makes them God's possession, and vouches for this covenant. "You shall be holy, for I the Lord your God am holy" (Lev. 19:2), and "I the Lord, I who sanctify you, am holy" (Lev. 21:8)—this is the foundation on which this covenant rests. All other laws that the people are given and asked to keep in righteousness have the holiness of God and of God's community as their prerequisite and their goal.

Just as God, the holy one, is separated from anything common,[5] and from sin, so too is the community of God's holy realm. God has chosen it. God has made it the community of the divine covenant. In this realm of holiness God has reconciled and purified it. Now this place of holiness is the temple, which is the body of Christ. The body of Christ thus is the fulfillment of God's will to establish a holy community. Set apart from world and sin to be God's own possession, the body of Christ is God's realm of holiness in the world. It is the dwelling place of God and God's Holy Spirit.

How does this come about? How, out of sinful human beings, does God create a community of saints that is totally separated from sin? How can God be defended against the accusation of being unrighteous, if God enters into a relationship with sinners? How can the sinner be righteous and God still remain righteous?

God is justified by God; God supplies the proof of divine righteousness. The cross of Jesus Christ works the miracle of God's self-justification. Now God is justified before God and before us (Rom. 3:21ff.).[6] The

---

[3.] The NRSV reads "sanctuary."

[4.] Verses 11-13, 17. The phrase "the earth swallowed them" in verse 12 refers to the Egyptians. Exodus 15 contains markings in Bonhoeffer's Luther Bible.

[5.] The word *gemein* in German can mean "common"—as opposed to "upper-class"—or it can mean "vulgar," "crude," or even "mean." [JG/GK]

[6.] "God providing God's own justification" [*Selbstrechtfertigung Gottes*] is a phrase listed in Bonhoeffer's topical index of the 1937 edition of *Nachfolge*. In his copy of the Nestle edition of the Greek New Testament, Bonhoeffer placed question marks next to verses 21, 25,

goal for the sinner is to be separated from sin and yet to be able to live   271
before God. However, it is only through death that the sinner can be
separated from sin. The sinner's very life is enmeshed in sin to such an
extent that deliverance from sin can be brought about for the sinners
only through their death. God can remain righteous only by killing the
sinner. And yet is the goal for the sinner to live and to be holy before
God? How can this come about?

It comes about by God becoming human. In God's Son, Jesus Christ,
God assumes our flesh. In Christ's body, God carries our human flesh
into death on the cross. God kills the Son of God who bears our flesh;
and with the Son, God kills everything that bears the name of earthly
flesh. Now it is evident that no one is good but the triune God,[7] that
no one is righteous but God alone. Now, through the death of God's
own Son, God has supplied the terrible proof of the divine righteousness (ἔνδειξις τῆς δικαιοσούνης αὐτοῦ, Rom. 3:26).[8] In the judgment
of wrath on the cross, God had to deliver all of humanity unto death so
that God *alone* would be righteous. God's righteousness is revealed in the
death of Jesus Christ. The death of Jesus Christ is the place where God
has supplied the gracious proof of God's own righteousness, the only
place from that moment on where God's righteousness dwells. Whoever
could participate in this death would thereby also participate in God's
righteousness. But now Christ has assumed *our* flesh, and in his body has
borne *our* sin onto the wood of the cross (1 Peter 2:24).[9] What happened to him happened to all of us. He took part in our life and in our
dying, and thus we came to take part in his life and his dying. If God's
righteousness required Christ's death as its proof, then we are with Christ

---

and 26 of Romans 3 to indicate his reservations about Luther's interpretive translation of
the phrase δικαιοσύνη θεοῦ [God's righteousness] as "righteousness before God." Bonhoeffer, in disagreement with Luther, understands Rom. 3:21ff. similarly to Barth's interpretation in *The Epistle to the Romans:* "By committing himself to men and to the world which has
been created by him and by his unceasingly accepting them and it, he justifies himself to
himself" (93). Cf. Klapproth's notes, *NL* B 15, 3 (16–20) (*DBW* 14:326–27).

[7.] See Mark 10:18.

[8.] See Hegel, *Lectures on the Philosophy of Religion:* "The ultimate self-emptying of
the divine idea: 'God has died, God himself is dead' is a monstrous and dreadful notion,
which presents to the imagination the most unfathomable abyss of separation" (202 [trans.
altered]). Bonhoeffer's copy contains markings throughout this passage. He discussed this
passage in *CF* (*DBWE* 3):34–35.

[9.] 1 Peter 2:24 reads "sins" instead of "sin." The Nestle edition of the Greek New Testament lists Rom. 6:11, which has "sin" in the singular, as a cross-reference for this verse. In
his edition of Nestle, Bonhoeffer has underlined this cross-reference several times.

272

at the place where God's righteousness dwells, at his cross, for he bore
our flesh. As those who have been killed, we thus come to take part in
God's own righteousness in Jesus' death. God's righteousness, which
causes us sinners to die, is, in Jesus' death, God's righteousness for us.
Since in Jesus' death God's righteousness is established, and we are
included in Jesus' death, God's righteousness is established for us as
well. God proves God's righteousness, demonstrating "that God alone
is righteous and that God justifies the one who has faith in Jesus" (Rom.
3:26).[10] Thus the justification of sinners consists in God *alone* being
righteous and sinners being totally and utterly unrighteous, rather than
in granting sinners their own righteousness alongside that of God. Every
desire to possess our own righteousness as well cuts us off completely
from being justified by God's own, unique righteousness. God alone is
righteous. Looking at the cross, we recognize this as the judgment which
has been rendered over us as sinners. Those who in faith see themselves
included in Jesus' death on the cross, the place where as sinners they are
condemned to die, receive God's righteousness, which triumphs in this
very place. They are made righteous precisely as those who neither can
be nor desire to be righteous themselves, but who recognize that God
alone is righteous. For as human beings we cannot be made right and
ready before God[11] except in recognizing that God alone is righteous
and we are sinners throughout. The question of how, as sinners, we can
be righteous before God is really the question of how, in our encounter with God, God *alone* can be righteous. Our justification is grounded
exclusively in God's justifying God, "so that you [God][12] may be justified in your words, and prevail in your judging" (Rom. 3:4).

The only thing that matters is God's victory over our unrighteousness,
that God alone be the one who is righteous. This victory of God has been
won in the cross. This is why this cross is not only judgment but reconciliation (ἱλαστήριον,[13] v. 25) for all who believe that, in the death of
Jesus, God alone is righteous, and in that way recognize their sin. It is

---

[10.] Bonhoeffer's citation of this verse deviates from Luther's translation and the
NRSV by including the ἐκ, "out of," from the Greek text.

[11.] In German, the expression *recht fertig gemacht*, "to be made ready," is a play on
words on *rechtfertig gemacht*, the term for "to be justified." Bonhoeffer had used this rather
unusual expression before in his exegesis of 1 Cor. 13:13 (*DBW* 13:403 [*GS* 5:559]).

[12.] Bonhoeffer inserts the name "God" for emphasis in Paul's quotation from Ps.
51:6 [NRSV 51:4].

[13.] NRSV: "atonement."

God's righteousness which brings about this reconciliation (προέθετο,[14] v. 25). "God was in Christ, reconciling the world to himself" (2 Cor. 5:19ff.).[15] "[God was] not counting their sin against them"[16]—but instead bore the sin, and as its consequence suffered the death of the sinner. "God has set up the word of reconciliation among us."[17] This message seeks to find faith, the faith that God alone is righteous and in Jesus has become our righteousness. However, between Christ's death and the message of the cross lies Christ's resurrection. Only as the cross of the risen one can his cross have power over us. The message of the one who was crucified is always already the message of the one who did not remain in death's bondage. "So we are messengers on behalf of Christ, since God is making his appeal through us; we entreat you on behalf of Christ, be reconciled to God."[18] The message of reconciliation is Christ's own word. He is the risen one who, in the word of the apostle, gives witness of himself as the one who was crucified: find yourselves included in Jesus Christ's death, and thus in God's righteousness which in his dying is bestowed on us as free gift. Those who will find themselves in Jesus' death see the righteousness of God alone. "For our sake God made him to be sin who knew no sin, so that in him we might become the righteousness of God."[19] The innocent one is killed because he bears our sinful flesh; he is being hated and cursed by God and the world; he is made sinful for the sake of our flesh. But in his death we find God's righteousness.

We are in him by virtue of his incarnation. He died for us so that we who are sinners would in him become God's righteousness, precisely as sinners who are pronounced free from sin by virtue of the righteousness of God alone. If in God's eyes Christ has become our sin, which must undergo judgment, then we have in him become righteousness—but this is most certainly not our own righteousness (ἰδία δικαιοσύνη, Rom. 10:3;

[14.] NRSV: "God put forward." Cf. *DBW* 14:328 (*GS* 4:203): God "divides the divine self for the sake of God's own righteousness. God suffers by offering up Christ, who sheds his blood for our atonement (προέθετο)."

[15.] The NRSV reads "in Christ God was reconciling the world to himself."

[16.] Again, as in 1 Pet. 2:24, in 2 Cor. 5:19 Bonhoeffer substitutes the singular, "sin," in place of the plural, *Sünden* or "sins."

[17.] The NRSV of 2 Cor. 5:19 reads: "[God has been] entrusting the message of reconciliation to us."

[18.] 2 Corinthians 5:20. [The NRSV has "So we are ambassadors for Christ."] [JG/GK]

[19.] 2 Corinthians 5:21.

Phil. 3:9). Rather, in a very strict sense, this is solely the righteousness of God. Thus, God's righteousness is such that we as sinners become God's righteousness. Our, or rather God's, righteousness (Isa. 54:7)[20] is such that God alone is righteous and we are sinners, accepted by God. God's righteousness is Christ himself (1 Cor. 1:30). And Christ is "God with us," "Immanuel" (Isa. 7:14), God, our righteousness (Jer. 33:16).

274

The proclamation of Christ's death is for us the proclamation of our justification. What incorporates us into the body of Christ, that is, into his death and resurrection, is the sacrament of baptism. Just as Christ died once and once only, so we are baptized and justified once and for all. Both baptism and justification are unrepeatable events in the strictest sense.[21] What can be repeated is only the recollection of what happened to us once and for all; it is, in fact, not only capable of, but in need of, daily repetition.[22] Nevertheless, such recollection is something different from the actual content of the event to which this recollection refers. There is no repetition possible for whoever loses the content of the event. The Letter to Hebrews is right (6:5f. and 10:26f.). If the salt has lost its taste, how can its saltiness be restored?[23] Those who are baptized are told "Do you not know . . . ?" (Rom. 6:3; 1 Cor. 3:16 and 6:19) and "So you also must consider yourselves having died away to sin and alive to God in Christ Jesus" (Rom. 6:11).[24] Everything has already taken place, not only on the cross of Jesus, but also as far as you are concerned. You have been separated from sin, you have died, you are justified. God has thus completed God's work. Through righteousness, God has established God's realm of holiness on earth. This realm of holiness is named Christ or the body of Christ. The separation from sin has been

---

[20.] The text of *Nachfolge* erroneously cites Isa. 54:7, instead of Isa. 51:7. Matthew 5:11 contains an allusion to this verse.

[21.] Bonhoeffer comments on the preceding "once and for all" (ἐφάπαξ); see above, 210, editorial note 21.

[22.] Wolf-Dieter Zimmermann's notes on Bonhoeffer's New Testament lectures in the third course, 1936, contain the Greek term καθ᾽ ἡμέραν [daily] from 1 Cor. 15:31 (*NL* B 9, 5 [21]). Cf. Luther's comments on "baptism by water" in his Small Catechism, where he speaks of "dying [daily] with all sins," and daily "rising as a new human being" (*The Book of Concord*, 349).

[23.] Matthew 5:13.

[24.] NRSV [trans. altered]. Bonhoeffer's translation slightly deviates from Luther's Bible or the NRSV. His use of the German *abgestorben*, "died away," rather than Luther's *gestorben*, "died," places an emphasis on the ἀπό, "way from," in the Greek original. See above, page 209.

accomplished by the sinner's death in Jesus Christ. God has a community which has been justified, and thus freed from sin. It is the community of the disciples of Jesus, the communion of saints. They have been accepted into God's holy realm, indeed they are God's holy realm, God's temple. They have been taken out of the world and live in a new space of their own in the midst of the world.

From now on, Christians in the New Testament are only named "the saints."[25] The other conceivable name, "the just," is not used. It is not equally capable of describing the full content of the gift received. It rather refers to the unrepeatable event of baptism and justification. True, the recollection of this event is in need of daily repetition. It is also true that the saints remain justified sinners. But together with the unrepeatable gift of baptism and justification and its daily recollection, Christ's death also warrants for us another gift, namely, the preservation of the life of those who are justified until judgment day. Living within this divine preservation is the process of sanctification.[26] Both gifts, justification as well as sanctification, spring from the same source, namely, Jesus Christ, the crucified one (1 Cor. 1:2 and 6:11). Both gifts have the same content, namely, community with Christ. Both gifts belong inseparably together. However, just because of this connection between them, they are not simply one and the same. While justification appropriates to Christians the deed God has already accomplished, sanctification promises them God's present and future action. Whereas, in justification, believers are being included in the community with Jesus Christ through Christ's death that took place once and for all, sanctification, on the other hand, preserves them in the sphere into which they have been placed. It keeps them in Christ, within the church-community. While the primary issue in justification is our relationship to the law, the decisive factor in sanctification is our separation from the world in expectation of Christ's coming again. While justification incorporates the individuals into the church-community, sanctification preserves the church-community together with all the individuals. Justification liberates believers from their sinful past. Sanctification makes it possible for them to stay close to Christ, to persevere in their faith, and to grow in love. It is perhaps possible to

275

[25.] This term is part of the title of Bonhoeffer's doctoral dissertation, *Sanctorum Communio.*

[26.] Klapproth's notes in *NL* B 9, 6 (14) makes the explicit comment: "'Sanctification,' not 'holiness.'"

think of the relation between justification and sanctification as analogous to the relation between creation and preservation. Justification is the new creation of the new human being.[27] Sanctification is their preservation and safekeeping unto the day of Jesus Christ.

276   Sanctification is the fulfillment of the will of God, who says: "You shall be holy, for I am holy," and "I, the Lord, I who sanctify you, am holy."[28] This fulfillment is brought about by God the Holy Spirit, and in it God's work in us finds its completion. The work of the Holy Spirit is the "seal"[29] with which believers are being marked as God's own possession until the day of salvation. Just as before they had been held in bondage under the law as in a locked prison (Gal. 3:23), so now the believers are locked "in Christ," marked with God's own seal, the Holy Spirit. No one may break this seal. It has been secured by God, and the key is in God's hand. This means that God has now taken complete possession of those whom God has gained in Christ. The circle has been closed. In the Holy Spirit we have become God's own. Secured from the world by an unbreakable seal, the community of saints awaits its final deliverance. The church-community moves through the world like a sealed train passing through foreign territory.[30] Just as Noah's ark had to be covered "inside and out with pitch" (Gen. 6:14) in order to be preserved throughout the flood, so does the journey of the sealed church-community resemble the passage of the ark through the floodwaters.[31] The goal of this sealing-off is redemption, deliverance, salvation (Eph. 4:30; 1:14; 1 Thess. 5:23; 1 Peter 1:5 *et passim*) on the day of Christ's second coming. Those who have been sealed are being assured of reaching their goal by a pledge, which is none other than the Holy Spirit, ". . . so that we, who were the first to set our hope on Christ, might live for the praise of his

---

[27.] See above, pages 217–18. In *Creation and Fall*, Bonhoeffer had already used the categories of death and resurrection for his interpretation of creation ex nihilo (*CF* [*DBWE* 3]: 34f.).

[28.] The biblical references Lev. 19:2 and 21:8, which were quoted at the beginning of this chapter, are here taken up once again.

[29.] The notes of Wolf-Dieter Zimmermann from 1936 record Bonhoeffer's opinion that "2 Cor. 1:22 σφραγίς [seal] and πνεῦμα [spirit] are parallel" (*NL* B 9, 5 [22]).

[30.] This image brings to mind to a German audience the train in which Lenin, with the help of the German Secret Service, in 1917 passed through Germany on his way from Switzerland to Russia. Since the 1920s, sealed trains traveling to East Prussia had been passing through the "Polish corridor."

[31.] In *NL* B 9, 6 (15) Klapproth writes that ". . . the 'ark' has already departed. But it is still possible to fall out!"

glory. In him you also, when you had heard the word of truth, the gospel of your salvation, and had believed in him, were marked with the seal of the promised Holy Spirit. The Holy Spirit is the pledge of our inheritance toward redemption as God's own people, to the praise of *his* glory" (Eph. 1:12-14).

277

The sanctification of the church-community consists in its being separated by God from that which is unholy, from sin. Its sanctification consists in having become God's own chosen people through being sealed off, in having become God's earthly dwelling place, the place from which judgment and reconciliation go forth to all the world. Sanctification means that Christians now are completely oriented toward and preserved unto the day of Christ's future coming, toward which they travel.

For the community of saints this implies three things. *First,* its sanctification will manifest itself *in a clear separation from the world.*[32] Its sanctification will, *second,* prove itself through *conduct* that is *worthy* of God's realm of holiness. And, *third,* its sanctification will be *hidden in waiting* for the day of Jesus Christ.

Sanctification is therefore possible only within the visible church-community. That is the *first point.* The visibility of the church-community is a decisive characteristic of sanctification. The church-community's claim to a space of its own within this world, and the concomitant separation from the space of the world, attests that the church-community is in the state of sanctification. For the seal of the Holy Spirit seals off the church-community from the world. By the power of this seal, God's church-community must insist on God's claim to the whole world. At the same time, it must claim a specific space for itself within the world, thus drawing a clear dividing line between itself and the world. Since the church-community is the city on the hill, the 'polis'[33] (Matt. 5:14), established on this earth by God and marked with a seal as God's own, its "political" character is an inseparable aspect of its sanctification. The "political ethics"[34] of the church-community is grounded solely in its

---

[32.] On the issue of "separation from the world" see above, page 16. [JG/GK]

[33.] In the following, Bonhoeffer uses 'political' in allusion to the Greek term πόλις for 'city' (or 'civic community', 'society'). Cf. Harnack's use of *Politie* (*The Mission and Expansion of Christianity in the First Three Centuries,* 1:326f.). See Zimmermann's notes in *NL* B 9, 5 (51): "πόλις, living one's own life with Christ with one's own commandments (when we are disobedient and recognize our sin, we find the grace of forgiveness within the church)."

[34.] This is the title of a 1932 book by Friedrich Gogarten. It was critically reviewed by Bonhoeffer early in 1933 in his series of lectures on recent theology (*DBW* 12:162–68).

278   sanctification, the goal of which is that world be world and community be community, and that, nevertheless, God's word goes out from the church-community to all the world, as the proclamation that the earth and all it contains is the Lord's.[35] That is the 'political' character of the church-community. A merely personal sanctification which seeks to bypass this openly visible separation of the church-community from the world confuses the pious desires of the religious flesh with the sanctification of the church-community, which has been accomplished in Christ's death and is being actualized by the seal of God. It is the deceptive pride and the false spiritual desire of the old, sinful being that seeks to be holy apart from the visible community of Christians. Contempt for the body of Christ as the visible community of justified sinners is what is really hiding behind the apparent humility of this kind of inwardness. It is indeed contempt for the body of Christ, since Christ was pleased visibly to assume my flesh and to carry it to the cross. It is contempt for the community, since I seek to be holy apart from other Christians. It is contempt for sinners, since in self-bestowed holiness I withdraw from my church in its sinful form. Sanctification apart from the visible church-community is mere self-proclaimed holiness.

Sanctification through the seal of the Holy Spirit always places the church in the midst of struggle.[36] The struggle is in the last resort the struggle over this seal, to prevent its being broken, either from within or from without. It is the struggle that seeks to prevent the world from wanting to be church, and the church from wanting to be world. The struggle of the church for the earthly space which has been given to the body of Christ is the church's sanctification. Separation of the world from the church, and separation of the church from the world, is the holy struggle of the church for God's sacred realm on earth.

This sacred realm is possible only within the visible church-community. But, and this is the *second point,* by the fact of its being separated from the world, the church-community lives within God's sacred realm. Likewise, in the midst of the church-community there still lives a piece of the world within this sacred realm. This is why the saints are called to act in all things in a manner which is worthy of their calling and of the gospel (Eph. 4:1; Phil. 1:27; Col. 1:10; 1 Thess. 2:12). However, the only

---

[35.] Ps. 24:1; an allusion to this verse is found in Acts 17:24.

[36.] Bonhoeffer's index of the 1937 edition of *Nachfolge* contains the entry: "*Struggle* of the church, see sanctification."

way they will be worthy is by daily reminding themselves of the gospel from which they live. "But you were washed, you were sanctified, you were justified" (1 Cor. 6:11). To live out of this daily reminder is what constitutes sanctification for the saints.[37] For the message by which they are called to be worthy is the message that the world and the flesh have died; that they have been crucified and have died with Christ on the cross and in their baptism; that sin can no longer rule since its royal power has already been broken;[38] and that it is, therefore, no longer possible for a Christian to sin. "Those who have been born of God do not sin" (1 John 3:9).

The break has been made. The "former" way of life (Eph. 4:22) has been brought to an end. "For once you were darkness, but now in the Lord you are light" (Eph. 5:8). Formerly, they committed the shameful and "unfruitful works of the flesh."[39] Now, the Holy Spirit produces in them the fruit of sanctification.

Christians must therefore no longer be called "sinners," provided sinners are understood as those who live subject to the power of sin (ἁμαρτωλοί; for the only exception, see Paul's self-designation in 1 Tim. 1:15). Rather, Christians were once sinners, godless, enemies (Rom. 5:8, 10, and Gal. 2:15, 17). But now they are saints for the sake of Christ. As saints, they are reminded and admonished to be what they are. They are not required in their sinful state to be holy. That would be an impossibility, a complete relapse into the attempt to earn salvation by works and thus be blasphemy against Christ. Instead, the saints are called to be holy. For they are sanctified in Christ Jesus through the Holy Spirit.

The life of the saints stands out in contrast against a terribly dark background. The dark works of the flesh are completely brought into the open by the bright light of life in the Spirit: "adultery, fornication, impurity, licentiousness, idolatry, sorcery, enmities, strife, jealousy, anger, quarrels, dissensions, factions, hatred, murder, drunkenness, carousing, and

279

[37.] Cf. Luther, Smaller Catechism (*The Book of Concord*, 348f.). See Zimmermann's notes in *NL* 9, 5 (21): "It is very conspicuous how little Paul has to say about *daily* sin and daily forgiveness of sin. Sin is borne and forgiven within the church-community" (*DBW* 14:609).

[38.] See Rom. 6:14a, which Bonhoeffer underlined in his copy of Nestle. In *NL* B 25 (6) Bethge's notes read: "transferred from the κυριότης [royal reign] of sin to the κυριότης of Christ . . . those who confess their sin, *they* are without sin" (see *DBW* 4:338).

[39.] See Eph. 5:11; Gal. 5:19.

[40.] This list diverges significantly from that in the NRSV and the Luther Bible, particularly by including adultery; the Nestle Greek New Testament notes that such an inclusion is based an alternate reading found in some manuscripts. [JG/GK]

things like these" (Gal. 5:19-21).[40] All these no longer have any place in
280 the community of Christ. They have been dismissed, judged on the cross,
and brought to an end. From the very beginning Christians are told that
"those who do such things will not inherit the kingdom of God" (Gal.
5:21; Eph. 5:5; 1 Cor. 6:9; Rom. 1:32). These sins separate us from eternal salvation. If one of these vices is, nevertheless, discovered within the
church-community, then the consequence must be exclusion from the
community's life altogether (1 Cor. 5:1ff.).

It is striking that the so-called catalogs of vices largely agree on the sins
they list. Topping the list is nearly always the sin of fornication (πορνεία),
which is incompatible with the new life of a Christian. What follows most
frequently is the sin of greed (πλεονεξία, 1 Cor. 5:10; 6:10; Eph. 4:19; 5:3,
5; Col. 3:5; 1 Thess. 4:4ff.[41]), which in some cases can be combined with
the former as "impurity" and "idolatry" (1 Cor. 5:10; 6:9; Gal. 5:3,[42] 19;
Col. 3:5, 8). Mentioned next are the sins against love for brothers and
sisters, and finally the sin of excessive self-indulgence.[17]

¶It is certainly no accident that fornication is the first sin mentioned
in these lists. The reason for this is not to be found in the particular cul-
tural context of the time, but in the particular nature of this sin. Fornication is the recurrence of Adam's sin, of the craving to be like God,[43]
the aspiration to be the creator of life, the desire to rule rather than
serve. It is the sin in which we transgress the boundaries God has set for
us, and in which we abuse God's creatures.[44] It was Israel's sin to deny
the faithfulness of its Lord again and again, and "by engaging in fornication with idols" (1 Cor. 10:7[-8]), Israel became dependent on them.
Fornication is first and foremost a sin against God the Creator. For a
Christian, however, it is also a particularly flagrant way of sinning against
281 the body of Christ itself, for a Christian's body is a member of the body
of Christ. It belongs to Christ alone. Bodily union with a prostitute

---

17. The origin of this catalog of vices is perhaps the saying of our Lord in
Mark 7:21f.

[41.] More precisely, 1 Thess. 4:3-7.

[42.] This reference is erroneous. *NL* A 55, 19 (*DBW* 14:729) adds "Eph. 5:3f." to the
list of references mentioned here.

[43.] Genesis 3:5.

[44.] See Bonhoeffer's commentary on Gen. 3:7 after his discussion on eating from
the tree of the knowledge of 'good' and 'evil': "Knowing about tob and ra is not to begin
with an abstract knowledge of ethical principles; on the contrary it starts out as sexuality,
that is, as a perversion of the relation of one human being to another" (*CF* [*DBWE* 3]:125).

destroys the spiritual communion [Gemeinschaft] with Christ. All those who rob Christ of their bodies and lend them to sin have separated themselves from him. Fornication is sin against one's own body. However, Christians must know that their body is also the temple of the Holy Spirit who dwells in them (1 Cor. 6:13ff.). Their bodies are in such intimate communion [Gemeinschaft] with Christ that Christians cannot with their bodies belong also to the world. The community of the body of Christ prohibits the sin against one's own body. The fornicator cannot escape the wrath of God (Rom. 1:29; 1 Cor. 5:1f.;[45] 7:2; 10:7; 2 Cor. 12:21; Heb. 12:16; 13:4). Christians are chaste; they surrender their body completely to the service of the body of Christ. They know that with the suffering and death of Christ's body on the cross their own bodies are also affected, and they are given over to death. Being in community with the tortured and transfigured body of Christ liberates Christians from disorderliness in matters of bodily life. The unbridled passions of the body die a daily death in this community. With discipline and chastity Christians use their bodies exclusively to serve and to build up the body of Christ, the church-community. This also holds true within a Christian marriage, which is itself thus transformed into a part of the body of Christ.

Greed is related to fornication. An insatiable desire is what they both have in common, and it is what lets the greedy person become enslaved to the world. God's commandment says you shall not covet.[46] Fornicators and greedy people are nothing but desire. Fornicators desire to possess another human being. The greedy desire to possess the things of this world. They seek power and authority, but in so doing they become slaves of the world, to which their hearts cling. Both fornication and greed bring us into contact with the world in a way that stains and defiles us. Both are idolatry, since in either case our hearts no longer belong to God and Christ, but to the coveted goods of our own world.   282

But those who create their own god and their own world, those who allow their own desire to become their god, must inevitably hate other human beings who stand in their way and impede their designs. Strife, hatred, envy, and murder all have the same source: they spring from our own selfish desire. "Those conflicts and disputes among you, where do

---

[45.] The 1937 edition of *Nachfolge* reads: "1 Cor. 1:5f." In the 1937 edition of the book, the number of erroneous biblical references in this chapter was relatively high.

[46.] In *NL* A 55, 19 (*DBW* 14:731), Bonhoeffer's notes pointed out: "10. commandment (Exod. 20:17)."

they come from? Do they not come from your cravings that are at war within you?" (James 4:1f.). Fornicators and greedy persons cannot know love for fellow human beings. They live out of the darkness of their own hearts. By sinning against the body of Christ, they sin against their kindred. The body of Christ makes fornication and love mutually exclusive. The body which I cut off from the community of the body of Christ cannot serve my neighbor. And again, the lack of respect for my own body and for other human beings necessarily leads to an insolent and godless life of excessive self-indulgence, drunkenness, and gluttony.[47] Those who lack respect for their body become slaves to their own flesh, and "their belly will be their God" (Rom. 16:18).[48] The ugliness of this sin consists in the desire of the dead flesh to pamper itself, thus dishonoring us even in our external appearance. All those who live a life of excessive self-indulgence have no part in the body of Christ.

For the church-community this entire world of vices is a thing of the past. It has separated itself from those who indulge in these vices, and is called to do so again and again (1 Cor. 5:9ff.). For "what fellowship is there between light and darkness?" (2 Cor. 6:14ff.). With the latter are "the works of the flesh";[49] with the former is "the fruit of the Spirit" (Gal. 5:19ff.; Eph. 5:9).

What is the meaning of fruit? The "works" of the flesh are many, but there is only one "fruit" of the Spirit. Works are accomplished by human hands, but the fruit sprouts and grows without the tree knowing it. Works are dead, but fruit is alive and the bearer of seeds which themselves produce new fruit. Works can exist on their own, but fruit cannot exist without a tree. Fruit is always something full of wonder, something that has been created. It is not something willed into being, but something that has grown organically. The fruit of the Spirit is a gift of which God is the sole source. Those bearing this fruit are as unaware of it as a tree is of its fruit. The only thing they are aware of is the power of the one from whom they receive their life. There is no room for praise here, but only the ever more intimate union with the source, with Christ. The saints themselves are unaware of the fruit of sanctification they bear. The left

283

[47.] Bonhoeffer focuses primarily on Gal. 5:19-21, as he indicated at the beginning of his discussion of the "catalog of vices."

[48.] Allusion to Phil. 3:19. The NRSV translates Rom. 16:18 as, "For such people do not serve our Lord Christ, but their own appetites."

[49.] Galatians 5:19.

[50.] Matthew 6:3.

hand does not know what the right hand is doing.[50] If they become curious to know something in this matter, if they decide to engage in self-contemplation, then they would have already torn themselves away from the root and their time of bearing fruit would have passed. "The fruit of the Spirit is love, joy, peace, patience, kindness, generosity, faithfulness, gentleness, and self-control" (Gal. 5:22). It is this passage that sheds the clearest light on the sanctification of the individual, as well as on the holiness of the church-community. The source of both of them is one and the same, namely, community with Christ, community in one and the same body. Just as the separation from the world is visibly accomplished only in an ongoing struggle, so personal sanctification also consists in the struggle of the Spirit against the flesh.[51] In their own lives, only the saints see strife, hardship, weakness, and sin. And the more maturity they gain in the state of sanctification, the more they recognize themselves as being overcome, as those who are dying according to the flesh. "Those who belong to Christ Jesus have crucified the flesh with its passions and desires" (Gal. 5:24). They still live in the flesh. But because of this very fact, their whole life must now be an act of faith in the Son of God who has begun his own life in them (Gal. 2:20). Christians die daily (1 Cor. 15:31). Even if their flesh is suffering and passing away, their inner being will be restored day by day (2 Cor. 4:6).[52] The dying of the saints according to their flesh is grounded solely in the fact that through the Holy Spirit Christ has begun his own life in them. The saints die in Christ and in his life. Now they no longer need to seek their own self-chosen sufferings with which once again simply to reassure themselves in their flesh. Christ is their daily death and their daily life.

This is why they can fully rejoice in the fact that those who are born of God are no longer able to sin,[53] that sin no longer rules over them, that they have died to sin and now live in the Spirit.[18] "There is therefore

284

---

18. "'Nevertheless I live,' says the believer. 'I live under God's eyes. I live in God's grace before God's judgment seat. I live enfolded by God's favor, light, and love. I have been completely freed from all my sins. My accounts show no outstanding or unpaid debts. The law no longer demands anything of me. It no longer compels me. It no longer condemns me. I am righteous before my God, just as God is righteous. I am holy just as my God is holy. I am perfect just as my Father in heaven is perfect. God's complete favor enfolds me. It is the ground on

[51.] Cf. Gal. 5:17.
[52.] The correct reference is 2 Cor. 4:16.
[53.] 1 John 3:9.

nothing to condemn in[55] those who are in Christ Jesus" (Rom. 8:1).[56] God is pleased with God's saints. For it is none other than God who is at work in their struggle and their dying. In so doing, God brings their sanctification to fruition. The saints should be completely confident that there is fruit, even though it remains deeply hidden from them. However, this does not mean—under the umbrella of the message of forgiveness—that fornication, greed, and hatred of human kindred could once again take hold within the Christian community. It is also wrong to think that the fruit of sanctification could remain invisible. But even where it does become widely visible, where the world, when looking at the Christian community, is compelled to say, as in the earliest days of Christianity, "See how they love one another,"[57] it is especially there that the saints will look exclusively and constantly to the one to whom they belong. And, unaware of their goodness, they will ask for the forgiveness of their sins. These very same Christians, who embrace the truth that sin no longer

285

---

which I stand, the shelter in which I find safety. I am lifted and carried by the full measure of God's own blessedness and peace. This is where I can breathe freely, where I find myself eternally content. Sin is no longer something I have or commit. My conscience is clear, and I know that I am walking in God's ways and doing God's will. I know that I am fully in accord with God's will, whether I am walking or standing, sitting or lying down, sleeping or waking. Whatever I think or speak is also in accord with God's will. Wherever I am, whether far afield or at home, I am in accord with God's gracious will. I am pleasing to God whether I am at work or at rest. My debt has been canceled for eternity; and new debts, which would require canceling, I am no longer able to incur. I am well protected in God's grace, and am no longer able to sin. No death will be able to kill me. I live forever just like all the angels of God. My God will no longer be angry with me or rebuke me. I am forever delivered from God's coming wrath. The evil one will no longer lay a hand on me, the world will never again catch me in its traps. Who will separate us from the love of God? If God is for us, who can be against us?'" (Kohlbrügge).[54]

[54.] This excerpt from a sermon by Kohlbrügge is found in *Quellwasser* (37), a collection of daily meditations. The text for Kohlbrügge's reflections is Gal. 2:20.

[55.] Luther's translation reads: "on."

[56.] The NRSV reads: "There is therefore now no condemnation for those who are in Christ Jesus."

[57.] Tertullian, *Apologeticus* 39. The reference is found in Harnack, *The Mission and Expansion of Christianity*, 2:9. Klapproth, in commenting on Acts 2:44f., also refers to John 13:34f.: "The enthusiasts, especially Schwenckfeld [1489–1561], have used this argument as a criticism of the Lutheran notae ecclesiae [signs or "marks" by which the church is to be recognized]!" (*NL* B 9, 6 [12]).

rules over them and that the believer no longer sins, will also confess that "if we say that we have no sin, we deceive ourselves, and the truth is not in us. If we confess our sins, God is faithful and just in forgiving us our sins and cleansing us from all unrighteousness.[58] If we say that we have not sinned, we make God a liar, and God's word is not in us. My little children, I am writing these things to you so that you may not sin. But if anyone does sin, we have an advocate with the Father, Jesus Christ, who is the righteous one" (1 John 1:8—2:1). "Forgive us our sins" is what the Lord himself has taught them to pray.[59] And he instructed them to forgive one another without ceasing (Eph. 4:32; Matt. 18:21ff.). By forgiving one another in brotherly and sisterly love, Christians make room for forgiveness by Jesus within their community. They no longer see the other as the one who has harmed them, but as the one for whom Christ has interceded on the cross pleading for forgiveness. They encounter one another as those who have been sanctified by the cross of Christ. Through dying daily under this cross, their thinking, speaking, and their bodies are being sanctified. It is under this cross that the fruit of sanctification grows.

The community of saints is not the 'ideal' church-community of the sinless and the perfect. It is not the church-community of those without blemish, which no longer provides room for the sinner to repent. Rather it is the church-community that shows itself worthy of the gospel of the forgiveness of sins by truly proclaiming God's forgiveness, which has nothing to do with forgiving oneself. It is the community of those who have truly experienced God's costly grace, and who thereby live a life worthy of the gospel which they neither squander nor discard.

This implies that forgiveness can only be preached within the church-community of saints, where repentance also is being preached; where the gospel is not separated from the proclamation of the law; where sins are not only and unconditionally forgiven, but where they also are retained. For it is the will of our Lord himself not to give what is holy, the gospel, to dogs,[60] but to preach it only under the safeguard of the call for repentance. A church-community which does not call sin sin will likewise be unable to find faith when it wants to grant forgiveness of sin. It commits a sin against what is holy; it leads a life unworthy of the gospel. It is an

286

[58.] Bonhoeffer's citation varies slightly at this point from the NRSV.

[59.] Matthew 6:12.

[60.] Matthew 7:6.

unholy church-community because it squanders the Lord's costly forgiveness. It is not enough to lament the general sinfulness of human beings, even within their good works; that is not preaching of repentance. Rather, specific sins have to be named, punished, and sentenced. That is the proper use of the power of the keys[61] (Matt. 16:19; 18:18; John 20:23) which the Lord entrusted to his church, and about which the reformers still spoke so emphatically.[62] The key that binds and retains sins must be employed within the church-community, too, not only for the sake of what is holy, but also for the sake of the sinners, and for the sake of the church-community itself. For the church-community to live a life worthy of the gospel, it must maintain the practice of *church discipline*. Just as sanctification brings about the separation of the church-community from the world, so it must also bring about the separation of the world from the church-community. One without the other will remain spurious and false. Being separated from the world, the church-community must exercise internal church discipline.

The aim of church discipline is not to create a community of those who are perfect. Its sole aim is to build up a community of those who truly live under God's forgiving mercy. Sinners within the church-community must be warned and disciplined, so that they not forfeit their salvation and thereby misuse the gospel. The baptismal grace can be received only by those who repent and profess their faith in Jesus Christ. The grace of the Lord's Supper can be received only by those who are "able to distinguish" (1 Cor. 11:29) between the true body and blood of Christ for the forgiveness of sins, and some other meal which may have a symbolic meaning or some other kind of character. This, in turn, implies one's being able to give evidence of one's understanding of the faith. It implies that we either "examine" ourselves or submit to an examination by another Christian to determine whether we truly desire Christ's body and blood, and his forgiveness. This *faith examination* [*Glaubensverhör*] is coupled with *confession* [*Beichte*], in which Christians seek and receive the assurance that their sins are forgiven. Here God provides the sinner with the help to avoid the danger of self-deception and self-forgiveness. In the confession of sin before another Christian,[63] the flesh dies together with its pride. It is

287

[61.] Cf. Bonhoeffer's earlier letter to Erwin Sutz in which he uses the Latin term *potestas clavium* (*DBW* 11:89 [*GS* 1:31f.]).

[62.] See the Augsburg Confession, article 25 (*The Book of Concord*, 61–63), and the Smalcald Articles (ibid., 287–318).

[63.] Cf. *DBW* 14:910f. (*GS* 4:405f.). See also *LT* (*DBWE* 5):108–18.

surrendered into shame and death with Christ, and through the word of forgiveness a new human being who is confident of God's mercy comes into being. The use of confession thus needs to be part of the life of the saints. It is a gift of God's grace whose misuse cannot go unpunished. In confession, we receive God's costly grace. Here Christians become like Christ in his death. "Therefore, when I urge you to go to confession, I am simply urging you to be a Christian" (Luther, Larger Catechism).[64]

The whole life of the church-community is permeated by discipline. There is an order of gradual levels, the reason for which is that discipline is to be exercised in the service of mercy. The proclamation of the word with regard to both keys[65] remains the sole basis for exercising church discipline. This proclamation is not confined to congregational worship services. Rather, the bearer of church office is never relieved of this commission. "Proclaim the message; be persistent whether the time is favorable or unfavorable; exercise discipline, warn, and exhort[66] with the utmost patience in teaching" (2 Tim. 4:2). That is the first level of church discipline. It ought to be immediately obvious that only such sins can be punished here that have become public. "The sins of some people are conspicuous so that they can be judged beforehand, while the sin[67] of others will only become apparent later" (1 Tim. 5:24). Church discipline thus spares the sinner from the punishment of the last judgment.

288

However, if church discipline already falters on this first level, namely, the office bearer's daily pastoral ministry, then everything that follows is thereby open to question. For the second level is for members of the church-community mutually to admonish one another as brothers and sisters: "teach and admonish one another" (Col. 3:16; 1 Thess. 5:11, 14). Admonition also includes comforting the fainthearted, supporting the weak, and being patient with all people (1 Thess. 5:14). For this is obviously the only way to struggle against daily temptation in the church-community and against falling away from it altogether.

[64.] From the concluding section entitled "A Brief Exhortation to Confession" (*Book of Concord*, 460 [*WA* 30/1:238, 1f.]). In 1938, in looking back on the experience of Finkenwalde, Bonhoeffer wrote: "Confession is following after [Beichte ist Nachfolge]," that is, discipleship (*LT* [*DBWE* 5]:112).

[65.] The keys to loose and to bind; cf. *DBW* 14:829f. (*GS* 3:369). The following passage, up until Bonhoeffer's note 20 on page 274, is almost identical with Bonhoeffer's "theses" 8 and 9 on "the power of the keys and church discipline" (*DBW* 14:836–43 [*GS* 3:374–81]).

[66.] Bonhoeffer's citation differs at this point from the NRSV, which has "keep an eye on those who cause dissensions and offenses." [JG/GK]

[67.] The Luther Bible and the NRSV follow the Greek plural here. Bonhoeffer prefers the singular "sin" in accordance with Rom. 6:11.

Where such mutual brotherly and sisterly service is no longer alive in the church-community, it will also be hardly possible to reach the third level in the right way. For if a member of the community nevertheless commits a sin of word or deed which becomes known, then the community must have the strength to initiate the process of real church discipline against this member. That process also is a long journey. First, the church-community has to muster the courage to separate itself from the sinner. "Have nothing to do with that person" (2 Thess. 3:14); "part company with them"[68] (Rom. 16:17); "do not even eat with such a one" (Lord's Supper?) (1 Cor. 5:11); "avoid them" (2 Tim. 3:5; 1 Tim. 6:5). "Now we command you, beloved, in the name of our Lord Jesus Christ (!), to keep away from believers who lead a disorderly life[69] and not according to the tradition they received from us" (2 Thess. 3:6). This course of action by the church-community is intended to let the sinners "blush with shame" (2 Thess. 3:14) in order to win them back. It certainly also includes their temporary exclusion from the activities of the church-community. However, this avoidance of known sinners is not yet meant to be a complete suspension of any community with them. Rather, the church-community

289 which separates itself from the sinners is called to continue to confront them with the word of admonition. "Do not regard them as enemies, but admonish[70] them as believers" (2 Thess. 3:15). The sinners still remain believers, and for that very reason they receive the discipline and admonition of the church-community. Church discipline flows out of merciful human kinship [Brüderlichkeit]. It is with gentleness that the defiant must be disciplined and the wicked be borne, so that "God may perhaps grant that they will repent and come to know the truth, turn sober again,[71] and escape from the snare of the devil, allowing themselves to be held captive by God to do his will" (2 Tim. 2:25f.).[72] The form of this admonition will have to vary depending on the individual sinner. But the goal of leading the sinner to repentance and reconciliation will always be the same. If a sin can be kept in confidence between you and the sinner, then you shall not make it public. Rather you ought to exercise discipline and ask that person to repent in private, and thereby "you have regained a brother or sister."[73] But if that person does not listen to you and

---

[68.] Bonhoeffer's citation differs at this point from the NRSV.

[69.] The NRSV reads: "believers who are living in idleness."

[70.] The NRSV reads: "warn."

[71.] This phrase is missing in the NRSV.

[72.] The NRSV reads: "having been held captive by him to do his will." The citation is from both verse 25 and verse 26.

[73.] Cf. *DBW* 14:838 (*GS* 3:376). Matt. 18:15 reads: "your brother."

persists in her or his sin, then you should, again, not make the sin public but try to find one or two other private witnesses (Matt. 18:15f.). Witnesses are first of all necessary to corroborate the fact of a sin having been committed. If the facts cannot be proven, and the person denies them, then the whole case should be left up to God. The witnesses are not inquisitors! The second reason to find additional witnesses is the sinner's stubborn refusal to repent. The secrecy with which the discipline is exercised is intended to make repentance easier for the sinner. If the person in question still refuses to listen, or if the sin has by now already become public knowledge within the church anyway, then it is up to the whole church-community to admonish and call on the sinner to repent (Matt. 18:17; cf. 2 Thess. 3:14). Those sinners that hold an office within the church ought to be put on trial only if the accusation is brought by two or three witnesses.[74] "As for those who sin,[75] rebuke them in the presence of all, so that the rest also may stand in fear" (1 Tim. 5:20). Now it is the entire church-community, together with the ordained minister, which is called upon to exercise the office of the keys. This public declaration requires that both the church-community itself and its ordained minister be publicly represented. "In the presence of God and of Christ Jesus and of the elect   290
angels, I implore[76] you to keep these instructions without prejudice, doing nothing on the basis of partiality" (1 Tim. 5:21), for now God's own judgment is about to be passed on the sinner. If the sinners repent, and publicly confess their sins, then they are granted the forgiveness of all their sins in the name of God (cf. 2 Cor. 2:6ff.).[77] But if the sinners persist in their sin, the church-community must retain their sin in the name of God. This, however, entails exclusion from all forms of life together with the church-community. "Let such a one be to you as a Gentile and a tax collector" (Matt. 18:17). "Truly I tell you, whatever you bind on earth will be bound in heaven, and whatever you loose on earth will be loosed in heaven. . . . for where two or three are gathered in my name, I am there among them" (Matt. 18:18ff.). The exclusion from the church-community merely confirms an already existing fact, namely, that these are unrepentant sinners who are "self-condemned" (Titus 3:11). It is not the church-community which passes judgment on them; rather, they have passed judgment on themselves. Paul speaks of this complete exclusion

---

[74.] Cf. 1 Tim. 5:19.

[75.] The NRSV reads: "persist in sin."

[76.] The NRSV reads: "warn."

[77.] 2 Corinthians 2:10 in the Luther Bible reads: "[forgiveness] in Christ's stead." The NRSV does not translate "forgiveness in Christ's stead," but instead speaks of the apostle Paul forgiving others "for your [the Corinthians'] sake in the presence of Christ."

from the church as a handing-"over to Satan" (1 Cor. 5:5; 1 Tim. 1:20). The guilty persons [Schuldige] are being handed back to the world where Satan reigns and causes death. (Here, Paul does not think of capital punishment as in Acts 5, as is evident when comparing 1 Tim. 1:20 with 2 Tim. 2:17 and 4:15.) The offenders have been expelled from the body of Christ because they have separated themselves from it. They no longer possess any rightful claim with regard to the church-community. However, even this ultimate act exclusively serves the goal of salvation for the persons concerned, that their "spirit may be saved in the day of the Lord" (1 Cor. 5:5), and that through being disciplined "they may learn not to blaspheme anymore"[78] (1 Tim. 1:20) For sinners to be restored to the church-community or to find salvation remains the goal of church discipline. It remains a pedagogical act. The declaration of the church-community will certainly stand for eternity if the sinner does not repent. However, this declaration with which the church-community must take away the sinner's salvation is just as certainly the final offer of life together with the church-community and of salvation.[79] 19 20

291

---

19. Church discipline always is exercised in the service of mercy. However, beyond church discipline as such, even beyond handing over the impenitent sinner to Satan, the New Testament still knows the curse or the 'anathema' as the most terrible of punishments. It no longer has the sinner's salvation as its goal. Rather, it is the proleptic pronouncement of the divine judgment. Its Old Testament equivalent is the 'cherem'[80] [ban] under which the godless are placed. Those under the ban are killed and thus irrevocably excluded from God's community. This implies two things. First, God's community is no longer in any position to

20. Doctrinal discipline [Lehrzucht] differs from church discipline [Gemeindezucht] insofar as the latter results from sound doctrine, that is, the proper use of the keys, whereas the former deals with the misuse of doctrine itself. False doctrine poisons the well from which the life of the church-community and church discipline spring. To sin against true doctrine is therefore more serious than sins of conduct. Those who rob the church-community of the gospel deserve unreserved condemnation, but those who sin in their conduct can count on the gospel being there for them. Doctrinal discipline applies primarily to the bearers of the teaching office of the church. Everything depends on making sure that the

[78.] The NRSV does not have the word "anymore." Paul is speaking here of Hymenaeus and Alexander, whom he has "turned over to Satan" because of their blasphemy.

[79.] In accordance with Matt. 18:17 and 1 Cor. 5:11, Bonhoeffer understood church discipline as a "dissolution of community" which represents "the final offer of community" (see *DBW* 14:676 [*GS* 2:238]).

The sanctification of the church-community thus proves itself by a conduct which is worthy of the gospel. The church-community produces the fruit of the Spirit and is subject to the discipline of the scriptural word. In all that, it remains the church-community of those whose sanctification is Christ alone (1 Cor. 1:30) and who journey toward the day of his coming.

---

bear and absolve those placed under the ban. This is why they are completely handed over to God. This means that those under the ban are both accursed and holy at the same time, precisely because they are in God's hands. As those who are accursed they now belong to God alone, which is why the church-community is no longer able to seek their salvation. Romans 9:3 supplies proof that being pronounced 'anathema' means being cut off from salvation. 1 Corinthians 16:22 permits the conclusion that 'anathema' has eschatological dimensions. Galatians 1:8f. states that the 'anathema' is pronounced over those who through their preaching intentionally seek to destroy the gospel itself. It is certainly no accident that teachers of false doctrine are addressed by the only passage in scripture which pronounces the 'anathema' over specific people. Doctrina est coelum, vita terra (Luther).[81]

office of teacher is conferred only on those who are 'didaktikos', that is, qualified to teach (1 Tim. 3:2; 2 Tim. 2:24; Titus 1:9) or "able to teach others also" (2 Tim. 2:2), and that no one is rashly ordained by the hasty laying on of hands lest that person's guilt fall back on the one who ordained that person (1 Tim. 5:22). Doctrinal discipline thus begins before a person is called to the teaching office of the church. Nothing less than the life and death of congregations depend on being utterly conscientious in this matter. However, doctrinal discipline does not end with being ordained to the church's teaching office; rather, it only begins at that point. Even a trustworthy office bearer such as Timothy[82] has to be admonished continuously to preserve the sound and wholesome doctrine. To that end he is especially encouraged in the reading of scripture in order to avoid the grave danger of going astray (2 Tim. 3:10; 3:14; 4:2; 2:15; 1 Tim. 4:13, 16; Titus 1:9; 3:8). In addition, he has to be admonished to lead an exemplary life: "Pay close attention to yourself and to your teaching" (1 Tim.4:13f.;[83] Acts 20:28). It is not humiliating for Timothy to be admonished to remain chaste, humble, impartial,

---

[80.] See Kittel, *Theological Dictionary of the New Testament*, 1:354–56, on ἀνάθεμα, the "curse."

[81.] "Teaching is heavenly, life is earthly." Bonhoeffer cites from Luther's 1531/1535 "Lectures on Galatians" (*LW* 27:41 [*WA* 57:13]; also in *WA* 40/2:51, 8f.). The following note is identical to "thesis" 9 of Bonhoeffer's lecture on the power of the keys and church discipline (*DBW* 14:841–43 [*GS* 3:379–81]).

[82.] Regarding the passages from Paul's letters to Timothy, see esp. *DBW* 14:963–66 (*GS* 4:352–57).

[83.] More precisely, verses 13-16; the quote is 1 Tim. 4:16a.

292   This brings us to the *third* hallmark of true sanctification. All sanctification is directed toward being able to stand firm on the day of Jesus
Christ. "Pursue . . . holiness[,] without which no one will see the Lord"
(Heb. 12:14).[85] Sanctification always relates to the end of time. Its goal
is not to pass the test when judged by the world or even by the person
being sanctified, but to pass the test before the Lord. In their own eyes
and in the eyes of the world the holiness of the saints may appear as sin,
293   their faith as unbelief, their love as cruelty, and their discipline as weakness. Their true holiness remains hidden. But Jesus Christ himself is preparing his church-community so that it will be able to stand before him.
"Husbands, love your wives, just as Christ loved the church and gave
himself up for her, in order to make her holy by cleansing her with the
washing of water by the word, so as to present the church to himself in
splendor, without a spot or wrinkle or anything of the kind—yes, so that
she may be holy and without blemish" (Eph. 5:25-27; Col. 1:22; Eph. 1:4).

---

and hardworking. The discipline of pastors must thus precede any church discipline among the congregation. Pastors have the task of teaching the sound
doctrine in their congregation and to oppose any distortion. Wherever an obvious distortion appears, pastors ought to command those who promote it "not
to teach any different doctrine" (1 Tim. 1:3), for pastors are invested with the
teaching office and therefore have the authority to command. In addition, they
are to warn and remind people to avoid wrangling over words (2 Tim. 2:14).
If someone is being identified as a teacher of false doctrine, that person is to
receive "a first and second admonition." If these are ignored, then the relation
to such heretical people is to be severed (Titus 3:10; 1 Tim. 6:4f.), for they lead
the church-community astray (2 Tim. 3:6f.). "Everyone who does not abide in
the teaching of Christ, [NRSV: but goes beyond it,] does not have God."[84]
Such false teachers also are to be excluded from life together in one's house
and refused the customary greeting among believers (2 John 10). False teachers
are the embodiment of the Antichrist. They alone are identified as Antichrist,
not those who commit sins of conduct. To them alone is the 'anathema' in Gal.
1:9 addressed. Doctrinal discipline [Lehrzucht] and church discipline [Gemein-
dezucht] are related in that, on the one hand, there is no church discipline
without doctrinal discipline. On the other hand, there is no doctrinal discipline
which will not inevitably lead to church discipline. Paul accuses the Corinthians
of seeking to create schisms out of arrogance while neglecting to exercise church
discipline (1 Cor. 5:2). Such a separation between issues of doctrine and issues of
conduct within the church-community is impossible.

[84.] 2 John 9.
[85.] Klapproth's notes in *NL* B 9, 6 (14) (*DBW* 14:728) refer to "Matt. 5" (v. 8) in this
context.

Only the sanctified church-community is able to stand before Jesus Christ. He who reconciled God's enemies and laid down his life for the godless did this in order that his church-community remain holy unto the day of his second coming. This happens by the church being sealed with the Holy Spirit. The saints are being sealed within the church-community's realm of holiness and preserved unto the day of Jesus Christ. On that day they are not to be found defiled and full of shame, but they will appear before him holy and blameless in spirit, soul, and body (1 Thess. 5:23). "Do you not know that the unrighteous[86] will not inherit the kingdom of God? Do not be deceived! Fornicators, idolaters, adulterers, male prostitutes, sodomites, thieves, the greedy, drunkards, revilers, robbers—none of these will inherit the kingdom of God. And this is what some of you used to be. But you were washed, you were sanctified, you were justified in the name of the Lord Jesus Christ and in the Spirit of our God" (1 Cor. 6:9-11). Therefore, do not count on God's grace if you intend to persist in sin! On the day of Jesus Christ only the sanctified church-community will escape the wrath of God. For the Lord will judge us each according to our works[87] without partiality.[88] For each person's works will become apparent, and to each the Lord will give "recompense for what has been done in the body, whether good or evil" (2 Cor. 5:10; Rom. 2:6ff.; Matt. 16:27). Whatever has not already received its judgment here on earth will not remain hidden on judgment day, but must come to light. Who will then stand firm? Those whose works are found to be good. Not the hearers but the doers of the law shall be justified (Rom. 2:13). According to the Lord's own saying, only those who do the will of his heavenly Father shall enter the kingdom of heaven.[89]

Since we shall be judged according to our works, we stand under the command to do the 'good work'.[90] The fears we have about doing good works as a pretext to justify our evil works[91] is a notion which certainly is foreign to scripture. Scripture never sets faith over against the good

294

[86.] The NRSV reads: "wrongdoers."

[87.] See Matt. 25:31-46.

[88.] Romans 2:11.

[89.] Matthew 7:21.

[90.] Klapproth's notes in *NL* B 9, 6 (21) (*DBW* 14:618) say: "In place of the good 'work' [in James], Paul then uses the term καρπός ('fruit')"; see above, page 266.

[91.] See Harnack's statement that "the 'common person' [in Protestant circles] enjoyed hearing that 'good works' were unnecessary, indeed even dangerous for their soul" (*What Is Christianity?* 287 [trans. altered]).

work such that the good work is seen as destroying faith; rather, it is the evil work which hinders and destroys faith. Grace and deeds belong together. There is no faith without the good work, just as there is no good work without faith.[21] [92] Christians need to do good works for the sake of their salvation. For whoever is found doing evil works shall not see the kingdom of God. Thus the good work is the goal of being a Christian.[93] In this life, there is only one thing of real importance, namely, how we can give a good account of ourselves in the last judgment. And because all persons will be judged according to their works, it is of utmost importance that Christians be prepared to do good works. Thus our becoming a new creation in Christ also has as its goal the doing of good works. "For by grace you have been saved through faith, and this is not your own doing; it is the gift of God—not the result of works, so that no one may boast. For we are God's work,[94] *created in Christ Jesus for good works,* for which God has prepared us beforehand to be our way of life" (Eph. 2:8-10; cf. 2 Tim. 2:21; 3:17; Titus 1:16; 3:1, 8, 14). On this point everything is crystal clear. Our goal is to do the good work which God demands. God's law remains in effect and must be fulfilled (Rom. 3:31). This is being accomplished through the good work. However, there is but *one* work which deserves that designation, namely, God's work in Christ Jesus. We have been saved through God's own work in Christ, rather than through our own works. Thus we never derive any glory from our own

---

21. Paul and James differ in that James cuts off the possibility of boasting for those who humbly believe, while Paul does the same for those who humbly do good works. James does not intend to deny that we are justified by faith alone. Rather, he seeks to draw believers themselves away from a dangerous security they expect from their own faith and instead to point them to the work of obedience, thus truly humbling them. It is the concern of both Paul and James that we truly live by grace and not by our own faculties.

[92.] In *NL* B 9, 5 (32) (*DBW* 14:613), Zimmermann's notes cite the following references: "Rom. 3:28-31; James 2:17ff." In *NL* B 9, 6 (20) (*DBW* 14:613, note 80), Klapproth writes: "Contradiction [between Paul and James] only if Paul's doctrine of justification is not understood properly."

[93.] Klapproth's notes, *NL* B 9, 6 (21) (*DBW* 14:614, note 88) explain that for a person to be τέλειος means "being determined, focused on a single goal; not simultaneously aiming for two goals; it means not being δίψυχος [with two souls]." See James 1:4, 8, which Bonhoeffer underlined in his copy of the Nestle edition of the Greek New Testament. See Matt. 5:48 (τέλειος, "perfect") and 6:22 ("single-minded," where the NRSV reads "healthy").

[94.] The NRSV reads: "what he has made us."

works, for we ourselves are God's work. But this is why we have become a new creation in Christ: to attain good works in him.

All our good works are nothing but God's own good works for which God has already prepared us. Thus good works are, on the one hand, demanded of us for the sake of our salvation; and they are, on the other hand, always only the works which God is doing in us. They are God's gift. It is indeed we who are required to persist in carrying out good works; it is we who are called to good works at any moment. And yet we know that with our good works we could never stand fast before God's judgment, but that it is Christ alone and his work to which we cling in faith. Thus to those who are in Christ Jesus, God promises good works with which they will be able to stand fast on that day; God promises to preserve them in the state of sanctification unto the day of Jesus. All we can do is to trust in this promise of God because it is God's word, and then go and persist in carrying out the good works for which God has prepared us.

Our good work is thus completely hidden from our eyes. Our sanctification remains hidden from us until the day when everything will be revealed. Those who attempt to see something here, who want to see their own identity revealed rather than wait in patience, will already have had their reward. In the very midst of the presumably visible progress in our sanctification in which we would like to rejoice, we are most of all called to repent and to recognize our works as thoroughly sinful. However, we are called to rejoice ever more in our Lord. God alone knows our good works, while we know only God's good work and listen to God's command. We journey under God's grace, we walk in God's commandments, and we sin. There is indeed no denying the fact that the new righteousness, the sanctification, the light which ought to shine remains completely hidden from us. The left hand does not know what the right hand is doing.[95] But we have faith and trust that "the one who began the *good work* in us[96] will bring it to completion by the day of Jesus Christ" (Phil. 1:6). On that day, Jesus Christ himself will reveal to us the good works of which we had been unaware. Without knowing it, we have fed him, provided him with drink, given him clothes, and visited him;

296

[95.] These are allusions to Matt. 5:16 and 6:2f.
[96.] The NRSV reads: "a good work among you."

and without knowing it, we have turned him away. On that day, we will be greatly astonished, and we will recognize that it is not our works which endure here but only the work which God, in God's own time, accomplished through us without our intention and effort (Matt. 25:31ff.). Once again, the only thing left for us is to look away from ourselves and to look to the one who has already accomplished everything for us, and to follow this one.

Those who have faith are being justified; those who are justified are being sanctified; those who are sanctified are being saved on judgment day.[97] This is not because our faith, our righteousness, and our sanctification, to the extent that they are ours, would be anything other than sin. Rather, it is because Jesus Christ has been made our "*righteousness* and *sanctification* and *redemption,* in order that those who boast, boast in the Lord" (1 Cor. 1:30).[98]

[97.] See Barth's statement about "the impossible, the eschatological possibility" that human beings are "being saved as those who are lost, justified as those who cannot be justified, raised to life from the dead" (*The Epistle to the Romans*, 415).

[98.] The NRSV reads: Jesus Christ "became for us . . . righteousness and sanctification and redemption, in order that, as it is written, 'Let the one who boasts, boast in the Lord.'" Bonhoeffer quotes from verses 30 and 31.

Chapter Thirteen

The Image of Christ

"Those whom he foreknew he also predestined to be conformed to   297
the image of his Son, in order that he might be the firstborn within a
large family" (Rom. 8:29).[1] To those who have heard the call to be disciples of Jesus Christ is given the incomprehensibly great promise that
they are to become like Christ. They are to bear his image as the brothers
and sisters of the firstborn Son of God. To become "like Christ"—that
is what disciples are ultimately destined to become. The image of Jesus
Christ, which is always before the disciples' eyes, and before which all
other images fade away, enters, permeates, and transforms them,[2] so
that the disciples resemble, indeed become like, their master. The image
of Jesus Christ shapes the image of the disciples in daily community.
For disciples, it is not possible to look at the image of the Son of God in
aloof, detached contemplation; this image exerts a transforming power.
All those who submit themselves completely to Jesus Christ will, indeed
must, bear his image. They become sons and daughters of God; they
stand next to Christ, their invisible brother, who bears the same form as
they do, the image of God.

God once created Adam in God's own image.[3] In Adam, God sought
to observe this image with joy, as the culmination of God's creation, "and
indeed, it was very good."[4] In Adam, God recognized the divine self.
Thus, from the beginning, it is our unfathomable mystery as human
beings that we are creatures and yet are called to be like the Creator. As

---

[1.] The Luther Bible reads "that they should be like the image . . ."; "like" is the translation of a Greek term (σuμμόρφους) which contains "form" (μορφή) as one of its constituent
elements. Concerning 'image Christology', see Irenaeus, *Adversus haereses* 4.37, conclusion
and demonstratio 22.

[2.] See Rom. 12:2.

[3.] Genesis 1:27.

[4.] Genesis 1:31.

created human beings, we are called to bear the image of the uncreated
God. Adam is "like God." In gratitude and obedience, Adam now ought to
bear his secret of being creature and yet God-like. The lie of the serpent

298   was to suggest to Adam that he would still have to become like God, and
to do so by his own deed and decision.[5] That was when Adam rejected
grace and instead chose his own deed. The mystery of his nature, of being
creature and yet God-like, was what Adam wanted to solve by himself. He
wanted to become what, from God's perspective, he already was. That was
the fall. Adam became "like God"—sicut deus[6]—in his own way. Having
made himself into a god, he now no longer had a God. He now ruled
alone as creator-god in a world bereft of God and subdued.[7]

But the puzzle of human existence remains unresolved. Human
beings have lost their own, God-like essence, which they had from God.
They live now without their essential purpose, that of being the image
of God. Human beings live without being truly human. They must live
without being able to live. That is the paradox of our existence and the
source of all our woes. Since then, the proud children of Adam have
sought to restore this lost image of God in themselves by means of their
own efforts. But the more seriously and devotedly they strive to regain
what was lost, and however convinced and proud they are of their apparent victory in achieving this, the deeper the contradiction to God grows.
Their distorted form, which they modeled after the image of the god of
their own imaginative projections, resembles more and more the image
of Satan, even though they may be unaware of this. The image of God, as
the Creator's gracious gift, has been lost on this earth.

But God keeps on looking at God's lost creature. For the second
time, God seeks to create the divine image in us. God wants to be
pleased with the creature once again. God seeks the divine image in us,
in order to love it. But God cannot find it except by assuming, out of
sheer mercy, the image and form of the lost human being. God must
conform to the human image, since we are no longer able to conform
to the image of God.

The image of God should be restored in us once again. This task
encompasses our whole existence. The aim and objective is not to renew

---

[5.] See Gen. 3:5.

[6.] "Like unto God." See Bonhoeffer's theological interpretation of Genesis 1–3,
DBWE 3 (*CF*):112–14.

[7.] See Gen. 3:5; *DBWE* 3 (*CF*): 120.

human thoughts about God so that they are correct, or that we would subject our individual deeds to the word of God again, but that we, with our whole existence and as living creatures, are the image of God. Body,   299 soul, and spirit, that is, the form of being human in its totality, is to bear the image of God on earth. God is well pleased with nothing less than God's own perfect image.

The image springs from real life, the living primordial form. Form is thus being shaped by form. The prototype from which the human form takes its shape is either the imaginative form of God based on human projection, or it is the true and living form of God which molds the human form into the image of God. A reshaping, a 'metamorphosis' (Rom. 12:2; 2 Cor. 3:18), a transformation has to take place if, as fallen human beings, we are to become again the image of God. The question is how it can become possible that human beings could be transformed into the image of God.

Since fallen human beings cannot recover and assume the form of God, there is only *one* way to find help. It is none other than God, who assumes human form and comes to us. The Son of God who, in the form of God, lived with the Father, empties himself of this divine form and comes to human beings in the form of a servant (Phil. 2:5ff.). Changing one's form, something which was not possible for human beings, now takes place within God. God's own image, which had remained with God through eternity, now assumes the image of the fallen, sinful human being. God sends the divine Son in the likeness of sinful flesh (Rom. 8:2f.).[8]

God sends God's Son—that is the only way to find help. Neither a new idea nor a better religion would suffice to accomplish this goal.[9] A human being comes to us human beings. Every human being bears an image. Our bodies and lives manifest themselves visibly. As a human being we are not merely word, thought, or will. Rather, before and in all

---

[8.] The ὁμοίωμα σαρκός—Christ as "the true image of the human 'sarx' [flesh]"—is a theme which Bonhoeffer developed in his 1933 Christology lectures, *CC* 106–13 (*DBW* 12:343–48 [*GS* 3:235–38]).

[9.] See Bonhoeffer's comment in his 1933 Christology lectures that "the incarnation of God may not be thought of as derived from an idea of God, in which something of humanity already belongs to the idea of God—as in Hegel" (*CC* 105 [*DBW* 12:342 (*GS* 3:234)]). In Bonhoeffer's words, "a notion like this mistakes the whole human being who is reality in history," God who became human, for "an idea of humankind" (*DBW* 12:322 [*GS* 3:212]). The Christology lectures ended with a meditation on who the one who became human really is [see *CC* 102–13 (*DBW* 12:340–48 [*GS* 3:231–42]).

of these, we are a human being, a form, an image, a brother or sister. A
300   human being thus develops not only a new way of thinking, willing, and
doing things, but a new image, a new form. In Jesus Christ, God's own
image has come into our midst in the form of our lost human life, in
the likeness of sinful flesh. God's own image becomes revealed in Jesus'
teaching and in his deeds, in his life and in his death. In him God has
created anew the divine image on earth. The incarnation, Jesus' word
and deed, and his death on the cross are integral elements of this image.
It is an image different from the image of Adam in the original glory of
paradise. It is the image of one who places himself in the very midst of
the world of sin and death, who takes on the needs of human flesh, who
humbly submits to God's wrath and judgment over sinners, who remains
obedient to God's will in suffering and death; the one born in poverty,
who befriended and sat at table to eat with tax collectors and sinners,[10]
and who, on the cross, was rejected and abandoned by God and human
beings—this is God in human form, this is the human being who is the
new image of God!

We know, however, that the marks of suffering, the wounds of the
cross, have now become the signs of grace on the body of the risen and
transfigured Christ;[11] and we are aware that the image of the crucified
will forever live in the glory of the eternal high priest, who in heaven
intercedes for us before God.[12] On Easter morning Jesus' form of a
servant was changed into a new body of heavenly form and radiance. But
whoever, according to God's promise, seeks to participate in the radiance and glory of Jesus must first be conformed to the image of the obedient, suffering servant of God on the cross. Whoever seeks to bear the
transfigured image of Jesus must first have borne the image of the crucified one, defiled in the world. No one is able to recover the lost image of
God unless they come to participate in the image of the incarnate and
crucified Jesus Christ. It is with this image alone that God is well-pleased.
Only those who allow themselves to be found before God in the likeness
of this image live as those with whom God is well pleased.

To be conformed to the image of Jesus Christ is not an ideal of real-
301   izing some kind of similarity with Christ which we are asked to attain. It is
not we who change ourselves into the image of God. Rather, it is the very

---

[10.] Matthew 9:10f.
[11.] John 20:19f.
[12.] See Heb. 2:17 *et passim*.

image of God, the form of Christ, which seeks to take shape within us
(Gal. 4:19). It is Christ's own form which seeks to manifest itself in us.
Christ does not cease working in us until he has changed us into Christ's
own image. Our goal is to be shaped into the entire *form* of the *incarnate,*
the *crucified,* and the *transfigured one.*

Christ has taken on this *human form.* He became a human being
like us. In his humanity and lowliness we recognize our own form. He
became like human beings, so that we would be like him. In Christ's
incarnation all of humanity regains the dignity of bearing the image
of God. Whoever from now on attacks the least of the people attacks
Christ, who took on human form and who in himself has restored the
image of God for all who bear a human countenance. In community
with the incarnate one, we are once again given our true humanity.
With it, we are delivered from the isolation caused by sin, and at the
same time restored to the whole of humanity. Inasmuch as we participate in Christ, the incarnate one, we also have a part in all of humanity,
which is borne by him. Since we know ourselves to be accepted and
borne within the humanity of Jesus, our new humanity now also consists
in bearing the troubles and the sins of all others. The incarnate one
transforms his disciples into brothers and sisters of all human beings.
The "philanthropy" (Titus 3:4) of God that became evident in the incarnation of Christ is the reason for Christians to love every human being
on earth as a brother or sister. The form of the incarnate one transforms the church-community into the body of Christ upon which all of
humanity's sin and trouble fall, and by which alone these troubles and
sins are borne.

The form of Christ on earth is the *form of the death* [*Todesgestalt*] of
the crucified one. The image of God is the image of Jesus Christ on the
cross. It is into this image that the disciple's life must be transformed.
It is a life in the image and likeness of Christ's death (Phil. 3:10; Rom.
6:4f.). It is a crucified life (Gal. 2:19). In baptism Christ engraves the
form of death on his own. Having died to the flesh and to sin, Chris-   302
tians are now dead to this world, and the world is dead for them (Gal.
6:14). Those who live out of their baptism live out of their death. Christ
marks the life of his own with their daily dying in the struggle of the
spirit against the flesh, and with their daily suffering the pains of death
which the devil inflicts on Christians. It is the suffering of none other
than Jesus Christ that all of his disciples on earth have to endure. Christ
honors only a few of his followers with being in the most intimate com-

munity with his suffering, that is, with martyrdom. It is here that the life of the disciple is most profoundly identical with the likeness of Jesus Christ's form of death.

¶It is by Christians' being publicly disgraced, having to suffer and being put to death for the sake of Christ, that Christ himself attains visible form within his community. However, from baptism all the way to martyrdom, it is the same suffering and the same death. It is the new creation of the image of God through the crucified one.

All those who remain in community with the incarnate and crucified one and in whom he gained his form will also become like the *glorified and risen one*. "We will bear the image of the heavenly human being" (1 Cor. 15:49).[13] "We will be like him, for we will behold him as he is" (1 John 3:2).[14] The image of the risen one will transform those who look at it in the same way as the image of the crucified one. Those who behold Christ are being drawn into Christ's image, changed into the likeness of Christ's form. Indeed, they become mirrors of the divine image. Already on this earth we will reflect the glory of Jesus Christ. The brilliant light and the life of the risen one will already shine forth from the form of death of the crucified one in which we live, in the form of sorrow and cross. The transformation into the divine image will become ever more profound, and the image of Christ in us will continue to increase in clarity. This is a progression in us from one level of understanding to another and from one degree of clarity to another, toward an ever-increasing perfection in the form of likeness to the image of the Son of God. "And all of us, who with unveiled faces let the glory of the Lord be reflected in us, are thereby transformed into his image from glory to glory" (2 Cor. 3:18).[15]

303

This is the indwelling of Jesus Christ in our hearts. The life of Jesus Christ here on earth has not yet concluded. Christ continues to live it in the lives of his followers. To describe this reality we must not speak about

---

[13.] Bonhoeffer's citation differs from the NRSV which reads: "We will also bear the image of the man of heaven." [JG/GK]

[14.] The NRSV, like Luther, translates this as "see him"; Bonhoeffer translates the verb as in Matt. 5:8.

[15.] [Bonhoeffer's citation differs from the NRSV which reads: "And all of us, with unveiled faces, seeing the glory of the Lord as though reflected in a mirror, are being transformed into the same image from one degree of glory to another."] [JG/GK] He also deviates slightly from the Luther translation. Bonhoeffer's translation of μεταυορφούμεθα as "transformed," *umgestaltet*, is more accurate than Luther's *verklärt*.

our Christian life but about the true life of Jesus Christ in us. "It is no longer I who live, but it is Christ who lives in me" (Gal. 2:20). The incarnate, crucified, and transfigured one has entered into me and lives my life. "Christ is my life" (Phil. 1:21).[16] But together with Christ, the Father also dwells in me; and both Father and Son dwell in me through the Holy Spirit. It is indeed the holy Trinity who dwells within Christians, who permeates them and changes them into the very image of the triune God.[17] The incarnate, the crucified, and the transfigured Christ takes on form in individuals because they are members of his body, the church. The church bears the incarnate, crucified, and risen form of Jesus Christ. The church is, first of all, Christ's image (Eph. 4:24; Col. 3:10), and through the church so too are all its members the image of Christ. Within the body of Christ we have become "like Christ."

It now becomes understandable that the New Testament calls us again and again to be "like Christ" (καθὼς Χριστός). We are to be like Christ because we have already been shaped into the image of Christ. Only because we bear Christ's image already can Christ be the "example"[18] whom we follow. Only because he himself already lives his true life in us can we "walk just as he walked" (1 John 2:6), "act as he acted" (John 13:15), "love as he loved" (Eph. 5:2; John 13:34; 15:12), "forgive as he forgave" (Col. 3:13), "have the same mind that was in Jesus Christ" (Phil. 2:5), follow the example he left for us (1 Peter 2:21), and lose our lives for the sake of our brothers and sisters, just as he lost his life for our sake (1 John 3:16). Only because he was as we are can we be as he was. Only because we *already* are made like him can we be "like Christ." Since we have been formed in the image of Christ, we can live following his example. On this basis, we are now actually able to do those deeds, and in the simplicity of discipleship, to live life in the likeness of Christ. Here simple obedience to the word takes place. I no longer cast even a single glance on my own life, on the new image I bear. For in the same moment that I

304

[16.] The NRSV reads "living is Christ."

[17.] See *NL* A 57, 3 (*DBW* 14:444), concerning the *"indwelling of the Trinity"*: *"The space of Christ existing as church-community* is thus also the space of the Holy Spirit in those who believe. Only as such is the space of Christ *real.*" See *DBWE* 3 (*CF*):164 and 76–79 and Schmid, *The Doctrinal Theology of the Evangelical Lutheran Church* (141 and 154–55, n. 18).

[18.] See Kierkegaard's comment, underlined by Bonhoeffer in his copy, that for the disciples, Christ is "the example [Vorbild] (toward which single individuals are to orient themselves, all the while admitting honestly where they really are)" (*Søren Kierkegaard's Journals and Papers*, 2:350–51). The German term translated as "example," *Vorbild,* is a composite of the term "image," *Bild,* which Bonhoeffer uses throughout this passage.

would desire to see it, I would lose it. For it is, of course, merely the mirror reflection of the image of Jesus Christ upon which I look without ceasing.[19] The followers look only to the one whom they follow. But now the final word about those who as disciples bear the image of the incarnate, crucified, and risen Jesus Christ, and who have been transformed into the image of God, is that they are called to be "imitators of God."[20] The follower [Nachfolger] of Jesus is the imitator [Nachahmer] of God. "Therefore be imitators of God, as beloved children" (Eph. 5:1).

[19.] 2 Cor. 3:18 (see above, pages 107–8, concerning Matt. 5:8).

[20.] Luther translates μιμηταί in Eph. 5:1 as "follower" or "disciple." Bonhoeffer's translation of this term as "imitator" recalls the term *imitatio,* or "imitation," and comes, quite remarkably, at the end of a book dedicated to the theme of discipleship, *Nachfolge.* In 1938 Bonhoeffer quoted Thomas à Kempis's *Imitatio Christi* in *Life Together* (see *LT* [*DBWE* 5]:81, 85, 89). He read the Latin original during his imprisonment in Tegel. In German the phrase *imitatio Christi* is translated as *Nachfolge Christi.*

MARTIN KUSKE AND ILSE TÖDT

EDITORS' AFTERWORD
TO THE GERMAN EDITION

DIETRICH BONHOEFFER'S exposition of the Sermon on the Mount cap-
tures the reader's attention today just as it did fifty years ago. *Disciple-ship,* however, is a book that needs to be seen within a specific context. Bonhoeffer did not intend it to be a piece of "timeless truth"; rather, he sought to uncover the specific truth for *"today."*[1] Statements which tes-tify to concrete truth have, nonetheless, the inherent capacity to inspire us ever anew.

The outline of this afterword will follow the chronological sequence of events in Bonhoeffer's life before, during, and after the writing of this book. We will then examine the subsequent reception of *Discipleship.*

I

Bonhoeffer's most extensive comments on the Sermon on the Mount from his time as a theological student are found in a catechetical lesson plan for a confirmation class.[2] In this document Bonhoeffer has one of the pupils make the statement: "Matt. 5:39ff. seems to say that accepting the commandment to love our neighbor implies refraining from all resis-tance against evil." In the mouth of the teacher he puts the sentence: "Love's intention is to overcome evil. . . . Where has the commandment of the Sermon on the Mount reached its limit?" And the pupil answers: "It has reached the limit wherever its fulfillment does not overcome but instead strengthens evil."[3]

[1.] Cf. *NRS* 162; also *TF* 98 (*DBW* 11:331f.).
[2.] See "Meditation und Katechese über die Ehre" (*DBW* 9:585–98).
[3.] Ibid., 595f.

During those years Matt. 5:39 was the subject of an intense debate. The verse was used, for example, by the sociologist Max Weber in 1919 in a lecture entitled "Politics as Vocation." Weber quoted this verse as proof that the Sermon on the Mount cannot serve as a basis for political decisions. This statement was aimed against Christian pacifism. Initially, this whole debate had been started by the Russian poet Count Leo Tolstoy (1828–1910). The Luther scholar Karl Holl[4] noted that Tolstoy, in his reading of the Synoptic Gospels, had found Jesus' saying "do not resist evil" in the Sermon on the Mount (Matt. 5:39) to be the "key" to the "meaning of Christ's teaching." Holl added the critical comment that "people today always associate the 'Sermon on the Mount' exclusively with Tolstoy."[5] Voicing similar concerns, the Lutheran theologian Paul Althaus wrote: ". . . we cannot stand by idly and let the new Christian radicalism, by invoking the name of Jesus and the Sermon on the Mount, confuse the conscience of Christians with regard to law, nation, government, and military service."[6]

308

When Bonhoeffer was assistant pastor in Barcelona, he shared the concerns of these theologians. "It is the most serious misunderstanding," the twenty-two-year-old stated in one of his three addresses to the congregation, "to turn the commandments of the Sermon on the Mount once again into a law by applying them literally to the present." "The whole life of someone like Count Tolstoy, and many others beside him, was based on this misunderstanding."[7] Pacifism as a principle must be mistaken. During a war I "cannot escape the painful decision whether to deliver my own brother or my own mother into the hands of the aggressor, or whether to be compelled to raise my hand against the enemy." And given such a case, my obligation is to do the latter, for "God has given me to my mother and to my nation . . . that is part of the divine order, for God created the nations."[8]

Based on his understanding of the 'orders of creation', Bonhoeffer during this period apparently regards it as impossible to accept the command of the Sermon on the Mount in simple obedience.[9] Whenever he

<hr/>

[4.] Holl, *Der Osten,* 433 and 446.

[5.] Holl, *Luther,* 252, note 1.

[6.] Althaus, *Religiöser Sozialismus,* 32.

[7.] In 1928. *NRS* 45 (*DBW* 10:332).

[8.] *DBW* 10:337 (*GS* 5:171).

[9.] In advocating this point of view, the young theologian is simply affirming the position of others rather than speaking from his own established conviction; see *DB-ER* 119–20.

touches on the topic of God's will for us in these Barcelona addresses, Bonhoeffer employs language which rings of unhappiness and constraint: "We thus see Jesus tread across the bleak heights of an unyielding demand placed before humanity. Who will dare to join him on this path? Who will follow him along this way [seine Nachfolge antreten]?"[10]

However, through a personal encounter Bonhoeffer came to rethink this whole question of Christian pacifism. During his year of study at Union Theological Seminary in New York in 1930–31, Bonhoeffer formed a friendship with Jean Lasserre, a Frenchman his own age. As a Frenchman, Lasserre was a citizen of a nation that many Germans at the time considered to be the "archenemy." Lasserre lived his life in strict obedience to the commandment for peace that Jesus had given in the Sermon on the Mount. This made a significant impression on Bonhoeffer.[11] However, the encounter with the pacifist Lasserre in itself does not yet sufficiently explain the fact that Bonhoeffer would very soon understand discipleship [Nachfolge] and the Sermon on the Mount in a very different way than he had during his time in Barcelona.

Bonhoeffer alluded to this event of personal transformation in a letter which was written during a period of intense internal struggles.[12] Referring back to an incident sometime before 1933, he wrote:

> Back then I was terribly alone and left to my own devices. It was quite awful. Then a change took place, a change that transformed my life and set its course in a new direction to this very day. I arrived at the Bible for the first time. Again, that is a terrible thing to admit. I had already preached quite often, I had seen much of the church, and both talked and written about it. But I had not yet become a Christian. In a wild and untamed way I was still my own master. . . . In all my abandonment I was nevertheless quite pleased with myself. It was the Bible which liberated me from this, especially the Sermon on the Mount. Since then everything has changed. I could clearly feel it, and even other people around me noticed it. It was a great liberation. It became clear to me that the life of a servant of Jesus Christ has to belong to the church, and step by step it became ever more evident just how far this had to go. Then came the painful situation of 1933. It only confirmed the new direction in which I was heading. And I now also found other people who shared the same vision and goal. The renewal of the church and the ministry became my supreme concern. . . .

[10.] *DBW* 10:310 and 294f. (*GS* 5:143f. and 126).

[11.] See *DB-ER* 152–54. Lasserre's 1953 book was published in English translation as *War and the Gospel.*

[12.] See *DB-ER* 506.

310 Very shortly before, I had still passionately attacked the position of Christian pacifism during a debate in which Gerhard[13] also was present. Now I suddenly came to recognize it as self-evident. And this process continued, step by step. I no longer saw or thought anything else anymore.[14]

Here Bonhoeffer recalls a date that could be pinpointed on a calendar. However, after reading this letter it would not have

> crossed anyone's mind to ask about this debate, and when and where it had taken place. All of us were much too shocked and disturbed by this turn toward pacifism. . . . And even if one were able to understand it, and follow the logic behind what at that time was a highly dangerous thought, one did not have the inner freedom to suppress the great fears for someone who actually held these convictions.[15]

The vast majority shied away from pacifism as if it were a monstrous threat. But for Bonhoeffer pacifism had suddenly become something that was self-evident.

From the winter semester of 1931–32 through the summer semester of 1933 Bonhoeffer taught as a lecturer [Privatdozent] at the University of Berlin. It was most likely during this period that a document entitled "Christ and Peace"[16] was written. It contains a number of remarkably close parallels to Bonhoeffer's later book *Discipleship*. In these lecture notes we no longer find any trace of "the bleak heights of an unyielding demand."[17] Instead, Jesus' call to follow him comes to us "with the promise of the Beatitudes." "Simple obedience is unaware of good and evil. It simply consists in following Jesus and in doing what he commands as something that is self-evident." For Christians it is "self-evident" that the commandments "You shall not kill" and "Love your enemies" do not

---

[13.] Gerhard Jacobi did not recall this debate when Eberhard Bethge asked him about it in 1964.

[14.] Letter from Finkenwalde dated January 27, 1936 (*DBW* 14:113 [*GS* 6:367f.]).

[15.] Letter to the German editors by Elisabeth Bornkamm dated November 18, 1983. In this letter she also states: "In the spring of 1932, I became a student pastor-in-training under Jacobi's supervision. After 1½ years I advanced to become a regular assistant pastor [Vikarin] (which at that time was the highest ecclesiastical status for women in the Confessing Church; this included being ordained by the Confessing Church with Franz Hildebrandt being one of the ordainers)."

[16.] *TF* 93–95 (*DBW* 17:116–20); see *DB-ER* 208–10. Bethge's research indicates that this document is most likely a set of notes by Jürgen Winterhager, taken during an address by Bonhoeffer to an ecumenical student forum. These notes were definitely written *after* July 1932, presumably in December of that year.

[17.] *DBW* 10:310 (*GS* 5:143).

allow them to do military service in war.[18] A set of notes from 1936, 311
taken by one of his seminarians during a Bonhoeffer lecture in Finkenwalde, contains a number of terms that echo this document—terms
such as "Christian conscientious objection to war," "simple obedience,"
"justification of the sinner, not justification of sin," "cheap grace," and
others.[19] Both in 1932 in Berlin and later in Finkenwalde, Bonhoeffer
emphasized the liberation, the ease, and the joy involved in discipleship.
God's commandment creates peace in those who receive it, a peace that
cannot remain confined to the inner person alone.

From 1931 on Bonhoeffer was an active participant in the Ecumenical Movement. German theology professors criticized this "promotion
of international friendship by the churches"[20] as dishonest, "so long
as the others are waging a murderous policy against our people."[21]
But Bonhoeffer had by now come to understand that even the "most
sacred ties" of the natural world, such as nation [Volk] and family, are
not so unconditionally binding as the commandment of the one Lord,
a commandment which is addressed to people of all nationalities in the
church. On August 28, 1934, at the ecumenical conference on the Danish island of Fanø, Bonhoeffer insisted that the community of the church
is called to proclaim God's commandment of peace in such a way that it
will be heard by the nations.[22] At the same conference, Jean Lasserre
presented the resolutions of the youth caucus regarding both conscientious objection to war and the universality of the church.[23] Nearly all
the German youth delegates had studied under Bonhoeffer in Berlin.[24]

From the outset it was clear to Bonhoeffer that the call to discipleship,
although unmistakably addressed to the individual, would place that
individual within a community and within the public arena. During his
pastorate in London from October 1933 to April 1935, Bonhoeffer, as
a member of the Confessing Church, wrote a set of "spiritual exercises"

[18.] *TF* 95 (*DBW* 17:117–18).

[19.] Zimmermann's notes in *NL* B 9, 5 (49–51) (see *DBW* 14:620–22).

[20.] An ecumenical organization founded in 1914 was called Weltbund für Freund-
schaftsarbeit der Kirchen, the World Alliance for Promoting International Friendship
through the Churches.

[21.] Quoted from *DB-ER* 195. This refers to Paul Althaus and Emmanuel Hirsch in
1931.

[22.] See *NRS* 289–92 (*DBW* 13:298–301).

[23.] See *NRS* 292–94 (*DBW* 13:193–96 [*GS* 1:209–11]) and *DB-ER* 391. See also *DBW*
13:197.

[24.] *DB-ER* 389–91.

expounding the Sermon on the Mount. Peter, who through the gracious call of Jesus has embarked on the path of obedient discipleship, is the same Peter who confesses Jesus as the Christ. The Confessing Church must likewise be the church engaged in discipleship.[25] This event of Peter's call, in which the church also is called, was then also the introductory topic for Bonhoeffer's New Testament lectures at Zingst in the spring of 1935.

312

II

During the period in which Bonhoeffer worked on *Discipleship*, Germany, by all external appearances, experienced a tremendous boom. Before 1933 a great many Germans felt that Germany had been treated shamefully by the powers that had been victorious in World War I. But now steps were taken "to wipe out the humiliation of Versailles." Among these steps was the introduction of mandatory military service in the spring of 1935.[26] Then, in 1936, the Olympic Games in Berlin presented a picture of Germany's grandeur to the world.

However, there were also other images that did not fit into this respectable picture. In the summer of 1936 an American visitor took a picture of a sign that was posted in a bookstore in Berlin. The sign read, in doggerel lines: "After the end of the Olympiad / we'll beat the CC (Confessing Church) to a pulp. / Then we'll chuck out the Jew. / The CC will end too."[27] With unbridled arrogance and brutality, the National Socialist movement was charging forward to the future it claimed to usher in.

The Confessing Church

During these years up until 1937, church life in Germany experienced a number of significant turning points. Since Hitler's takeover on January 30, 1933, the National Socialist revolution had sought to force all elements of society, including the churches, into line [Gleichschaltung]

[25.] In a 1934 letter that was presumably addressed to the circle around Gerhard Jacobi, Bonhoeffer wrote similarly: "The confessing Peter was the Peter who followed Jesus, and at the same time the Peter who was called to undergo suffering" (*NL* A 41, 10 [*DBW* 13:177]). See also Bonhoeffer's 1934 sermon on Jer. 20:7 (*DBW* 13:347–51 [*GS* 5:505–9]).

[26.] Cf. *DB-ER* 431.

[27.] *DB-ER* 536 (*DBW* 14:217 [*GS* 2:280f.]).

with the ideology and structures of the Nazi party. This included the demand that Christians discriminate against their fellow Jewish citizens and against other groups that had been branded as "enemies of the people" [Volksfeinde]. In September 1933, Ludwig Müller was installed as Reich Bishop [Reichsbischof] of a Protestant Reich Church [Reichs-   313
kirche] which was indeed directly dependent on the National Socialist regime. However, the German Christians whose teachings were adapted to the Nazi regime became subject to sharp criticism within the church in Germany. The "Theological Declaration," adopted at the Confessional Synod in Barmen at the end of May 1934, became the foundation of the Confessing Church. At the Confessional Synod in Dahlem on October 19 and 20, 1934, this church then adopted its own "emergency statutes" [Notrecht] and renewed its claim to be the legitimate Protestant church in Germany. The Reich Church, on the other hand, tried to stigmatize the Confessing Church as illegal, and to treat it accordingly.

The Confessing Church nevertheless gained significant weight within German Protestantism, forcing the Nazi regime to a fundamental change of direction in its church policy. On July 16, 1935, the government established the Reich Ministry for Church Affairs [Reichskirchenministerium], headed by Hanns Kerrl. The independence of the church seemed to be asserted by means of establishing a Reich church commission chaired by the respected General Superintendent Wilhelm Zoellner, as well as state and provincial commissions. The state's publicly declared intention was to "bring peace" [Befriedung] to the church. This meant practically, however, that the Church Struggle was designated to disappear from the public sphere, and together with it the Confessing Church's confession that did not have the 'proper' relationship to National Socialism. On September 24, 1935, the Reich government enacted a Law for the Protection of the German Protestant Church [Gesetz zur Sicherung der Deutschen Evangelischen Kirche], which was soon followed by a number of ordinances that specified its implementation. The fifth of these ordinances, issued on December 2, 1935, made it illegal for any "groups" to exercise any functions pertaining to church government or administration. With this move, the state for its part had now eliminated the legal status of the Confessing Church, its governing body, the Council of Brethren [Bruderrat], and all of the Confessing Church's institutions. This included the seminaries for pastors-in-training [Predigerseminare]. The education of pastors-in-training was nevertheless continued by the Confessing Church. The number of the "illegals," as the young theologians involved were called, grew in the course of time to about seven hundred. But the temptation to obtain "legal status" through the state-sanctioned church commissions also continued to grow.

When in the winter of 1936–37 Wilhelm Zoellner dared to oppose the extreme position of German Christians, he found himself the target of the Secret Police [Geheime Staatspolizei, abbreviated as Gestapo]. He tendered his resignation on February 12, 1937. In 1937 Hitler buried his expectation that he could enlist the churches to help generate support for his political and military goals. The immunity of many Christians against the National Socialist ideology, with its religious implications, was simply too strong. From now on the regime no longer concealed its unyielding determination to force the churches into line with National Socialism. The thirteenth ordinance specifying the implementation of the Law for the Protection of the German Protestant Church was issued on March 20, 1937. It established the Reich Ministry for Church Affairs not only as the body to exercise governmental oversight over the churches, but also as the highest authority for questions of internal church government.[28] Reich Bishop Müller had long since become a totally irrelevant figure. The state's and the Nazi party's instruments of power were now employed to "eliminate confessional influences from public life" [Entkonfessionalisierung] and by pressure and terror to strike against those who would still insist that the church remain independent. A wave of arrests was launched, aiming at members of the Confessing Church. This new government tactic finally also led to the closure of the Finkenwalde seminary for pastors-in-training. The Secret Police closed the seminary at the end of September 1937, acting on orders from Heinrich Himmler, the SS National Leader [Führer] and Chief of the German police.[29]

The Narrow Path of the Church Struggle

The Council of Brethren, as the church government of the Confessing Church of the Old Prussian Union, had entrusted the leadership of one of its seminaries for pastors-in-training to Dietrich Bonhoeffer. Albrecht Schönherr was a member of the first course of seminarians in 1935.[30]

[28.] Cf. *DB-ER* 575–76.

[29.] *DB-ER* 584–85 (see *DBW* 15:13).

[30.] Schönherr belonged to the "Bonhoeffer circle" of students that had formed in Berlin in 1932; cf. *DB-ER* 208.

He gives a brief summary of the sentiment among the young theologians:

> All of us had assumed the risk of a rather insecure existence. What held and carried us was the conviction that in the summer of 1934 the Confessional Synod of Barmen had spoken the truth with its six theses, and that the Synod of Dahlem which followed that same fall had applied these truths to the church at the practical level. Back then the Council of Brethren of the Confessing Church, out of a sense of responsibility for our future, was hesitant to act. But we expected and demanded of them that they would take themselves and us seriously, or rather that they would take the separating truth of the word of God seriously. This meant practically that they would take us confidently and fully under their care with an education that the state considered illegal.[31]

315

In the "spiritual exercises" from his London period, Bonhoeffer had placed less emphasis on this *separating* power of the word of God than he did later in Finkenwalde. The section on Matt. 7:1-12, for example, was originally entitled "The Right Way to One's Neighbor." When revising the manuscript for publication, Bonhoeffer now chose "The Community of Disciples Is Set Apart" as the title for the entire chapter on Matthew 7. The Confessing Church adopted its own order, and in so doing separated itself from the Reich Church government and the National Socialist regime. The third thesis of the Theological Declaration of Barmen from 1934 states that such a stance must be part of the witness of the church. The Christian church, "as a church of pardoned sinners, has to witness in the midst of a sinful world, with its faith as with its obedience, with its message as with its order, that it belongs solely to him [Jesus Christ, its Lord], and that it lives and wants to live solely from his comfort and from his direction in the expectation of his appearance."[32] When over the years the true cost of maintaining an independent church order over against the Hitler regime became more and more apparent, a "Lutheran" objection began to be heard. It argued that "it was a Reformed way of thinking to place such a legalistic weight on church order."[33] Bonhoeffer nevertheless could not avoid the conclusion that the narrow path the church had entered with its decisions in Barmen and Dahlem was indeed the mandated path of discipleship. In Finkenwalde

---

[31.] Unpublished lecture, "Predigt und Predigtlehre Dietrich Bonhoeffers," delivered at the Section of Theology at the Humboldt University in Berlin on March 11, 1981.

[32.] Leith, *Creeds of the Churches,* 520f.

[33.] Bonhoeffer, "Irrlehre in der Bekennenden Kirche?", 1936. (*DBW* 14:706 [*GS* 2:269f.]).

he therefore wrote that "wherever the church order is being manipulated from the outside, it becomes the constitutive element of the church-
community; for in it the visible form of the Holy Spirit itself is being
attacked."[34] Bonhoeffer's book *Discipleship* expounded the third thesis
of the Barmen Declaration in such a way that its truth became undeni-
able, even beyond the historical context of the Church Struggle in the
Third Reich.

316

Those members of the Confessing Church who held fast to this decision of the church walked into an uncertain future. They did so with the
same "irresponsibility" with which Peter had stepped onto the water. In
that situation it was tempting to have second thoughts and shy away from
the initial decision, or, like the third of the would-be disciples in Luke
9:57-62, to add a "but let me first": I intend to follow, but allow me first
to submit myself to the state-sanctioned church commissions (and thus
renounce the binding authority of the decisions taken in Barmen and
Dahlem).[35] It was in January 1936 that the first pastoral candidate at
Finkenwalde took that step of gaining security by "becoming legal." "In
the period that followed, almost every Finkenwalde course lost a member
who went to the committees or, as they said, 'went over to the consis-
tory.'"[36] In the fourteenth letter from Finkenwalde, Bethge reported
that one of the brothers had submitted himself to the authority of a commission "without having talked about this with us or even with Brother
Bonhoeffer only. . . . In the previous summer semester [he] had still
added his signature to a declaration of our brotherhood entitled 'Do you
want to consummate it in the flesh?'"[37] The Finkenwalde community
reacted to such cases not with self-righteous accusations but with a sense
of deep concern. What was tragic was the fact that here people knowingly
abandoned a path which they had come to understand as the path they
were called to follow. Bonhoeffer's statement, "All those who knowingly
separate themselves from the Confessing Church in Germany separate
themselves from salvation,"[38] generated a lot of criticism in the pews.
What those critics failed to hear was the (pastoral) qualifier "knowingly."

[34.] *NLA* 57, 3 Pt. II 12 (*DBW* 14:460).

[35.] Hanfried Müller contends that Bonhoeffer's commentary on Luke 9:61 in *Dis-cipleship* can be understood as a warning against choosing that option; see *Von der Kirche zur Welt*, 199.

[36.] *DB-ER* 503.

[37.] Letter of November 30, 1936 (*NL* A 48; cf. *DB-ER* 574–75).

[38.] Bonhoeffer, "Zur Frage der Kirchengemeinschaft", 1936 (*WF* 93f. [*DBW* 14:676]; also in *TF* 166).

It indeed took a great deal of courage to stick without compromise to the decisions the Confessing Church had made in Barmen and Dahlem. However, statements from imprisoned members of the Confessing Church, such as the one in a letter from Willi Brandenburg,[39] agreed with Bonhoeffer's own conviction: discipleship is grace. For the sake of that grace Bonhoeffer reminded those entrusted to his care that they had "been marked with a seal" [Versiegelung] and were subject to "church discipline" [Gemeindezucht]; he impressed on them that it was not advisable for them to jump from the ark on which they were being carried. So that they would not do harm to their souls, Bonhoeffer placed the obligation to follow the narrow path on all those who would listen to him. But as time went on, he also continued to maintain community with those Finkenwalde seminarians whom he considered as having gone astray. In the end, before being killed on the Eastern front in 1942, Willi Brandenburg had also succumbed to the pressure of becoming "legalized."[40]

317

Reaching an Understanding with Karl Barth

When Bonhoeffer began to revise his *Discipleship* manuscripts, he decided to write a letter to Karl Barth. Almost three years had gone by since their last written exchange. "Truth be told, the whole period was on my part really a continuous and quiet wrestling with your theological position, and, therefore, I had to remain silent for a while," Bonhoeffer wrote in his letter to Barth on September 19, 1936.[41] He reported that the young theologians at the seminary in Finkenwalde were dealing with the very same questions that had lately been on his own mind, namely, how to understand the Sermon on the Mount and Paul's doctrine of justification and sanctification. He then made reference to a remark that Barth had made one night in 1931, at an open evening for students at his home in Bonn. According to Bonhoeffer, Barth had remarked with great seriousness that he sometimes felt he should, rather than delivering lectures, instead "corner" individual students "like the old Tholuck and ask them

---

[39.] Brandenburg was a member of the "Bonhoeffer circle" of students in Berlin; a copy of his letter from prison, when he was not yet a seminarian at Finkenwalde, was enclosed with the tenth circular letter from Finkenwalde from July 22, 1936 (*DBW* 14:201–3 [*GS* 3:496–98]); see *WF* 67ff.

[40.] See Brandenburg's letter from October 5, 1941, cited in *DB-ER* 693 (*DBW* 16:321 [*GS* 2:593]).

[41.] *WF* 116 and *TF* 430 (*DBW* 14:235).

the question, 'How is it with your soul?' The deep need in this area
has not been met since, not even by the emergence of the Confessing
Church."[42] In light of this task, Bonhoeffer wrote, he would value
Barth's counsel.

In a letter from October 14, Barth responded that he was looking forward "with openness, but also not without a certain amount of concern"
to the results of Bonhoeffer's reflections "on the inexhaustible theme
of justification and sanctification." "What comes to mind are the Religious Socialists, the Wuppertal Pietists in the decade before the Church
Struggle, . . . and finally the members of the Oxford Group,[43] including
Emil Brunner." What all of them had in common, according to Barth,
was a "withdrawal from the initial focus on a christological-eschatologi-
cal reality in favor of some realizations within humanity's own sphere—
which actually are always abstract." Barth now saw Bonhoeffer engaged
in an attempt to try to capture this "possibility envisioned by Tholuck"
in a "theoretical-practical system." Barth had read what he called an
"Instruction on Scripture Meditation" from Finkenwalde, Barth went on,
in which, just as in Bonhoeffer's letter, he did not like "the fundamental
distinction between theological study and devotional practice" and "a
difficult-to-define smell of a monastic eros and pathos."[44]

The official author of this "Anleitung zur täglichen Meditation"
(Instructions in Daily Meditation)[45] was Eberhard Bethge, whose 1937
copy of *Discipleship* included the text by Vilmar on Matt. 5:48. In the draft
of his book Bonhoeffer's biblical exposition incorporated this "devotional"
text as well as others by Kohlbrügge and Luther taken from breviaries.[46]
This may have occurred in reaction to Barth's letter.[47] In any case, Bonhoeffer expected that a meditative approach to the theme of discipleship
would lead to the very same results as an approach based on sober scientific exegesis, rather than end up in some sort of emotional movement.

318

[42.] *WF* 117 and *TF* 431 (*DBW* 14:237).

[43.] A group founded by Frank Buchmann after his conversion in 1908; the name of
the group was changed to Moralische Aufrüstung, or Moral Rearmament, in 1938. See also
the letter of October 24, 1936 (*DBW* 14:256 [*GS* 1:46f.]).

[44.] *WF* 121 (*DBW* 14:252f. [*GS* 2:289f.]).

[45.] See *WF* 57–61 (*DBW* 14:945–50 [*GS* 2:278–82]); a copy was included in the eighth
circular letter from Finkenwalde dated May 22, 1936.

[46.] Christian Köckert, following a suggestion by Franz Hildebrandt, drew the attention of the German editors of the present volume to a collection of meditations by Luther
which were compiled by Karl Witte.

[47.] See the letter of October 24, 1936 (*DBW* 14:255f. [*GS* 1:46]).

Literary Dialogue Partners

In *Discipleship,* Bonhoeffer very rarely makes explicit mention of the person with whose thought he engages at a particular point. Those interested in theology were at any rate sufficiently able to recognize 319 Bonhoeffer's conversation partners, even if these were not explicitly mentioned by name. An example is Barth's 1922 commentary on Romans, from which Bonhoeffer clearly quoted the image of the 360-degree turn. He then connected this image with the ὡς μὴ (to have "as though they had not") from 1 Cor. 7:29-31, the key concept in Rudolf Bultmann's understanding of Christian existence.

In the introduction to *Discipleship* one name is mentioned explicitly: Kierkegaard. Bonhoeffer had already cited a book of collected writings by Kierkegaard in the manuscript he brought from London for his "Discipleship" lectures at the Finkenwalde seminary. When revising the manuscript for publication, he once again returned to that book as a rich resource. It was Bonhoeffer's hope that Kierkegaard's polemic against the Danish state-established Lutheranism of the nineteenth century would help stir up the also predominantly Lutheran German Protestant Church. To counter the temptation of simply caving in to the interference of the National Socialist regime in church government required the use of sharp language. In his 1968 doctoral dissertation, Traugott Vogel identified the Kierkegaard edition Bonhoeffer must have used. In fact, Eberhard Bethge then found the volume, annotated by Bonhoeffer's own hand, in the collection of Bonhoeffer's books that Bethge had inherited.

Some Lutherans charged that the Confessing Church under the leadership of the Council of Brethren was prone to "Dahlemite tendencies" (i.e., tendencies which held fast to the emergency statutes adopted at the Confessional Synod in Dahlem). However, these Lutheran objections did not prevent Bonhoeffer from remaining faithful to those valid insights he had gained from Lutheran theologians. Both in *Sanctorum Communio* and in *Act and Being* he already had drawn on Karl Holl's extensive articles on Luther, in particular "Der Neubau der Sittlichkeit" (The reconstruction of morality).[48] From Holl, Bonhoeffer learned that the category of 'possibility' has no proper place in theology.[49] On certain

---

[48.] Holl, *Luther,* 155–287.
[49.] Ibid., 234f.

issues he also agreed with Paul Althaus, for example, with Althaus's
Lutheran theological critique of "Religious Socialism," even though
Althaus and Elert expressed other views during the Third Reich which
ran directly counter to the course to which Bonhoeffer held fast.[50]

320   With similar resolve Bonhoeffer criticized the ethics of the Swiss
Reformed theologian Emil Brunner, even though in matters of church
politics he received support from the Reformed quarter.[51] On April
28, 1934, Bonhoeffer wrote a letter from London to Erwin Sutz. In it he
already indicated that his reflections on the Sermon on the Mount had
convinced him of the necessity to engage in a discussion with Brunner's
book, *The Divine Imperative*.[52] In *Discipleship*, without explicitly referring
to Brunner, Bonhoeffer then warned not to stifle the obedience of discipleship under the bushel of "bourgeois" conventions. Yet in spite of
these reservations Bonhoeffer, in his 1936 chapter, "The Call to Discipleship," inserted Brunner's dual thesis that obedience consists in faith in
God's promise and that true obedience is faith.[53]

Bonhoeffer's reception of Tholuck's book *Commentary on the Sermon
on the Mount* appears at first sight equally ambiguous. A copy which had
originally belonged to Carl Weiszäcker (1822–99) had been given to the
seminary in Finkenwalde by a donor from the Rhineland. Bonhoeffer
began to refer to the book after the summer course of 1936. He wove the
conversation with this literary partner into the text of his "spiritual exercises," which he had brought with him from London. Tholuck inspired
Bonhoeffer to include a number of remarkably erudite footnotes and
annotations in his own book. Examples of the former are the first two
footnotes in the section on the Beatitudes; an example of the latter, the
explication of the oath in antiquity. However, Bonhoeffer also sharply
criticized this respected and influential theologian when he termed Tholuck's invocation of John 18:23 against Matt. 5:39, for example, as "evil
thoughtlessness." Bonhoeffer examined and respected the thoughts of
others in the way he had already defined in his doctoral dissertation:
". . . it remains our task to preserve the insight, without making the
same mistake."[54] Even his literary conversation partners he intended
"to judge not as persons but only as far as their objective decisions and

---

[50.] See, e.g., *DB-ER* 306, 435.
[51.] See, e.g., *DB-ER* 520–26.
[52.] See *DBW* 13:128f. (*GS* 1:40).
[53.] See Brunner, *The Divine Imperative*, 81.
[54.] See *SC* (*DBWE* 1):74 on the philosophy of spirit in idealist philosophy.

actions were concerned," [55] in this case the formation and expression of their thoughts.

In preparation for *Act and Being,* his Habilitationsschrift, Bonhoeffer had thoroughly studied Erich Przywara's book *Religionsphilosophie katholischer Theologie.* At the time, this book was considered "a blueprint for solving the world's problems," as Christoph von Hase, Bonhoeffer's cousin and fellow student, recalls. On page 30, Przywara quotes the "harsh word of the author of the 'Nachfolge Christi' that 'it is better to experience remorse than to know its definition.'" In his copy, Bonhoeffer marked this statement with an exclamation mark in the margin. This reference to the *Imitatio Christi* [*Nachfolge Christi*] by Thomas à Kempis might be one reason why Bonhoeffer chose the title *Discipleship* [*Nachfolge*] for his own book.

321

III

The conclusion of Bonhoeffer's work on *Discipleship* almost coincided with the closure of the seminary in Finkenwalde and the end of his work there. When on the first Sunday of Advent 1937 Bonhoeffer wrote a dedication in Eberhard Bethge's copy of *Discipleship,* he thanked him for "two and a half years of life together in faithful community in Finkenwalde."[56] During the Advent season of 1937 Bonhoeffer also dedicated a copy of the book to Martin Niemöller, who had been imprisoned since July 1, 1937: ". . . as an expression of gratitude from a fellow Christian. A book which he [Niemöller] would be able to write better than the author."[57] In his circular letter for Christmas that year, Bonhoeffer wrote to the former students at Finkenwalde that "since the book appeared in print, I have often dedicated it in spirit to all of you. That I did not do so explicitly on the title page is due to the fact that I did not want to claim your support for my own thoughts and theology—our community has another foundation."[58] At the conclusion of the opening chapter Bonhoeffer had written the "invisible dedication" of the book to all those who recognize with amazement that costly grace is at the same time merciful grace.

[55.] See *DBW* 14:108 (*GS* 2:211).

[56.] *DB-ER* 452.

[57.] *WF* 163f. (*DBW* 15:21 [*GS* 2:307]). See *DB-ER* 452 and 579–80.

[58.] *DBW* 15:15 (*GS* 2:525); see *DB-ER* 452.

Early Reactions to Discipleship

During the Third Reich readers knew that a real engagement with the thoughts of *Discipleship* would necessarily entail practical consequences for their own lives. Here Bonhoeffer had exposed the seductive, comfortable understanding of grace which was pervasive throughout German Protestantism and that had caused the *Volkskirche* to get weak, losing the strength and vitality that the church of the Reformation once had. This painful truth apparently did not permit a merely intellectual engagement with this book at the time. Consequently, no extensive reviews were published. However, the book itself made the rounds rather quickly.[59] In the midst of the Church Struggle this reflection on the biblical and theological foundations of the church was seen as a call to arms pointing in the right direction.

In villages in Eastern Pomerania Bonhoeffer quietly continued the training of pastoral candidates for the Confessing Church in "collective pastorates" [Sammelvikariate]. Heinz Fleischhack, a member of the first "secret" course in Groß-Schlönwitz, recalls:

> For Christmas [1937] Dietrich Bonhoeffer gave each of us [seven] candidates who had found ourselves in this place a copy of *Discipleship*—bound in that snow-white cover. And throughout the following months, Bonhoeffer continued to deal with this book. It served as the basis for his regular Bible studies at the Prussian Landowners' gatherings [Junkerkonvent] at the home of Mrs. von Kleist-Retzow. When we studied 1 Corinthians 13 in our Bible content course, Bonhoeffer emphasized that *this* kind of love does go hand in hand with discipleship. *Discipleship* thus became the determining influence for my own theological existence.[60]

The encounter with Bonhoeffer and with his exposition of the call to discipleship shaped many of these young theologians for the rest of their lives. It strengthened them in their courage freely to live out their faith, and in their ability to discern clearly when resistance was called for.

In the years that followed, the pastors of the Confessing Church became subject to an increasing, indeed almost unbearable, pressure to become "legalized." Gerhard Krause, who was a candidate in the fourth course in Finkenwalde and had come to embrace the idea of legalization, wrote to Bonhoeffer on February 18, 1939:

[59.] See *DB-ER* 453.
[60.] Letter to the German editors by Heinz Fleischhack on March 11, 1983.

In preparation for the Prussian Synod I have reread fairly long sections of your *Discipleship,* because I wanted to keep the possibility of reversing my opinion. But you are quite right when you write of the "bottomless pit of theological dissent" between us. . . . open to changing back to my former views. But you are right, of course, when in your letter you talk about the "unfathomable theological disagreement between us." . . . In your doctrine of justification and even more so in your doctrine of the church . . . , I sense errors that I have only seen elsewhere in Catholic theology.[61]

323

Together with a pastoral colleague, Krause drafted a theological position paper which sharply disagreed with Bonhoeffer's views while being supportive of those in the Confessing Church who were seeking legalization.[62]

It was still possible for Bonhoeffer to teach five more courses in Eastern Pomerania. Then in March of 1940 the Gestapo, the Secret Police of the Nazi authorities, finally also closed this last refuge.[63]

Discipleship *and Bonhoeffer's* Ethics

From the late fall of 1940 Bonhoeffer was employed by the Munich branch of the Abwehr, the German military counterintelligence. He was thus part of the circle of conspirators against Hitler which had formed at the Berlin headquarters of the Abwehr. During the winter months of 1940–41, Bonhoeffer was a guest at the monastery of Ettal in Bavaria. From there he wrote, among other things: "In the public readings here, they have included *Life Together,*[64] and for the Christmas celebration here at the monastery yesterday, I'm told, also some passages from *Discipleship.* That is rather gratifying, isn't it?"[65]

In Ettal, Bonhoeffer worked on his *Ethics.* The first partial manuscripts for the proposed book had already been written in the summer and fall of 1940, and further sections followed until 1943. In the very first of these manuscripts, entitled "Christ, Reality, and the Good," Bonhoeffer referred back to *Discipleship.*[66] Quite unlike his early academic publica-

---

[61.] *DB-ER* 617; *DBW* 15:152(*GS* 6:440).

[62.] Cf. *DB-ER* 615–19.

[63.] See *DB-ER* 589.

[64.] *Life Together,* which reflects on the experience in Finkenwalde, had been written by Bonhoeffer in September and October 1938 at the Göttingen home of his twin sister, Sabine Leibholz, who together with her family had just emigrated.

[65.] Letter from Bonhoeffer dated December 26, 1940 (*DBW* 16:102 [*GS* 2:588]).

[66.] *E* 199 (*DBW* 6:48). Regarding the problems of the sequence and chronology of the *Ethics* manuscripts, see the new critical edition, *DBW* 6:13–22.

tions, this book continued to engage his thinking in a rather striking way. In *Discipleship* he had reached the conclusion that the church must be physically visible, occupying space in the world. Along that same line, Karl Barth, in a letter to Bonhoeffer from October 14, 1936, had warned against the retreat into a sphere of human "piety."[67] In the first of his *Ethics* manuscripts Bonhoeffer now vigorously argued against the theological scheme of two spheres. The danger of such a scheme, he charged, was the mistaken notion that the church and the world would statically exist side by side as "two separate realms," with the church thereby abdicating its coresponsibility for the state of justice and injustice within society.[68]

In both the first and the second of his *Ethics* manuscripts, Bonhoeffer took up a term which he had introduced in the final section of *Discipleship*, namely, the term "the incarnate one" [der Menschgewordene]. In the final pages of *Discipleship*, Bonhoeffer had spoken about the form of Jesus Christ as consisting of three dimensions. In his manuscript entitled "Ethics as Formation," especially, he now spoke quite similarly about "the incarnate, crucified, and risen one."[69]

In the manuscript "History and the Good," Bonhoeffer revisited a train of thought which had already caused some surprise among those who had sat in on his lectures at Finkenwalde. There, specifically in his exposition of Matt. 6:1-4, he had already spoken about how the good happens like the action of a sleepwalker, when disciples are following Jesus. In *Ethics*, the concept of 'discipleship' [Nachfolge] is replaced by a strictly theological understanding of the term 'responsibility' [Verantwortung]: "The good, as the responsible act, is carried out without knowing about the good."[70] In his Finkenwalde lectures, Bonhoeffer had hinted at the notion of the 'passivity', understood in a theological sense, of the active human being. In his *Ethics* this concept now became indispensable for

---

[67.] See *WF* 120 (*DBW* 14:251 [*GS* 2:289]).

[68.] See *E* 193–200 (*DBW* 6:41–50).

[69.] *E* 72–86 (*DBW* 6:69–86). This manuscript was written right after the manuscript entitled "Christ, Reality, and the Good." In a manuscript drafted during his stay in Ettal, Bonhoeffer dealt with the concept of 'situation' and in that context referred to "*Discipleship*, chapter 1" (*E* 140 [*DBW* 6:160]). "Chapter 1" (like the reference "in the first chapter" in Bonhoeffer's letter from the second Sunday of Advent 1943, *LPP* 157 [*DBW* 8:226]) refers to the chapter "The Call to Discipleship," rather than to the introductory chapter entitled "Costly Grace."

[70.] *E* 245 (*DBW* 6:285). Regarding the harmful knowledge of good and evil which is part of our fallenness, see *CF* 87–93 (*DBW* 3:82–87) and *E* 21–24 (*DBW* 6:301–4).

him.[71] In the last of his *Ethics* manuscripts, on which he was working when he was arrested on April 5, 1943, Bonhoeffer describes God's commandment as an "angel guiding our steps while we are asleep."[72]

During his work on the *Ethics* manuscripts, Bonhoeffer was deeply engaged "in the worldly sphere." He expressed surprise about the fact that he was able to live "for days without the Bible." The option of forcing himself to read the Bible appeared to him "not as obedience, but as an act of auto-suggestion." "I know that I only have to open my own books to hear all the things that can be said against all of this. I also do not intend to justify myself, but I recognize that I have had periods which were 'spiritually' much richer . . . ; however, since I have the impression that in this matter some kind of breakthrough is imminent for me, I simply let things take their course and do not fight it."[73]

325

Bonhoeffer's Final Word on Discipleship

In his prison letters from the summer of 1944, Bonhoeffer further explored a question which he had already raised in the preface to *Discipleship*. It was the question of how to live a life of discipleship (or how to have "faith," to say it in other words) as a person working in the world. In the letter from July 18, 1944, Bonhoeffer contemplated the different ways we are "dragged into" following Jesus Christ, and came to understand that this experience is never a partial or merely "religious" act; "'faith' is something whole, involving all of one's life."[74]

On July 20, 1944, the attempt on Hitler's life failed. The following day, with the threat to his own life now greater than ever, Bonhoeffer wrote a letter to Eberhard Bethge. In it he recalled a conversation he had had with Jean Lasserre in 1931: "We were asking ourselves quite simply what we wanted to do with our lives. He said he would like to become a saint (and I think it's quite likely that he did become one). At the time I was very impressed, but I disagreed with him, and said, in effect, that I should

---

[71.] See *E* 245 (*DBW* 6:285): "The free act ultimately recognizes itself as God's act. . . ." See also *E* 55f. (*DBW* 6:340–41).

[72.] See *E* 279 (*DBW* 6:389) and the "Ethics" note in *NL* A 75, no. 107.

[73.] Letter to Eberhard Bethge from June 25, 1942 (*TP* 138 [*DBW* 16:325]); see also *TF* 499. Cf. Bethge's comment that "these statements have to be understood against the background of a kind of mutual agreement into which we had entered, namely, the agreement to commit ourselves" to keeping the daily rhythm of living with the Bible as they had done in Finkenwalde (*Bekennen und Widerstehen*, 204).

[74.] *LPP* 362 (*DBW* 8:537).

like to learn to have faith. For a long time I didn't realize the depth of
the contrast. I thought I could acquire faith by trying to live a holy life,
or something like it. I suppose I wrote *Discipleship* as the end of that
path. Today I can see the dangers of that book, though I still stand by
what I wrote. I discovered later, and I'm still discovering right up to this
moment, that it is only by living completely in this world that one learns
to have faith. One must completely abandon any attempt to make something of oneself, whether it be a saint, or a converted sinner, or a church-
man (a so-called priestly type!), a righteous person or an unrighteous
one, a sick person or a healthy one. By this-worldliness I mean living
unreservedly in life's duties, problems, successes and failures, experiences and perplexities. In so doing we throw ourselves completely into
the arms of God, taking seriously, not our own sufferings, but those of
God in the world—watching with Christ in Gethsemane. That, I think, is
faith; that is *metanoia*;[75] and that is how one becomes a human being, a
Christian (cf. Jer. 45!)."[76]

The hopes of the conspirators had been dashed. As if having briefly
put down all his work to take a short break, Bonhoeffer in this letter
spoke simply and calmly about the identity of his own self. Sometime
before 1933, this self had gratefully given up all attempts to make something of itself. To lead something like a holy life is a legitimate aspiration
in the sphere of the penultimate. It is certainly nothing less than that,
but it is also nothing more. For a self who is aware of how radically different the ultimate is, the striving for sanctification is without danger.
Things only become dangerous if the penultimate is being confused with
the ultimate. On December 5, 1943, Bonhoeffer had written to Bethge:

> We live in the sphere of the penultimate, and have faith in the ultimate,
> do we not? Lutherans (so-called!) and Pietists would get goose bumps even
> thinking such a thought. But it is the truth, nevertheless. In *Discipleship* (in
> the first chapter) I have only hinted at this idea, but subsequently did not
> fully develop it. Now this must wait for a later time.[77]

[75.] Greek for "repentance, change of heart."

[76.] *LPP* 369f. (*DBW* 8:542). As his meditation-Bible, Bonhoeffer used an edition of
the translation by Luther. In it, Jeremiah 45, which consists of only five verses, is marked
with numerous underlinings and marginal notes: ". . . Thus says the Lord: I am going to
break down what *I* have built, and pluck up what *I* have planted—that is, *my whole land*. And
you are seeking great things *for yourself*? Do not seek them; for I am going to bring disaster
upon all [marginal note by Bonhoeffer: "just and unjust"] flesh, says the Lord; but I will
give you *your soul* as a *prize of war* in every place to which you may go" (Jer. 45:4f.).

[77.] *LPP* 157 (*DBW* 8:226).

This "hint" in *Discipleship* to which Bonhoeffer refers in his letter is found in the chapter "The Call to Discipleship." Here Bonhoeffer states that the first step, which we are capable of taking by our human freedom, is that of hearing and acting in the sphere of the penultimate. He asserts, however, that this first step still falls short of 'discipleship' in the full sense. Nonetheless, without taking this first step, the one who is being called cannot learn to have faith. On the day after the failed coup   327 attempt, Bonhoeffer was calmly learning to have faith as a coconspirator fully living in this world. He knew that Christ in Gethsemane prayed that the cup might pass, and it does pass; but its passing consists precisely in undergoing God's suffering in the world.[78]

Bonhoeffer's final comments on *Discipleship* later proved to be both unsettling and reassuring to the pastors he trained at Finkenwalde and in Eastern Pomerania. Heinz Fleischhack admitted that, when reading the prison letters which had been published in 1951, he had "become repeatedly concerned" until he finally read Bonhoeffer's statement that he still stood behind the book as he always had.[79] Many of these pastors have been haunted by the question of whether, in the end, Finkenwalde might have been only a temporary phase in Bonhoeffer's life. Eberhard Bethge spoke for them when he said: "For us the big discovery was Dietrich Bonhoeffer the theologian and the devout man, the Bonhoeffer of meditation and prayer, the person who lectured on 'discipleship' to us." For Bethge himself it then became "a sometimes painful, yet also important process of growth to come to realize that the Bonhoeffer whom we had met in Finkenwalde could be viewed as a mere interlude by his own family."[80] In the letter from July 21, 1944, Bonhoeffer indeed indicates that for him *Discipleship* marked the conclusion of a particular chapter in his journey. The "spiritual exercises" had led him into a community which was quite different from the community of his own family. His later journey led him, through changed circumstances, into that circle of the Bonhoeffer family which was deeply involved in the conspiracy. Bonhoeffer experienced that discipleship takes place one step at a time; each step marks a new entrance into discipleship. He considered the totality of one's life's journey, including his own, to be in the hands of the one who calls us into discipleship.

[78.] See above, page 90.
[79.] Letter to the German editors from March 11, 1983.
[80.] See Bethge, *Bekennen und Widerstehen*, 203f.

328

IV

Academic-theological reviews of *Discipleship* were not published until after 1945. The first and most extensive of these came from the pen of Karl Barth.[81]

Karl Barth and Discipleship

Barth's 1955 review of *Discipleship* starts out almost euphorically. "By far the best" of what has been written about "human sanctification" and the "call to discipleship," Barth wrote, came from a man who "sought to make [discipleship] a reality in his actions, and who in his own way did indeed succeed in that endeavor."[82] Barth then referred to Bonhoeffer's opening chapters ("The Call to Discipleship," "Simple Obedience," and "Discipleship and the Individual") and to his exposition of the Sermon on the Mount. "In the New Testament sense it is not possible to be a pacifist merely in principle; one can only be a pacifist *in practice.* However, all those who are being called to discipleship must watch whether in practice they can really ignore or avoid becoming a *pacifist!* "[83]

In a later passage, Barth cites a quote from Kohlbrügge which Bonhoeffer had used in *Discipleship.* With it Barth illustrates his concern that Kohlbrügge's statements sound as if spoken on a psychological level. Accordingly, this makes it "at least somewhat difficult not suddenly to hear almost perfectionist notes in them."[84] Barth's worries in 1936, over how Bonhoeffer might deal with the subject of 'sanctification', had apparently not entirely been laid to rest.

In a later paragraph Barth emphasizes, first, that the "act of love" is carried out by human beings facing God, rather than being "God's puppets-on-a-string."[85] This is a critical allusion to the Platonic allegory of

---

[81.] *Church Dogmatics*, 4/2:499–613, esp. 533–53. On September 24, 1988, Hinrich Stoevesandt from the Karl Barth Archive indicated to the editors that an examination of Barth's copy of *Discipleship* leaves it unclear whether he had already studied the book in a preliminary way when writing the passage in *Church Dogmatics* 2/2:566–75. That volume of Barth's *Church Dogmatics* had been published in 1942.

[82.] Ibid., 533f.

[83.] Ibid., 550.

[84.] Ibid., 576.

[85.] Ibid., 786.

the puppet-on-a-string that can be manipulated by the golden cord to   329
which it is attached.[86] Barth has reservations about Bonhoeffer's interpretation of Matt. 6:3f., which likens the act of love to the behavior of
a "sleepwalker."[87] Using imagery from Plato's cave allegory,[88] Barth
then writes two pages later: Those who by the work of the Holy Spirit
have come to act in love "come out into the open like cave-dwellers—
squinting a little since the sun out there is so bright, and worried a little
since out there it is also windy and rainy at times; but they do come
out." And they simply are who they are, "having abandoned the mistaken
notion that they belonged to themselves."[89] Barth might have thought
with a "squinting" look at Bonhoeffer's statements that maybe this is
what Bonhoeffer had meant to say.

Discipleship *in Bonhoeffer Research*

Hanfried Müller's doctoral dissertation from 1961 is the first comprehensive presentation of Bonhoeffer's theology as a whole published in
German. In it, Müller sees *Discipleship* within its historical context as the
rebuke of the clause "but first let me go . . ." (Luke 9:61). According to
Müller, Bonhoeffer's contemporaries associated the following issues with
this phrase: "to achieve the official recognition of the Confessing Church
by the state, to restore the internal peace within the church, to deal with
the question of financial security, and to become 'legalized.'"[90] Müller's analysis asserts that Bonhoeffer's book, rather than *consisting* of two
parts, *falls apart* in two pieces.[91] Bonhoeffer's careful correlation of Part
One and Part Two is obviously not easy to detect at first sight.

   In his analysis of the entire Bonhoeffer opus, Ernst Feil has pointed
out that during the period of writing *Discipleship*, Bonhoeffer's thinking
was characterized by both a christological concentration and a "negative" relationship of the Christian to the world.[92] Feil interprets this as

---

[86.] Plato, *Laws* 644c ff., 803b ff.
   [87.] Ferenc Lehel recalls that Bonhoeffer had used the "image of the sleepwalker" in
that context; see Heinz Eduard Tödt, *Wie eine Flaschenpost*, 248.
   [88.] *Politics* 514ff.
   [89.] *Church Dogmatics* 4/2:787.
   [90.] Hanfried Müller, *Von der Kirche zur Welt*, 199.
   [91.] Ibid., 230f.
   [92.] Feil, *The Theology of Dietrich Bonhoeffer*, 76–82.

330 Bonhoeffer's attraction to a genuine monastic life, an attraction which
at the time played an important part in Bonhoeffer's biography.[93] Feil
also considers it surprising that Bonhoeffer concludes his book about
listening to the word with an allusion to the *seeing*, the "beholding of
God."[94] These reflections in the final chapter, entitled "The Image of
Christ," were never presented by Bonhoeffer in his lectures in Finkenwalde. He certainly considered them part of the "Discipline of the Secret"
[Arkandisziplin].

Over the years, numerous Bonhoeffer studies have appeared within
the expansive arena of the Protestant and Roman Catholic world. Many of
them include an appraisal of *Discipleship,* and especially of the theological
understanding of the world which Bonhoeffer develops in this book.[95]
Discipleship is much more closely linked with Bonhoeffer as a person than
a work usually is with its author. It is, therefore, a book which no Bonhoeffer scholar can disregard.[96] To give an example of a dissenting
voice which could already be heard in 1939,[97] let us finally mention
yet another study. Gerhard Krause's article on Dietrich Bonhoeffer in
the *Theologische Realenzyklopädie* directs the reader's attention to Bonhoeffer's seminar in Berlin in 1932–33. The "exercises" in this seminar,
Krause argues, "reproduced Thomas à Kempis's *Imitation of Christ.*"[98]
"A 'conceptual framework' that was 'intentionally different from that of
the Reformation' "[99] was, according to Krause, "directed against the students of Luther." However, due to the "traces of mysticism" which Krause
perceives in *Discipleship,* Bonhoeffer was "hardly successful" in prevailing

---

[93.] Ibid., 128f.

[94.] Cf. ibid., 81f. For the majority of the cross-references to Bonhoeffer's work as a
whole, the editors are indebted to Ernst Feil.

[95.] For an indirect discussion with Hanfried Müller on this point, see Feil, *The Theology of Dietrich Bonhoeffer,* 125–38; for explicit discussions of Ernst Feil's position, see Peters,
Die Präsenz des Politischen in der Theologie Dietrich Bonhoeffers, 57, and Strunk, *Nachfolge Christi,*
205f.

[96.] The bibliography in this volume lists a selected number of such scholarly contributions.

[97.] See Krause's letter from February 18, 1939 (*DBW* 15:150–54 [*GS* 6:439–42]).

[98.] Krause, *Theologische Realenzyklopädie* 7:60; see the student notes of the seminar
from February 22, 1933, which contain the key word "exercise" [Exercitium] (*NL* Appendix B 2, 3 [47–50]) (*DBW* 12:198–99).

[99.] See *DBW* 13:171 (*GS* 6:296): "The time has now come when, due to a partial recov-
ery of Reformation theology, we must once again turn our attention to the Sermon on the
Mount—although it must be understood differently than it was during the Reformation."

over these opponents.[100] This assessment points indirectly and without
Krause's intention to the theologically central issue in *Discipleship*. In his   331
criticism of modern Protestant church life and Protestant theology, Bonhoeffer, in the spirit of the Reformation, went back to the Bible itself. He
pointed to issues in the Sermon on the Mount and in the texts that deal
with discipleship that we had repressed or almost forgotten. In so doing,
Bonhoeffer gave new relevance to justification and sanctification, the
central tenets of the Reformation.

On the Journey to Reality

In 1976 the Geneva center of the World Council of Churches hosted a
conference on the seventieth anniversary of Bonhoeffer's birth. In his
address for the occasion, Carl Friedrich von Weizsäcker outlined his
thoughts about how Bonhoeffer's *Discipleship* is bound to continue to
accompany us on our journey through history. "Bonhoeffer had been
entrusted with a group of pastoral candidates nearly his own age with
whom he lived together in a communal setting. He had the courage to
offer to them, and even impose on them, some of the ancient rules of
monastic life which in every age have proven helpful to those engaged
in a serious effort to live that life. Among these rules were a set pattern
for each day, a prayer liturgy, and a humble rediscovery of some practices in the infinitely rich field of meditation. The fact that Bonhoeffer
introduced these rules and practices in the face of firmly set Protestant
prejudices against them exemplifies, in my judgment, the very same
'courage to be real' which, in the final phase of his theological development, led him in the apparently opposite direction of embracing a
sense of 'worldliness.' His own life became a living example of Bonhoeffer's conviction that the Christian life can become more worldly
only by becoming more spiritual, and more spiritual only by becoming
more worldly. Both of these movements are intended to break down
the protective mechanisms that prevent us from facing our own fear of
ourselves."[101]

[100.] Krause, *Theologische Realenzyklopädie* 7:60; see also *DBW* 15:152 (*GS* 6:440), which
has already been mentioned.

[101.] Von Weizsäcker, "Thoughts of a Nontheologian on Dietrich Bonhoeffer's Development," in *The Ambivalence of Progress*, 166, in which von Weizsäcker coins the phrase "the
journey toward reality [Reise zur Wirklichkeit]" (163).

Above all, as a "spiritual" book, von Weizsäcker argued, *Nachfolge* contains indispensable insights into how to live responsibly in the world, and thus insights for the political arena. "I would like to assume that someday our world will know a political landscape in which certain problems that still face us today will no longer be around—such as the problem that sovereign powers can start wars. However, such a scenario will be the result of a political construct which perhaps in many ways will more resemble the Roman Empire than the heavenly kingdom envisioned by the Quakers. At the same time, I do not believe that such a political construct can be anything other than plain barbarism, unless it is born out of a striving for the absolute"[102]—or, to say it in terms of Bonhoeffer's *Discipleship*, out of the disciplined effort to carry out the will of the One to whom alone unreserved obedience is due.[103]

In the spiritual and the intellectual arena, too, according to von Weizsäcker, there will be the need to dismantle defense mechanisms with which groups of people anxiously seek to guard their special status over against others.[104] In the modern world it is no longer tenable to hold the view that "reality consists [only of one's own culture] and that everything else is nothing but the 'context' of that reality. If you are a Lutheran because your parents were Lutherans, does that allow you to conclude that Roman Catholics are wrong? If you are a Christian because you were born in Europe, does that permit you to determine that Buddhists are wrong? And if you are religious because you were nurtured in a religious tradition, does that give you the right to assume that nonbelievers are wrong?"[105] But whoever has discovered unmistakable truth in one of the traditions will want to refrain from trivializing any of the other traditions. A book such as *Discipleship*, which was written with the author's clear focus on the source of his own faith tradition, has the practical effect of making the boundaries between the Christian denominations more permeable. In addition, it helps to tear down barriers of anti-Jewish prejudice. Moreover, it leads us closer to thresholds the crossing of which toward mutual understanding we are not yet able to envision. The community into which the coming of costly grace calls us extends far beyond the confines of the "Christian West."

[102.] Von Weizsäcker, "Gedanken eines Nichttheologen," *Genf '76*, 59.

[103.] In his Luther Bible, Bonhoeffer has underlined the term "discipline" in verses such as Prov. 4:13: "Keep hold of discipline; do not let go of it; guard it, for it is your life."

[104.] See von Weizsäcker, "Thoughts of a Nontheologian on Dietrich Bonhoeffer's Development," in *The Ambivalence of Progress*, 171.

[105.] Von Weizsäcker, "Gedanken eines Nichttheologen," *Genf '76*, 55f.

Chronology of Discipleship

February 4, 1906
Dietrich Bonhoeffer and his twin sister, Sabine, born in Breslau, Germany

Summer semester 1923
Bonhoeffer begins a year of theological study at the University of Tübingen

Early summer 1924
Bonhoeffer travels to Rome and North Africa with his brother Klaus

June 1924–July 1927
Bonhoeffer studies theology at Friedrich-Wilhelm University, Berlin

July 1927
Acceptance of *Sanctorum Communio* for Bonhoeffer's licentiate in theology at Friedrich-Wilhelm University, Berlin

February 1928
Bonhoeffer serves as assistant pastor at the German congregation, Barcelona

July 1930
Acceptance of *Akt und Sein* [*Act and Being*], Bonhoeffer's *Habilitationsschrift* or qualifying thesis for a teaching position at Friedrich-Wilhelm University, Berlin

September 1930
Abridged first edition of *Sanctorum Communio* published by Trowitzsch und Sohn, Berlin

September 1930–Summer 1931
Postgraduate year as a Sloane Fellow at Union Theological Seminary, New York

August 1931
Bonhoeffer begins his post as lecturer on the theological faculty of Friedrich-Wilhelm University, Berlin

September 1931
Publication of *Akt und Sein*

November 15, 1931
Bonhoeffer's ordination at St. Matthias Church, Berlin

Summer semester 1932
Bonhoeffer lectures at Friedrich-Wilhelm University, Berlin, on "The Nature of the Church"

Fall 1932
Bonhoeffer delivers talk on "Christ and Peace" to German Student Christian Movement in Berlin

January 30, 1933
Adolf Hitler made chancellor of Germany

April 1933
Bonhoeffer's article on "The Church and the Jewish Question"

Summer 1933
Bonhoeffer's Christology lectures and seminar on Hegel's philosophy of religion at Friedrich- Wilhelm University, Berlin

September 1933
Preliminary work with Pastor Martin Niemöller to organize the Pastors' Emergency League

October 17, 1933
Bonhoeffer begins his pastorate for German-speaking congregations at the German Evangelical Church, Sydenham, and the Reformed Church of St. Paul in London

March 14, 1934
Decree by Reich Bishop Müller to close the Old Prussian preachers' seminaries

May 29–31, 1934
Organizational meeting of Confessing Church in Barmen, Germany; adoption of the Barmen Declaration

August 28, 1934
Bonhoeffer delivers his sermon, "The Church and the People of the World," at the ecumenical conference in Fanø, Denmark

Autumn 1934
Opening of the first preachers' seminary of the Confessing Church at Bielefeld-Sieker

December 1934–March 1935
Bonhoeffer visits Anglican monasteries in Britain

March 10, 1935
Bonhoeffer takes leave of his London parishioners

April 26, 1935
Bonhoeffer travels to the site of the Confessing Church's seminary at Zingst by the Baltic Sea

April 29, 1935
Opening of the preacher's seminary of the Confessing Church at Zingst; Bonhoeffer gives first lecture on the New Testament

June 24, 1935
Confessing Church Seminary relocated to Finkenwalde in Pomerania

September 15, 1935
Nuremberg Laws cancel citizenship for German Jews and prohibit marriage between Jews and Aryans

December 2, 1935
Confessing Church's training centers, examinations, and ordinations declared illegal by the state

February 1936
Bonhoeffer gives the last of his weekly, hour-long classes on "Discipleship" during the winter semester at Friedrich-Wilhelm University, Berlin

April 22, 1936
Bonhoeffer lectures in Finkenwalde, "On the Question of the Church Community"

August 5, 1936
Bonhoeffer's authorization to teach on the faculty of the Friedrich-Wilhelm University, Berlin, is withdrawn

August 26, 1937
Bonhoeffer completes work on *Nachfolge*

Mid-October 1937
Finkenwalde Seminary closed by action of the Gestapo

November 1937
Publication of *Nachfolge*

December 5, 1937
Collective pastorates begin in Köslin and Gross-Schlönwitz, replacing the Confessing Church seminaries

February 1938
Bonhoeffer makes initial contacts with leaders of the political resistance to Hitler: Canaris, Oster, Beck, and Sack

April 20, 1938
All pastors in Germany on active duty ordered to take the oath of allegiance to Hitler in recognition of his birthday

September 9, 1938
Bonhoeffer and Bethge help the family of Sabine and Gerhard Leibholz escape Germany into Switzerland

September 30, 1938
Munich agreement between Hitler, Chamberlain, Daladier, and Mussolini

September–October 1938
Bonhoeffer writes *Gemeinsames Leben* while staying at the Leibholz's former home

November 9–10, 1938
Kristallnacht: destruction of hundreds of synagogues and thousands of Jewish-owned shops in Germany, arrests of an estimated 35,000 Jews

1939
Publication of *Gemeinsames Leben* as volume 61 of *Theologische Existenz heute*

June 2–July 27, 1939
Bonhoeffer's second trip to the United States

September 1, 1939
German troops invade Poland; Great Britain and France declare war on Germany

1940
Chr. Kaiser Verlag publishes second edition of *Nachfolge*

April 5, 1943
Bonhoeffer is arrested and incarcerated in Tegel prison

April 9, 1945
Bonhoeffer is executed together with Canaris, Oster, Sack, Gehre and Strünck at Flossenbürg Concentration Camp

1948
SCM Press publishes an abridged English edition of *Nachfolge* entitled, *The Cost of Discipleship*

1949
First United States edition of *The Cost of Discipleship*

1955
In his section on "The Call to Discipleship" in his *Church Dogmatics* IV/2 Karl Barth states that "the best that has been written on the subject is to be found in Bonhoeffer's *The Cost of Discipleship*" (533).

1959
Second, unabridged edition of *The Cost of Discipleship* published by SCM Press

1960
Macmillan publishes the second unabridged edition of *The Cost of Discipleship*

1961
Chr. Kaiser Verlag publishes the seventh edition of *Nachfolge*

1963
Macmillan publishes paperback edition of *The Cost of Discipleship*

1964
SCM Press publishes paperback edition of *The Cost of Discipleship*

1981
Publication of the twelfth edition of *Nachfolge* with an "Afterword" by Eberhard Bethge

1989
Publication of the new critical German edition of *Nachfolge*, as Dietrich Bonhoeffer Werke 4

1994
Publication of a revised second edition of *Nachfolge*, Dietrich Bonhoeffer Werke 4

1995
Simon and Schuster issues Touchstone paperback edition of *The Cost of Discipleship*

Bibliography

1. Literature Used by Bonhoeffer

Althaus, Paul. *Der Geist der lutherischen Ethik im Augsburgischen Bekenntnis.* Munich: Chr. Kaiser, 1930. *NL* 4.1.

————. *Kirche und Volkskampf: Die Völkische Wille Im Licht des Evangeliums.* Gütersloh: C. Bertelsmann, 1928. *NL* 2 C 4.1b.

————. *Religiöser Sozialismus: Grundfragen der christlicher Sozialethik* (Religious socialism: Basic questions of Christian social ethics). Vol. 5, *Studien des apologetischen Seminars in Wernigerode* (Studies of the apologetics seminar in Wernigerode). Gütersloh: Bertelsmann, 1921. *NL* 4, 2.

Barth, Karl. *Der Römerbrief.* 2d ed. of the new, rev. ed. of 1922. Munich: Chr. Kaiser, 1923. English translation: *The Epistle to the Romans.* Translated from the 6th German ed. by Edwin C. Hoskins. London: Oxford University Press, 1933, 1960.

Die Bekenntnisschriften der evangelisch-lutherischen Kirche. Vol. 1. Edited and published in the anniversary year of the Augsburg Confession. Göttingen: Vandenhoeck & Ruprecht, 1930. *NL* 2 C 3. English translation: *The Book of Concord: The Confessions of the Evangelical Lutheran Church.* Edited and translated by Theodore G. Tappert, in collaboration with Jaroslav Pelikan, Robert H. Fischer, and Arthur C. Piepkorn. Philadelphia: Fortress Press, 1959.

Bengel, Johann Albrecht. *Gnomon: Auslegung des Neuen Testamentes in fortlaufenden Anmerkungen.* Vol. 1, *Evangelien und Apostelgeschichte.* Published originally in Latin in 1742; German translation by C. F. Werner. Basel, 1876. [Uncorrected printing from the 3d ed., Berlin-Stuttgart, 1959.] English translation: *Gnomen of the New Testament.* Revised and edited by Andrew R. Fausset. 5 vols. Philadelphia: Smith, English & Co., 1860.

Die Bibel oder die ganze Heilige Schrift des Alten und Neuen Testaments nach der deutschen Übersetzung D. Martin Luthers (The Bible or the entire Holy Scriptures of the Old and New Testaments according to the German translation of Dr. Martin Luther). Supervised by the Commission of the Deutsche Evangelische Kirchenkonferenz. Mitteloktav ed. Stuttgart, 1911. *NL* 1 A 6,

The Book of Concord. See above, *Die Bekenntnisschriften der evangelisch-lutherischen Kirche.*

Bornhäuser, Karl Bernhard. *Die Bergpredigt: Versuch einer zeitgenössischen Auslegung* (The Sermon on the Mount: An essay toward a contemporary interpretation). Gütersloh: Bertelsmann, 1927. *NL* 1 D 2.

Brunner, Emil. *Das Gebot und die Ordnungen: Entwurf einer protestantisch theologischen Ethik.* Tübingen: Mohr (Paul Siebeck), 1932. *NL* 4, 6. English translation: *The Divine Imperative.* Translated by Olive Wyon. Philadelphia: Westminster Press, 1947.

—————. *Der Mittler: Zur Besinnung über den Christusglauben.* Tübingen: Mohr (Paul Siebeck), 1927. *NL* 3 B 15. English translation: *The Mediator.* Translated by Olive Wyon. New York: Macmillan Press, 1934.

Evangelisches Gesangbuch für Brandenburg und Pommern (Protestant hymnbook for Brandenburg and Pomerania). Berlin and Frankfurt an der Oder: Provinzialkirchenräte von Brandenburg und Pommern, 1931.

Gogarten, Friedrich. *Politische Ethik: Versuch einer Grundlegung* (Political ethics: Essay toward a foundation). Jena: Diederichs, 1932. *NL* 4 14.

Harnack, Adolf von. *Lehrbuch der Dogmengeschichte.* 3 vols. Tübingen: Mohr, 1909–10. *NL* 2 C 4 17. English translation: *History of Dogma.* Translated by E. B. Speiers and Neil Buchanan from the 3d German ed. 5 vols. New York: Russell & Russell, 1958.

—————. *Die Mission und Ausbreitung des Christentums in den ersten drei Jahrhunderten.* Leipzig: J. C. Hinrichs, 1902, 1924. The latter edition is found in *NL* 2 C 1, 11. English translation: *The Mission and Expansion of Christianity in the First Three Centuries.* 2 vols. Translated and edited by James Moffat. 2d rev. and enl. ed. New York: Harper, 1962.

—————. *Das Wesen des Christentums: Sechzehn Vorlesungen vor Studierenden aller Facultäten im Wintersemester, 1899/1900 an der Universität Berlin gehalten.* Leipzig: J. C. Hinrichs, 1926. *NL* 3 B 30. English translation: *What Is Christianity?* Translated by Thomas Bailey Saunders. New York: Harper, 1957.

Hegel, Georg Wilhelm Friedrich. *Sämtliche Werke* (Collected works). Edited by Georg Lasson. Vol. 12, *Begriff der Religion* (Concept of religion).

Leipzig: 1925; Vol. 14, *Die absolute Religion* (The absolute religion). Leipzig: Felix Meiner Verlag, 1929. *NL* 7 A 26.

————. *Vorlesungen über die Philosophie der Religion.* Edited by Georg Lasson. Vol. 1, Leipzig, 1925; Vol. 3, Leipzig; 1929. *NL* 7 A 26. English translation: *Lectures on the Philosophy of Religion.* 3 vols. Edited by Peter C. Hodgson. Translated by R. F. Brown, P. C. Hodgson, and J. M. Stewart, with the assistance of J. P. Fitzer and H. S. Harris. Berkeley: University of California Press, 1984–87. Vol. 3 was previously published as *The Christian Religion.* Edited and translated by Peter C. Hodgson. Based on the edition by Georg Lasson. Missoula, Mont.: Scholars Press, 1979. [Bonhoeffer's quotations from the Lasson edition of the *Vorlesungen über die Philosophie der Religion* pose a peculiar problem in English translation. Lasson's edition was an editorial reconstruction of the various preceding versions of Hegel's text; because of this, it has been largely abandoned as a reliable source in contemporary editions of Hegel. Thus, there are no contemporary English translations of vols. 1 and 2 of the *Philosophie der Religion* that follow Lasson's edition closely. English-language citations to these two volumes, therefore, refer the reader when possible to Peter Hodgson's three-volume edition, *Lectures on the Philosophy of Religion.* However, in many cases there simply are no exact parallels to citations from Lasson's text in Hodgson's three-volume edition; in these cases only the Lasson edition's pagination has been given in editorial notes. To further complicate matters, Lasson's edition of vol. 3 of the *Philosophie der Religion* was the basis of Hodgson's earlier edition of vol. 3, *The Christian Religion.* Despite Hodgson's own subsequent misgivings about the use of Lasson's edition as a textual basis, we have used that text when providing English-language parallel references to vol. 3 of Lasson's edition simply because *The Christian Religion* is the only modern edition of vol. 3 of *Philosophie der Religion* that substantially follows Lasson's text.]

Holl, Karl. *Luther.* Vol. 1 of *Gesammelte Aufsätze zur Kirchengeschichte* (Collected essays on church history). Tübingen: Mohr, 1923.

Kierkegaard, Søren. *Der Einzelne und die Kirche: Über Luther und den Protestantismus* (The individual and the church: On Luther and Protestantism). Translated and with a foreword by W. Kütemeyer. Berlin: Kurt Wolff Verlag/Der Neue Geist Verlag, 1934. *NL* 7 A 40.

Kittel, Gerhard, ed. *Theologisches Wörterbuch zum Neuen Testament.* 7 vols. Stuttgart: W. Kohlhammer Verlag, 1933–64. English translation: *Theo-*

logical Dictionary of the New Testament. 10 vols. Translated and edited by Geoffrey W. Bromiley. Grand Rapids, Mich.: Eerdmans, 1964–76.

Kohlbrügge, Hermann Friedrich. *Quellwasser: Tägliche Andachten aus den Predigten von Pastor Dr. H. F. Kohlbrügge* (Water from the spring: Daily meditations from the sermons of Pastor Dr. H. F. Kohlbrügge). Edited by Theodor Stiasny. Personal publication, 1931. *NL* 5 F 13.

Luther, Martin. *Disputationen Dr. Martin Luthers in den Jahren 1535–1545 an der Universität Wittenberg gehalten* (Dr. Martin Luther's disputations at the University of Wittenberg during the years 1535–45). Edited by Paul Drews. Göttingen: Vandenhoeck and Ruprecht, 1895. *NL* 2 C 3, 19.

————. *Dr. Martin Luthers Briefwechsel* (Dr. Martin Luther's exchange of letters). Revised by Dr. E. L. Enders and continued by G. Kawerau. Frankfurt am Main: Evangelischer Vereins, 1884–1932.

————. *Luthers Vorlesung über den Römerbrief 1515–1516.* Vol. 1 of *Anfänge der reformatorischen Bibelauslegung.* Edited by J. Ficker. Pt. 2, *Die Scholien.* Leipzig: Dieterichscher Verlag, 1925. *NL* 1 D 24. English translation: *Lectures on Romans, LW* 25. Edited by Hilton C. Oswald. "Glosses": chaps. 1–2, translated by Walter G. Tillmanns; chaps. 3–16, translated by Jacob A. O. Preus. "Scholia": chaps. 1–2, translated by Walter G. Tillmanns; chaps. 3–15, translated by Jacob A. O. Preus.

————. *Werke: Kritische Gesamtausgabe.* Weimar: H. Böhlau, 1883–. English translation: *Luther's Works.* 55 vols. Vols. 1–30 edited by Jaroslav Pelikan. St. Louis: Concordia, 1958–67. Vols. 31–55 edited by Helmut Lehmann. Philadelphia: Muhlenberg Press and Fortress Press, 1957–67.

Müller, Johannes. *Die Bergpredigt—verdeutscht und vergegenwärtigt* (The Sermon on the Mount—translated into German and updated). Munich: C. H. Beck, 1929. *NL* 3 B 59.

Müller, Ludwig. *Deutsche Gottesworte: Aus der Bergpredigt verdeutscht* (God's word in German: The Sermon on the Mount translated into German). Weimar: Verlag Deutsche Christen, 1936. *NL* 2 C 4 33.

Nestle, Eberhard, ed., revised by Erwin Nestle. *Novum Testamentum Graece et Germanice: Das Neue Testament griechisch und [Luther-] deutsch* (The New Testament in Greek and [Luther's] German). 13th ed. Stuttgart: Privilegierte Württembergische Bibelanstalt, 1929. *NL* 1 A 4.

Ein neues Lied: Ein Liederbuch für die deutsche evangelische Jugend (A new song: A songbook for Protestant youth). Edited by Reichsverband weiblicher Jugend. Berlin 1933.

Ritschl, Albrecht. *Unterricht in der christlichen Religion.* Bonn: 1903. English translation: *Instruction in the Christian Religion.* Translated from the 4th

German ed. by Alice Mead Swing. In Albert Temple Swing, *The Theology of Albrecht Ritschl.* New York: Longmans, Green, 1901.

Schlatter, Adolf. *Die Theologie der Apostel* (The theology of the apostles). Stuttgart: Calwer, 1922.

Schlier, Heinrich. *Christus und die Kirche im Epheserbrief* (Christ and the church in the Letter to the Ephesians). Beiträge zur historischen Theologie 6 (Contributions to historical theology 6). Tübingen: Mohr, 1930.

Schmid, Heinrich. *Die Dogmatik der evangelisch-lutherischen Kirche dargestellt und aus den Quellen belegt.* Gütersloh: Gütersloher Verlagshaus, 1893. *NL* 3 B 65. English translation: *The Doctrinal Theology of the Evangelical Lutheran Church.* Translated by Charles A. Hay and Henry E. Jacobs. Philadelphia: Lutheran Publishing Society, 1889.

Schmidt, Kurt Dietrich, ed. *Die Bekenntnisse und grundsätzlichen Äußerungen zur Kirchenfrage* (The confessions and foundational declarations on the church question). Vol. 2, *Das Jahr 1934.* Göttingen: Vandenhoeck & Ruprecht, 1935. *NL* 2 C 4 2 b.

Schmidt, Traugott. *Der Leib Christi: Eine Untersuchung zum urchristlichen Gemeindegedanken* (The body of Christ: An examination of the early church's concept of the church-community). Leipzig and Erlangen: A. Deichert, 1919.

Seeberg, Reinhold. *Lehrbuch der Dogmengeschichte.* 4 vols. Leipzig: A. Deichertischer Verlag, 1913–23. *NL* 2 C 4. 44. English translation: *Textbook of the History of Doctrines.* Translated by Charles E. Hay. 2 vols. in 1. Grand Rapids, Mich.: Baker Book House, 1956.

Tholuck, August. *Die Bergpredigt.* 4th rev. and enl. ed. Gotha, 1856. *NL* 1 D 32. English translation: *Commentary on the Sermon on the Mount.* Translated from the 4th rev. and enl. ed. by the Reverend R. Lundin Brown, M.A. Edinburgh: T. & T. Clark, 1860.

Troeltsch, Ernst. *Die Soziallehren der christlichen Kirchen und Gruppen. Gesammelte Schriften.* Vol. 1, pt. 1. Tübingen: Mohr (Paul Siebeck), 1912. English translation: *The Social Teaching of the Christian Churches.* Translated by Olive Wyon, with a foreword by James Luther Adams. 2 vols. Louisville: Westminster/John Knox, 1992.

Weber, Max. *Die protestantische Ethik und der Geist des Kapitalismus.* Vol. 1 of *Gesammelte Aufsätze zur Religionssoziologie.* Tübingen: Mohr (Paul Siebeck), 1920. English translation: *The Protestant Ethic and the Spirit of Capitalism.* Translated by Talcott Parsons. New York: Charles Scribner's Sons, 1976.

Westcott, B. F., and F. J. A. Hort. *The New Testament in the Original Greek.* Cambridge and London, 1886.

Witte, Karl, ed. *Nun freut euch lieben Christen gemein: Luthers Wort in täglichen Andachten* (Now rejoice you dear Christians together: Luther's word in daily worship services). Berlin, 1934. *NL* 5 F 23.

2. Literature Consulted by the Editors

Andersen, Dorothea, Gerhard Andersen, Eberhard Bethge, and Elfriede Vibrans, eds. *So ist es gewesen: Briefe im Kirchenkampf 1933–1942 von Gerhard Vibrans, aus seinem Familien- und Freundeskreis und von Dietrich Bonhoeffer* (The way it was: Letters during the German Church Struggle of 1933–42 from Gerhard Vibrans, his circle of family and friends, and Dietrich Bonhoeffer). Gütersloh: Chr. Kaiser/Gütersloher, 1995.

Balthasar, Hans Urs von. *Die grossen Ordensregeln: Lectio Spiritualis* (The great rules of order: Spiritual reading). Vol. 12. Einsiedeln: Johannes, 1974.

Barth, Karl. *Die kirchliche Dogmatik.* 4 vols. Munich and Zurich: Chr. Kaiser and Evangelischer Verlag, 1932–67. English translation: *Church Dogmatics.* Edited by G. W. Bromiley and T. F. Torrance. Translated by G. T. Thomson. 4 vols. Edinburgh: T. & T. Clark, 1956–77.

———. *Das Wort Gottes und die Theologie: Gesammelte Vorträge.* Munich: Chr. Kaiser, 1924. *NL* 3 B 11. English translation: *The Word of God and the Word of Man.* New York: Harper and Brothers, 1957.

Bethge, Eberhard. *Bekennen und Widerstehen: Aufsätze, Reden, Gespräche.* Munich: Chr. Kaiser, 1984.

———. *Dietrich Bonhoeffer: Theologe—Christ—Zeitgenosse: Eine Biographie.* Munich: Chr. Kaiser, 1967, 1989. English translation: *Dietrich Bonhoeffer: A Biography.* Rev. ed. Edited and revised by Victoria Barnett. Minneapolis: Fortress Press, 2000.

———. "Dietrich Bonhoeffer und die Juden." In *Konsequenzen: Dietrich Bonhoeffers Kirchenverständnis heute,* edited by E. Feil and I. Tödt, 171–214. Internationales Bonhoeffer Forum 3. Munich: Chr. Kaiser, 1980. English translation: "Dietrich Bonhoeffer and the Jews." In *Ethical Responsibility,* edited by John D. Godsey and Geffrey B. Kelly, 43–96.

―――. *Friendship and Resistance: Essays on Dietrich Bonhoeffer.* Geneva: WCC Publications; Grand Rapids, Mich.: Eerdmans, 1995.

―――. "The Legacy of the Confessing Church: Transporting Experience across Historical Turning Points." *Church & Society* (July/August 1995): 78–92.

―――. "Nachwort" (Afterword) to *Nachfolge,* by Dietrich Bonhoeffer, 283–304.

Bobert-Stützel, Sabine. *Dietrich Bonhoeffers Pastoraltheologie* (Dietrich Bonhoeffer's pastoral theology). Gütersloh: Kaiser/Gütersloher, 1995.

Bonhoeffer, Dietrich. "Christologie." *GS* 3:116–242 [also published in *DBW* 12:279–348]. English translation: *Christ the Center.* A new translation by Edwin H. Robertson. London: Collins [U.K. title: *Christology*]; San Francisco: HarperCollins, 1978.

―――. *Dietrich Bonhoeffer Werke.* Edited by Eberhard Bethge et al. 16 vols. Munich: Chr. Kaiser, 1987–99. English translation: *Dietrich Bonhoeffer Works.* Edited by Wayne Whitson Floyd, Jr., et al. 16 vols. Minneapolis: Fortress Press, 1995–.

1. *Sanctorum Communio: Eine dogmatische Untersuchung zur Soziologie der Kirche.* Edited by Joachim von Soosten. Munich: Chr. Kaiser, 1986. English translation: *Sanctorum Communio: A Theological Study of the Sociology of the Church.* Edited by Clifford J. Green. Translated by Reinhard Krauss and Nancy Lukens. Minneapolis: Fortress Press, 1998.

2. *Akt und Sein: Transzendentalphilosophie und Ontologie in der systematischen Theologie.* Edited by Hans-Richard Reuter. Munich: Chr. Kaiser, 1988. English translation: *Act and Being: Transcendental Philosophy and Ontology in Systematic Theology.* Edited by Wayne Whitson Floyd, Jr. Translated by H. Martin Rumscheidt. Minneapolis: Fortress Press, 1996.

3. *Schöpfung und Fall.* Edited by Martin Rüter and Ilse Tödt. Munich: Chr. Kaiser, 1989. English translation: *Creation and Fall.* Edited by John W. de Gruchy. Translated by Douglas Stephen Bax. Minneapolis: Fortress Press, 1996.

4. *Nachfolge.* Edited by Martin Kuske and Ilse Tödt. Gütersloh: Chr. Kaiser, 1989; 2d ed., 1994.

5. *Gemeinsames Leben: Das Gebetbuch der Bibel.* Edited by Gerhard L. Müller and Albrecht Schönherr. Munich: Chr. Kaiser, 1987. English translation: *Life Together.* Edited by Geffrey B. Kelly. Translated by Daniel W. Bloesch. *The Prayerbook of the Bible: An Introduction to the Psalms.* Edited by Geffrey B. Kelly. Translated by James H. Burtness. Minneapolis: Fortress Press, 1995.

6. *Ethik.* Edited by Ilse Tödt, Heinz Eduard Tödt, Ernst Feil, and Clifford Green. Gütersloh: Chr. Kaiser, 1992, 1998.

7. *Fragmente aus Tegel.* Edited by Renate Bethge and Ilse Tödt. Munich: Chr. Kaiser, 1994.

8. *Widerstand und Ergebung.* Edited by Christian Gremmels, Eberhard Bethge, and Renate Bethge, assisted by Ilse Tödt. Munich: Chr. Kaiser, 1998.

9. *Jugend und Studium, 1918–1927* (Youth and education, 1918–27). Edited by Hans Pfeifer, with Clifford Green and Carl Jürgen Kaltenborn. Munich: Chr. Kaiser, 1986.

10. *Barcelona, Berlin, Amerika: 1928–1931.* Edited by Reinhart Staats and Hans Christoph von Hase, assisted by Holger Roggelin and Matthias Wünsche. Munich: Kaiser, 1991.

11. *Ökumene, Universität, Pfarramt: 1931–1932.* Edited by Eberhard Amelung and Christoph Strohm. Gütersloh: Chr. Kaiser, 1994.

12. *Berlin: 1932–33.* Edited by Carsten Nicolaisen and Ernst-Albert Scharffenorth. Gütersloh: Chr. Kaiser, 1997.

13. *London: 1933–1935.* Edited by Hans Goedeking, Martin Heimbucher, and Hans-Walter Schleicher. Gütersloh: Chr. Kaiser, 1994.

14. *Illegale Theologen-Ausbildung: Finkenwalde 1935–1937.* Edited by Otto Dudzus and Jürgen Henkys, assisted by Sabine Bobert-Stützel, Dirk Schulz, and Ilse Tödt. Gütersloh: Chr. Kaiser, 1996.

15. *Illegale Theologen-Ausbildung: Sammelvikariate 1937–1940.* Edited by Dirk Schulz. Gütersloh: Chr. Kaiser, 1998.

———. *Ethik.* Arranged and edited by Eberhard Bethge, 1949, restructured 1963. Munich: Chr. Kaiser, 1985. English translation: *Ethics.* Translated by Neville Horton Smith. New York: Macmillan, 1965; New York: Simon and Schuster, 1995.

———. *Gesammelte Schriften* (Collected works). Edited by Eberhard Bethge. 6 vols. Munich: Chr. Kaiser, 1958–74.

———. *Meditating on the Word.* Edited and translated by David McI. Gracie. New York: Cowley, 1987.

———. *Nachfolge.* Munich: Chr. Kaiser, 1937, 1940. Newly reprinted, 1961; reprinted with an afterword by Eberhard Bethge, 1981, 1987. English translation: *The Cost of Discipleship.* Translated by Reginald H. Fuller, foreword by Bishop George K. A. Bell of Chichester, memoir by Gerhard Leibholz. London: SCM, 1948. With a preface by Reinhold Niebuhr, New York: Macmillan, 1949. (Both the 1948 and the 1949 editions were abridged.) 2d unabridged ed. with translation revised by Irmgard Booth, London: SCM, 1959; New York: Macmillan, 1960. Paperback ed. (with different pagination), New York: Macmillan, 1963; London: SCM, 1964. First Touchstone ed., New York: Simon and Schuster, 1995.

———. *No Rusty Swords: Letters, Lectures, and Notes, 1928–1936.* Edited and with an introduction by Edwin H. Robertson. Translated by Edwin H. Robertson and John Bowden. London: Collins; New York: Harper, 1965.

———. *Prayers from Prison.* Interpreted by Johann Christoph Hampe. Translation of previously untranslated material by John Bowden. London: Collins; Philadelphia: Fortress Press, 1978.

———. *Preface to Bonhoeffer: The Man and Two of His Shorter Writings.* Edited and translated by John D. Godsey. Philadelphia: Fortress Press, 1965.

———. *Spiritual Care.* Edited, translated, and with an introduction by Jay C. Rochelle. Philadelphia: Fortress Press, 1985.

———. *A Testament to Freedom: The Essential Writings of Dietrich Bonhoeffer.* Edited by Geffrey B. Kelly and F. Burton Nelson. San Francisco: HarperCollins, 1990; rev. and expanded ed., 1995.

———. *True Patriotism: Letters, Lectures, and Notes, 1939–1945.* Edited by Edwin H. Robertson. Translated by Edwin H. Robertson and John Bowden. London: Collins; New York: Harper, 1973.

———. *The Way to Freedom: Letters, Lectures, and Notes, 1935–1939.* Edited by Edwin H. Robertson. Translated by Edwin H. Robertson and John Bowden. London: Collins; New York: Harper, 1966.

———. *Widerstand und Ergebung: Briefe und Aufzeichnungen aus der Haft.* Edited by Eberhard Bethge. Munich: Chr. Kaiser, 1951; exp. ed., 1970, 1985. English translation: *Letters and Papers from Prison.* Edited by Eberhard Bethge. Translated by Reginald H. Fuller; translation revised by Frank Clarke et al. Additional material translated by John Bowden for the enl. ed. published in London: SCM, 1971; New York: Macmillan, 1972; New York: Simon and Schuster, 1997.

———. *Worldly Preaching: Lectures on Homiletics.* Edited and translated with critical commentary by Clyde F. Fant. New York: Crossroad, 1991.

Bonhoeffer, Dietrich, and Maria von Wedemeyer. *Love Letters from Cell 92: The Correspondence between Dietrich Bonhoeffer and Maria von Wedemeyer, 1943–45.* Translated by John Brownjohn. Nashville: Abingdon Press, 1995.

Büchmann, Georg. *Geflügelte Worte: Der Zitatenschatz des deutschen Volkes gesammelt und erläutert* (Familiar quotations: The treasury of quotations of the German people collected and expanded). Frankfurt: 1864, 1986.

Bultmann, Rudolf. *Jesus*. Tübingen: Mohr (Paul Siebeck), 1926. English translation: *Jesus and the Word*. Translated by Louise Pettibone Smith. New York: Scribner's, 1958.

Calvin, Jean. *Institutio,* 1559. Edited by P. Barth and G. Niesel. English translation: *Institutes of the Christian Religion*. Vols. 20–21 of *The Library of Christian Classics*. Edited by John T. McNeill. Translated by Ford Lewis Battles. Philadelphia: Westminster Press, 1960.

Catechismus ex Decreto Consilii Tridentini ad Parochos Pii Quinti Pont. Leipzig: 1840. *NL* 6 B 7. Translated into German as *Katechismus nach dem Beschlusse des Konzils von Trient für die Pfarrer: Auf Befehl der Päpste Pius V. und Klemens XIII.* Edited and translated according to the Roman edition of 1955, with an index of terms. Kirchen and Sieg: 1970. English translation: *Catechism of the Council of Trent*. Translated by J. Donavan. Dublin: James Duffy, 1914.

Claudius, Matthias. *ASMUS omnia sua Secum portans oder Sämtliche Werke des Wandsbecker Boten* ("ASMUS omnia sua Secum portans" or the collected works of "Der Wandsbecker Bote"). Berlin: 1941; reprint of the 1st ed., 1774–1812, Munich: 1976.

Clements, Keith. *A Patriotism for Today: Dialogue with Dietrich Bonhoeffer*. Bristol: Bristol Baptist College, 1984.

——. *What Freedom? The Persistent Challenge of Dietrich Bonhoeffer*. Bristol: Bristol Baptist College, 1990.

Day, Thomas I. *Dietrich Bonhoeffer on Christian Community and Common Sense*. Lewiston, N.Y.: Edwin Mellen Press, 1982.

de Gruchy, John. *Bonhoeffer and South Africa: Theology in Dialogue*. Grand Rapids, Mich.: Eerdmans, 1984.

——. "Bonhoeffer's English Bible." *Dialog* 17, no. 3 (summer 1978): 211–15.

——. *Dietrich Bonhoeffer: Witness to Jesus Christ*. London: Collins; Minneapolis: Fortress Press, 1988.

——, ed. *Bonhoeffer for a New Day: Theology in a Time of Transition*. Grand Rapids, Mich.: Eerdmans, 1997.

——, ed. *The Cambridge Companion to Dietrich Bonhoeffer*. Cambridge: Cambridge University Press, 1999.

Deharbe, Joseph. *Catechism of Christian Doctrine*. New York: Fr. Pustet, 1901.

Elliott, J. K. *The Apocryphal New Testament*. Oxford: Clarendon Press; New York: Oxford University Press, 1993.

Elshtain, Jean Bethge. "Caesar, Sovereignty, and Bonhoeffer." In *Bonhoeffer for a New Day: Theology in a Time of Transition.* Edited by John W. de Gruchy, 223–35.

Evangelisches Gesangbuch in den Gliedkirchen der Evangelischen Kirche in Deutschland, seit 1992 (Protestant Church hymnbook for use in the member churches of the Protestant Churches in Germany since 1992).

Feil, Ernst. *Bonhoeffer Studies in Germany: A Survey of Recent Literature.* Philadelphia: International Bonhoeffer Society, English Language Section, 1997.

————. *The Theology of Dietrich Bonhoeffer.* Translated by H. Martin Rumscheidt. Philadelphia: Fortress Press, 1985.

Flex, Walter. *Der Wanderer zwischen beiden Welten.* Munich: C. H. Beck.

Floyd, Wayne Whitson, Jr. "Revisioning Bonhoeffer for the Coming Generation: Challenges in Translating the *Dietrich Bonhoeffer Works.*" *Dialog* 34, no. 1 (1995): 32–38.

————. "The Search for an Ethical Sacrament: From Bonhoeffer to Critical Social Theory." *Modern Theology* 7, no. 2 (January 1991): 175–93.

————. *Theology and the Dialectic of Otherness: On Reading Bonhoeffer and Adorno.* Lanham, Md.: University Press of America, 1988.

Floyd, Wayne Whitson, Jr., and Clifford J. Green. *Bonhoeffer Bibliography: Primary Sources and Secondary Literature in English.* Evanston, Ill.: American Theological Library Association, 1992.

Floyd, Wayne Whitson, Jr., and Charles Marsh. *Theology and the Practice of Responsibility: Essays on Dietrich Bonhoeffer.* Valley Forge, Pa.: Trinity Press International, 1994.

Glenthøj, Jørgen. *Dokumente zur Bonhoeffer Forschung, 1928–1945* (Documents on Bonhoeffer Research, 1928–1945). Munich: Chr. Kaiser, 1969.

Godsey, John D. "The Doctrine of Love." In *New Studies in Bonhoeffer's Ethics.* Edited by William J. Peck, 189–234.

————. "The Legacy of Dietrich Bonhoeffer." In *A Bonhoeffer Legacy.* Edited by A. J. Klassen, 161–69.

————. *The Theology of Dietrich Bonhoeffer.* Philadelphia: Westminster Press, 1960.

Godsey, John D., and Geffrey B. Kelly. *Ethical Responsibility: Bonhoeffer's Legacy to the Churches.* Lewiston, N.Y., and Toronto: Edwin Mellen Press, 1981.

Green, Clifford J. "Human Sociality and Christian Community." In *The Cambridge Companion to Dietrich Bonhoeffer*. Edited by John W. de Gruchy.

————. *The Sociality of Christ and Humanity: Dietrich Bonhoeffer's Early Theology, 1927–1933*. Missoula, Mont.: Scholars Press, 1975. Reprint, *Bonhoeffer: A Theology of Sociality*. Grand Rapids, Mich.: Eerdmans, 1999.

Gunkel, Hermann and Leopold Zscharnack, editors. *Die Religion in Geschichte und Gegenwart*. 2d ed. 5 vols. Tübingen: Mohr (Paul Siebeck), 1927–32.

Harnack, Adolf von. *Marcion: Das Evangelium vom fremden Gott. Eine Monographie zur Geschichte der Grundlegung der katholischen Kirche*. Leipzig: J. C. Hinrichs'sche Buchhandlung,1921. Reprint, Darmstadt: 1960. English translation: *Marcion: The Gospel of the Alien God*. Translated by John E. Steely and Lyle D. Bierma. Durham, N.C.: Labyrinth Press, 1990.

Hennecke, Edgar, and Wilhelm Schneemelcher, eds. *Neutestamentliche Apokryphen*. Vol. 2. Tübingen: Mohr (Paul Siebeck), 1971. English translation: *New Testament Apocrypha*. Edited by R. McL. Wilson. Translated by A. J. B. Higgins et al. 2 vols. Philadelphia: Westminster Press, 1963–65.

Herrmann, Wilhelm. *Die sittlichen Weisungen Jesu* (The moral directives of Jesus). Göttingen: Vandenhoeck & Ruprecht, 1904, 1907. Also published in *Schriften zur Grundlegung der Theologie* (Writings on theological foundations), edited by Peter Fischer-Appelt, 1:200–241. Munich: Chr. Kaiser, 1966.

Hertlein, Friedrich Karl, ed. *Iuliani imperatoris quae supersunt praeter reliquias apud Cyrillum omnia* (All the works of the Emperor Julian that survive except the fragments in Cyril). Vol. 1, *Bibliotheca Teubneriana, Lipsiae* (The Teubner series [of classical texts]). Leipzig: 1875.

Hildebrandt, Franz. *Est: Das lutherische Prinzip* (The Lutheran principle). Göttingen: Vandenhoeck & Ruprecht, 1932.

Höfer, Josef, and Karl Rahner. *Lexikon für Theologie und Kirche*. Freiburg: Herder, 1957–67.

Holl, Karl. *Der Osten* (The east). Vol. 2 of *Gesammelte Aufsätze zur Kirchengeschichte* (Collected essays on church history). Tübingen: Mohr (Paul Siebeck), 1928.

Huber, Wolfgang. "Feindschaft und Feindesliebe: Notizen zum Problem des 'Feindes' in der Theologie" (Enmity and love of enemies: Observations on the problem of the "enemy" in theology). *Zeitschrift für Evangelische Ethik* 26 (1982): 128–58.

Ignatius von Loyola. *Geistliche Übungen: Nach dem spanischen Urtext.* Translated from the original Spanish by J. Feder, S.J. 5th ed. Regensburg: 1932. *NL* 6 B 26. English translation: *The Spiritual Exercises of St. Ignatius.* Translated by Louis J. Puhl. Westminster, Md.: Newman Press, 1951.

Kelley, James Patrick. "The Best of the German Gentiles: Dietrich Bonhoeffer and the Rights of Jews in Hitler's Germany." In *Remembering for the Future,* edited by Yehudi Bauer et al., 1:80–92. New York: Pergamon Press, 1989.

Kelly, Geffrey B. "Bonhoeffer and the Jews: Implications for Jewish-Christian Reconciliation." In Kelly and Weborg, eds., *Reflections on Bonhoeffer,* 133–66.

———. "Bonhoeffer's Theology of History and Revelation." In *A Bonhoeffer Legacy,* edited by A. J. Klassen, 89–130.

———. "The Influence of Kierkegaard on Bonhoeffer's Concept of Discipleship." *Irish Theological Quarterly* 41, no. 2 (April 1974): 148–54.

———. "An Interview with Jean Lasserre." *Union Seminary Quarterly Review* 27, no. 3 (spring 1972): 149–60.

———. *Liberating Faith: Bonhoeffer's Message for Today.* Minneapolis: Augsburg, 1984.

———. "Prayer and Action for Justice: Bonhoeffer's Christocentric Spirituality." In *The Cambridge Companion to Dietrich Bonhoeffer,* 246–68. Edited by John W. de Gruchy.

———. "Rechtfertigung in der 'Nachfolge': Eine Klarstellung" (Justification in *Discipleship:* A clarification). In *Wie eine Flaschenpost,* edited by Heinz Eduard Tödt, 304–8. Munich: Chr. Kaiser, 1979.

———. "Sharing in the Pain of God: Dietrich Bonhoeffer's Reflections on Christian Vulnerability." *Weavings* 7, no. 4 (July/August 1993): 6–15.

Kelly, Geffrey B., and John Weborg, eds. *Reflections on Bonhoeffer: Essays in Honor of F. Burton Nelson.* Chicago: Covenant Publications, 1999.

Kierkegaard, Søren. *The Journals of Søren Kierkegaard: A Selection.* Edited and translated by Alexander Dru. London and New York: Oxford University Press, 1938.

———. *Søren Kierkegaard's Journals and Papers.* Vols. 1–4. Edited and translated by Howard V. Hong and Edna H. Hong. Bloomington: Indiana University Press, 1967–75.

Klassen, A. J., ed. *A Bonhoeffer Legacy: Essays in Understanding.* Grand Rapids, Mich.: Eerdmans, 1981.

Krüger, Martin. *Ausgewählte Märtyrerakten: Sammlung ausgewählter kirchen- und dogmengeschichtlicher Quellenschriften* (Selected acts of the martyrs:

Collection of selected primary source writings on church and the history of dogma). Vol. 3. New series. Tübingen: 1965.

Kuske, Martin. *Das Alte Testament als Buch von Christus: Dietrich Bonhoeffers Wertung und Auslegung des Alten Testaments.* Berlin: Evangelischen Verlagsanstalt, 1970. English translation: *The Old Testament as the Book of Christ: An Appraisal of Bonhoeffer's Interpretation.* Translated by S. T. Kimbrough Jr. Philadelphia: Westminster Press, 1976.

Lasserre, Jean. *War and the Gospel.* Translated by Oliver Coburn. Scottdale, Pa.: Herald Press, 1962.

Leith, John H., ed. *Creeds of the Churches.* Garden City, N.Y.: Doubleday and Co., 1963.

Lifton, Robert Jay. *The Nazi Doctors: Medical Killing and the Psychology of Genocide.* San Francisco: HarperCollins, 1986.

Loewenich, Walther von. *Luthers Theologia crucis.* Munich: Chr. Kaiser, 1929, 1933. English translation: *Luther's Theology of the Cross.* Translated by Herbert J. A. Bouman. Minneapolis: Augsburg, 1976.

Lovin, Robin. "Biographical Context." In *New Studies in Bonhoeffer's Ethics,* edited by William J. Peck, 67–101.

———. "Dietrich Bonhoeffer: Responsibility and Restoration." In Lovin, *Christian Faith and Public Choices: The Social Ethics of Barth, Brunner, and Bonhoeffer,* 156–78. Philadelphia: Fortress Press, 1984.

Lutheran Book of Worship. Minneapolis: Augsburg Publishing House, 1978.

The Lutheran Hymnary. Minneapolis: Augsburg, 1935.

Matthews, John W. "Responsible Sharing of the Mystery of Christian Faith: *Disciplina Arcani* in the Life and Theology of Dietrich Bonhoeffer." *Dialog* 25, no. 1 (winter 1986): 19–25.

Nachlaß Dietrich Bonhoeffer: Ein Verzeichnis. Archiv—Sammlung—Bibliothek (Dietrich Bonhoeffer's literary estate: A bibliographical catalog). Edited by Dietrich Meyer and Eberhard Bethge. Munich: Chr. Kaiser, 1987.

Neander, August. *Das Leben Jesu in seinem geschichtlichen Zusammenhange und seiner geschichtlichen Entwicklung.* Hamburg: 1837. English translation: *The Life of Jesus Christ in Its Historical Connexion and Historical Development.* Translated from the 4th German ed. by John McClintock and Charles E. Blumenthal. New York: Harper, 1870.

Nelson, F. Burton. "Bonhoeffer and the Spiritual Life: Some Reflections." *Journal of Theology for Southern Africa* 30 (March 1980): 34–38.

———. "God's Guest on Earth: A Model for Sojourning Discipleship." *Sojourners* 13, no. 5 (May 1984): 27.

————. "The Life of Dietrich Bonhoeffer: A Chapter from the Modern Acts of the Apostles." In *The Cambridge Companion to Dietrich Bonhoeffer*, edited by John W. de Gruchy, 22–49.

————. "The Relationship of Jean Lasserre to Dietrich Bonhoeffer's Peace Concerns in the Struggle of the Church and Culture." *Union Seminary Quarterly Review* 40, nos. 1–2 (1985): 71–84.

Noth, Martin. *Das System der zwölf Stämme Israels: Beiträge zur Wissenschaft vom Alten und Neuen Testament* (The system of the twelve tribes of Israel: Contributions to the scientific study of the Old and New Testaments). Stuttgart: W. Kohlhammer, 1930.

Pangritz. Andreas. *Dietrich Bonhoeffers Forderung einer Arkandisziplin: Eine unerledigte Anfrage an Kirche und Theologie* (Dietrich Bonhoeffer's demand for a discipline of the secret: An unanswered inquiry for the church and theology). Pahl-Rugenstein Hochschulschriften Gesellschafts- und Naturwissenschaften (Pahl-Rugenstein University scientific writings on society and nature) 259. Cologne: Pahl-Rugenstein Verlag, 1988.

Peck, William J. "The Role of the Enemy in Bonhoeffer's Life and Thought." In *A Bonhoeffer Legacy*, 345–61. Edited by A. J. Klassen.

————, ed. *New Studies in Bonhoeffer's Ethics*. Lewiston, N.Y., and Queenston, Ontario: Edwin Mellen Press, 1987.

Przywara, Erich. *Religionsphilosophie katholischer Theologie: Handbuch der Philosophie Sonderausgabe* (The philosophy of religion of Catholic theology: The handbook of philosophy). Special ed. Munich and Berlin: Oldenbourg, 1927. *NL* 7 B 20.

von Rad, Gerhard. *Der Heilige Krieg im alten Israel: Abhandlungen zur Theologie des Alten und Neuen Testaments* (The holy war in ancient Israel: Discourses on the theology of the Old and New Testaments). 3d ed. Vol. 20. Göttingen: Vandenhoeck & Ruprecht, 1958.

Raiser, Konrad. "Bonhoeffer and the Ecumenical Movement." In *Bonhoeffer for a New Day*, edited by John W. de Gruchy, 319–39.

Rasmussen, Larry, with Renate Bethge. *Dietrich Bonhoeffer: His Significance for North Americans*. Minneapolis: Fortress Press, 1990.

Ritschl, Albrecht. *Die Entstehung der altkatholischen Kirche: Eine kirchen- und dogmengeschichtliche Monographie* (The origin of the old Catholic church: A monograph on church history and the history of dogma). Bonn: Mareus, 1850.

Ruinart, Thierry. *Acta primorum martyrum sincerum & selecta.* Amsterdam: 1713.

Schlatter, Adolf. *Der Evangelist Matthäus: Seine Sprache, sein Ziel, seine Selbständigkeit* (Matthew the Evangelist: His language, his purpose, his independence). Stuttgart: Calwer, 1929.

Schmitt, Jakob. *Von den Geboten* (On the commandments). Vol. 2 of *Erklärung des mittleren Deharbe'schen Katechismus zunächst für die mittlere und höhere Klasse der Elementarschulen* (Explanation of the middle-level Deharbe catechism, primarily for use in the higher classes of the elementary schools). Freiburg im Breisgau: 1874.

Schweitzer, Albert. *Kultur und Ethik.* Munich: Beck, 1923. English translation: *Christianity and Ethics.* Translated by John Naish. London: A. & C. Black, Ltd., 1923.

Sohm, Rudolf. *Die geschichtlichen Grundlagen* (The historical foundations). Vol. 1 of *Kirchenrecht* (Canon law). Leipzig: 1892.

Sorum, Jonathan D. "Cheap Grace, Costly Grace, and Just Plain Grace: Bonhoeffer's Defense of Justification by Faith Alone." *Lutheran Forum* 27, no. 3 (August 1993): 20–23.

———. "The Eschatological Boundary in Dietrich Bonhoeffer's *Nachfolge.*" Ph.D. diss., Luther Northwestern Theological Seminary, 1994.

The Talmud of Babylonia: An Academic Commentary. Yoma. English. A. Chapters 1–2; B. Chapters 3–5; C. Chapters 6–8. Translated by Jacob Neusner. Atlanta, Ga.: Scholars Press, 1994.

Theologische Realenzyklopädie: Abkürzungsverzeichnis (Theological specialist encyclopedia: Index of abbreviations). Arranged by Siegfried Schwertner. Berlin and New York: Walter de Gruyter, 1976.

Thomas à Kempis. *Imitatio Christi. Werke.* Vol. 2, edited by M. J. Pohl. Freiburg: 1904. *NL* 11 8. English translation: *The Imitation of Christ.* Edited and introduced by Harold C. Gardner. Garden City, N.Y.: Doubleday, 1955.

Tödt, Heinz Eduard. *Theologische Perspektiven nach Dietrich Bonhoeffer.* Gütersloh: Kaiser/Gütersloher, 1993.

———, ed. *Wie eine Flaschenpost: Ökumenische Briefe und Beiträge für Eberhard Bethge* (Like a bottled message cast upon the waters: Ecumenical letters and articles in honor of Eberhard Bethge). Munich: Chr. Kaiser, 1979.

Tödt, Ilse, ed. *Dietrich Bonhoeffers Hegel Seminar, 1933.* From the student notes of Ferenc Lehel. Internationales Bonhoeffer Forum 8. Munich: Chr. Kaiser, 1988.

Vilmar, August Friedrich Christian. *Zur neuesten Culturgeschichte Deutschlands* (On the most recent history of German culture). Scattered papers reassembled by Vilmar. Pt. 1: *Politisches und Sociales* (Political and social). Frankfurt am Main and Erlangen: 1858.

Weiss, Bernhard. *Das Leben Jesu.* Vol. 1. Berlin: 1884. English translation: *The Life of Christ.* Translated by John Walter Hope. 3 vols. Edinburgh: T. & T. Clark, 1883–1909.

Wind, Renate. *Dietrich Bonhoeffer: A Spoke in the Wheel.* Translated by John Bowden. Grand Rapids, Mich.: Eerdmans; London: SCM, 1991. [U.K. title: *A Spoke in the Wheel: A Life of Dietrich Bonhoeffer.*]

Winkworth, Catherine. *The Chorale Book for England.* London: Longman, Green, Longman, Roberts and Green, 1863.

————. *Lyra Germanica.* Second Series: The Christian Life. London: Longman, Brown, Green, Longmans and Roberts, 1858.

Zerner, Ruth. "Bonhoeffer on Discipleship and Community." *Lutheran Forum* 30, no. 2 (May 1996): 35–38.

————. "Dietrich Bonhoeffer and the Jews: Thoughts and Actions, 1933–1945." *Jewish Social Studies* 37, nos. 3–4 (summer–fall 1975): 235–50.

————. "Dietrich Bonhoeffer's Views on the State and History." In *A Bonhoeffer Legacy,* edited by A. J. Klassen, 131–57.

Zimmermann, Wolf-Dieter. *Wir nannten ihn Bruder Bonhoeffer: Einblicke in ein hoffnungsvolles Leben* (We called him Brother Bonhoeffer: Insights into a hope-filled life). Berlin: Wichern, 1995.

————, ed. *Begegnungen mit Dietrich Bonhoeffer.* Munich: Chr. Kaiser, 1964, 1969. English translation: *I Knew Dietrich Bonhoeffer: Reminiscences by His Friends.* Edited by Wolf-Dieter Zimmermann and Ronald Gregor Smith. Translated by Käthe Gregor Smith. London: Collins; New York: Harper, 1966.

3. Other Literature Related to *Discipleship*

Alemany, José. *Realidad y Fe Cristiana: Una aproximación desde la Teología de D. Bonhoeffer* (Reality and Christian faith: An approximation based on the theology of D. Bonhoeffer). Santiago: 1979.

Altenähr, Albert. *Dietrich Bonhoeffer—Lehrer des Gebets: Grundlagen für eine Theologie des Gebets bei Dietrich Bonhoeffer* (Dietrich Bonhoeffer—Teacher of prayer: Foundations for a theology of prayer based on Dietrich

Bonhoeffer). Studien zur Theologie des geistlichen Lebens (Studies on the theology of the spiritual life) 7. Würzburg: Echter Verlag, 1976.

Barth, Karl. *Die Kirchliche Dogmatik.* Vol. 4/2, *Die Lehre von der Versöhnung,* 603–26. Zurich: Evangelischer Verlag, 1964. English translation: *Church Dogmatics.* Vol. 4/2, *The Doctrine of Reconciliation.* Translated by G. W. Bromiley. Edinburgh: T. & T. Clark, 1958.

Brocker, Mark. "The Community of God, Jesus Christ, and Responsibility: The Responsible Person and the Responsible Community in the Ethics of Dietrich Bonhoeffer." Ph.D. diss., University of Chicago Divinity School, 1996.

de Lange, Frits. "Grond onder de voeten: Burgerlijkheid bij Dietrich Bonhoeffer. Ein theologische studie" (Ground under one's feet: Civic responsibility according to Dietrich Bonhoeffer. A theological study). Ph.D. diss., University of Kampen, Netherlands, 1984.

————. *Wachten op het verlossende Woord: Dietrich Bonhoeffer en het spreken over God.* Baarn, The Netherlands: Ten Have, 1995. English translation: *Waiting for the Word: Dietrich Bonhoeffer on Speaking about God.* Grand Rapids, Mich.: Eerdmans, 2000.

Dumas, André. *Une Théologie de la réalité: Dietrich Bonhoeffer.* Geneva: Éditions Labor et Fides, 1968. English translation: *Dietrich Bonhoeffer: Theologian of Reality.* Translated by Robert McAfee Brown. New York: Macmillan, 1971.

Green, Barbara. "Introduction to *Who Is Jesus Christ for Us Today? Dietrich Bonhoeffer, after Fifty Years,* edited by Barbara Green." *Church & Society* (July/August 1995): 1–7.

————. "Poore Foolische Friend: Bonhoeffer, Bethge, Vibrans, and a Theology of Friendship." In Kelly and Weborg, *Reflections on Bonhoeffer,* 185–98.

Green, Clifford J. "Soteriologie und Sozialethik bei Bonhoeffer und Luther" (Soteriology and social ethics in Bonhoeffer and Luther). In *Bonhoeffer und Luther: Zur Sozialgestalt des Luthertums in der Moderne* (Bonhoeffer and Luther: On the social shape of Lutheranism in modern times), edited by Christian Gremmels, 93–128. Internationales Bonhoeffer Forum 6. Munich: Chr. Kaiser, 1983.

Harrelson, Walter. "Bonhoeffer and the Bible." In *The Place of Dietrich Bonhoeffer: Problems and Possibilities in His Thought,* edited by Martin E. Marty, 115–142. New York: Association Press, 1962; London: SCM, 1963.

Kelley, James Patrick. "Revelation and the Secular in the Theology of Dietrich Bonhoeffer." Ph.D. diss., Yale University, 1980.

Kramer, Rolf. "Grenzen einer Nachfolge-Ethik" (Limits of a discipleship ethics). *Theologia Viatorum* 15 (1979/80): 61–72.

Krause, Gerhard. "Dietrich Bonhoeffer (1906–1945)." *Theologische Realenzyklopädie* 7:55–66.

Kuske, Martin. *Weltliches Christsein: Dietrich Bonhoeffers Vision nimmt Gestalt an* (Being a worldly Christian: Dietrich Bonhoeffer's vision takes shape). Berlin and Munich: Evangelischen Verlagasanstalt and Chr. Kaiser, 1984.

Lange, Ernst. "Kirche für andere: Dietrich Bonhoeffers Beitrag zur Frage einer verantwortbaren Gestalt der Kirche in der Gegenwart" (The church for others: Dietrich Bonhoeffer's contribution to the question of a responsible form of the church today). In *Kirche für die Welt: Aufsätze zur Theorie kirchlichen Handelns* (Church for the world: Essays on the theory of church action), edited by R. Schloz, 19–62. Munich: Geinhausen, 1981.

Lehmann, Paul L. "Paradox of Discipleship." In *I Knew Dietrich Bonhoeffer,* edited by Wolf-Dieter Zimmermann and Ronald Gregor Smith, 41–45.

———. "Politik der Nachfolge" (Politics of discipleship). *Evangelische Theologie* 32 (1972): 560–79.

Löhr, Christian. "Das Verständnis des Friedens in Dietrich Bonhoeffers Auslegung der Bergpredigt" (The understanding of peace in Dietrich Bonhoeffer's explanation of the Sermon on the Mount). In *Bonhoeffer-Studien,* edited by A. Schönherr and W. Krötke, 98–112. Berlin: Evangelischen Verlagsanstalt, 1985.

Marlé, René. *Bonhoeffer: The Man and His Work.* Translated by Rosemary Sheed. New York: Newman Press; London: Geoffrey Chapman, 1968.

Marsh, Charles. *Reclaiming Dietrich Bonhoeffer: The Promise of His Theology.* New York and Oxford: Oxford University Press, 1994.

Mengus, Raymond. *Théorie et pratique chez Dietrich Bonhoeffer* (Dietrich Bonhoeffer's theory and practice). Paris: Éditions Beauchesne, 1978.

Mödlhammer, Johann Werner. *Anbetung und Freiheit: Theologisch-anthropologische Reflexionen zur Theologie Dietrich Bonhoeffers* (Worship and freedom: Theological-anthropological reflections on the theology of Dietrich Bonhoeffer). Salzburg: Otto Müller, 1976.

Morawska, Anna Maria. *Chrzéscijanin w Trzeciег Rzeszy* (The Christian in the Third Reich). Warsaw: 1970.

Müller, Christine-Ruth. *Dietrich Bonhoeffers Kampf gegen die nationalsozialistische Verfolgung und Vernichtung der Juden* (Dietrich Bonhoeffer's struggle against the Nazi persecution and annihilation of the Jews). Heidelberger Untersuchungen zu Widerstand, Judenverfolgung und Kirchenkampf (Heidelberg research on the resistance movement, the persecution of the Jews, and the Church Struggle) 5. Munich: Chr, Kaiser, 1990.

Müller, Gerhard Ludwig. *Bonhoeffers Theologie der Sakramente* (Bonhoeffer's theology of the sacraments). Frankfurter Theologische Studien 28. Frankfurt am Main: Knecht, 1979.

Müller, Hanfried. *Von der Kirche zur Welt: Ein Beitrag zu der Beziehung des Wort Gottes auf die societas in Dietrich Bonhoeffers theologische Entwicklung* (From the church to the world: A contribution to the relation of the word of God to society in Dietrich Bonhoeffer's theological development). Leipzig and Hamburg-Bergstedt: Reich, 1966.

Müller, Norbert. "Gesetz und Evangelium bei Bonhoeffer" (Law and gospel with Bonhoeffer). In *Bonhoeffer Studien,* edited by A. Schönherr and W. Krötke, 51–60.

Ott, Heinrich. *Reality and Faith: The Theological Legacy of Dietrich Bonhoeffer.* Translated by Alex A. Morrison. Philadelphia: Fortress Press, 1972.

Pangritz, Andreas. *Karl Barth in der Theologie Dietrich Bonhoeffers: Eine notwendige Klarstellung.* Berlin: Alektor, 1989. English translation: *Karl Barth in the Theology of Dietrich Bonhoeffer.* Translated by Barbara Rumscheidt and H. Martin Rumscheidt. Grand Rapids, Mich.: Eerdmans, 2000.

Peck, William J. "From Cain to the Death Camps: An Essay on Bonhoeffer and Judaism." *Union Seminary Quarterly Review* 38, no. 2 (winter 1973): 158–76.

Pelikan, Herbert Rainer. *Die Frömmigkeit Dietrich Bonhoeffers: Dokumentation, Grundlinien, Entwicklung* (The piety of Dietrich Bonhoeffer: Comments, foundations, development). Vienna: Herder, 1982.

Peters, Tiemo Rainer. "Jenseits von Radikalismus und Kompromiß: Die politische Verantwortung der Christen nach Dietrich Bonhoeffer" (Beyond radicalism and compromise: The political responsibility of Christians according to Dietrich Bonhoeffer). In *Verspieltes Erbe? Dietrich Bonhoeffer und der deutsche Nachkriegsprotestantismus,* edited by Ernst Feil, 94–115. Internationales Bonhoeffer Forum 2. Munich: Chr. Kaiser, 1979.

————. *Die Präsenz des Politischen in der Theologie Dietrich Bonhoeffers: Eine historische Untersuchung in systematischer Absicht* (The presence of the political in the theology of Dietrich Bonhoeffer: A historical inquiry with a systematic aim). Gesellschaft und Theologie: Systematische Beiträge (Society and theology series: Systematic contributions) 18. Munich and Mainz: Chr. Kaiser and Matthais-Grünewald, 1976.

Rothuizen, Gerard Th. *Aristocratisch Christendom: Over Dietrich Bonhoeffer. Leven, Verzet, Ecumene, Theologie* (Aristocratic Christianity: Over Dietrich Bonhoeffer. Life, resistance, ecumenism, theology). Kampen: J. H. Kok, 1969.

Schijndel, H. J. van. *Religie, Geloof, Disciplina Arcani* (Religion, faith, the *disciplina arcani* [discipline of the secret]). Kampen: J. H. Kok, 1979.

Schönherr, Albrecht. "Leib Christi und Nachfolge bei Dietrich Bonhoeffer" (The body of Christ and discipleship with Dietrich Bonhoeffer). In Schönherr, *Horizont und Mitte: Aufsätze, Vorträge, Reden, 1953–1977* (The horizon and the center: Essays, lectures, talks, 1953–77), 149–63. Berlin and Munich: Evangelische Verlagsanstalt and Chr. Kaiser, 1980.

Schönherr, Albrecht, and Krötke, Wolf, eds. *Bonhoeffer-Studien: Beiträge zur Theologie und Wirkungsgeschichte Dietrich Bonhoeffers. Im Auftrage des Bonhoeffer-Komitees beim Bund der Evangelischen Kirchen in der Deutschen Demokratischen Republik* (Bonhoeffer Studies: Essays on the theology and history of the influence of Dietrich Bonhoeffer. Commissioned by the Bonhoeffer Committee at the Alliance of the Protestant Churches in the German Democratic Republic). Berlin: 1985.

Strohm, Christoph. *Theologische Ethik im Kampf gegen den Nationalsozialismus: Der Weg Dietrich Bonhoeffers mit den Juristen Hans von Dohnanyi und Gerhard Leibholz in den Widerstand* (Theological ethics in the struggle against Nazism: The path of Dietrich Bonhoeffer with the jurists Hans von Dohnanyi and Gerhard Leibholz in the resistance movement). Heidelberger Untersuchungen zu Widerstand, Judenverfolgung und Kirchenkampf (Heidelberg research into the resistance movement, the persecution of the Jews, and the Church Struggle) 1. Munich: Chr. Kaiser, 1989.

Strunk, Reiner. *Nachfolge Christi: Erinnerungen an eine evangelische Provokation* (Following Christ: Looking back on a Protestant provocation). Munich: Chr. Kaiser, 1981.

Torrance, Thomas F. "Cheap and Costly Grace." *Baptist Quarterly* 22 (1968): 290–311.

Vogel, Traugott. "Christus als Vorbild und Versöhner: Eine kritische Studie zum Problem des Verhältnisses von Gesetz und Evangelium im Werke Søren Kierkegaard" (Christ as exemplar and reconciler: A critical study on the problem of the relationship of law and gospel in the works of Søren Kierkegaard). Excursus: "Spuren Kierkegaards in Bonhoeffers 'Nachfolge'" (Traces of Kierkegaard in Bonhoeffer's *Discipleship*), 297–303. Ph.D. diss., Humboldt University, Berlin, 1968.

Walker, Hamish Norman. "The Incarnation and Crucifixion in Bonhoeffer's 'Cost of Discipleship.'" *Scottish Journal of Theology* 21, no. 4 (December 1968): 407–15.

Weizsäcker, Carl Friedrich von. "Gedanken eines Nichttheologen zur theologischen Entwicklung Dietrich Bonhoeffers" (Thoughts of a nontheologian on the theological development of Dietrich Bonhoeffer). In *Genf '76: Ein Bonhoeffer Symposion* (Geneva '76: A Bonhoeffer symposium), edited by Hans Pfeifer, 29–50, with the ensuing discussion edited by Ernst Feil, 51–67. Internationales Bonhoeffer Forum 1. Munich: 1976. Also published in *Der Garten des Menschlichen: Beiträge zur geschichtlichen Anthropologie*, 454–78. Munich and Vienna: C. Hanser, 1977. English translation: *The Ambivalence of Progress: Essays on Historical Anthropology.* New York: Paragon, 1988.

Wendel, Ernst Georg. *Studien zur Homiletik Dietrich Bonhoeffers: Predigt—Hermeneutik—Sprache* (Studies on the homiletics of Dietrich Bonhoeffer: Preaching, hermeneutics, language). Hermeneutische Untersuchungen zur Theologie (Hermeneutic research into theology) 21. Tübingen: Mohr (Paul Siebeck), 1985.

Woelfel, James. *Bonhoeffer's Theology: Classical and Revolutionary.* Nashville: Abingdon Press, 1970.

Wüstenberg, Ralf Karolus. *Glauben als Leben: Dietrich Bonhoeffer und die nichtreligiöse Interpretation biblischer Begriffe.* Frankfurt: Peter Lang, 1996. English translation: *A Theology of Life: Dietrich Bonhoeffer's Religionless Christianity.* Translated by Douglas Stott. Grand Rapids, Mich.: Eerdmans, 1998.

INDEX

OF SCRIPTURAL REFERENCES

INDEX

OF NAMES

INDEX

OF SUBJECTS

GREEK TERMS

ἄνθρωπος, καινός. *See* new person
ἁπλοῦς. *See* simple
ἀπό (away from). *See* justification
δεῖ. *See* must
δικαιοσύνη (ἰδία). *See* righteousness (own)
εἰς (into). *See* baptism
ἐκκλησία. *See* church-community; church
ἐκ τοῦ πονηροῦ. *See* Satan/satanic
ἐν (in). *See* Christ
ἐξουσία. *See* authority
ἔσχατον. *See* end/last thing
ἐφάπαξ. *See* once, for all time
καθ' ἡμέραν. *See* daily
καθώς (like). *See* Christ
καρπός. *See* fruit
κοινωνία. *See* community
μορφή. *See* form
περιπατεῖν. *See* journeying
περισσόν. *See* extraordinary
πλεονεξία. *See* greed
πνεῦμα. *See* spirit
πορνεία. *See* adultery
σάρξ. *See* flesh
σύν (with). *See* Christ
σφραγίς. *See* seal/sealing
τέλειος and δίψυχος. *See* schisms, in the church and perfection

τέλος. *See* end/last thing
ὑπέρ (for). *See* Christ
ὑπερ-ὑπο. *See* above-below
ὡς μή. *See* having, as if one did not have

---

a priori, 207
above-below, 240. *See also* authority; slavery
abstinence, 249
Abwehr resistance circle, ix, 305
acculturation, 8
Act and Being, 2, 6, 18–19, 51, 150, 301, 303, 321
action/inaction, 150, 182
activism, 108
activity/passivity, 109, 145
admonition, 243, 263, 271–72, 275, 276
adoration, 154
adultery, 125, 127, 263–64, 277
alcoholism, 65
alienation, 123. *See also* estrangement
allegiance, 116, 127, 138, 150, 179–80
almsgiving, 146
anathema, 275, 276
anger, 122–23, 263–64
Antichrist, 103, 247, 276
Anti-Christianity, 37
Apocalypse, 194

353

EDITOR AND TRANSLATOR BIOGRAPHIES

WAYNE WHITSON FLOYD, JR. (Ph.D., Emory University) is visiting professor and director of the Dietrich Bonhoeffer Center at the Lutheran Theological Seminary at Philadelphia, a Dean's Fellow in the Religion Department of Dickinson College, and serves as Canon Theologian for the Episcopal Cathedral of St. Stephen in Harrisburg, Pennsylvania. He is the author of *The Wisdom and Witness of Dietrich Bonhoeffer* (Fortress Press, 2000) and *Theology and the Dialectics of Otherness: On Reading Bonhoeffer and Adorno* (University Press of America, 1988); he co-authored with Clifford Green the *Bonhoeffer Bibliography: Primary Sources and Secondary Literature in English* (American Theological Library Association, 1992); and he co-edited with Charles Marsh *Theology and the Practice of Responsibility: Essays on Dietrich Bonhoeffer* (Trinity Press International, 1995). Dr. Floyd's articles on Bonhoeffer have appeared in *Union Seminary Quarterly Review, The Lutheran, Modern Theology, Religious Studies Review, Dialog, Modern Theology,* and *Christian Century* and numerous anthologies.

JOHN D. GODSEY (D. Theol., University of Basel, Switzerland) is Emeritus Professor of Systematic Theology at Wesley Theological Seminary in Washington, D.C. He is the author of *The Theology of Dietrich Bonhoeffer* (Westminster Press, 1960, the first monograph published on Bonhoeffer's theology). He is also author of *Preface to Bonhoeffer* (Fortress Press, 1965). He is co-editor of *Ethical*

Responsibility: Bonhoeffer's Legacy to the Churches (Edwin Mellen Press, 1981). He was a founding member of the International Bonhoeffer Society, English Language Section, and served on its Board of Directors until his retirement in 1992. In 1964–1965 Dr. Godsey was a Fulbright Research Scholar at the University of Göttingen, Germany. He served as President of the American Theological Society from 1985 to 1986.

BARBARA G. GREEN (M.Div., Yale Divinity School; postgraduate study University of Heidelberg, German) is executive director of the Churches' Center for Theology and Public Policy in Washington, D.C. From 1983–1998 she served as policy advocate in the Washington Office of the Presbyterian Church (USA). From 1977–1981 she was liaison representative of the National Council of Churches in the USA to the Federation of Protestant Churches in the GDR, based in Berlin, Germany. She serves on the board of the Dietrich Bonhoeffer Works English edition, the International Bonhoeffer Society, English Language Section, and chairs the International Advisory Committee of the German Protestant Kirchentag movement. She is an ordained clergywoman in the Presbyterian Church (USA). She has edited the monograph, *Who Is Jesus Christ for Us Today? Dietrich Bonhoeffer after Fifty Years.*

GEFFREY B. KELLY (S.T.L., S.T.D., University of Louvain, Belgium, LL.D., North Park University, Chicago) is professor of systematic theology, chairperson of the Department of Religion, and director of the Lasallian Leadership Institute at La Salle University, Philadelphia. Elected president of the International Bonhoeffer Society, English Language Section, in 1992, Dr. Kelly is the author of *Liberating Faith: Bonhoeffer's Message for Today* (Augsburg Publishing House, 1984). He has co-edited *Ethical Responsibility: Bonhoeffer's Legacy to the Churches* (Edwin Mellen Press, 1981), *A Testament to Freedom: The Essential Writings of Dietrich Bonhoeffer* (HarperSanFrancisco, 1995) and *Reflections on Bonhoeffer: Essays in Honor of F. Burton Nelson* (Covenant Press, 1999). He has written numerous articles on Bonhoeffer appearing in such journals as *Dialog,*

Union Seminary Quarterly Review, Ephemerides Theologicae Lovanienses, Princeton Seminary Bulletin, The Irish Theological Quarterly, America, and *Weavings.*

REINHARD KRAUSS (Ph.D., University of St. Andrews) began his theological education at the universities of Tübingen and Bonn. His doctoral research on Karl Barth's concept of religion and its indebtedness to nineteenth-century liberal theology was published as *Gottes Offenbarung und Menschliche Religion: Eine Analyse des Religionsbegriffs in Karl Barths Kirchliche Dogmatik mit besonderer Berücksichtigung F. D. E. Schleiermachers* (Edwin Mellen, 1992). Dr. Krauss's interest in Dietrich Bonhoeffer's life and thought is rooted in his own German background and the experience of growing up in postwar Germany. His appreciation for Bonhoeffer's theology has deepened over time both through translating Bonhoeffer texts and through seeking to apply Bonhoeffer's insights in parish ministry. Since 1986 Dr. Krauss has lived and worked in the United States and currently serves as Co-Pastor of St. Luke's Presbyterian Church in Rolling Hills Estates, California. He is also a member of the Editorial Board of the Dietrich Bonhoeffer Works and serves on the translation teams for Bonhoeffer's *Sanctorum Communio* and *Ethics.*